THE GUINNESS BOOK OF THE **CAR**

THE GUINNESS BOOK OF THE *Car*

Anthony Harding
Warren Allport
David Hodges
John Davenport

GUINNESS BOOKS

Editor: Honor Head
Design: Alan Hamp

© Anthony Harding, David Hodges, Warren Allport & John Davenport and Guinness Superlatives Ltd, 1987

Published in Great Britain by Guinness Superlatives Ltd, 33 London Road, Enfield, Middlesex

Typeset in 10/12pt Century Schoolbook by Fakenham Photosetting Ltd, Fakenham, Norfolk Printed and bound in Great Britain by Hazell, Watson & Viney Ltd, Aylesbury, Bucks

'Guinness' is a registered trade mark of Guinness Superlatives Ltd

The Guinness book of the car.
    1. Automobile driving – Miscellanea
    I. Harding, Anthony   II. Hodges, David
    III. Davenport, John   IV. Allport, Warren
    796.7'09'04   GV1021

    ISBN 0–85112–806–8

Page 1 Baby Austin: Sir Herbert at the wheel of the 1922 Seven 'Chummy'.

Page 2 Earl Howe's Mercedes-Benz being hoisted onto the quay at Calais from Southern Railway's *Autocarrier*, the first cross-Channel car ferry, in 1931.

CONTENTS

INTRODUCTION

'If the horse hadn't been invented first, there wouldn't have been anything for the automobile to replace.' – Groucho Marx.

To save both time and patience, shall we assume the emergence of Man and his subsequent invention of the wheel, and then move on a few hundred millenia? To the time when men who had become rich and powerful got tired of walking on their own two feet and so employed the muscle power of the less industrious to bear or haul litters, palanquins, that four-legged taxi known as the sedan chair, and rickshaws. Draught animals – oxen, horses, mules and dogs – pulled carts, wagons, sledges and, eventually, coaches. A bonus with this type of power unit was that when it could no longer work it could be eaten, given a modicum of culinary expertise – which is more than could be said of a worn-out Volkswagen Beetle!

The mid-18th century saw steam power harnessed to road vehicles, and very soon the steam carriage became a practical means of passenger transport – only for it to be damned by the horse lobby and overtaken, both literally and economically, by a variety of internal combustion gas-engined devices. The first of these was pioneered successfully by Karl Benz, of Mannheim, in 1884. The horseless carriage, and very soon the Motor Industry, came into being, for better or for worse.

Over the next 30 years, engineers thought hard and wrought mightily, and nobody has summed up this immensely important period of automotive development as soundly and succinctly as the late Laurence Pomeroy Jr, son of the eminent Vauxhall designer in the salad days of that marque, and a distinguished motoring writer: 'From 1885 to 1895 men struggled to make the car go. From 1895 to 1905 they contrived to make it go properly. Between 1906 and 1915 they succeeded in making it go beautifully.'

During World War I little was done to further motor car design, but a great deal to improve aircraft engines. Thus up-market engines of the early 20s soon came to benefit from the metallurgical advances and aero-engine technology of the war years, while chassis and suspension design on Edwardian lines persisted on most cars through to the late 1930s, and on some mass-produced cars until after World War II.

During the 1930s, some rather dreadful cars were produced in the cheaper ranges, with a 55–60 mph/88–96 kph maximum speed allied to handling reminiscent of a sailing dinghy. At the other end of the spectrum, expensive cars had lovely engines, longer wheelbases and stiffer chassis, providing the bases for some of the finest aesthetic flowerings of the coachbuilders' arts, tailored to owners' whims and physique. Nevertheless, no Bentley was blessed with independent front suspension until 1939, while with 4¼ litres an open aluminium-bodied Rolls–Royce struggled to reach 80 mph/129 kph on the flat.

Mixed trio at Monaco in 1985 – Lauda in a McLaren heads Patrese in an Alfa Romeo and Piquet in a Brabham.

When Adolf Hitler had been seen off after another war, the late 1940s saw the car makers labouring to get back into business – building their pre-war designs for a hungry market whilst getting their brave new models, or maybe a dangerously complacent variation on an old theme, into production.

Recovery took time, but the following decades saw most significant advances – unitary body/chassis construction, all-round independent suspension, disc brakes and so on. These gradually became commonplace on mass-produced family cars and, in the twenty-odd years since, some icing has been put on the cake – but what proper motorist ever really needed to be wet-nursed by synthetic female sirens, servicing lights *et al*, telling him 'when he should blow his nose....'?

In the widest area of motoring – that is to say getting around and about on one's own business and pleasure – the private motorist and his vehicle seem always to have been sitting targets for harassment from over-zealous busy-bodies and bureaucrats. Threatened with horse-whipping in the early days, then suffering speed traps, compulsory registration numbers, 'Road Fund' income never spent on highways, swingeing taxation on fuel – plus 'buckle that belt, clamp that wheel, blow into this and you'll land in jail' (apologies to Jerome Kern) – the would-be do-gooders have had a field day at motorists' expense since the beginning. And matters will not improve....

Competitive motoring was almost inevitable as soon as two horseless carriages came together; organized motoring sport began as early as 1894 and has generally flourished ever since. Perhaps the races of the 19th century were more akin to modern rallies, but then many modern rallies are really motor races, are they not? *Plus ça change*. Unhappily, the glamour of some of the traditional road-races has been lost – but, just occasionally, ghosts of the great contests between factory teams may be discerned (if they are viewed through sufficiently powerful rose-coloured spectacles) in some of the events of the current Formula One circus, with its tinsel, artificial atmosphere and rapacious ring masters and performers.

That erudite, astringent motoring historian (and no mean amateur racing driver to boot) 'Sam' Clutton once observed that 'there is no historical fact about motoring history that cannot be proved wrong'. Thus the present contributors find themselves wide open – on the ropes almost – to a real pasting from the International Nit-picking Brigade. Whilst they have striven tirelessly to get their facts as correct as they know how, there are probably readers who may well be able to put them to rights on some points. Their comments will truly be welcomed and errors corrected in future editions. We hope there will be but few of the former and many of the latter!

Now follows an arbitrary, catholic selection of some interesting historical and technical highlights (plus a few sidelights perhaps) covering around two hundred-odd years of the ancestry of personal transportation, the men who designed and built it; and also of those who sported with it for fun – or their own rewards – and your entertainment.

A ROAD CAR CHRONOLOGY

1769

Nicholas-Joseph Cugnot (1725–1804) designed a steam truck, for transporting cannon of the French Army, which was commissioned by the Minister of War. It was built at the Paris Arsenal, in the grounds of which its first tests were held. It proved capable of about 2½ mph/4 kph but it had to stop every 15 minutes for its boiler to be refilled by hand.

1771

Cugnot's second, and full-size, steam vehicle was designed for a payload of 4–5 tons. Again it was built and tested at the Paris Arsenal. It ran quite well, but is said to have run into a low stone wall on

Ancestor: Cugnot's second steam tractor.

one of its trials, thus providing the world's first motor accident. Alas, by this time the Government had lost interest in the project, which was shelved. This vehicle may still be seen today in the Conservatoire Nationale des Arts et Métiers in Paris.

1801

The world's first passenger-carrying vehicle was the steam locomotive built in England by the great Cornish engineer and steam vehicle pioneer, Richard Trevithick (1771–1833). It proved capable of transporting seven or eight passengers up the 1:5/20% gradient of Camborne Beacon (about 550 ft/168 m) in Cornwall, on Christmas Eve. Improved versions followed, and in...

1803

Richard Trevithick, in conjunction with Andrew Vivian, now designed and patented his reliable and controllable 'Celebrated London Carriage'. Its mechanical parts were manufactured in Cornwall and then sent to London by ship. There they were

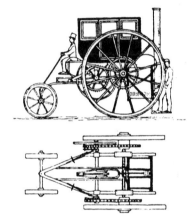

West Country-bred: Richard Trevithick's 'Celebrated London Carriage'.

assembled and fitted with coach-like bodywork. This enclosed steam-powered vehicle was capable of 10 mph/16 kph. Financial support did not materialize however, and this practical carriage was dismantled in 1804.

1805

Oliver Evans, of Maryland, USA, produced a dubious steam-driven dock pontoon on wheels, which he proceeded to drive about 1½ miles/2 km from his workshop in Philadelphia to the river, by arranging to power a single wheel of the carrying frame by belt and pulley from the 5 hp engine of the pontoon. Evans had taken out a patent on steam wagons in 1787, but this was the first time he had actually got down to building one.

1824

The first four-wheel-drive vehicle to be built was Timothy Burstall and John Hill's steam coach. It is said to have weighed over 7 tons which limited its speed to a maximum of 4 mph/6.5 kph.

1826

Samuel Brown of Brompton, London, who had patented a 'gas-vacuum' engine working on coal gas, adapted one of them to make a road vehicle. This carriage climbed Shooter's Hill at Blackheath, but as its twin cylinder engine (12 in × 24 in/30 cm × 61 cm) of 5431 in^3/89 litres, gave but 4 hp, it was comfortably out-performed by steam carriages and was much more expensive to run. Thus it came to nought.

1828

The first vehicle to incorporate a differential in its transmission was reputedly a steam carriage built by a Frenchman, Marcel Pecquer.

1840

Francis Hill's steam coach travelled from London to Hastings and back without mechanical trouble – the first time 100 miles/160 km (actually 128 miles) was thus covered. Forty more years were to pass before this feat was surpassed.

1860

The first successful two-stroke gas engine was patented by Etienne Lenoir of Belgium. In 1862 he built a very experimental gas-engined vehicle which managed to achieve about 2 mph/3 kph over a short distance.

1865

The Locomotives on Highways Act ('Red Flag Act') was passed by the British Government. It was intended to regulate the use of heavy traction engines pulling large loads. It required that every road locomotive must have 'three persons in attendance' – one to steer, one to stoke and one to walk ahead bearing a red flag to warn oncoming traffic and help with restive horses. The maximum speeds permitted were 4 mph/6.4 kph in open country and 2 mph/3.2 kph in towns.

1873

Amédée Bollée, a bell-founder of Le Mans, France, ran his practical 12-seater steam brake *L'Obéissante*. It featured an efficient elliptical cam steering system and independent front suspension.

Le Mans steam brake: Amédée Bollée, *père*'s 'L'Obéissante'.

1875

Until recent years, it was thought that an Austrian Jew named Siegfried Markus (1831–98) had a claim to the title of 'inventor of the motor car' as he was credited with having built a vehicle powered by a gas engine in this year. Now, however, it has been established that the device was in fact built by Messrs Marky, Bronovsky and Schulz in 1888–9 at Adamsthal, and thus Markus was comfortably preceded by Karl Benz (q.v.).

1877

The first practical 'four-stroke' engine was patented by the Otto and Langen Company of Deutz, Germany. Much of the design work was carried out by Gottlieb Daimler (q.v.) and Wilhelm Maybach (q.v.) who both worked for the company, which they left in 1882 to set up on their own at Cannstatt.

George B. Selden, an American, made a provisional application for a patent on his design for a powered road vehicle. However, the patent was not completed until 1895. Investigations brought about by legal battles in the USA over the 'Selden Patent' have shown that the vehicle itself, which it was claimed had been built in 1877, was not in fact made until 1905 – in which year the longest run of which it proved capable was 1400 ft/426 m.

1884/5

Karl Benz of Mannheim, Germany, built himself a two-seater tricycle powered by a four-stroke gas engine, which worked quite well. Benz thus became the most worthy contender for the vexed title of 'Inventor of the Motor Car'.

Karl Benz at the helm of his epoch-making four-stroke, gas-engined tri-car.

American pioneer: Charles Duryea at the controls of the brothers' landmark vehicle.

1885

The first pneumatic car tyre was produced in France by André Michelin. Later he demonstrated some on a Peugeot car which he entered in the Paris–Bordeaux race of 1895. He had his vicissitudes – 22 spare tubes were fitted in 730 miles/1174 km, and the crew lost count of the number of punctures they repaired.

1886

Nikolaus A. Otto's patent for the principle of the four-stroke engine was broken, thus allowing other designers like Karl Benz to develop such engines without first paying expensive licence fees to the Deutz works.

The first four-wheeled petrol-driven car with a four-stroke engine was built by Daimler and Maybach at Cannstatt, their 'landmark' vehicle being known today as the 'Cannstatt-Daimler'. However, there was to be no commercial production of Daimler cars before 1891.

1887

Karl Benz actually sold an improved version of his 1885 three-wheeler to one Emile Roger, a Parisian engineer.

The first true electric car was built by Magnus Volk of Brighton, Sussex, England, whose electric tramway along the seafront to Black Rock was the first of its kind open to the public. (Raffard had converted a tricycle to electric propulsion six years before.)

1888

Emile Roger now took the French agency for Karl Benz's cars – the 'Motor Industry' was under way!

The Butler tricycle was the first automobile to have a float-feed carburettor.

1893

The first experimental petrol-powered car in the USA was demonstrated by Frank and Charles Duryea. Although this was not indisputably the first American car, the Duryea brothers certainly set up the first US company to manufacture cars for sale in 1894, and 13 were completed in 1896.

1894

Emile Levassor of France designed the Panhard which was the forerunner of the modern car, with front-mounted engine driving the rear wheels via clutch and gearbox.

Gottlieb Daimler and Wilhelm Maybach invented the atomizing carburettor.

The Benz 'Velo' became the world's first production car and accounted for most of the 67 Benz vehicles produced in this year.

1895

The first all-British four-wheeled petrol car was designed and built by the Lanchester brothers, Frederick and George (q.v.), in Birmingham. Their first production car went on the market in 1900.

The Lanchester Brothers: 'Dr Fred' (driving) with 'Mr George' (passenger) in their 1897 creation.

Right At Reigate, Surrey, 1896: Church Street looks different now from when the Emancipation Run cars passed through *en route* to Brighton.

1902 White steamer: between 1896 and 1939 some 180 different makes of car were steam-driven. Most were short-lived and of American manufacture.

1896

The 'Emancipation Act' recognized a class of 'light locomotive', waived the ridiculous 'three in attendance rule' and allowed a speed of 12 mph/19 kph on roads in Great Britain. (See 1865.)

The first in-line four-cylinder engine was built by Panhard et Levassor of France for racing, and Dr Frederick Lanchester (q.v.) completed his first horizontally-opposed ('flat') four-cylinder engine.

The Daimler Company was formed in Great Britain at Coventry to manufacture French and German patented cars under licence. It was the first so to be.

1897

First Land's End to John o' Groats by car was achieved by *The Autocar* magazine's editor Henry Sturmey. The 4½ hp Coventry-Daimler averaged nearly 10 mph/16 kph for the 929 miles/1495 km.

First front-wheel-drive car was the Austrian Graf-und-Stift, which was powered by a single-cylinder de Dion engine. It was soon followed by the French Latil, in 1898/9.

Magneto ignition was first employed in Britain by Lanchester.

The electric front-drive Kriéger device was introduced. The idea was that the horse, shafts and front axle were removed from the carriage, and the French Kriéger 'power-pack' (plus a hundred-weight or two of batteries of course) wheeled in.

The Shell Transport and Trading Company was formed to sell petrol. It amalgamated with Royal Dutch in 1906.

The Australian Horseless Carriage Syndicate built the aptly-named 'Pioneer' – not the country's first horseless carriage though, as the steam-powered Shearer had appeared eight years earlier, nor indeed its first internal-combustion-engined vehicle as Knight-Eaton had adapted a bicycle in 1897.

1898

Wilhelm Maybach successfully developed the honeycomb radiator.

Schrader invented the now-universal car tyre valve with its removable core.

1899

The first car with independent front suspension was the French Decauville 3½ hp Voiturelle, with transverse leaf-spring and sliding pillars.

'Petrol' was first used as a word to describe the petroleum spirit supplied by the Carless, Capel and Leonard Company at the suggestion of Frederick Sims, who imported the first Daimler to the United Kingdom. Since then this trade name has become common usage.

1900

The first four-wheel-drive car in the USA was built by Charles Cotta of Illinois. It was steam-powered and its drive was achieved by a compensating chain gear. (See 1824.)

The Thousand Miles Trial was an ambitious event for its day. Sixty-five entrants started from London *en route* to Bristol, up the west coast and across to Edinburgh. The cars then returned via the east coast and Midlands. Twenty-three cars finished the course.

1901

The first American car to be manufactured in quantity was the 'curved dash' Oldsmobile, designed by Ransom Olds (q.v.).

The first car to combine the 'modern' features of pressed-steel chassis, honeycomb radiator and gate gearchange was the 35 hp Mercedes.

1902

The first petrol-fuelled four-wheel-drive vehicle was the vast 8.7 litre Dutch Spyker which was built as a racing car. It was powered by the first six-cylinder automotive engine and was also the first car to have four-wheel braking. Spykers came from Trompenburg near Amsterdam.

The first straight-eight cylinder engine was the 40 hp unit built by CGV (Charron, Girardot and Voigt) in Paris for a racing car. In 1903 Clement Ader built the first automotive V8. Buffum built a racing car with a flat-8 engine in 1904, and in the following year Hewitt introduced flat-8 and V8 engines in production models.

The forerunner of the modern motor caravan was built on a Panhard chassis to the order of one Doctor Lehwess, who planned a world tour in it, but it failed before reaching the borders of European Russia.

1903

The first coast-to-coast crossing of the USA by car was made by a Winton. The journey took 65 days,

'Old Scout' and 'Old Steady': a brace of 'curved dash' Oldsmobiles, probably taking part in the first transcontinental (USA) race of 1905. (See 1901.)

One of the first three Royce experimental cars outside the works of Royce Ltd., Cooke Street, Manchester, in 1904.

for 20 of which the car was immobile for repairs, mainly due to bad road conditions.

The Motor Car Act raised the speed limit in Great Britain to 20 mph/32 kph but brought in the requirements of driving licences and registration numbers. (See 1865 and 1896.)

The first Australian motoring organization, the Australian Automobile Club, was formed in Sydney. The national Australian Automobile Association did not come into being until 1924.

Parsons non-skid chains were introduced in January. They fitted over tyres like the snow chains of today.

1904

Frederick Henry Royce's (q.v.) first experimental car took to the road on 1 April, and the momentous meeting with the Hon. C. S. Rolls was arranged by Henry Edmunds at the Midland Hotel, Manchester, in May. Later, in London, Rolls showed the car to his partner, Claude Johnson.

The first true automatic transmission was introduced by Sturtevant, of Boston, Massachusetts, USA, though a British Hutton had run with a Barber variable transmission a year before. Sturtevant then standardized it on their range in 1905. This company was short-lived however.

The first motor vehicle known to have been made in Japan was a twin-cylinder, chain-driven, ten-seat steam car built by Torao Yamaba.

First use of a tubular backbone chassis was on the little British Rover 8 hp air-cooled model.

The first British six-cylinder car was the 30 hp Napier which had its cylinders cast in pairs. It was shown at the Crystal Palace Motor Show in February.

1905

The foundation of the Automobile Association (AA) whose 'scouts' job it was to warn motorists of concealed police 'speed traps'.

Detachable and interchangeable wheels or rims were introduced. Heretofore punctured or damaged tyres had to be dealt with at the side of the road with the wheels remaining attached to the car. Among them were the Rudge-Whitworth wire wheel and the Michelin detachable rim.

Schrader produced the first tyre pressure gauge. Tyre pressures had previously been largely a matter of guesswork.

1906

Rolls-Royce introduced their 40/50 hp six-cylinder 'Silver Ghost' model at the Olympia Show in November. It was a milestone in the history of automobile design.

1907

A supercharged engine was first built – for racing purposes – by the Chadwick Company of USA. It was not used in their production models however.

The first amphibious car in the modern sense was demonstrated by a Parisian inventor called Ravailler. It was later taken to America where it was named 'Water–Land I'. (See 1805.)

The first home-made petrol-engined Japanese car was the Takuri. It was mostly designed by Komanosuke Uchiyama, for the Automobile Trading Company of one Shintaro Yoshida, who had been involved in the car trade in the USA. The Type 3 production model had a twin-cylinder, horizontally-opposed, 1850 cc engine imported from the USA, with transmission by cone-clutch, two-speed gearbox and chain-drive. Its configuration was strongly influenced by contemporary European practice – particularly that of Darracq and Laurin et Klément.

Henry Ford 'invented' the mass-production of cars: Model T bodies and chassis meet on the line for the first time.

1908

The immortal Model T Ford – first of the 'Peoples' Cars' – was introduced in October. Its production continued until 1927 when total production had reached 16,536,075 vehicles – a record number which stood until 1972 (q.v.). The Model T was the first four-cylinder car with a detachable cylinder head.

Coil and distributor ignition was first introduced by Delco of USA.

First interchangeability of standard parts was introduced by the Cadillac Company of USA, who won the Dewar Trophy. Three of their single-cylinder cars were dismantled, their parts scrambled, and then re-assembled, all under RAC supervision. The hybrids then ran 500 miles/805 km non-stop at Brooklands Motor Course.

1909

The Knight sleeve-valve engine was adopted for the Daimler 38 and 48 hp models.

1910

The first production car *successfully* to be fitted with four-wheel brakes was the Scottish Argyll. It used a diagonal control system invented by the French engineer Henri Perrot. In this year Allen-Liversidge four-wheel brakes were fitted by Arrol-Johnston, Crossley, Spyker, Sheffield-Simplex and Thames cars, but they had to be discarded within a year as the main brake control rod passed through the steering pivot and thus could lock the steering when the brakes were applied!

The first manufacturer to offer closed bodies as standard equipment was Cadillac of USA.

The first bolt-on wheels of modern type were marketed by the Sankey Company of Great Britain.

1911

Electric starting and lighting was introduced by the Cadillac Company of USA as standard specification. It was developed by C. F. Kettering of General Motors.

1912

The Morris Oxford, with a White and Poppe 1018 cc engine, was launched by William Morris (q.v.) of Cowley, Oxford. It became known as the 'bull-nose' Morris and served as Britain's answer to Henry Ford's Model T until the birth of Herbert Austin's cobby little 'Seven' in 1922.

The first genuine 'light car' was the Singer Ten, with a 4-cylinder 1089 cc engine and combined gearbox and rear axle.

The British Ever-ready Company announced a spring-recoil starter which fitted into the starting handle dog. It was wound by the engine and, when released by a pedal, turned the engine over eight times at 300 rpm. A number was fitted to Austin cars.

1913

The Australian commercial vehicle manufacturers Caldwell-Vale built a four-wheel-drive cross-country car. Later it was claimed to be the first car intended for off-road use. In one form it also had four-wheel steering.

1914

The first American water-cooled V8 engine, designed by Henry Leland (q.v.), is claimed to have been fitted by the Cadillac Company. However, some might press the earlier claims of De Dion Bouton (6.1 litres) and the 1905 3.5 litre Rolls-Royce units among others. Nevertheless Leland's engine was put into successful series production.

The Lancia Company of Turin, Italy, claimed to be the first European manufacturer to provide full electrics as standard, on their Theta model.

1915

Packard's Twin Six (V12) model was the first American car to have alloy pistons.

Bull-nose: the Morris 'Oxford' and 'Cowley' models, with side-valve engines and 3-speed gearboxes, provided stodgily reliable transport from 1912. A 1923 'Cowley'.

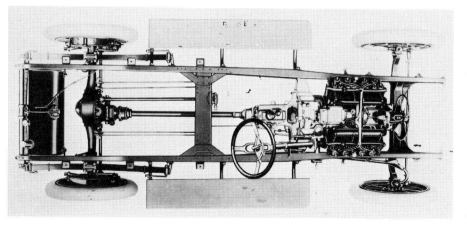

Cadillac chassis, 1914: V8 engine in two blocks of four cylinders (79 × 130 mm/3.1 × 5.1 in. = 5098 cc./311 cu. in.; output 70 bhp @ 2400 rpm) in unit with gearbox. Note right-hand drive chassis, featuring electric starting and lighting, central gear-change and handbrake.

Thermostatic control of the cooling system was introduced by Cadillac.

1916

The first production series 12-cylinder engine appeared on the Packard Twin Six.

Parisian Renault taxis were commandeered to move troops to the Western Front for the Battle of the Marne.

The first mechanical windscreen wipers were introduced in America, on Willys-Knight cars among others.

The first all-steel car tourer bodywork was offered in the USA by Dodge. It was made by the Budd Coachwork Company of Troy, Michigan.

1917

A push-button electric gear selector, known as the Cutler-Hammer Magnetic Gear Shift, was introduced on Premier car models. This company was based at Indianapolis, USA, though this obvious automotive name was also used by Austrian, British and German manufacturers.

1918

The Chevrolet Motor Company, USA, and the Chevrolet Motor Company of Canada joined the General Motors Corporation.

1919

The first production series straight-8 engine appeared on the Type 8 Isotta-Fraschini of Italy.

The Alvis Company of Coventry was founded by T. G. John.

La Dolce Vita: the straight-8 Isotta-Fraschini was Italy's luxury production car of the 1920s.

First servo-assisted front-wheel braking came on the Type H6 Hispano-Suiza designed by Marc Birkigt (q.v.).

The 3-litre Bentley prototype was given its début at the Olympia Show and created a minor sensation. (See W. O. Bentley, page 35.)

The first Australian car to be built in volume was the Australian Six, with a proprietary engine which proved to be its Achilles heel. 'Volume' in this case was relative, production reaching no more than three cars a week during the company's five-year life.

1920

General Motors Research Corporation, forerunner of G.M. Research Laboratories, was founded.

1921

First hydraulic four-wheel brakes were fitted to Duesenberg Model A straight-8 models (USA). The first mass-produced car to fit them was the Chrysler 70 of 1924.

The first catalogued supercharged cars were two Mercedes models exhibited at the Berlin Motor Show.

The Tri-Continental Corporation ('Trico') of Buffalo, N.Y., USA, introduced its arcuate-type (bowed) vacuum-operated windscreen wiper motor. This gradually replaced their hand-operated 'Crescent Cleaner' in the 20s until, by 1937, it was standard equipment on all passenger cars manufactured in the USA.

The first left-hand drive option by a British manufacturer was offered by the Lanchester Company on cars for the American market.

The first series production car with swing-axle rear suspension was the rear-engined saloon car from Germany designed by Dr Edmund Rumpler. It had a 'teardrop' plan-form which gave it a drag coefficient of 0.28, despite its height and partly-exposed wheels. Drag figures of this order were not matched on production road cars until the 1960s, when Lotus achieved 0.29 with the first Elite, and another quarter of a century passed before 0.28 was claimed for a mass-production saloon, the Renault 25.

1922

First 'Million Year' for any car manufacturer: Ford of America delivered 1,216,792 units of their Model T.

Top Tropfenwagen: Dr Rumpler's 'teardrop' saloon car was a forerunner of his rear-engined G.P. Benz design of 1923.

Above All-time low: they never came cheaper than the Briggs & Stratton 'Buckboard' of 1922.

Daimler Dinosaur: one of a few special 'Double-Six' chassis built in 1930.

The cheapest-ever car was built by the Briggs and Stratton Company of Milwaukee, Wisconsin, USA. Their 'Red Bug Buckboard' was offered at $125–150, then about £25–30.

The great little Austin Seven – first British 'Peoples' Car' – started production. It continued until 1938, by which time nearly 300,000 had been built. It is remembered today by elderly motorists with similar affection to that afforded the earlier 'bull-nose' Morris. (See 1912.)

The first car to be fitted with a Marconiphone radio set was a Daimler.

The automatic choke was introduced by Cadillac of USA.

Barker headlamps which moved mechanically for dipping were fitted to Alvis and Morris cars among others.

1923
Budd all-steel saloon bodywork was adopted by Dodge, USA. (See 1916.)

1924
Double-filament headlamp bulbs were introduced in America.

1925
The pioneer Mercedes and Benz Companies of Germany amalgamated to found the great firm of Daimler-Benz AG. The Daimler concern had changed its name to Mercedes in 1901 in an effort to overcome the anti-German prejudice of the important French market, following the Franco-Prussian war.

First known use of an oil-pressure warning light was on the Italian Fiat 509 model.

1926
USSR's first private car to be designed and built on home ground was the NAMI-1 – a small twin-cylinder tourer.

The first British V12 engine powered the Daimler 'Double-Six'. It had a capacity of 7136 cc and sleeve-valves. The vast chassis had a wheelbase of 12 ft 11½ in/3.9 m.

Arrow direction indicators on either side of number plates appeared on British 14/40 Talbots.

Car heaters operating off the cooling system appeared first in the USA, though foot-warmers similarly supplied were to be found on pre-1900 Cannstatt-Daimlers of Germany.

The first car with safety glass windows as standard equipment was offered by Cadillac, USA.

1927
The first London–Brighton Commemoration Run was organized by the *Daily Sketch* newspaper. This annual event is restricted to cars built before 31 December 1904. It 're-enacts' the celebratory London-to-Brighton outing of the Motor Car Club when the 'Emancipation Act' of 1896 put paid to the 'Red Flag Act' of 1865.

1928
The first front-wheel drive car with all-independent suspension was the 12/75 Alvis of Great Britain.

Sweet Sixteen: Cadillac V16 unit, 1932.

British Innovator: the f.w.d./i.f.s. Alvis 12/75.

The first synchromesh gearboxes were fitted to La Salle and Cadillac cars in the USA.

The last private car to be offered with solid tyres was the British Trojan Type XL.

The first mass-produced estate car was offered by Ford, USA, on their Model A chassis.

1930

The first 16-cylinder engines in private cars powered the V16 Bugatti Type 47 (very few were built), and the V16 Cadillac and Marmons of 1930/31, both of which were marketed in series. Around the same time, prototypes of Bucciali and Peerless were built and shown but they were never produced commercially.

The British Daimler Company of Coventry pioneered their fluid-flywheel transmission with steering-column selector. The system was used on all their models from 1932 to 1956.

1931

Front-wheel drive with transverse engine lay-out originated on the twin-cylinder 490 cc D.K.W. (*Das Kleine Wunder*) F1 model from Germany. (See 1959.)

1932

The last catalogued steam-powered private car was the Doble, built by Abner Doble in California, USA. His F-type swansong had a flash boiler at the front and a four-cylinder horizontal engine geared directly to the back axle. It went very well but was expensive to buy and difficult to maintain.

Abner Doble's personal E24 steamer. These Dobles weighed over two tons, did around 90 mph/144 kph and cost $12,000 (£2400) in their day.

1933

The first all-synchromesh gearbox to be fitted as standard appeared on the British Alvis Speed Twenty model.

Semaphore-type direction indicators were introduced in Great Britain on Morris cars.

1934

Citroën of France's 4-cylinder *Traction Avant* was the first front-wheel drive car with unitary chassis/body construction.

The first coil-spring independent front-suspension lay-out was introduced by Cadillac, USA.

1935

A straight-12 engine was designed by Gabriel Voisin (q.v.) of France. With a capacity of six litres, its two rear cylinders protruded back into the driving compartment as far as the instrument panel. The straight-12 was the last Voisin model to carry his distinctive winged radiator mascot.

The first headlamp flashers appeared on the Fiat 1500 model in Italy.

1936

The first diesel-engined private car to be offered for sale was the Mercedes-Benz 260D from Germany.

The first pop-up headlamps were a feature on the innovative Cord Model 810 from USA. They had to be wound-up manually however.

1937

Screen washers were offered as an option on American Studebaker cars.

1938

The year of the foundation of the longest-ever production run – that of the ubiquitous Volkswagen 'Beetle', designed by Dr Ferdinand Porsche (q.v.).

Sponsored by Adolf Hitler's Government as the 'Peoples' Car', it was publicized by the Reich as the *KdF Wagen* (*Kraft durch Freude* = Strength Through Joy) which was the slogan of the Nazi movement. (See 1962.)

The first steering-column gear-change (allied to a normal manual box) was introduced in the USA by Cadillac.

VW type 38 prototypes in Berlin. Designed to cost under 1000 *Reichmarks* (10–11 per £ sterling) and be available at weekly instalments of 5 marks, there were 169,741 savers in the KdF car scheme in December 1938.

1939

The first Bentley car with independent front suspension was the Mark V 4¼-litre model.

'Winker' turn indicators, developed by the Guide Lamp Division of the General Motors Corporation, were introduced by Buick of USA.

1940

The first modern-type automatic transmission was an option offered by General Motors of USA, as 'Hydramatic' drive on their Oldsmobile models, and also on Cadillacs in 1941.

First air-conditioning system on a car was offered by Packard, USA.

The Bantam Car Company, of Butler, Pennsylvania, USA (who built the British Austin Seven under licence) delivered a batch of 70 four-wheel-drive light military scout cars for trials by the Army. Eight of them had four-wheel steering as well. These cars became known world-wide as the ubiquitous Jeeps (G.P. = General Purpose). In 1941 the Ford and Willys Companies took up Jeep production using the latter company's engines. Bantam had employed Continental 4-cylinder units.

Two-speed windscreen wipers were offered on American Chrysler models.

The General Motors Corporation produced its 25,000,000th car on 11 January.

1941

The first four-wheel-drive private car in series production was the 3.5 litre 6-cylinder GAZ-61 from the USSR. It followed upon very limited edition designs from the USA (1900) and Holland (1902), by Cotta and Spyker respectively.

Red Star: the 4-w-d GAZ-61.

Wartime Daimlers feature all-independent suspension!

Below Impeccable low-drag styling is a Bristol *sine qua non*: the 401 saloon of 1948.

OHY 401

1942

The American Nash 600 sedan had full unitary construction with a box section frame welded directly to the body – for the first time on a cheap American car.

1942/3

The Daimler Company of Coventry, England, were producing their four-wheel-drive, all-independently sprung scout cars and armoured cars, with engines of 2.5 and 4.1 litres respectively, fluid flywheels and epicyclic gears. The armoured car was the first Daimler with disc brakes.

Civilian car production was now virtually at a standstill in European countries . . . .

1944

Volvo of Sweden introduced their PV444 1.4-litre model – the first Volvo to sell in any numbers outside Scandinavia. It formed the basis of their post-war production and survived until 1965.

1945

Renault of Billancourt, Paris, France, was nationalized. In 1944 Louis Renault (q.v.) had been accused of collaboration with the Germans.

The Bristol Aeroplane Company launched its Car Division. The first of this superlative line of cars was their aerodynamic Type 400 2-litre.

1946

First British car to have a steering-column gear change was the Triumph 1800 model.

First Indian-built private car was the Hindusthan Ten. It was identical to the 10 hp Morris Series M, and the forerunner of a series of Morris models to be built by Hindusthan Motors.

1947

The Standard Motor Company of Coventry brought out their first truly new post-war design – the Vanguard. With its outstanding 2-litre, 4-cylinder engine, three-speed gearbox with steering-column change and full-width six-seater 'fastback' body, it was a very significant British family car of its day.

The deathless Aston Martin Company was acquired by the tractor manufacturer, David Brown. The new company's second model, the DB2, was powered by the W. O. Bentley-designed 2.6-litre ohc Lagonda engine.

1948

Saw the introduction of the Land Rover four-wheel-drive cross-country vehicle – as a 'stop-gap' design to see the Company into its post-war conventional car programme. It is as popular as ever to this day and has now sold a total of approximately 1.5 million units at home and abroad to 1986 – and it soldiers on! Diesel engines were fitted optionally from 1958, and the V8 petrol-engined version came in 1979. The more sophisticated Range Rover, with coil-spring suspension, has been available since 1970 and around 160,000 have been sold.

The Jaguar XK120 was the Star of the Show at Earl's Court. It was then the world's fastest production car, with a top speed of 120 mph – but not the greatest of stoppers.

Show Stopper: the twin ohc, 3½ litre Jaguar XK120 made a sensational début at £988 (+ £275 Purchase Tax).

Standard Style-setter: this leading design for its day was well-named 'Vanguard'.

The world's first radial tyre; the steel braced Michelin X.

1949

The Alex Issigonis-designed Morris Minor 8 hp appeared. Compact yet roomy, and with torsion bar suspension, it set new road-holding standards for its day. Not excluding the Mini, it is Sir Alex's (q.v.) favourite brainchild.

The French 2CV Citroën was introduced (though a prototype had been produced as early as 1936). From its original concept as a 'peasant's car' the 'Tin Duckling' is now a 'cult car', and thrives after a run of nearly forty years.

Key starting, as distinct from pressing a button, was pioneered by Chrysler of USA.

1950

Jet 1, the first of a series of Rover gas turbine cars, appeared. It was the world's first successful turbo car, with rear-mounted 200 bhp engine in a Rover

The first torque converter-type automatic transmission to be offered on an American passenger car was introduced by Buick.

The first radial-ply tyre was marketed – the Michelin X. The first car to be fitted with them was the Citroën *Traction Avant*.

Reliable tubeless tyres were marketed in USA by Goodrich.

The first car to be mass-produced in Australia, by General Motors, was the 2.2-litre 6-cylinder Holden FX type. It cost £A675.

Right Early bird: the 1939 prototype Citröen 2CV 'Tin Duckling' did rather resemble a small corrugated-iron shed on wheels. . . .

Alex Issigonis' Morris Minor was the first British post-WW II cheap car to match, or surpass, its Continental competitors.

Swoosh! – the Rover Jet 1, with 2-seater convertible body modified from that of a '75' P4 piston-engined production model.

75 chassis. In 1952 it was timed at 151.965 mph/ 244.5 kph over a flying kilometre.

Ford of Dagenham first used the MacPherson strut (combined coil-spring and damper) front suspension. It was devised by Earle S. MacPherson, an engineer at Ford, Dagenham, and was used on nearly every Ford Europe car thereafter.

Tinted glass windows became available on Buick models in USA.

1951

The Chinese Government, under Mao Tse-tung, produced their first private car prototype. It was referred to as 'The People's Car'.

Modern-type power steering was offered on the Chrysler Imperial models in America.

1952

Modern-type disc brakes, of Dunlop design (British patent 688382, for a disc fixed to a rotating hub and clamped by piston-operated pads on each side) were fitted to the Jaguar entries in the Mille Miglia. Manufacture was subsequently licensed to Girling and Bendix. Developed originally for the C-type racing Jaguar and used to win Le Mans in 1953, they were fitted as standard to the 1954 D-types and to the Austin-Healey 100S the same year. Triumph sports cars had front discs in 1956 and the Jensen 541 got 4-wheel disc brakes that autumn. The Jaguar XK150 was provided with discs in the spring of 1957. Early attempts at disc brakes date back to the British Lanchester of 1903.

1953

The first American sports-car in the modern idiom was the Chevrolet Corvette. It was also the first series-production car with a fibreglass body.

The first tubeless tyres to be marketed in Great Britain were manufactured by Dunlop.

1954

The first British diesel-engined private car was a version of the Standard Vanguard Phase II.

First petrol-engined private car with fuel injection as standard was the 3-litre, gull-wing-doored Mercedes-Benz 300SL from Germany.

Cadillac (USA) became the first manufacturer to adopt power-assisted steering as standard throughout its range.

Sport Leicht: the glamorous 300SL Mercedes required circumspection of the enthusiastic amateur driver.

1955

First production car with front-wheel disc brakes and self-levelling suspension was the Citroën DS of France. Its monocoque body was also the first with detachable body panels.

1956

The Rover T3, turbo-engined, 4-wheel-drive coupé, with a glass fibre body, was presented at the Earl's Court Show.

Renault's Dauphine model was the first French car to sell over two million units.

1957

The first car fitted with air suspension was the Cadillac Eldorado Brougham model.

First cars with twin paired-headlamps (four headlamps) were the Lincoln and Cadillac models.

The 1000 cc Toyota Corona was launched in May (see also 1986 and 1987).

1958

The world's first production car with unitary body/chassis construction in glass fibre was Colin Chapman's (q.v.) Lotus Elite from Great Britain.

Avant-garde; 1955: Citroën's Gallic expertise allied high-pressure hydraulics to both brakes and suspension, with very advanced aerodynamics as a bonus.

Plastic Pioneer: Anthony Colin Bruce Chapman's glass-reinforced plastic Lotus Elite.

Horse-collar: Ford's Edsel 'Citation' model was a misnomer to say the least!

First British saloon car with disc brakes all-round was the Daimler Majestic. Automatic transmission was standard.

The year of the Ford Edsel – perhaps the greatest flop ever dealt by a world-wide major manufacturer. Launched by the Lincoln-Mercury Division of Ford, Detroit, Edsels had V8 engines of 5.9 or 6.7 litres. Their appearance was of quite startling vulgarity even by the standards of American automobiles of the day. With a wrap-round windshield, prolific fins, loads of flashy chromium plating and a radiator reminiscent of a horse's neckwear, only 35,000 were sold in the first six months, and the Edsel was out of production by 1960 – a triumph for the taste of US buyers at last!

1959

The fabulous 'Mini' was launched, as the Austin Seven/Morris Mini Minor, on 26 August, at the price of £496–19s–2d. Over 5,000,000 had been sold by mid-February, 1986. The millionth was built in February 1965, and the two millionth on 19 June 1969. This first transverse-engined, front-wheel drive, monocoque small car was the inspired design of Sir Alexander Issigonis (q.v.).

The last of the production straight-8-engined cars was the Z.I.S. from the Soviet Union. The American straight-8 Packard had been phased out in 1955.

America's first production rear-engined car was the notorious Chevrolet Corvair, which formed the platform for Ralph Nader's safety campaign. The latter ultimately resulted in the introduction of Federal Safety Standards for cars sold in the USA.

1960

All-wooden unitary construction was first used in production application by Jem *Mar*sh and Frank *Cost*in on the original Marcos GT coupés. It had been experimented with on the prototype cars of Frederick and George Lanchester (q.v.) in 1922/23, and also in Australia by Marks-Moir in 1923.

1961

Jaguar Cars of Coventry, England, introduced their epoch-making E-type sports-car – the first 150 mph production car.

The Morris Minor achieved a million sales in January. It was the first British car so to do.

The first American V6-cylinder passenger car engine was introduced by Buick.

The first Israeli private car was the Sabra, designed to suit local conditions by Reliant of Tamworth, Warwickshire, England. Ilin of Haifa had, however, been assembling American Kaisers from 1951.

Glas of Germany's 1004 coupé was the first production car to employ cogged-tooth belt-drive to its overhead camshaft.

Space efficiency, or four in a shoe box? Cutaway 1959 Mini: the 'bent-wire' gearlever was later replaced by a shorter, remote one.

The British Triplex Company introduced zone-toughened safety glass.

1962

Hydrolastic suspension, the invention of Alec Moulton, appeared for the first time on the Issigonis Austin/Morris 1100 models with transverse engines, front-wheel drive and bodies designed by Pininfarina (q.v.).

The Rover T4 turbo-engined front-wheel drive car was seen at the Earl's Court Motor Show. Its bodywork served as a prototype for the conventionally piston-engined Rover 2000 model which was launched the following year.

First ever 'Million Year' for a European manufacturer was scored by the Volkswagen 'Beetle' from Wolfsburg, West Germany. The 20 millionth 'Beetle' came off the production line in Mexico in May 1981. 20,630,000 had hatched out by January 1986.

On 14 March, General Motors produced the 75,000,000th US-made vehicle.

1963

The Rover 2000 model, brainchild basically of the late Peter Wilkes and Spencer King, was the first European car to sport a bowl-in-piston engine.

N.S.U. of West Germany started production of their Wankel rotary-engined 'Sports Spyder' two-seater roadster. The power unit gave 50 bhp from the equivalent of approximately 500 cc.

1964

Ford of Detroit unleashed their 'Planned Miracle' – the Mustang, in April. Prosaic though it was mechanically, its cosmetics made it 'the star of one of the most remarkable automobile success stories of modern times'. This astute example of automotive packaging was the brainchild of Lee Iacocca, then General Manager of Ford Division, and now the Boss at Chrysler, USA. He is a trained engineer but, above all, an exceptionally sales-orientated one, selling 400,000 units of a new model within a year, and 1.5 million in the first three years.

First fully automatic air-conditioning system was Cadillac's 'Climate Control'.

1965

Introduction of compulsory exhaust emission controls were introduced in California, USA. These were latterly applied to the other 47 States in 1968.

Brake stop-lamps were made compulsory on vehicles in the United Kingdom. The Law also decided that all new cars must have flashing turn-indicators from 1 September.

The ten millionth Volkswagen 'Beetle' was built.

The largest front-wheel drive production car was the Oldsmobile Toronado at 17 ft 7 in long/5.3 m with a 6.9 litre engine giving 385 bhp. This monster was joined a year later by a Cadillac version called the Eldorado.

Iacocca's Miracle: 1964 Ford Mustang.

1966

Turkey built its first passenger car in Istanbul by Otosan. It was designed by the Reliant Motor Company of Tamworth, as a two-door saloon powered by a 1200 cc Ford engine.

Forerunner of the 'buggy'-type vehicle was the Meyers-Manx. It was built on a VW 'Beetle' floorplan and appeared in California, USA.

First four-wheel drive car with anti-lock braking was the British Jensen FF model. It used the Dunlop-designed Maxaret system.

The millionth Ford Mustang was produced on 2 March, after a run of one year, eleven months and twenty-three days – a record for that time.

The first widespread use of plastics for external car body parts was pioneered by the Pontiac Company, USA, with plastic radiator grilles and smaller items.

1967

B. F. Goodrich in USA invented the space-saver spare tyre which was inflated by a can of freon gas. It was first supplied as standard equipment on the Pontiac Firebird of that year.

The Peykan started a little-noticed but remarkable production run that was to last 20 years and see the millionth vehicle produced in 1984, its specification very little changed from the first. Peykans were in fact Hillman Hunters supplied in 'knocked down' kit form to Iran, where they accounted for almost the entire market – in 1986 it was reported that first prize in a lottery was a place on a waiting list for a Peykan.

General Motors produced the 100,000,000th US-made vehicle on 21 April.

1968

The Triumph 2.5-litre PI model was the first British family car to be fitted with fuel injection – by Lucas.

The British Leyland Motor Corporation was the first UK manufacturer to make a million vehicles in a year. They produced 1,001,105 units, which included 867,067 cars.

The first small four-wheel-drive vehicle with a transverse engine was the Austin Ant. It was intended as a more practical successor to the Moke, but only 30 prototypes were built before British Leyland company realignments led to the Group abandoning the market for light 4-w-d cars, which

Japanese manufacturers were later to find very worthwhile.

Mercedes-Benz of Stuttgart were the first European manufacturers to fit electronic (rather than mechanical) fuel injection, of Bosch design, to their cars.

Michelin of France introduced their XAS assymetric radial tyre. Deep zigzag grooves came on the inside and centre of the tread, with a very narrow cut-out on the built-up outside shoulder of the tyre.

The Jensen Motor Company of West Bromwich, Birmingham, were the first British manufacturer to offer Lucas quartz-iodine (now quartz-halogen) headlamp bulbs as standard equipment on their Interceptor and FF models.

1969

The US Government introduced their Federal Safety Standards nationwide.

Ford of Dagenham fulfilled 'The Car You Always Promised Yourself' – their Capri! It was a sporty GT version of the best-selling Cortina family saloons which first appeared in 1962.

Rover's innovatory 2000 series cars were the first to be offered with a Triplex safety glass roof panel as a factory-approved extra.

Ford of Detroit offered Kelsey-Hayes anti-lock braking system with rear wheel sensors to prevent wheels locking under retardation.

1970

The British Ford company exported the millionth Cortina and, shortly afterwards in July, produced the two millionth example.

Head restraints to car seats became compulsory in the USA.

1971

Sweden's Saab 99 model was the first car to be fitted with the headlamp wash/wipe system.

1971/2

Apollo Missions 15, 16 and 17 to the Moon (26/7/71; 16/4/72; 7/12/72) carried with them the Lunar Roving Vehicle (LRV), a four-wheel battery-powered car. It was a lightweight engineering triumph and enabled the astronauts greatly to increase the areas of surface exploration they could undertake. If driven hard it would attain a top speed of 10.5 mph/17 kph on the level.

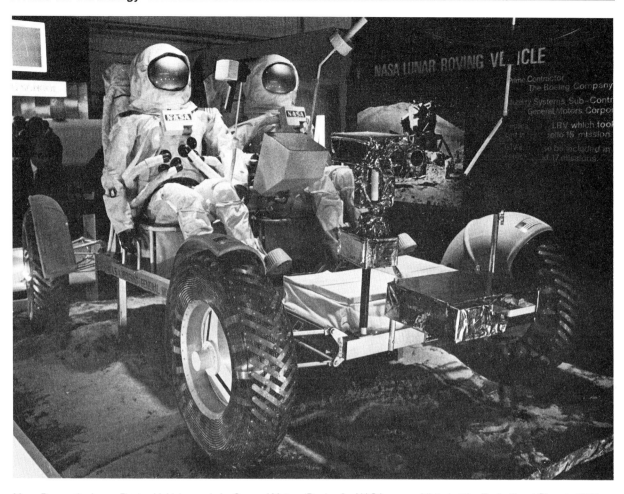

Moon Buggy: the Lunar Roving Vehicle, made by General Motors/Boeing for NASA, was exhibited at the Earl's Court Show in 1971, complete with piano-wire tyres and dummy astronauts.

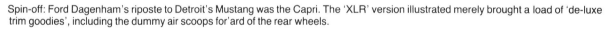

Spin-off: Ford Dagenham's riposte to Detroit's Mustang was the Capri. The 'XLR' version illustrated merely brought a load of 'de-luxe trim goodies', including the dummy air scoops for'ard of the rear wheels.

On Apollo 17 it covered a total distance of 18 miles/ 29 km, though its astronaut drivers never ventured farther than the 5.5 miles/9 km from the Lunar Module to which they would be able to return on foot should the LRV break down.

The first wheeled vehicle on the Moon was USSR's Lunokhod I which landed on 17 November 1970. It was, however, earth-controlled and unmanned. It moved around the Mare Imbrium for about 6.5 miles/10.5 km.

1972

Volkswagen 'Beetle' sales reached 15 million and in 1973 exceeded the previous record held by the Ford Model T of 16,536,075 units of an individual model.

1973

First turbocharged production car was the BMW 2002 Turbo model from Germany.

General Motors in the USA offered the first 'air-bag' safety cushion restraint on a production car.

1974

The first 5-cylinder-in-line engine fitted in a private car came in the Mercedes-Benz 300D (3-litre diesel) model.

1975

Rolls-Royce's Camargue model was the first car in the world to be fitted with automatic bi-level (cool head – hot feet) air-conditioning.

1976

Quickest first million production of an individual model – 31 months – was achieved by the Volkswagen Golf. Its production started in 1974.

1977

First 5-cylinder-in-line petrol-powered engine was fitted by Audi of Germany in their 100 GL5E model.

1978

First American 'compact' cars with front-wheel drive were the Dodge Omni and Plymouth Horizon from Chrysler.

1979

Polymer Research ran its first 'plastics' engine, a 2.3-litre unit which weighed a mere 176 lb/ 79.8 kg. Structural parts such as the block were made of graphite-reinforced plastic and smaller items such as tappets and piston rings from Tor-

lon, while components subject to greatest heat and stress (from combustion chambers to crankshaft) were still metal. Polimotor worked to prove their plastics engines with a series of racing units, including a 750 bhp turbo V6 suitable for Indycar racing.

1980

The first mass-production car with permanent four-wheel drive was the Audi Quattro. Its 5-cylinder 2144 cc turbocharged engine delivered 200 bhp. However it was preceded by the up-market Jensen FF model in 1966 (q.v.).

Japanese car production overtook that of the USA for the first time, when they made 7,000,000 units, nearly a quarter of the world's total for the year.

1981

B.M.W. (Bayerische Motoren Werke) of Munich introduced an on-board computer on their 5-Series models indicating to the driver that it is time for a service – the interval varying according to his personal driving methods.

Das Kindermädchen: on their 1981 5-series cars, B.M.W. introduced service interval indicator lights, to be re-set by their dealers . . . .

1982

The first 'compact' car produced by the great Daimler-Benz Company of Stuttgart was the Mercedes-Benz 190 model. In 1983 they introduced a diesel-engined version of this car with an encapsulated engine for silencing purposes.

The Opel Corsa was General Motors' first European small car with front-wheel drive. It has been sold in Britain as the Vauxhall Nova since 1983.

Production of the Morris Ital was discontinued. It was the last model to bear the famous name of William Morris (q.v.).

1983

The General Motors Corporation and Toyota of Japan formed a new company in the USA to build the Chevrolet Nova, at Freemont, California. It was called NUMMI (New United Motor Manufacturing Incorporated).

Polyglot Popular: Opel's Corsa in Germany and Vauxhall's Nova in Britain are built in a new American General Motors works in Spain.

1984

Jaguar Cars of Coventry was privatized from the British Leyland Group on 9 August. Its dynamic Chairman and Chief Executive, Sir John Egan, had taken over the then slack reins of the company in 1980, with outstanding results.

First Italian car with anti-lock braking system as standard was the Ferrari 412.

First American turbocharged front-wheel drive sports-car was the Chrysler Laser/Dodge Daytona.

'All-American' Laser: Chrysler's conception of a mid-80s sports-car, for home consumption.

1985

The fastest-ever road cars were tested authentically. The Ferrari Testa Rossa was road-tested by both the German magazine *Auto Motor und Sport* and the British *Motor* magazine. It achieved a top speed of 180 mph/289.7 kph, while the latter's figures 0–60 and 0–100 mph (0–96.5 and 0–160.9 kph) were 5.8 and 12.7 sec. respectively. Britain's *Autocar* road test of the Lamborghini Countach 5000S showed a maximum of 179.2 mph/287.7 kph with 0–60 mph (0–96.5 kph) in 4.9 sec and 0–100 mph (0–160.9 kph) in 10.6 sec. In parenthesis, the British magazine *Fast Lane* claims to have wrung 190 mph/305 kph from a Lamborghini Countach *quattrovalvole*, while Aston Martin claim 186 mph/298 kph for their Vantage Zagato model.

The Ford Granada model range became the first to have anti-lock brakes as standard on all models.

1986

Fuel injection and anti-lock brakes were first fitted by Rolls-Royce on their European models for the October Motor Show at the National Exhibition Centre at Birmingham.

Alpha and Omega: 1957 Toyota Corona and 1986 Corolla models – with 10 million sales separating them....

Ultimate? Rolls-Royce Phantom VI limousine (6750 cc V8), with Mulliner Park Ward coachwork on, perhaps, the last of the traditional separate chassis – the bonnet is centre-hinged as well!

Toyota passed two production milestones in the same year – cumulative production of the Corolla range reached 10 million (albeit the 1986 cars were very different from the original Corolla, especially as the model had become a front-wheel drive type in 1983), whilst Corona production passed five million (in its first year, 1957, Corona production was 3450 cars and the peak came in 1975 when 317,000 were built).

First car with height-adjustable belts to both front and rear seats was the General Motors Vauxhall Carlton GL.

Nissan became the first Japanese manufacturer to build cars in Britain, at Washington, Co. Durham.

1987

The most expensive British standard production car is the Rolls-Royce Phantom VI limousine at £195,595.83 including tax. The special State Landaulette version can cost over twice as much.

The cheapest new car purchaseable in Britain is the Fiat 126, 652 cc two-door model at £2431.

France's Citroën AX economy car goes into production.

Toyota Corona total cumulative production topped 6,000,000 units in 29 years, only seven months after reaching the five million mark (see 1957 and 1986).

February saw the demise of the Ford Capri. Launched in 1969 (q.v.), it did Ford Europe proud, with total sales of 1,886,647 units, to which must be added a final fling of 1038 'special edition' 280 Injection models – all finished in 'Brooklands' green.

The German magazine *Auto Motor und Sport* road tested the very-limited production Porsche 959 at a maximum speed of 197 mph/317 kph. About 20 cars have been built and orders confirmed for a further 250.

MOTORING MEN

1 Designers

Herbert Austin

Herbert Austin, British (1866–1941) was employed by the Wolseley Sheep Shearing Machine Company in Australia before he became involved with the automobile. When he returned to his native land in 1895, his employers became interested in the new-fangled horseless carriage and Herbert designed for them a brace of tri-cars between 1896 and 1898. A prototype four-wheeler Wolseley came the year after, production thereof starting in 1900. Later Austin fell out with the Board over engine design policy and thus opted to set up his own company in Birmingham in 1906. The Austin Motor Company prospered and was Britain's largest car producer by the outbreak of WWI. In the immediate post-war years, Austin had his problems, but the Company's failing fortunes were restored by the introduction of the 'Baby' Austin Seven in 1922. It rapidly became a best-seller in Great Britain, as well as being built under licence in Germany as the B.M.W., in France as the Rosengart and in the USA as the Bantam. Herbert's cobby little Seven is as much a milestone in British motoring history as was Henry Ford's Model T in the United States. The Austin Motor Company continued to manufacture good, solid, reliable, well-engineered (if a trifle dull) vehicles right up to WWII. Austin himself was knighted in 1917 and he became 1st Baron Austin of Longbridge in 1936.

Walter Owen Bentley, British (1888–1971) trained as a locomotive engineer at Doncaster, an apprenticeship which is reflected in the solidity of his motor-car designs. Before WWI he imported, and raced, French D.F.P. cars, fitting some of them with aluminium pistons. During hostilities, he designed two successful rotary aero-engines for the Admiralty. He showed his prototype sports-car (F. T. Burgess of Humber assisted in its design) in 1919. He marketed it two years later and, sales being meagre, sought to boost them by turning again to racing. The saga of the 'Bentley Boys', their cars and many famous victories, has become an oft-told and evergreen motoring legend.... Design-wise, suffice here to say that, when 'W.O.', as he was known, required his Dreadnought chassis to go faster, he 'sent out for more litres...'. Thus the capacities of his sports-cars increased from the 2996 cc of the 'Three Litre' model, through the 4398 cc of the '4½' and 6597 cc of the 'Speed Six', to the 7983 cc of the superb '8-Litre'. Reliability ensued.... Alas the Bentley Motors Company was somewhat under-financed from its outset and the industrial depression of 1930 saw W.O.'s firm taken over by Rolls-Royce (again competition from Napier) for £125,175. Bentley now completed his contract by going to work at Derby on developing the 3½- and 4¼-litre 'Rolls-Bentleys' of the middle 1930s. On his release in 1935 he went to Lagonda, as Technical

Director, where he designed the lovely V12 model but unfortunately its proper development was halted by WWII. The war over, he was responsible for the engines of the new Aston Martin/Lagonda which were now being manufactured under the aegis of David Brown of tractor fame.

Despite the fame of his name, and of the splendid cars that bear it, the reserved and gentlemanly W. O. Bentley never seems quite to have been blessed with the good fortune his talents deserved.

Karl Benz

Karl Benz, German (1844–1929) was the first man to build a series of cars to one practical design and then sell them to the public. His father was a locomotive driver and he died when Karl was two years old. The young Benz attended Karlsruhe Polytechnic where he studied engineering, and then he started a business in Mannheim in 1882, making stationary two-stroke gas engines of his own design. His first four-stroke was a two-seater tri-car with electric ignition, surface carburettor and belt drive – and it worked fairly well. He improved upon it however and, in 1887, he succeeded in selling a car to Emile Roger of Paris who, impressed, now took an agency to market Benz cars in France. Karl Benz's motor-car patent is dated 29 January 1886. His vehicles sold briskly by the standards of the 1890s but, alas, Karl was averse to moving with the times and stuck to his 'horseless-carriage' conception far too long. Thus his products were overtaken by those of more 'modern' designers (eg Maybach q.v.) after 1902.

Marc Birkigt

Marc Birkigt, Swiss (1878–1953) was born in Geneva and orphaned at 11; his grandmother sent him to the Ecole de Mécanique whence he graduated with distinction in engineering and physics. After his military service, Birkigt went to Paris, and thence to Barcelona in 1899, where he became interested in motor vehicles while he was working in electrical engineering.

With finance provided by one Damien Mateu, the Hispano-Suiza Company was registered in 1904, and production started with lorries as well as passenger cars. Later its aero-engines, designed by Birkigt, powered large numbers of Allied aircraft in both world wars.

Birkigt's most distinguished automobile designs were the 4-cylinder T-head 'Alfonso' model (1910), which was followed in 1919 by the great, innovatory, 37.2 hp, 6.5-litre, 6-cylinder car with a single overhead-camshaft, light-alloy cylinder block and 4-wheel brakes. This landmark was followed by the 8-litre 'Boulogne' (1923) which was one of the pre-eminent luxury cars of the mid-20s. Next, in 1931, came Marc's masterpiece – the magnificent 9.4-litre V12 Type 68, which later became available in 11,310 cc form in 1934, with 250 bhp – and a price of £3750 in the England of that day, with fairly prosaic coachwork! Production of the Type 68 continued up to 1939 when Birkigt returned to Paris and aero-engines until France fell. Nevertheless, manufacture of the 20 mm Hispano-Suiza cannon continued in Britain and armed Spitfires, Hurricanes and Beaufighter aircraft.

After the war, the Bois Colombes (Paris) and Barcelona (Spain) factories were sold, the latter producing commercial vehicles and also the short-lived Pegaso luxury sporting cars of *Wilfredo Ricart*. Marc Birkigt never really got going again post-war. He decided to enjoy family life on his estate outside Geneva. He was a quiet, retiring man, a perfectionist who liked walking, hunting and Wagner's music – cost accountants were anathema to him, and his Hispano-Suiza Company was the only marque of the 20s and 30s which one might mention in the same breath as Rolls-Royce.

Ettore Bugatti, Italian (1882–1947) was Italian by birth, German by

Ettore Bugatti

nationalization and he lived in France. He trained as an artist, turned to engineering, and then became one of the original thinkers in the field of automobile design. He worked for the De Dietrich and Mathis Companies, before building cars bearing his own name in a disused dye works at Molsheim, Alsace, in 1909. Surprisingly, the first of these was a small, 1200 cc, 4-cylinder, ohc-engined car, designated the Type 13, which performed very well. However it was beautifully made, and thus expensive, at a time when most small cars were cheap and nasty.

Ettore became a proponent of the straight-8, ohc engine (his WWI aircraft engine was a double-straight-8) and the 2-litre Type 30 car of 1923 set the pattern for the majority of his designs in the 20s – which included the vast Type 41 '*La Royale*', a white elephant of 12¾-litres and 14 ft 2 in/4.2 m 5 cm wheelbase in the production versions (15 ft/3 m the prototype). Bugatti was the first-ever manufacturer to sell Grand Prix cars commercially, and his classically handsome Type 35 racing car, and its derivatives, were also powered by straight-8 engines.

In 1934 came his last touring design – the 3.3-litre, twin ohc Type 57, which, with 130 bhp on tap and an excellent chassis, was well able to hold its own with (or even pass) the contemporary Rolls-Bentley of 3½-litres capacity.

Ettore Bugatti has been described by the pundits as 'an artist first, a mechanical genius second, and an engineer last of all', while that 'in his life and his artistic approach to mechanical problems, he was really a man of the Regency era, born out of his time'. Add to this *Grand Seigneur, bon viveur* and bloodstock fancier, and Ettore Bugatti comes up as a colourful character. Alas production of his cars never got back under way after WWII.

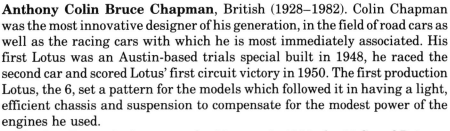

Anthony Colin Bruce Chapman, British (1928–1982). Colin Chapman was the most innovative designer of his generation, in the field of road cars as well as the racing cars with which he is most immediately associated. His first Lotus was an Austin-based trials special built in 1948, he raced the second car and scored Lotus' first circuit victory in 1950. The first production Lotus, the 6, set a pattern for the models which followed it in having a light, efficient chassis and suspension to compensate for the modest power of the engines he used.

Colin Chapman

The first Lotus single-seater, the 12, came in 1956; the 16 Grand Prix car was raced in 1958; the widely-successful rear-engined 18 was built in Formula Junior and Grand Prix forms (a first Grand Prix victory came at Monaco in 1960); the trend-setting monocoque 25 appeared in 1963. Collaboration with one Ford company culminated in the Indianapolis 500 victory in 1965; collaboration with another brought the DFV engine, first used in the Lotus 49. Among the Grand Prix designs produced under Chapman's direction were the classic 72 and the ground effects 78 and 79, while along the way there had also been gas-turbine racing cars and four-wheel-drive essays.

The relatively simple road-going sports-cars gave way to more up-market models in the 1970s, the Company introduced its own engine, while Chapman dabbled with power-boats and developed a 'think-tank' consultancy element at Lotus.

Colin Chapman died of a heart attack, but his Lotus team survived him, as did his Lotus Company in the face of many immediate problems.

Gottlieb Daimler, German (1834–1900) was the son of a Schorndorf baker who apprenticed his son to a gunsmith. Afterwards Gottlieb worked for various engineering concerns before joining the gas-engine firm, Otto &

Gottlieb Daimler

Langen of Deutz in 1872. Here he stayed for 10 years, during which time he designed the first workable four-stroke internal combustion engine, in which he was aided by Wilhelm Maybach (q.v.). The pair set up on their own as consultant engineers at Cannstatt in 1882, where they designed and built the first 'modern-type', petrol-fuelled car engine in 1883. The Daimler Motoren Gesellschaft was founded in 1890 producing ever-improving vehicles, later examples being built under licence by Panhard et Levassor and the British Daimler Company. In parentheses, the famous Daimler and Benz concerns were separate entities until their amalgamation in 1925 – by which time Gottlieb had been dead for a quarter of a century.

Comte Albert de Dion, French (1856–1946) was a Founder Champion of the horseless carriage, his interest initially being in steam-powered vehicles. He employed Georges Bouton to develop them, which he did successfully, with his partner Trépardoux. Later they built petrol-engined tricycles which sold well. In 1898 came their first small car, of which De Dion et Cie had sold 1500 examples by 1901. The Company also sold its engines to the scores of other manufacturers who mushroomed at this time. The Comte himself (Marquis, 1901) was a driving force in the Olympian *Automobile Club de France* – and a formidable duellist to boot.

Keith Duckworth

Keith Duckworth, British (1933–   ) is best known as the designer of the outstandingly successful Ford Cosworth DFV 3-litre Grand Prix engine, and as co-founder, and later chairman and chief engineer, of Cosworth Engineering Ltd. He entered the automotive world as a part-time worker at Lotus Cars, becoming their transmission development engineer until he had a disagreement with Colin Chapman (q.v.). Duckworth left Lotus and set up Cosworth Engineering with Mike Costin, in 1958. Initially they prepared racing engines, and then developed Formula Junior and Formula 2 power units on Ford bases. The DFV led to other very successful engines, such as the DFX. Cosworth now undertook development work for other companies, such as Daimler-Benz, but remained generally associated with Ford, and a substantial and sophisticated plant burgeoned at Northampton. Duckworth has remained genial and bluff – good social company, although he does not suffer fools gladly – but that mask does not conceal the technical shrewdness of a gifted engineer capable of applying cold logic to the solution of mechanical problems.

Enzo Ferrari

Enzo Ferrari, Italian (1898–   ) has been one of the outstanding personalities of motor sport for almost 60 years. He was not a designer, nor was he more than a fairly good racing driver, but he was a leading team manager and since the late 1940s has been the universally-known racing car constructor. For a quarter of a century he has been the patrician figure of racing.

His association with Alfa Romeo began in 1920 and he was responsible for Alfa Romeo's racing activities in the 1930s, his *Scuderia Ferrari* (formed in 1929) campaigning the official Alfa team until 1939, when he broke with the company. His own first car appeared in 1940 – a sports car, and it was wholly in character that a pair ran in the *Mille Miglia* that year – and after World War II he set up as a constructor in his own name. In Grand Prix racing he challenged the all-conquering Alfa Romeo team, eventually defeating it in 1951.

As Alfa Romeo withdrew, never to return as a major force, and Maserati faded in the second half of the 1950s, Ferrari became the foremost Italian racing marque. Ferrari's importance to national automotive prestige was underpinned by Fiat's financial support from the mid-1950s, resulting in a majority shareholding in Ferrari in the 1960s, when one of the conditions was that Enzo Ferrari remained in office. Fiat control has not constrained Ferrari – for example, when he has felt it best for his team he has not hesitated to employ British designers.

The early reputation of Ferraris tended to be built on sports cars – Ferraris won the Le Mans 24-hour Race nine times, and won 14 international sports car racing championships (under various titles). However, the team has contested only Grands Prix since the early 1970s, while the road cars have been a succession of high-performance GT machines.

Enzo Ferrari has survived many personal crises, particularly the death of his son Dino and accidents to many Ferrari drivers, and the sometimes vicious attacks of the Italian Press as well as the changing fortunes of racing, to maintain his marque and his racing programme at the highest level for four decades.

Henry Ford

Henry Ford, American (1863–1947) had no professional engineering training as such, but he was a natural-born mechanic whose ambitions lay in the manufacturing of a cheap yet reliable means of transport for a 'mass market'. His first motor vehicle – a crude quadricycle – was built in 1896. Henry worked for the Edison Company and the Detroit Automobile Company before setting up the first Ford Motor Company in 1901, having previously designed a couple of successful racing cars (in partnership with Tom Cooper) to help drum up the necessary finance. Gas buggies of Oldsmobile type were produced at first. Then came the immortal Model T in October 1908, (it was principally the design of James Cousens) and it proved to be a world-beater.

Now Ford set up the original 'mass production line' and also adopted a one-model policy. His Model T remained in production until 1927, by which time over 16½ million 'Tin Lizzies' had been sold. She was one of the great cars of all time.

Mauro Forghieri, Italian (1935–   ) presided over the technical aspects of Ferrari racing teams for a quarter of a century, bringing a wholly individualistic combination of automotive talent and Latin temperament to one of the less easy jobs in motor sport.

He gained an engineering degree before joining Ferrari in the late 50s. He was moved to the racing department as assistant to the volatile Carlo Chiti in 1960, took over from him late in 1961 and was occasionally displaced only to be hurriedly reinstated! Through to the early 70s he was responsible for Ferrari sports-car designs as well as Grand Prix cars. Whilst this led to some profitable cross-fertilization, it also over-stretched the resources of both man and teams.

Forghieri has not been a slave to Ferrari practices and traditions, unlike some of his colleagues, being quite prepared to adopt outside innovations, such as British-style chassis and suspension advances, even to getting some components (such as the first Ferrari monocoques) made outside Maranello; or bringing into the factory an experienced outside designer such as Harvey Postlethwaite. Outwardly, however, his cars have always carried the Ferrari stamp and been individualistic. They have frequently been successful, too, and have carried forward Ferrari's record of the greatest number of Grand Prix wins, which has remained unbroken through the 60s, 70s and into the second half of the 80s. Nevertheless, he was moved to take charge of Ferrari research and development in 1985.

Giorgetto Giugiaro, Italian (1938–   ) is one of the most outstanding car designers of the 70s and 80s. He has combined the conflicting requirements of fashion and engineering to produce integrated designs which incorporate new technical developments.

His styling education began at the Academia di Belle Arti in Turin, and in 1955 he took a job in Fiat's design department to pay for his studies. At the end of 1959 he joined Bertone's styling studio, working on the design of cars like the Gordon Keeble, Aston Martin DB4, Ferrari 250GT, Mazda 1000 and Fiat Dino coupé. A move to Ghia, as head of the styling department, followed in 1965. There he designed the Maserati Ghibli, De Tomaso Mangusta and Iso Rivolta Fidia.

At the beginning of 1968 Giugiaro set up his own company, Ital Design, with Aldo Mantovani and Luciano Bosio. An exponent of the wedge-shaped mid-engined high performance car, his Manta Bizzarini was shown at Turin in 1968, and was followed by other styling exercises leading to the design of the production Lotus Esprit in 1975. Other production car designs have been less exotic but, nevertheless, very successful. The Volkswagen Golf, Passat and Scirocco models, the Alfasud, Audi 80, Hyundai Pony, Fiat Panda and Lancia's Delta and Thema have all had the Giugiaro touch. Supercars have figured as well – the Maserati Bora, Merak and Quattroporte, the De Lorean and the BMW M1 among them, while the Lotus Etna (shown as a prototype in 1984) for the 1990s was also from his pen. Nor have all Giorgetto Giugiaro's designs been for cars – not long ago he designed a new specially-shaped pasta for an Italian food company!

Alex Issigonis

Alexander Arnold Constantine Issigonis, British (1906–   ) was born in Smyrna of Greek and Bavarian parents. He came to England in 1923 and learnt his engineering at Battersea Polytechnic, working in the Humber drawing office in the early 30s. In 1933 he built the Lightweight Special – a sprint car with an aluminium-faced plywood monocoque chassis, all-independent suspension and an 'Ulster' Austin Seven engine which he eventually supercharged. Alec moved to Morris in 1936 to work on suspension designs, and he stayed there throughout WWII on experimental vehicles for the Army. His highly successful post-war Morris Minor design was launched in 1948 and it sold over a million units up to 1961. After the Nuffield–Austin merger of 1952 Issigonis went to Alvis, where he worked on a V8-engined sporting family car which never went into production. Next he returned to Longbridge in 1956 and his most famous design, the brilliant Morris Mini Minor/Austin Seven economy car, with transverse engine and all-independent rubber-sprung suspension, appeared in 1959. It has now (1986) been in production for 27 years and has sold well over five million units.

Small is beautiful to Sir Alec Issigonis (C.B.E. 1964; K.B.E. 1969): 'I am still not much interested in large cars. A small one sets a tremendous challenge non-existent with a large one. Mr Royce had nothing to do!'

Vittorio Jano, Italian (1891–1965), who was born near Turin, was another of those great empirical engineers without formal training, save as a draughtsman. He started his career with the Rapid Company and then moved to the Fiat design department in 1911. There he became the pupil of the head-man, Carlo Cavalli. Jano helped in the organization of the highly-successful Fiat racing team of the early 20s, and was in charge of it by 1923. Then he left to join Alfa Romeo in Milan, commissioned to design and manage their new GP car to replace the ill-fated P1 of 1922/23, for the 1924 season.

Vittorio Jano

Jano now built Alfa the famous, 2-litre supercharged, straight-8, bull-nose car which won its very first race at Cremona, and many more thereafter up to 1932. It was known as the P2. Jano replaced it by the even more splendid Tipo B *monoposto*, or P3, which was just as much a winner as its predecessor. As a team manager, Vittorio is said to have been an equably-tempered man yet a strong disciplinarian. Racing cars aside, Jano was also responsible for those beautifully-engineered Alfa Romeo 6C1500 and 1750 series sports-cars which went into production in 1927; these were followed by his 8C2300 and 2900 sports-cars which between them won four consecutive Le Mans 24-hours (1931–4) and a brace of Mille Miglia (1932–3).

In 1938 Jano went back to Torino, but this time to Lancia as chief of the experimental department. After WWII he was involved from the outset in the Appia (1953–63) and Aurelia (1950–9) models, developing the latter touring-car into the 'hairy' 2-litre GT version which took both the Liége–Rome–Liége (1953), and Monte Carlo (1954) rallies. His swan-song as a designer was the V8 Lancia D50 GP car (with its distinctive pannier fuel tanks). Jano was now ahead of his time, and the cars had handling problems on the tyres of that day. Nevertheless the D50 scored its victories before Lancia withdrew from racing and the cars were handed over to Ferrari in 1955, Vittorio becoming a consultant to the Modena firm.

In his later years, he suffered the distress of seeing his brother die of cancer. While he was ill with but a bad bout of bronchitis, he became convinced that he, too, had the same disease, and *Commendatore* Vittorio Jano shot himself in bed on 13 March 1965.

Frederick William Lanchester, British (1868–1946). The son of an architect, he designed and built the first four-wheeled petrol vehicle of entirely British origin in 1895, assisted by his younger brother (q.v.). It was an esoteric motor-car designed from first principles. He founded the Lanchester Company in 1899 and commercial production began. 'Doctor Fred', as he was known, was always ahead of his time and his innovations include the fully-balanced engine, lightweight pistons, full pressure lubrication, a preselector semi-automatic gearbox, disc brakes and many more. He was also a pioneer aerodynamicist and, later, Consultant Engineer to the Daimler Company.

George Herbert Lanchester, British (1874–1970). George took over as Chief Designer at Daimler when his elder brother had a row with the Board and resigned in 1909. George was then responsible for all the 1910 to pre-1914 Lanchester models (in consultation with Fred). All the subsequent Lanchester designs up to the take-over by the Daimler Company in 1931 were his own, after which he joined the Daimler design staff and, latterly, worked for Alvis until WWII.

Hans Ledwinka, Austrian (1878–1967) was born at Klosterneuburg near Vienna, and he was apprenticed to his uncle to learn metal-working. He also attended the Vienna technical college, before joining the large Nesselsdorf railway coachworks in 1897, at a time when they happened to be experimenting with a horseless carriage based on the contemporary Benz, and young Hans proved to be of help in bringing it successfully to production by 1900. A year later he moved to the Friedmann firm in Vienna to help in the development of their steam-car, returning to Nesselsdorf in late 1905 as Director of its by now moribund 'car division'. Ledwinka managed to pull this round with his new models, powered by 4- and 6-cylinder engines with hemispherical combustion chambers and integral gearboxes, as well as by his work on the commercial vehicle side of the business.

In 1916 an altercation over new buildings allowed him to be tempted to take over the newly set-up automobile section of the great Steyr armaments factory. Here he designed both economy and luxury cars, introducing overhead camshafts and swing-axle suspension.

The most important phase of Hans Ledwinka's career began in 1921 when he again returned to Nesselsdorf – which was by this time called Koprivnice, Czechoslovakia – and the newly-formed Tatra Company. Here he worked on large and small air-cooled engines (both petrol and diesel), 'backbone' chassis, all-independent swing-axle suspension, and practical and acceptable streamlined bodywork. A crystallization of his design philosophy was the 2.9-litre, V-8 Tatra Type 87 car which, with a four-door streamlined saloon body, was credited with 100 mph top speed, allied to a consumption of 20.4 mpg, in 1937; a vehicle which was years ahead of its time.

Henry Leland

Henry Martyn Leland, American (1843–1932) was a master of precision engineering design in the machine tool field, who worked for the famous Brown & Sharpe Company of Providence, Rhode Island, before founding his own firm (with his son Wilfred) at Detroit in 1890. Leland, Faulconer & Norton produced tool and lathe grinders, milling machines and gear cutters of their own design. Around 1900 Leland began providing quiet gears for Oldsmobiles and advising upon, and improving, their engines. In association with the Detroit Automobile Company, Henry established the Cadillac Automobile Company in 1902 (see page 177), and its products under his aegis became synonymous with volume production allied to precision engineering standards of manufacture. Leland initiated electric lighting and starting as standard specification on his cars in 1912. His Cadillac Company joined William C. Durant's General Motors consortium in 1909. His famous V-8 cylinder engine design, which was loosely based on an unsuccessful 1910 De Dion Bouton unit, and the first Lincoln V8 of 1920, were the progenitors of all the many subsequent, highly-effective American V8 engines.

Emile Levassor

Emile Levassor, French (1844–1897) was the partner of René Panhard in a wood-working machinery business in Paris, until 1887, when they were commissioned to turn to building engines by one Edouard Sarazin, who held the licence for France. Sarazin died later that year and Emile married the widow in 1890.

An experimental Panhard-Levassor car, with belt-drive, preceded the 'classic' design of 1891, which had an upright Daimler engine, a pedal-operated clutch, shaft-drive and a sliding-pinion gearbox. This configuration, which became known as the 'Système Panhard', was widely copied by other manufacturers.

In the 1895 Paris–Bordeaux–Paris race, Emile Levassor won immortal fame for his magnificent, single-handed 48¾ hours drive to victory, averaging 15 mph/24 kph for 732 miles/1178 km.

William Lyons, British (1901–1985) was born in Blackpool, where he founded the Swallow Sidecar Company, in partnership with his friend William Walmsley, in 1922. Initially, the firm prospered in the motor-cycle field, but later stylish special car bodies were designed to fit Austin, Fiat and Standard chassis.

Lyons introduced his own car, the S.S. (with a Standard engine), in 1931. His products became known as 'S.S. Jaguars' in 1935 and a range of elegant,

William Lyons

yet inexpensive models, powered by 'bought-in' engines, continued up to WWII; the best-known and most sought-after today is the flamboyantly attractive two-seater 'S.S. 100' sports car.

An astute businessman, Bill Lyons also had an unerring eye for sleek and subtle styling, and he was personally responsible for the body designs of the XK120, and the Mark VII Jaguars and, in part, for the E-type sports-cars and the XJ6 saloons. His talent in this field received recognition in his appointment to Fellowship of the Royal Society of Arts and as a Royal Designer for Industry.

William Lyons was knighted in 1956. He relinquished his Managing Directorship of Jaguar Cars Ltd in 1968, though he remained its Chairman until 1972.

Wilhelm Maybach, German (1846–1929), who was in partnership with Gottlieb Daimler at Cannstatt, was mainly responsible for their 1901 design which has been called 'the prototype of the modern car'. Its specification comprised, for the first time ever in one vehicle, a pressed steel chassis, a gate-change gearbox and a honeycomb radiator – all innovatory features in that day – and Wilhelm's four-cylinder engine also used low-tension magneto ignition. The car was built at the behest of a Director of the firm, Emile Jellinek, and the subsequent line of Daimler products were thereafter renamed 'Mercedes', after his daughter, to counteract the anti-German feeling of the important French market of that time. Maybach founded his own concern in 1907 and became famous for his aero-engines and, to a lesser degree, for some beautifully-engineered, fast and complex, luxury motor-cars of the 20s.

Harry Armenius Miller, American (1875–1943) was born in Menomonie, Wisconsin, to a Canadian mother by a German father. At 14, he went to work for the local machine shop and, later, moved on to jobs in Minnesota, Oregon, Utah and San Francisco, where he gained some experience of the petrol engine. Harry turned out to be another empirical engineer – he built himself a motor-cycle in 1896, following this up with what may have been the original American marine outboard-motor a year later. Next he invented a new sparking plug and the 'Master' carburettor, a factory being set up for the latter's production in Indianapolis in 1911 – the year of the first '500' – where he became interested in racing. Soon he designed an improved carburettor – the Miller Type H – sold out in Indianapolis and manufactured it in Los Angeles. Here it became a 'best-seller' and was used extensively on racing cars. Harry Miller essayed his own 4-cylinder engine in 1916, but only six of them were built.

Harry Miller

During WWI the Miller carburettor was fitted on the Bugatti-designed 'parallel-8' aero engines made under licence in the USA by Duesenberg, and, when Harry started building his own racing engines by 1921, his first was a straight-8 and a modified version of the twin ohc Duesenberg unit as used in their Indianapolis '500' contenders. After a successful interim 2-litre engine with hemispherical combustion chambers, came the famous 1500 cc (91 cu in) front-wheel-drive, supercharged Millers of 1926. Fifty '91's were produced, mostly with rear-wheel-drive, and between them they dominated top-grade American racing for the next three years.

Harry Miller was an open-handed guy and something of a spendthrift – he was also a much better engineer than he was a businessman. Thus he went bankrupt in 1932. He became a very sick man but his design work continued (some of it for Ford) albeit less successfully, into the early 40s. His studies in the 20s had included all-independent suspension and a 4-wheel-drive car, while he was fortunate in those happier days to have the ardent support of two brilliant associates – *Leo Goosen*, the draughtsman, and *Fred Offenhauser*, the foreman mechanic. As for Harry himself, an acknowledged authority has described him as 'the greatest single figure in American motor-racing history, as well as one of the greatest automotive designers that the United States will ever produce'.

William Morris

William Richard Morris, British (1877–1963) set up as a bicycle-repairer when he was 16 years of age at Cowley St John, near Oxford. Later he went into the motor-cycle building business (1901) with a machine of his own design, but the venture did not prosper. Next he opened a garage – car sales, repairs, hire cars *et al*. This time he *was* successful and, in 1910, he planned his own economy car. Mainly constructed from bought-out components, the first production Morris 'Oxford' was ready in 1913. It was powered by a White and Poppe engine, sported the famous bull-nosed radiator, and gave 50 mph/80 kph with 50 mpg/227 mpl according to usage! Seeking more power for a four-seater model, Morris changed to the American (larger yet cheaper to buy) Continental engine for his 'Cowley' which appeared in 1915. When the post-war car boom deflated, everyone's sales slumped; yet Morris survived the crisis by reducing his prices when his rivals were increasing theirs or lying doggo.

Morris manufactured a very basic, yet sound, motor-car (as did Henry Ford of the USA, q.v.). Thus he won the confidence and support of British motorists desiring reliable, if stodgy, transportation. It made him a vast fortune over the years. Nevertheless, he was a great philanthropist and many thousands of people today have good reason to be grateful to Bill Morris, the late 19th-century youthful racing-bicyclist who became Sir William Morris (1939), Baron Nuffield (1934) and Viscount Nuffield (1938).

Ransom E. Olds, American (1864–1950) built a steam tri-car in 1893/94, and he followed this up with a gasoline-engined version in 1896. Production began in 1901 and his 'curved-dash' Oldsmobile gas buggy became famous, successful and widely-copied, in the USA. It featured a horizontal single-cylinder engine and two-speed epicyclic gearing, allied to a very high-pitched chassis with flexible springing for the rough-going for which it was designed to cope.

In 1904, altercations with his fellow directors caused Olds to sell out, leave the company and then set up another one to make Reo cars. Naturally his new products bore a strong resemblance to his earlier ones, but if anything they were rather better. Thus it seems unkind that the Reo never quite achieved the high reputation of the Oldsmobile. (Reo is, of course, derived from the man's initials.)

Battista Pininfarina, Italian (1893–1966) was one of the most outstanding car stylists and designers. He was born Battista Farina and quickly acquired the Piedmontese nickname 'Pinin' ('little one'), which explains why some of his cars were styled by Farina and some by Pininfarina. In June 1961 his name was officially changed to Pininfarina by decree of the President of the Italian Republic.

Pinin's first job was working for his brother Giovanni, who had founded Stablimenta Farina in the early 1900s. Before long he had met, and made friends with, Vincenzo Lancia and Enzo Ferrari. For a time both Farina and

Ferrari were active as racing drivers. A visit to America in 1922 gave Battista more modern coachbuilding ideas and, in 1930, he was persuaded by Vincenzo Lancia to launch out on his own.

Carrozzeria Farina was formed as a coachbuilding factory in Turin. It soon became noticed for innovations like the horizontal grille and inclined windscreen. A curved windscreen, faired-in headlamps and a long, sloping tail were seen in Farina's Lancia Aprilia aerodynamic coupé of 1936. By 1939 the company had 500 employees and bodied 800 cars a year.

After WWII Pinin Farina's design for the Cisitalia coupé with low bonnet, horizontal grille and integrated aerodynamic shape, was a milestone in car design. It led, in 1951, to the Lancia Aurelia B20 coupé which initiated the Grand Touring production car style, while the early co-operation between Pinin Farina and Ferrari can be traced back to the 1952 Ferrari 212 Inter, followed by the Testa Rossa in 1959.

Today, Pininfarina are Ferrari's 'house-stylists'. Family car design was not neglected, however, and the 1955 Peugeot 403, 1958 Austin A40 and 1962 BMC 1100 were all Pininfarina styled – in 1963 the PF Sigma design exercise anticipated car safety legislation.

Battista Pininfarina was created an Italian Cavaliere del Lavorno (Knight of Work) in 1953, given an Honorary Architecture Degree by the Politecnico di Torino in 1963, and the Legion d'Honneur by France in 1966. On Battista's death on 3 April 1966, his son Sergio became president of the Company.

Ferdinand Porsche

Ferdinand Porsche, Austro-Hungarian (1875–1952) was an engineering phenomenon whose career spanned over 40 years. Like F. H. Royce, Porsche started as an electrical engineer before he turned to automobiles, and was also a pioneer of petrol-electric transmissions. He became Managing Director of the Austro-Daimler Company in 1905 and was one of the best rally drivers of the day, competing successfully in the 1909 and 1910 Prince Henry Trials in Austro-Daimlers of his own design. A full list of all the fruits of Porsche's wonderfully creative mind is beyond the scope of this thumbnail sketch. However, this tough, down-to-earth, brusque man was responsible for the S-type Mercedes-Benz sports-cars (culminating in the 38/250 model of 1928), the V16 Auto Union Type C Grand Prix car of 1937 and the Volkswagen 'Beetle'. He also patented torsion bar suspension. Following these landmarks came the Germany Army 'Tiger' tank and the Daimler-Benz 601 aero-engine of WWII. The Doctor was interned by the Allies for two years after the war and he was released in 1947. Now he proceeded to design the flat-12, 4-w-d Cisitalia G.P. car of 1949, to say nothing of being involved in the gestation of the Model 356 of the marque which bears his name.... Small wonder that Ferdinand Porsche has been called 'the greatest and most versatile genius the motor-car has produced'.

Louis Renault, French (1877–1944) was the youngest of the three brothers who gave their name to Automobiles Renault Frères. The others were Fernand (1865–1910) and Marcel (1872–1903) who ran the family button manufacturing and drapery business in Paris. Louis preferred a small workshop in the grounds of their house at Billancourt. In 1898 he was working on a 'direct-drive' system to replace the currently-accepted transmission by belts and chains. He designed a proper gearbox with direct top, two indirects and reverse, with the drive being taken thence to the rear wheels via a prop-shaft and crown-wheel-and-pinion. Being ever short of funds, he stripped down his old De Dion tricycle and rebuilt it as a four-wheeled, two-seater *voiturette* incorporating his own gearbox. Some friends tried it out and, impressed, asked Louis to make some for them, but, broke as usual, he was in no position to build them. However, Fernand and Marcel were businessmen and saw the potential of Louis' invention. They decided to float a company, Renault Frères, which was founded in February 1899 to exploit the inventions of their young brother and to build vehicles, his 'direct-drive' being granted its patent in the same month. Poor Louis was not made a director of the company as he had no money and was considered too young! Fernand helped with administration and continued to run the drapery business; Marcel controlled the new company, while Louis was in charge of all engineering matters.

For publicity and development reasons, Louis and Marcel started to race their products. Marcel, though not so skilled a driver as his brother, won the 1902 Paris–Vienna race (after Louis' car had been badly damaged) but was killed in the disastrous Paris–Madrid event of 1903, after which Louis swore never to race again. Louis acquired the deceased's shares from Marcel's mistress to whom he had left them but Fernand continued as 'admin. man' and, in 1904, became chairman of Renault Frères, London, but his health deteriorated over the next few years until Louis was virtually running the show on his own. Now Louis bought out Fernand and became the sole owner of Renault Frères. When Fernand died, he changed the style to 'Automobile Renault – Louis Renault *Constructeur*'. He controlled the firm until his death, in mysterious circumstances, in 1944.

Frederick Henry Royce, British (1863–1933) was a brilliant engineer, without formal training, whose forte was not that of the innovator so much as an outstanding talent for improving vastly upon the original ideas of others. Royce had an electrical engineering business in Manchester in the 1890s. In 1903 he took to motoring and, in 1904, he built three experimental cars of his own whose excellence brought about the epoch-making meeting with the **Hon. Charles Stewart Rolls** (1877–1910) and the formation of the Rolls-Royce Company in 1906. Royce's 40/50 hp or 'Silver Ghost' model was launched in 1906 and is a landmark in the history of automobile engineering. Its refinement, quietness and reliability set new standards for its day; incredible longevity was also to be proved through the years .... Alas 'Henry Royce, Mechanic' as he modestly called himself, was a 'workaholic' who ruined his health in his enthusiasm. He became a baronet in 1931.

Henry Royce

Charles Rolls *Right*

Gabriel Voisin, French (1880–1973) who trained as an architect, was a successful pioneer aeronaut and aircraft manufacturer before he turned to designing and building motor-cars in 1919. A highly talented man, he was also an aerodynamicist, an inventor ... and a redoubtable womanizer! Voisin was a proponent of the Knight-type, double-sleeve valve engine which, in 4-, 6-, straight-8 and V-12 cylinder configurations (there was even a straight-12) powered all his cars. Voisins were notable for their light weight and 'stream-lined' bodies (which were frequently of unconventional appearance), these attributes being responsible for works cars taking 1st, 2nd, 3rd and 5th places in the fuel-consumption GP de Tourisme at Strasbourg in 1922 and an excellent fifth place, behind much more powerful rivals, in the 1923 French Grand Prix.

Voisin's passenger models acquired considerable chic among wealthy Frenchmen, and others, during the late 20s and early 30s but still his Issy-les-Moulineaux works closed at the end of 1935. Later, in 1945, Gabriel showed his versatility with his transverse-engined, f.w.d. 'Biscooter' which was the harbinger of Alec Issigonis's Mini (q.v.).

2 Racing Drivers

Mario Andretti

Mario Andretti, American (1940–). The most versatile driver in recent racing, Andretti has been successful at the highest levels in Grand Prix, track and endurance racing. He was USAC national champion in 1965, 1966 and 1969, won the Indianapolis 500 in 1969, was a leading figure in CART racing in the mid-1980s (champion in 1984). First drove in Formula 1 in 1968, in a Lotus, enjoyed some success with Ferrari F1 and sports-racing cars in 1970–2, then drove Alfa Romeo in sports-car events and Lola in F5000 before returning to the Grands Prix with Parnelli then rejoining Lotus in 1976. He built up a strong rapport with Colin Chapman, and his Lotus years culminated in the world championship in 1978, before the team slipped out of contention and Andretti spent a fruitless spell with Alfa Romeo. Back on the US tracks he was often in direct competition with his son Mike. Andretti competed in 128 Grands Prix, winning 12.

Alberto Ascari, Italian (1918–1955). Son of Antonio Ascari, a prominent member of the Alfa Romeo GP team in the 1920s who was fatally injured in a 1925 French GP crash, Alberto Ascari was the archetypical Italian racing driver of the immediate post-war era. Generally he drove for Ferrari, winning 13 Grands Prix in 1951–3 and taking the world championship in 1952–3. Then he joined Lancia, winning two secondary F1 races and the Mille Miglia before his inexplicable and fatal accident in a sports Ferrari he was unofficially testing at Monza.

Jack Brabham

Sir Jack Brabham, Australian (1926–). The taciturn Australian brought a rare mixture of skills to his races and his teams – boldness and finely developed tactical abilities, a shrewd business sense and sound mechanical knowledge. Among his rewards were three world championships, seven GP victories scored with Coopers and seven with his own Brabhams – in 1966 he became the first driver to win a world championship race in a car bearing his own name, in the French race at Reims. In 1970 he retired from single-seater racing (he has since been seen in other types of car) and later he sold his interest in the Brabham racing car company to his partner of many years, Ron Tauranac. He remained a frequent visitor to the North American and European tracks, where his sons Geoff and Gary were successful competitors in the 1980s. Sir Jack competed in 126 Grands Prix, winning 14.

Rudolf Caracciola, German (1901–1960). In a 30-year career, this calm Rhinelander was usually rated the top German driver, although this position was occasionally usurped, particularly by Lang and Rosemeyer. He had a tremendous success record, usually achieved with Mercedes-Benz (whose cars he drove to six German GP victories). He recovered from several serious accidents, notably in practice sessions for the 1933 Monaco GP and the 1946 Indianapolis 500, but his last, in a sports car at Berne in 1952, ended his career.

Jim Clark

Jim Clark, British (1936–1968). Clark was a driver with immense natural talent, who was universally respected by his colleagues in motor racing and the wider sporting world. He started racing saloons and sports cars in events local to his Scottish home in 1956 and four years later he joined Lotus, to begin an outstanding partnership with Colin Chapman. Clark first drove in Formula 1 in 1960, scored his first F1 victory in the non-championship Pau GP in 1961, his first championship race victory in the 1962 Belgian GP, and won his first world championship in 1963. That year he startled the Indianapolis establishment with a strong drive into second place in the 500, and in 1965 was the first European driver to win the race for 45 years. He was killed in an unexplained crash in a Formula 2 car at Hockenheim. Clark started in 72 Grands Prix and won 24.

Juan-Manuel Fangio, Argentinian (1911–   ). Fangio learned his craft in the rough school of South American city-to-city races, and became one of the greatest of single-seater drivers, with a Grand Prix start/finish record that remains unequalled: he started in only 51 GPs, qualified for a front row start position for 48 of them and won 24. He gained his first world championship driving for Alfa Romeo in 1949, won two more with Mercedes in 1954–5, a fourth with Ferrari in 1956 and a fifth championship driving Maseratis in 1957. He retired in 1958, but for many years after that was a regular visitor to Grands Prix, and demonstrated racing cars with great verve until health made him ease off in the early 1980s. Fangio was universally recognized as a great racing driver and admired as a quiet gentleman.

Juan-Manuel Fangio

Giuseppe Farina, Italian (1906–1966). Sometimes aloof, temperamental and impetuous, Farina at his best was brilliant. He started racing in the 1930s and drove for Alfa Romeo before and after World War II. He won five races with the classic Alfa 158, which so admirably complemented his driving style, in the year when he became first world champion, 1950. Farina also drove Maserati and Ferrari single-seaters with success, and had a fine record in sports-car racing. He died in a road crash in 1966. Started in 33 championship Grands Prix, won 5.

Emerson Fittipaldi, Brazilian (1946–   ). Like so many drivers of the recent generation, Fittipaldi started racing karts (he was a national champion in Brazil) then attracted wide attention as soon as he started racing in F Ford in Britain in 1968. Drives in F3 and F2 soon followed, and in 1970 he drove in his first GP, in Britain, and won his first GP, in the USA, both for Lotus. He continued with Lotus until 1973, winning his first world title in 1972, and he won the championship again, with McLaren, in 1974. He worked hard with the uncompetitive Copersucars from 1976 until 1979, had an equally fruitless season in a Fittipaldi in 1980, then abandoned the Grands Prix. He turned to single-seater racing in the USA, and won his first CART race in 1985. Started in 144 Grands Prix, won 14.

Anthony J. Foyt

Anthony Joseph Foyt, American (1935–). 'A.J.', the all-American driver of his generation, with great talent, abundant charm or loud fury, and chunky good looks, started racing midgets in the 1950s, first raced at Indianapolis in 1958 and first won the 500 in 1961 with an Offy roadster – the type of car to which he seemed wholly suited. A.J. accepted the new age of 'funny cars' reluctantly, but eventually built his own Coyotes and drove one to win the 500 for the fourth time, in 1977. His last victory in one of his Coyotes came in 1978 at Silverstone. He seemed to fade away but reappeared in the Indianapolis top ten in 1984. He also drove NASCAR stock cars (winning the Daytona 500) and sports cars: in a rare race outside North America he won at Le Mans with Dan Gurney in a Ford in 1967.

Mike Hawthorn, British (1929–1959). The first British driver to win a world championship, Hawthorn became prominent with his drives in an F2 Cooper in 1952 and won his first GP as a member of the Ferrari team in 1953. He won the championship as a Ferrari driver in 1958 – and scored in many sports car races – retiring after winning the championship. He was deeply upset by the death of his friend Peter Collins and retired from racing at the end of the season. Within three months he was killed in a road accident. Competed in 45 Grands Prix, won three.

Graham Hill

Graham Hill, British (1929–1975). Raced in Grands Prix during 18 seasons, with a gritty determination compensating for that last fraction of talent, where he was at a slight disadvantage in the company of a few contemporaries such as Clark and Stewart. He drove his first GP in a Lotus at Monaco – he was later to win that race five times – moved to BRM, and started winning GPs in 1962. That year he won his first world championship; his second came in 1968, when he was back with Lotus. After fighting his way back to fitness after a serious accident in 1969, Hill drove Brabhams in 1971–2, a Shadow in 1973, then the Lolas which led towards his becoming a constructor in his own right. He won many races away from the GPs, most notably the Indianapolis 500 and the Le Mans 24-hour Race. With other members of his F1 team, he was killed in an aircraft accident in 1975. Started in 176 Grands Prix, won 14.

Phil Hill

Phil Hill, American (1927–). The first American to win the world championship, Californian Hill was a fine sports car driver when he became a Ferrari F1 driver late in 1958, and a season of consistent high placings brought him the championship in 1960. That was his high point in single seaters, but he continued in sports cars until 1967. He retired from racing to concentrate on car restoration, and later driving and describing historic cars. Started in 48 Grands Prix, won three.

Denis Hulme, New Zealand (1936–). Tough, competent and professional, Denny Hulme worked hard through secondary categories for five years before getting his first F1 drive, with Brabham, in 1965. In 1967 he won his first GP at Monaco, and gained the championship, before joining the McLaren F1 and CanAm teams (CanAm champion in 1968 and 1970). Hulme continued in GPs until the end of 1974 and was still active in the following year as GPDA President, after which he seemed to retire to New Zealand. However, he 'reappeared' as a respected saloon car driver, and in 1986 co-drove the TT-winning Rover. Started in 112 Grands Prix, won eight.

James Hunt

James Hunt, British (1947–). A controversial world champion at the end of the 1976 season, Hunt shrugged off his early reputation as 'Hunt the Shunt' and proved that he could drive with great determination and real ability. He won his first GP, and the Hesketh team's only championship race, in 1975; moved to McLaren in 1976, and took the title after a season-long battle with Lauda (and the sport's officials). His title defence was at times spirited, but McLaren's cars were outclassed, and after a final effort with Wolf, Hunt retired in the middle of the 1979 season. Started in 92 Grands Prix, won 10.

Jacky Ickx, Belgian (1945–). One of the finest all-round drivers, Jacky Ickx was picked from F3 by Ken Tyrrell to drive in F2 and his 1967 F2 championship led to a Ferrari GP contract. He won his first GP that year, moved to Brabham then back to Ferrari in 1970–1 for his last GP victory. But it is for his sports-car racing that Ickx will be remembered, with marques such as Ford, Ferrari, Matra, Alfa Romeo and Porsche, and many victories. His six victories at Le Mans are outstanding (1969–75–76–77–81–82). By the 1980s he was in semi-retirement, involved with the re-establishment of Spa-Francorchamps, and indulging such pleasures as the Paris–Dakar raid. Started in 116 GPs, won eight.

Alan Jones

Alan Jones, Australian (1946–). Son of Stan Jones, leading Australian driver of the early 1950s, Alan Jones grafted towards an F1 drive through the first half of the 1970s, racing in F3, F Atlantic and F5000 before driving a private Hesketh, then for the Hill and Surtees teams, and scoring his first GP victory, in a Shadow in 1977. He drove for Williams 1978–81, mastering ground effects driving, and winning 12 races and the 1980 world championship. Then he 'retired' from the Grands Prix, but won the Australian national sports car championships and had two 'guest' GP drives. He returned to lead the Beatrice-Lola team, a little overweight and pungent in his comments as he battled to score just 4 points in 1986. At the end of that season he retired again from F1. Started in 116 Grands Prix, won 12.

Niki Lauda

Nikolaus-Andreas Lauda, Austrian (1949–). Perhaps the most professional driver in GP racing during the period after Jackie Stewart retired, Niki Lauda was very much his own man and had to make his own way up the conventional racing ladder towards Formula 1. He raced in F Vee, F3 and sports cars before graduating to F2 and a first GP in a March in 1971. Success came with Ferrari in 1974, when he scored his first GP win. He first won the world championship in 1975 and survived a horrifying and widely-publicized accident at the Nürburgring in the following year before regaining the title in 1978. He won two GPs in Brabhams in 1978 and none in 1979 before he abruptly retired during practice for the Canadian GP. McLaren tempted him back to racing in 1982, and he was champion for the third time in 1984, but won only one GP in 1985 and at the end of that season he retired again. Lauda started in 171 Grands Prix, won 25.

Bruce McLaren, New Zealander (1937–1970). This quiet man is now better remembered as a constructor, but in the 1960s he was a leading driver. McLaren won his first GP in 1959 and continued to drive for Cooper while his interest in sports-car racing grew – he won Le Mans in 1966, and the following year saw his McLaren CanAm cars win that championship for the first of four successive seasons. He won two F1 races in McLaren cars in 1968.

McLaren died in a test accident at Goodwood. Started in 101 championship races, won four.

Stirling Moss

Stirling Moss, British (1929–). Although ill-fortune denied him a world championship, Moss is rated among the greatest of drivers, a master of all circuit categories and at one time a prominent rally driver. He started racing in 1948 in the 500 cc Formula 3 and moved on to F2 and top-line sports-car racing (where he won the RAC TT seven times). In the GPs, his 1954 season with a Maserati earned him a drive with Mercedes-Benz and a first championship victory; seasons with Maserati, Vanwall and Rob Walker followed before a crash in a non-championship race at Goodwood in 1962 ended his main-line career. He subsequently appeared in historic car and saloon races, remaining a familiar figure in motor sport. Started in 66 championship GPs, won 16.

Felice Nazzaro, Italian (1881–1940). More than most early racing drivers, Nazzaro fits the modern pattern – he even built cars bearing his own name, and drove them to win important races in 1913–14. For most of his career, however, he was a Fiat man, winning the three main races of 1907 in their big cars, and scoring his second French GP victory in a very different Fiat in 1922. He raced in a GP for the last time in 1922, but remained with Fiat almost until his death.

Tazio Nuvolari

Tazio Nuvolari, Italian (1892–1953). 'Il Maestro', Nuvolari epitomized the brave, fiery and skilled Italian racing-driver of an era that is long in the past. He raced cars of many makes and sizes, from Bianchi in the 1920s to Ferrari in the 1940s, but is most often recalled for his exploits with Alfa Romeos in the mid-1930s, notably when he beat the mighty Mercedes and Auto Union teams in outclassed Alfas. Towards the end of the decade he drove Auto Unions to three GP victories. After World War II he led the 1947 Mille Miglia to within 90 miles of the finish, to be beaten by failing electrics – but the legend grew. A sick man, he drove his last race in a Cisitalia in 1950.

Richard Petty, American (1937–). Supreme NASCAR driver from the mid-1960s through to the early 1980s, 'King' Petty was the son of three-times national stock-car champion Lee Petty, and his own son, Kyle, was a rising NASCAR driver in the early 1980s. When he won the Firecracker 400 at Daytona in 1984, Richard Petty also scored his 200th Grand National victory (out of 944 starts). Petty Engineering usually ran GM cars, with Dodge, Buick, and Chevrolet of Pontiac badges, although it campaigned Fords in 1967, and year-in, year-out these were in STP colours.

Nelson Piquet

Nelson (Souto Maior) Piquet, Brazilian (1952–). A Brazilian kart champion, Piquet followed several of his countrymen to England, where he was national F3 champion in 1978. That year he first raced F1 cars – an Ensign, a McLaren and then a Brabham. He remained with the Brabham team until the end of 1985, winning his first GP with them at Long Beach in 1980, and the world championship in 1981 and 1983, when he was the first driver to take the title with turbocharged cars. His 1986 season was his most successful in terms of race victories – he won four GPs in Williams cars, but was only third in the championship table. By the end of that season he had started in 126 GPs, won 17.

Alain Prost, French (1955–). The first French driver to win the world championship, this quiet little man with the ultra-smooth driving technique has been one of the most successful drivers of the 1980s. European junior kart champion in 1973, he started racing cars in 1976, was European F3 champion in 1979, drove for McLaren in 1980, then moved to Renault, winning nine GPs in the French cars and scoring 134 championship points – more than any other driver in those three seasons. He returned to McLaren, to win seven GPs in 1984 and equal Clark's 1964 record, although he was only second in the championship. Prost clearly won the title in 1985, and snatched it back again by two points when he won the final race at Adelaide in 1986. That was his 105th GP, and he had won 25 of them.

Jochen Rindt, Austrian (1942–1970). A driver with great skill and courage, Rindt was virtually unknown when he beat the best in an F2 race at Crystal Palace in 1964. After that he won numerous F2 races, as well as the Le Mans 24-hour Race in 1965, but his F1 fortunes with Cooper and Brabham were poorly rewarded. He joined Lotus in 1969, winning his first GP in the USA; in 1970 he won five more but was fatally injured in a practice accident at Monza. His points score was not equalled before the end of that season, so he became the first driver to be awarded the championship title posthumously. Started in 60 Grands Prix, won six.

Keke (Keijo) Rosberg, Finnish (1948–). Noted for a flamboyant style that was actually a sign of fine car control, Rosberg made his way to the world championship along a conventional route – karts, F Vee and Super Vee, F Atlantic and F2. His first F1 drives were with Theodore Racing in 1978 (he drove their uncompetitive car to a surprise victory in the rain-soaked Silverstone International Trophy), and barren seasons followed with Wolf and Fittipaldi. He joined Williams in 1982, won his first championship race in the Swiss GP at Dijon and ended the year as world champion. He won four more GPs with Williams then joined McLaren for a less successful final season. Started in 114 GPs, won five.

Keke Rosberg (left) and Alain Prost

Bernd Rosemeyer, German (1910–1938). A rare driver, who made the move from motor-cycles straight into the seat of a GP car, in the Auto Union team, Rosemeyer raced one of the rear-engined cars for the first time early in 1935, and won his first GP in one four months later. In the next two seasons he often seemed to battle alone against the Mercedes team, and won nine major races.

races. Then his talent was squandered in a pointless record attempt on an autobahn.

Jody Scheckter, South African (1950–). Scheckter won an F Ford championship and 'Driver to Europe' award in his native South Africa in 1970, and built up an impressive record in F Ford and F3 before his GP debut in 1972. He won the US F5000 championship in the following year, and achieved GP notoriety by a rash manoeuvre at Silverstone which started a chain-reaction accident. He moved to Tyrrell and scored his first GP victory in 1973, then the only championship victory for that team's six-wheeled P34. He won three GPs with the Wolf team, moved on to Ferrari and won the championship in 1979 and retired at the end of a mediocre 1980 season. Contested 112 GPs, won 10.

Jackie Stewart

Jackie Stewart, British (1939–). Stewart enjoyed a scintillating Grand Prix career and then shrewdly built another career on the base of motoring and motor racing. As a driver he showed outstanding natural talent in his earliest days, drove F3 Coopers for Ken Tyrrell in 1964, joined BRM in 1965 and scored his first GP victory in Italy that year. From 1968 he again drove for Tyrrell, in Matras (1968–9, winning 9 GPs), March (1970, winning a single GP) and Tyrrells (1970–3, winning 15 GPs). He was world champion in 1969, 1971 and 1973, retiring before the last race of that season as a mark of respect for his young team-mate and nominated successor, Francois Cevert, who was killed in a US GP practice accident. Stewart started in 99 GPs, won 27.

John Surtees, British (1934–). Seven times world motor-cycle champion, John Surtees moved into cars in 1960, driving F Junior and moving on rapidly to Formula 1, driving Lotus, Cooper and Lola before joining Ferrari in 1963. He won the championship in 1964 with the Italian team, left it in 1966 to drive for Cooper (and, incidentally, win the first CanAm championship). He won one race for Honda in 1967, then had an unrewarding spell with BRM before he set up as a constructor. His cars were successful in F5000, and Hailwood drove Surtees' F2 cars to that championship in 1972, but there was only one F1 victory, in a non-championship race. Surtees became increasingly disillusioned, and eventually abandoned his GP effort at the end of the 1978 season, and soon gave up even the secondary programme that had kept Team Surtees alive. As a driver, Surtees had started in 111 GPs, won six.

The Unser family (American) is often referred to as a motor racing dynasty. The second and third generations have become best known, although the New Mexico dynasty was 'founded' by Louis and Jerry who built and raced their own dirt-track cars. Two of the second-generation brothers, Bobby and Al, had exceptionally long and successful careers (a third brother, Jerry, died after an Indianapolis practice accident in 1959). In 1985 Al Unser Snr took the Indycar championship from his son Al by just one point at the last race of the season.

Bobby Unser (1934–) first raced in 1949, became a full USAC competitor in 1964, started winning regularly with Eagles in 1967 and drove for the marque until 1975. Three-time Indy 500 winner, USAC champion in 1968 and 1974, winner in sprint cars and stock cars, many times the winner at Pike's Peak. He raced a GP car only once, a BRM in 1968. After his last successful Indycar spell, with Penske, he turned to team management in

Bobby Unser *Right*

Al Unser

1983, and has also been a race commentator. He returned to Pike's Peak in 1986, to drive an Audi to victory and break the climb record.

Al Unser (1939–) became the oldest driver ever to win the US championship, in 1985, and by that time he ranked third behind Foyt and Andretti in terms of all-time Indycar victories. Started racing stock cars, and attracted wider attention as runner-up to Bobby at Pike's Peak in 1960 (in 1964 he broke his brother's run of victories on the climb). Scored his first USAC win in 1968, won three times at Indianapolis, in 1978 becoming the first driver to win all three Indycar 500-mile races in a single season. He was also successful in F500, stock cars and CanAm.

Al Unser Jnr (1962–) shared an Indycar victory podium with his father for the first time in 1985. He raced sprint cars, then took his first national class title driving Formula Super Vee Ralts in 1981, won the CanAm title in 1982, raced Indycar Eagles and Marches in 1983–4, and gained his first victory in the category at Portland in 1984. He won two races in Lola T900s in 1985, and scored three second and three third places on his way to that championship confrontation with his father at Miami.

3 Rally Drivers

Rauno Aaltonen, Finnish (1938–). The man who, more than any other, deserves to be called the Flying Finn. From the age of 12, when he started racing hydroplanes in his native Turku, to 16, when he shifted to motor-cycles and went in for motocross, road racing and speedway, until 18, when he moved into cars, the man has always been a winner. His first rally was in 1956 in a Mercedes, but he bought a Saab the following year and by 1961 was Finnish champion. The same year he co-drove – literally – with Eugen Bohringer in the Mercedes team and won his home event, the 1000 Lakes, with a Mercedes.

In 1962, he was introduced to BMC and the Mini Coopers, though his first outing, on the Monte Carlo, nearly ended in fatality when he crashed and had

Rauno Aaltonen

to be dragged from the burning wreck by his co-driver, Geoff Mabbs. But by 1963 he was a full member of the team and finished third on the Monte and 1000 Lakes and second on the *Coupe des Alpes*. He nearly won the Liège in a Healey 3000, crashing out of the lead on the last night, but he came back the following year with a Healey to win the last on-the-road Liège.

But it was 1965, when he was European Champion, that was the peak of his career. He won in the Geneva, Czechoslovakia, Poland, the RAC and the Three Cities and was second on the 1000 Lakes.

In 1967 he achieved his ambition to win the Monte Carlo rally and in doing so won a prize of a free entry on the Safari. Thus started a quest that has not yet finished, for he persuaded BMC to send a Mini Cooper to the Safari, failed to finish and has been back every year since, mainly in Datsuns and Opels, to try and win it.

When BMC ceased to rally he got a contract with Lancia, for whom his best result was a second place on the 1969 San Remo. He then rallied for BMW and Fiat in Europe while trusting to Datsun for his Safari and Southern Hemisphere outings (he won the Southern Cross in 1977). He has finished many Safaris and has been second no less than three times for Datsun (1977, 1980, 1981) and once for Opel (1984).

Nowadays the Safari is his obsession, but sailing and teaching other people to drive are his relaxations. He does a lot of testing and developing for Opel and his BMC nickname of 'the Professor' seems as real now as it did then.

Eugen Bohringer, German (1923–   ). Learnt to drive on his father's tractor before graduating to motor-cycles before the 1939–45 war. Imprisoned in Russia, he did not see his native Stuttgart until the late 1950s. He started doing hill climbs and circuit races with Porsches and Alfa Romeos with a fair degree of success. Then, in 1960, the local Mercedes factory offered him a drive in their rally team as number two to Walter Schock; dutifully, Bohringer finished second to him on the Monte Carlo of that year. He won a *Coupe des Alpes* in 1960, one of only six awarded.

In 1961, he was eighth fastest on the Monte but the handicap put him 30th. He went on that year to be fourth on the Tulip and Acropolis and to win the Polish rally. A good result in the RAC would have won him the European championship but he left the road.

He did better still in 1962, with seven class wins from eight starts in championship rallies, wins on the Acropolis, Polish and Liège–Sofia–Liège and two second places which included the Monte Carlo Rally. The season ended again with a crash on the RAC but this time the championship had been won for Mercedes already.

The Mercedes effort was slowing down by 1963 but they did let Bohringer drive in two of his favourite events, the Acropolis and Liège–Sofia–Liège, both of which he won, the latter in the new 230SL sports car.

In 1965, Bohringer drove for the other Stuttgart factory, Porsche, and gave them an amazing second overall in the most severe weather seen on a modern Monte Carlo, with a 904 – virtually a race car. He drove a 906 in the *Coupe des Alpes* the same year but the car broke.

Bohringer's rally career was late in starting and short, like the man himself, but his victories on the Liège (endurance) and Acropolis (rough roads) compared with his performances on the tarmac, ice and snow of the Monte Carlo have made him an eternal champion of rallying.

John Buffum

John Buffum, American (1945–   ). During service with the USA Armed Services in Europe, Buffum became fascinated by rallies. He made an arrangement to rent an ex-works practice car from Porsche and, in the 12 months from April 1968, competed in 17 German regional rallies. He also drove in three internationals at the beginning of 1969, the Lyons–Charbonniers, *Neige et Glace* and Monte Carlo, on which latter event he finished 12th overall.

Back in the USA at the end of his service, he started racing with a Ford Escort Twin Cam in 1970 in the smaller class of SCCA Trans-Am. The car was built by Broadspeed and had a Hart engine. He had some success and in 1972 moved up to a BDA-engined Escort, which startled some Corvette drivers and enabled him to win the up-to-2.5 litre Trans-Am class in 1973. From two halves of crashed race Escorts, he built himself a rally car with which he was leading the Press-on-Regardless rally in 1972 until rolling. His nickname was created during this period – Stuff 'em Buffum!

In 1973, while still racing, he started to do more rallies with his second Escort and finished fourth overall on the Press-on-Regardless in its first World Championship year. But 1974 saw him back racing a BMW, this time in the IMSA Camel GT series and while the Rideau Lakes/Press-on-Regardless of that year were running, he was down racing in Mexico – and selling his BMW.

In 1975 he was summoned at the last minute to make up numbers on the *Criterium du Quebec* and finished second overall in what was virtually a road-going Porsche, which was a nice way to finish a year in which he had won his first SCCA rally championship with the Escort. In 1976 there occurred the SCCA and NARRA feud as to whose championship was going to be IT; Buffum chose NARRA and won their championship and the Quebec with an ex-works Porsche that had come to the USA for Zasada to drive in 1974.

In 1977 he started a five-year association with the Triumph importers and won four successive SCCA championships for them in TR7s (1977–8) and TR8s (1979–80). He finished fourth on the 1977 Quebec behind two works Fiats and a works Ford and in 1978 made the first of many forays to the RAC Rally, competing in an Escort. He had three tries with TR8s and in 1980 retired with just one stage to go while lying sixth.

With the Triumph programme stopping in 1981, Buffum swapped to Peugeots and finally Audis for the SCCA championship but could only make third by the end of the year. But the contact with Audi in North America firmed into a permanent arrangement which lasts to this day. He won the SCCA championship in an Audi Quattro in 1982, 1983, 1984, 1985 and 1986. He finished both the 1982 and 1983 RAC rallies in 12th and sixth places respectively and in 1984 he had his best World Championship result outside North America when he finished fifth on the Acropolis in a Quattro.

To date, Buffum has won 55 rallies in North America, ten USA Championships and has won the 'CanAm' Rally Cup no less than eight times. Respected and liked on both sides of the Atlantic, the boy from Burlington, Vermont is North American rallying personified.

Erik Carlsson, Swedish (1929–   ). Born in Trollhattan where Saabs are made, it was motor-cycles that first occupied Carlsson. In 1948 he was second in the *Motocross des Nations*. Then cars took his interest. Early rallies were done in VWs and Austin A40s, but in 1953 he co-drove a Volvo on the Swedish Rally. The following year he bought a Saab 92 and started winning his class in Southern Sweden. His aggressive driving on the little car was only ac-

Erik Carlsson

centuated by his own size. He frequently rolled the car and was dubbed 'Erik pa taket' or 'Erik on the roof'.

In 1957 he became a test driver for the Saab factory and for the first time had a full works car. He won the 1000 Lakes Rally that year and did his first Tulip Rally, where the underpowered Saab was outclassed. In 1958 he concentrated on ice racing and won the first of five Swedish national titles. In 1959 he won the Swedish and German rallies, but it was his win on the 1960 RAC Rally that really got him known internationally. He went on to win it three times in a row.

The Acropolis fell to him and the amazing two-stroke Saab in 1961 and he finished fourth overall on the Monte driving the 95 Estate car, that being the only model with a four-speed gearbox at the time. In 1962 he made an all-out attack on the European Championship, winning the Monte and the RAC, being second on the Geneva, and third on the Swedish and 1000 Lakes, but this was not enough to beat Bohringer.

In 1963 he started with a win in Monte Carlo but the year is memorable for his Safari drive, where a lead of an hour and a half came to nothing when he hit an anteater (and the animal won), and for his amazing second place on the Liège–Sofia–Liège.

In 1964 he married Pat Moss but still found time to win the San Remo, finish third on the Monte, second on the Safari, Polish and Geneva rallies, and again second on the Liège–Sofia–Liège. But that year he achieved his dearest ambition, which was to win a *Coupe des Alpes* in the 850 cc 75-bhp Saab that he had made so famous.

After that year Erik still did some rallies but with the end of the two-stroke era he moved over into Saab's promotions department and has worked for them as a full-time ambassador ever since. Just occasionally he let some of his old form show, as when he was leading the Baha 1000 in California in 1969 but was sidelined with a broken drive shaft.

Roger Clark

Roger Clark, British (1939–   ). The family business is a collection of garages in Leicestershire, so it was to cars at once that young Mr Clark's attention turned. He did his first rally in a Ford Thames van in 1956. British rallies at the time were highly navigational but the better events required considerable driving skill. Clark became East Midlands champion in 1961 and then began to go for bigger national events. It was on these in 1962, at the wheel of a Mini Cooper during a very icy winter, that he showed he had exceptional car control. A good run on the Tulip Rally and a second place on the Scottish Rally of 1963 led the new Reliant team to give him a try-out on the *Coupe des Alpes*, where he finished sixth in the GT class for them.

In 1964 he bought a Ford Cortina GT and promptly won the Welsh, Scottish and London rallies, ahead of the Ford works entries. But the hint was not taken and it was Rover who gave him his first works drives in 1964. On the Monte in 1965 he was sixth overall in a Rover 2000 and first in his category, after what must be one of the finest drives of his career. Ford lent him a car for the Tulip, where he failed to finish but did impress, and 1966 saw him in their fulltime employ.

To set out all of Roger Clark's results for Ford over the ensuing 13 years would be to depress other drivers. Suffice it to say that he has won all British internationals at least once and that includes two wins on the RAC Rally as a World Championship event (1972 and 1976). He also won the Acropolis and the Tulip and the Canadian Shell 4000 (1967), and has competed in rallies on all five continents. His successes have largely been in Escorts of one kind or another, but he did finish tenth (after leading) on the 1968 London–Sydney in a MkII Lotus Cortina and won his class on the 1969 Three Cities rally in a MkIV Zodiac. He was also one of the very few people to have ever competed in Ford's GT70 prototype, in which he retired in the *Ronde Cevenole* in 1971. He also won the RAC Rally Championship four times in Fords (1965, 1972, 1973, 1975).

Since retiring from the works Ford team in 1979, Roger Clark has driven a works-prepared TR8 on some British events (1980), a works Ford to tenth on the RAC Rally with a BBC presenter (1981), and finished 11th in a Rothmans Porsche on the RAC Rally in 1984. He has also established a boat-building business as well as working with his brother, Stan, to expand the family garage business to include Porsche, Lotus, Austin Rover and Renault franchises.

Skekhar Mehta

Shekhar Mehta, Kenyan (1945–). Born in Kampala, Uganda, Mehta's present residence in Kenya is thanks to a certain ex-President Amin, but if the number of times he has won the Safari is any guide, he should be an honorary Kenyan anyway. His first rally car was a BMW 1800 which he acquired in 1966. By the early 1970s he was driving Datsuns and made several appearances with them on British rallies. In 1971 he opened the account with a second on the Safari with a Datsun 240Z, their homage to the Healey 3000. They were difficult cars to handle but the irrepressible Mehta went on to come sixth with one on the 1972 Acropolis and then won the 1973 Safari with one. In Morocco that year he parked one in a dry river bed and broke an oil pump on the 1000 Lakes, while in a tiny (by comparison) Sunny he came 37th on the RAC.

In 1974 he drove for Lancia (everyone does at some time) and came 11th on the Safari with a Fulvia and fourth in San Remo with a Beta Coupé. In the Beta he retired on the Safari in 1975 and then reverted to Datsun, coming sixth in Morocco and seventh in Portugal with a Violet. The following year he won the Cyprus and was third in Australia, but had an accident on the Safari and a third on the Acropolis. In 1977 and 1978 he broke down on the Safari but in 1979 he embarked on a string of four successive victories for Datsun in that rally (1979, 1980, 1981, 1982). He also won the Kuwait Rally that year, which caused him to go back and win the Middle East Championship in 1980. In 1981 he was fifth in the Acropolis, second in Argentina and third in the Ivory Coast which, added to his Safari win, put him fifth in the World Championship.

In 1983 Datsun came along with their new 240RS but it was not to herald success for Mehta. He broke down on the Safari and it was an Audi that took him to his best placing that year, fourth in Argentina. He drove a Subaru on the 1984 Monte and finished a commendable 14th but was back in a 240RS for the Safari (fifth), Acropolis (seventh), Ivory Coast (third) and RAC (eighth). For 1985 he had a rare accident on the Safari, notched up fourth in Acropolis and Argentina and retired in New Zealand.

With Datsun/Nissan cars well outclassed in most rallies by the Group B four-wheel-drive supercars, they all but retired in 1986. Mehta lent his services to Peugeot for the Safari and did all the testing as well as driving on the event. He finished eighth in a 205 T16 after many problems. He and Nissan will find the Group A rules in 1987 more to their liking and, hopefully, he will take up his unequalled Safari record where he left off – five outright wins.

Hannu Mikkola

Hannu Mikkola, Finnish (1942–   ). This man, who has done more World Championship rallying than any other, has an active career spanning almost twenty years – and shows no sign of slackening yet. Born on the Eastern borders of Finland, he did his first rally at the age of 21 in a borrowed Volvo PV 544. By 1966 he was second in the Finnish Championship and drove a Lancia Fulvia on the Monte in 1967, retiring from sixth place when his co-driver lost the road book. In Finland he stuck to Volvos and was third in a 122S on the 1967 1000 Lakes and won the Finnish Championship for them in 1968. The same year he drove a Datsun to ninth in the Monte Carlo, then a Lancia Fulvia to second place on the Austrian Alpine just weeks before taking a factory Escort Twin Cam to outright victory on the 1000 Lakes. For 1969 he was in the Ford team and won both the Austrian and 1000 Lakes for them. But it was in 1970 that he really proved his worth to them; he won the London–Mexico, the Arctic and the 1000 Lakes (his hat-trick), all in various Escorts, and became internationally famous.

In 1971 he was only fourth on the RAC and elsewhere unreliable, but that was swiftly redeemed when he won the Safari, the first European to do so, with an Escort RS in 1972. He also won the Scottish that year, as if to underline his versatility. In 1973 he was fourth on the Monte and won the New Zealand, but little else went well and he retired on the RAC with a broken hand following an accident. In 1974 he won the 1000 Lakes yet again for Ford, but began to feel restless. In 1975 he drove several makes of cars; second in the Monte and Portugal with a Fiat 124 Abarth and winning the 1000 Lakes in a Toyota Corolla and in Morocco in a Peugeot 504. In 1976/77 he split his time between Toyota and Peugeot but had no major wins, only a very creditable second on the RAC in 1977.

In 1978 he rejoined Ford and won the RAC Rally, as well as finishing second in both Portugal and Sweden. The next year he was even more successful, his victories in Portugal, New Zealand and the RAC helping to sweep Ford to the manufacturer's title. He also won the Ivory Coast and was second on the Safari, driving a Mercedes 450 SLC which carried him to second place in the Drivers' Championship, one point behind his Ford team mate, Bjorn Waldegaard.

In 1980 he continued to drive both Mercedes and Ford, coming second in Argentina and third in New Zealand for Mercedes, fourth in Sweden, third in San Remo and second on the RAC for Ford. What no-one knew as they congratulated him on being second in the World Championship again was that he had signed a deal with Audi for 1981. To start with he struggled with the new car and team; he was 91st on the Monte, won in Sweden, had three straight retirements and then bounced back to be third in the 1000 Lakes, fourth in San Remo and to win the RAC. Things went better in 1982, with second places in the Monte and San Remo and wins in the 1000 Lakes and the RAC, but still he was only third in the World Championship.

It was 1983 in which he put it right and won the championship. Fourth in Monte was his worst result, with wins in Sweden, Portugal, Argentina and the 1000 Lakes and second places in the Safari, Ivory Coast and the RAC. And 1984 was almost as distinguished, with nothing lower than third (the Monte and the Safari) but only one win (Portugal) and one retirement (1000 Lakes). His reward was second in the World Championship.

For 1985 he reduced his commitment, allowing Blomqvist and Rohrl to take stage centre at Audi. He was fourth in Sweden but retired on the Safari, coming back with the Sport Quattro to set some sensational times on the 1000 Lakes before retiring with a blown engine, an experience to be repeated on the RAC. He did take the Sport Quattro to the USA and won the Olympus Rally in its debutante year. In 1986 he was third in the Monte and then pulled out of Portugal and, like Audi, stopped rallying while the Group B controversy raged. He even watched his beloved 1000 Lakes from a helicopter!

Hannu Mikkola has been rallying long enough to have been everything from a hell-raiser to an elder statesman; he has an enviable record at both long-distance and sprint events and he is always, but always, competitive.

Sandro Munari

Sandro Munari, Italian (1940–   ). Being the son of a farmer means starting out on tractors, but Munari soon graduated to karts and by 1960 was building his own. He moved into cars with an 850 Abarth which he used on hill climbs as well as for personal transport. He started rallying in 1964 but results eluded him. Invited to co-drive for Arnaldo Cavallari, a boyhood friend from Venice, in a Jolly Club Alfa Romeo GTA, he jumped at the chance to learn more. They won rallies in Italy and Austria together but Munari wanted to drive himself.

When the Lancia team was being formed in 1965, he offered his services and drove a Flavia on several internationals including the 1000 Lakes. He was very quick on special stages and was lying second on the Monte Carlo of 1966 until he misjudged a bend on the last night. In 1967 he was fifth on the Monte in a Fulvia and went on to win all the rallies of the Italian championship. However he really put himself in the record books when he won the *Tour de Corse* and nearly became the first man ever to finish unpenalized; he missed the vital time control by seconds only. That same year he won his class in races at Mugello (road circuit) and Nürburgring with a Fulvia and counted the experience as useful for his progress as a rally driver.

But that career was halted for a while. His car was involved in a road accident in Yugoslavia on the 1968 Monte Carlo when he relaxed his concentration; his co-driver was killed and he spent several months in hospital. In 1969 he made a spectacular comeback, winning the Italian championship again in a Fulvia, but results eluded him during 1970/71 when he had to be content to finish behind the Scandinavians in the team. In 1972, however, he did what none of them had been able to do and that was to win the Monte for Lancia in a 1600 cc Fulvia. The rest of the year was occupied with developing Lancia's new Stratos. In 1973 he started out winning the Costa Brava in a Fulvia, but as soon as the Stratos was homologated he was away on a string of major victories that included the Firestone and the *Tour de France* and gave him the European Championship.

In 1974 there was no Monte to win, but Munari did bring home a Fulvia third overall on the Safari before reverting to the Stratos to win the San Remo and the Rideau Lakes and finish third on the RAC Rally. In 1975 he started the hat-trick of Monte Carlo wins with the Stratos that made both him and it truly famous. He also notched up two excellent results on the Safari, second in 1975 and third in 1977, which proved that he was as good at the long events as he was at the speed events. In 1977 he won the FIA Cup that was the forerunner of the World Drivers' title but that was also the end of the Stratos era as a works car. Fiat had bought Lancia and now wondered why they ran two competition departments, especially as Fiat had won the World Manufacturer's title.

In 1977 he started with one last go at the Monte with the Stratos, but the engine blew, and by Portugal Munari was in a Fiat 131 Abarth with the others. He never really liked the car and failed to get a result. For the RAC he was given a Stratos again but retired with engine failure. In 1979 he marked time and finished tenth on the Safari with the Fiat 131, but his main rally career in Europe was now at an end. He has returned several times to the Safari, with a Dodge Ramcharger in 1981, a Porsche 911 in 1982, an Alfa Romeo GTV6 in 1983 and a Toyota Celica Turbo in 1984, but failed to finish.

For several years he has worked from his home in Bologna for a distributor of dairy products, combining it with appearances as Alfa Romeo team manager – but now *they* have been bought by Fiat.

Tony Pond

Tony Pond, British (1945–   ). Britain's own superstar did his first rally in a Hillman Imp in 1967. By 1969 he was doing more rallies, now in a Mini Cooper, and was winning restricted and national events. He later ascribed his ability to pace himself on longer rallies to early experience of all-night British events. By 1974, he had benefited from the Ford Escort Mexico championship and won the Mexico section of the Swedish Rally. He finished fourth on the Welsh Rally in an Escort RS and then was signed up by the new British Opel team. He retired in an Ascona on the RAC Rally of 1974, but the following year was fourth on the Scottish and third on the Welsh before shifting to a Kadett GT/E to finish fourth on the RAC Rally. In the middle of the year he also won the Tour of Britain in a private Escort RS 2000.

In 1976 he was signed by the emerging Leyland team and drove Dolomite Sprints and then TR7s, in which he showed well on the RAC Rally but broke down. In 1977 he won the *Boucles de Spa* in a TR7, was third in Elba, second on the Scottish and eighth on the RAC. The following year he gave the TR8 its first rally and first win on the Granite City and went on to win the Ypres and Manx, retire in Corsica and finish fourth on the RAC. He also made the first of many trips to Africa, where he won the Molyslip Rally in a GM Chevair.

He changed allegiance to Chrysler in 1979, coming fifth on the Welsh and fourth in San Remo before retiring on the RAC Rally and then returning to the Leyland camp. In 1980, with a TR8, he was fourth in the British Open Championship, winning the Manx and coming fourth in Scotland. In addition he won the Ypres and the Manx Stages, was second in Cumbria, seventh on the RAC and tenth in the European Championship. His Chevair drive also netted him two wins in Africa.

With the end of the TR8 in competition and a long gestation period for its replacement, the Metro 6R4, Pond stayed loyal to the factory and in return spent a lot of time racing for them, first in Metro Turbos (1983) and Rovers (1984/5). In return he was allowed to drive for other teams in Europe, principally Datsun. But first, in 1981, he drove a Vauxhall Chevette in the UK, where he came second in the British Open, winning the Scottish and the Manx. He also won the BBC TV Rallysprint, but, more importantly, he drove underpowered Datsuns to a staggering third overall in Corsica and a fifth in Portugal. In 1982 he drove a Datsun Violet to fourth overall on the Safari at his first attempt, while in 1983 he was sixth in Corsica and second in Spa with a Nissan 240RS. He drove his first Rover in a rally, the Manx, set fastest time on the first stage and then retired with a broken drive shaft. He was to return with this car after the saloon car racing season stopped in 1984 and finished third on the Manx, first in Group A and well ahead of many Group B cars.

It was 1984 that he made his first sorties in the new Metro 6R4, starting with the York Rally, where he led until retirement with engine problems. He also had a very short RAC Rally, ending it with a crash in the Rover on the very first stage.

In 1985 he campaigned a Rover Vitesse in the British Open Championship and won Group A four times out of six, but crashed on the Manx and lost the

Group A title. He won the first rally for the 6R4 on the Gwynnedd, won the first rally with the 400 bhp version (the Argyll Stages) and won the Audi Sport Rally just prior to the car's homologation and world debut on the RAC, where, to the delight of an ecstatic home crowd, he finished third overall. Unfortunately, the first full season of the 6R4 in the World Championship mainly brought retirements, while other people's accidents brought disillusion. It was not until his favourite, the Manx, that Pond had a reliable car and he won easily, but a rare mistake in San Remo cost him a good placing, and his sixth on the RAC was more indicative of car problems than his real ability.

At the end of the 1986 season Pond said that he wanted to go into racing; good though he is at that, he is still the best British rally driver and unlikely to concede the position if he can get the right car.

Jean Ragnotti

Jean Ragnotti, French (1945–). Farmer's son, practical joker and stuntman, Jean Ragnotti is currently the most successful French rally driver. He started out on motor-bikes, then drove a truck for a living, bought a second-hand R8 Gordini in 1967 and won the Vaucluse Rally. He went on to win his group six times in the same car the following year. In 1969 he started to be offered other people's cars to drive and drove an NSU and an Opel Kadett as well as the R8.

For 1970 he acquired a Kadett and won Group 1 ten times and was 11th overall on the Monte Carlo. Opel France signed him for 1971/2 and he rewarded them with a win in Group 2 on the Monte in 1971 and in Group 1 the following year. Elsewhere, though, luck seemed to have deserted him and he parted with Opel for 1973 to take up Formula 3, winning one race at Montlhéry at the end of the season. Earlier, he had driven an R12 Gordini to 15th on the Monte.

In 1974 he raced a March 2-litre prototype with some success and finished third in the Caledonian Safari with a BMW. At that time he started driving stunts for films and doing just such racing and rallying as offered itself. In 1975 he drove for the Alpine team on the Monte with an A110 and crashed, while in 1976 they gave him the responsibility of sorting out the A310. He came 50th on the Monte, retired in Portugal, the Acropolis and the RAC but scored a notable fourth in Corsica. During the shift of Alpine to Renault he drove a VW Golf on the 1977 Monte and finished 18th. He was seventh at San Remo with an R5 Alpine but retired with the new car on the RAC.

With Renault having established a rally team, he drove to second in the Monte in 1978 in an R5 Alpine and, amazingly, got one of these front-wheel-drive cars home third in the Ivory Coast Rally. The following year he was 11th in the Monte, fourth in the Acropolis and second in Corsica with the R5 Alpine and these results made him seventh in the World Championship for drivers. In the R5 Turbo, 1980 saw him as French champion and seventh in the European Championship after winning the Lorraine, coming second in Poland and fourth in both the *Criterium Alpin* and Antibes.

In 1981 he won the Monte Carlo and finished fifth on the RAC, while in 1982 he finally won the Corsica and was classified tenth in the World Drivers' ratings. In 1983 he was seventh in the Monte but did little else, Renault's efforts being focused on Formula 1. In 1984 he won the French Championship again, which included winning the *Tour de France* and the *Criterium Alpin*. He was fifth in Portugal, third in Corsica and eighth in the European Championship.

The R5 Turbo was now at a disadvantage to the spate of four-wheel-drive cars in rallies but Renault did bring out the Maxi Turbo, and Ragnotti responded by winning in Corsica for them on its World Championship debut in 1985. He also won the Ypres and the *Tour de France*. During 1986 he drove a Group A R11 on several internationals as a development exercise and won rallysprints in both France and Finland. However patience has its reward and, for 1987, he was announced as the leading driver in a Renault Group A team for the World Championship.

Sympathetic, irrepressible, interviewable and always quick, Ragnotti is France's best rally ambassador.

Walter Röhrl

Walter Röhrl, German (1947–   ). The maestro of rally drivers, Walter Röhrl is also the most contentious, especially where commercial interests clash with his personal views. Always keen on fitness, he started out as a skier before turning to motor cars. His first rally was in 1968 with a baby Fiat. His first major impression on the rally world was when, driving a Ford Capri, he astounded the establishment by leading the best of Europe on the Olympia Rally until retiring. In the same car he won the Baltic Rally and was second in Poland.

For 1973 he drove for the Opel tuner, Irmscher, and with an Ascona won in Czechoslovakia, Hungary and Rumania and was second in Austria, giving him second equal in the European Championship. That same year he drove a Commodore on the Monte and was 45th. In 1974 he did the European rallies again with an Ascona, won six times and emerged as clear champion. He also did the RAC and finished fifth overall.

For 1975 he joined Opel's team for the World Championship, but out of six starts he only had one finish – in first place on the Acropolis. By the end of the year Opel had moved from the Ascona to the Kadett GT/E and it was in this car that he finished fourth on the 1976 Monte. He did his first Safari but crashed and luck deserted him elsewhere as well. He did not fare much better in 1977, but his speed had been noted and he drove a Fiat 131 in Canada and San Remo. For 1978 he spent his first full year with the Italians and won the Acropolis and the Quebec for them, as well as being fourth in the Monte and sixth on the RAC. But there was much rivalry between Röhrl and team-mate Markku Alen, stirred by the separate Fiat/Lancia factions. Röhrl was given a Stratos to drive on occasion and won four rallies in Germany with it. In 1979 Röhrl's best result in the World Championship was second in San Remo, and he was eighth in both the Safari and the RAC and won four rallies again in Germany.

But 1980 was his year to be World Champion for Fiat. He won the Monte Carlo, in Portugal, in Argentina and in the San Remo and was second in both New Zealand and Corsica. He again won four rallies in Germany, the Hunsrück for the third consecutive time.

At this point Röhrl decided to leave the Italians and take up an offer from Mercedes, but no sooner was his signature dry than Mercedes pulled out of competition. Röhrl was left to do a few rallies in a Porsche and started doing a few endurance races. However 1982 saw him with a full Opel contract to drive their Group 4 Ascona 400 sponsored by Rothmans. He only failed to finish once (Portugal), won the Monte and the Ivory Coast and was never less than fourth in seven other World events. This gave him his second World Championship.

In 1983 he was back with the Italians, driving a Lancia Rally 037, after problems involving the Opel sponsors. He won the Monte Carlo for the third time, as well as the Acropolis and the New Zealand and was second in Corsica and San Remo. He was second in the World Championship. He also did some endurance racing for Lancia.

For 1984 he joined Audi and immediately gave them their first Monte Carlo victory (and his fourth), but a sixth in Portugal was the best of the rest. In 1985 he reduced the number of rallies that he did, coming second in the Monte, third in both Portugal and New Zealand and then took the Sport Quattro to a wonderful win against the odds in San Remo. In 1986 he started with a fourth place on the Monte in a Sport Quattro behind the similar car of Mikkola. His next event was then the infamous Portuguese, where Röhrl took a leading part in the drivers' 'rebellion'. For the rest of that season, both he and Audi were on the sidelines but a return is planned for 1987 with a Group A Quattro, starting with his best event, the Monte.

Jean-Luc Therier

Jean-Luc Therier, French (1944–   ). Eccentricity is supposed to be the prerogative of the English, but perhaps it extends to Normans as well! Therier is the best-loved of French rallymen, both for his results and for his sense of fun. He started out racing a Renault R8 in 1966 and finished third in the *Coupe Gordini*. In 1967 he took the same car rallying and won several national events, as well as keeping up the racing and winning a ride in an Alpine at Le Mans. He drove there again in 1968 and won his class. The same year he got a factory R8 and consistently won his class with it in French international rallies, but the revelation came in 1969 on the Monte Carlo, where he took a Group 1 R8 to fifth overall and first in group. He was immediately admitted to the inner circle of works Alpine drivers and, together with Jean-Pierre Nicolas and Jean-Claude Andruet, became one of their 'Musketeers'.

Early troubles came from driving the car too hard, often in pursuit of his more experienced colleagues, but then in 1970 he won both the Acropolis and San Remo rallies. He started well in 1971 with a second place on the Monte, which he had led until the last night, but then a pattern emerged of leading and retiring. In part this was due to his dislike of recce-ing, which he kept to the absolute minimum, but his talent was indisputable and he could improvise his driving along with the best of the Scandinavians. He proved this in 1973; after finishing fifth on the Monte he went to Sweden and drove on a rally that banned studs, finishing third overall. Then he won the Portuguese, the Acropolis and the San Remo – a major contribution to Alpine's World Championship that year.

In 1974 the Alpine team started to become Regie-mented and Therier drove an R17 on some events, finishing second in Morocco and winning a shortened Press-on-Regardless in the USA. His other task was to drive the new Alpine 310, with which he finished third in Corsica that year and won the *Ronde Cevenole* in 1975. Therier never really made the swap from Alpine-man to Renault-man, while family problems and his garage business made him focus his attention more at home. In 1978 he did a couple of rallies in a Triumph TR8 but mainly he rallied with Toyota, retiring in Sweden, Portugal, the Acropolis and RAC rallies with various mechanical problems. These were to persist in 1979 when his Toyota failed to finish in Portugal, the Acropolis and the RAC and, to add to the list, he retired on the Monte with a VW Golf in both 1979 and 1980. But in a private Porsche 911 he won the *Tour de Corse* in 1980 and campaigned it throughout 1981/2. Retirements on the Monte Carlo, in Portugal, Corsica and finally in San Remo showed that there was a big gap between works and private teams. They did get a third on the Monte in 1982 and in that same year he got a deal together to rally an R5 Turbo for the French Championship, which he won. He was also a fantastic second overall with the little Renault on the *Tour de France*, behind a Ferrari 308 and ahead of a Lancia 037.

He carried on with a Renault R5 Turbo in 1983 but with little success and his final World Championship result came in 1984 when he finished fourth on the Monte Carlo. In 1985 he had a horrendous accident during the Paris–Dakar and, though he survived with his life, his driving career was effectively finished. His spirit and his performances in the Alpine A110 will live on.

RACING AND RECORDS

1878

A contest between road locomotives in Wisconsin included a road race (as well as categories such as ploughing) in its 201 miles/323.4 km; a steam Oshkosh was the only entry to complete the course, in 33 hours 27 min.

1894

The Paris–Rouen Reliability Trial was the forerunner of rallies and races; 25 vehicles started the 78.75-mile/126.7-km run, a de Dion steam tractor with a semi-articulated passenger trailer setting the pace, averaging 11.6 mph/18.7 kph, but as it did not meet the regulations or the spirit of the contest first prize was awarded jointly to a Panhard and a Peugeot.

1895

First true motor race, the Paris–Bordeaux–Paris

over 732 miles/1178 km was contested by 22 starters. Nine finished, led by Emile Levassor in a Panhard. He completed the course in 48 hours 48 min (15 mph/24.1 kph).

Chicago *Times-Herald* contest was the *first motoring competition in the USA*, comprising a race and tests for efficiency. A Duryea won – the first car to compete and win on pneumatic tyres (André Michelin had used pneumatic tyres on his Peugeot in the Paris–Bordeaux–Paris, but failed to complete the course).

1896

A committee set up to organize the Paris–Bordeaux became the basis of the *Automobile Club de France* – the *first motor sports club* in the world.

1897

The 149-mile/239.7-km Marseilles–Nice–la Tur-

The de Dion steam tractor with semi-articulated passenger trailer which the Comte de Dion drove to put up the best time in the 1894 Paris–Rouen trial.

bie race saw *the only road victory to be gained by a steam vehicle*, a de Dion driven by the Comte de Chasseloup-Laubat (average 19.2 mph/30.89 kph). This event showed that automobile sport could exist in January on the Riviera; secondly, it was split into special stages; and lastly, on rain-soaked roads, Brunninghaus (Panhard) crashed into the *Café de Paris* in front of Monaco Casino, the first of many accidents at that spot.

1898

First hill climb run over a short course at Chanteloup, and won by Camille Jenatzy in an electric car (a hill climb had been run in 1897, but only as part of the Marseilles–Nice race). At the first organized sprint meeting, at Achères, the Comte de Chasseloup-Laubat set the fastest time in a Jeantaud electric vehicle, which became the first speed record. The most famous of the early sprint meetings were the Nice Speed Trials, run from 1899 until 1904, when Rigolly covered the flying kilometre in 23.6 sec (94.78 mph/152.50 kph). The nearest British equivalent was the sprint meeting organized at Bexhill-on-Sea, 1902–7 and again in the 1920s, while the more significant *Daytona Beach (USA) speed meeting was first run* in 1903.

Notable racing 'firsts' included the first races in Germany and in Belgium, the first marque race (for Mors cars), the first massed-start race (Paris–Bordeaux), the first fatal race accident (in the *Cir-*

cuit de Perigueux, when the Marquis de Montaignac and his mechanic were killed as their Landry et Beyrouc rolled), and the first of the great city-to-city races to cross frontiers. This was the 889-mile/1430-km Paris–Amsterdam–Paris, won by Charron on a Panhard at 26.9 mph/43.3 kph. The equivalent principal events in the succeeding years were: 1899, *Tour de France* over 1350 miles/2172.5 km, won by René de Knyff (Panhard) at 30.2 mph/48.6 kph; 1900, Paris–Toulouse–Paris, won by Levegh (Mors) at 40.2 mph/64.6 kph; 1901, Paris–Berlin over 687 miles/1105.5 km, won by Fournier (Mors) at 44.1 mph/70.9 kph; 1902, Paris–Vienna over 615 miles/989.7 km, won by Farman (Panhard) at 38.4 mph/61.7 kph; 1903, Paris–Madrid, stopped short at Bordeaux after a succession of accidents, when Gabriel (Mors) was declared the winner, having *averaged* 65.3 mph/105.06 kph over the 342 miles/550 km.

First lady to race in a car was a Madame Laumaille, driving a de Dion tricycle in the Marseilles–Nice race (she finished fourth in class, beating her husband!).

A world speed record, forerunner of the Land Speed Record, was established by the Comte Gaston de Chasseloup-Laubat, driving a Jeantaud electric car at Achères near Paris to record 39.24 mph/63.14 kph. Until 1964 only vehicles powered through the wheels were eligible, but the doors were then opened to jet- and rocket-propelled

The Michelin brothers, André and Edouard, in the 1895 Paris–Bordeaux–Paris race. Although their Peugeot was not classified as a finisher, it was important as the first car to compete on pneumatic tyres.

vehicles and speeds increased dramatically. Since 1964 there has been a separate record category for wheel-driven automobiles. In a record attempt two runs have to be made, in opposite directions, over a flying kilometre or mile course; this stipulation came into effect in 1911 and has ruled out some spectacular 'one-way' speeds. The record holders are:

	Driver	Car	Venue	Speed (mph/kph)
1898	G. de Chasseloup-Laubat	Jeantaud	A	39.24/63.14
1899	C. Jenatzy	Jenatzy	A	41.42/66.64
	G. de Chasseloup-Laubat	Jeantaud	A	43.69/70.29
	C. Jenatzy	Jenatzy	A	49.92/80.32
	G. de Chasseloup-Laubat	Jeantaud	A	57.60/92.68
	C. Jenatzy	Jenatzy	A	65.79/105.85
1902	L. Serpollet	Serpollet	N	75.06/120.77
	W. K. Vanderbilt, Junior	Mors	Ab	76.08/122.41
	H. Fournier	Mors	D	76.60/123.25
	M. Augières	Mors	D	77.13/124.10
1903	A. Duray	Gobron-Brillié	O	83.47/134.30
	A. Duray	Gobron-Brillié	D	84.73/136.33
1904	H. Ford	Ford	SC	91.37/147.01*
	W. K. Vanderbilt, Junior	Mercedes	Da	92.30/148.51
	L. E. Rigolly	Gobron-Brillié	N	94.78/152.50
	P. de Caters	Mercedes	O	97.25/156.47
	L. E. Rigolly	Gobron-Brillié	O	103.55/166.61
	P. Baras	Darracq	O	104.52/168.17
1905	A. Macdonald	Napier	Da	104.65/168.38*
	V. Héméry	Darracq	A-1S	109.65/176.43
1906	F. H. Marriott	Stanley	Da	121.57/195.61
1909	V. Héméry	Benz	B	125.95/202.65
1910	B. Oldfield	Benz	Da	131.27/211.19*
1911	R. Burman	Benz	Da	141.37/227.46*
1914	L. G. Hornsted	Benz	B	124.10/200.17**
1919	R. de Palma	Packard	Da	148.87/241.15*
1920	T. Milton	Duesenberg	Da	156.03/251.05*
1922	K. L. Guinness	Sunbeam	B	133.75/215.20
1924	R. Thomas	Delage	Ar	143.31/230.58
	E. Eldridge	Fiat	Ar	146.01/234.93
	M. Campbell	Sunbeam	P	146.16/235.17
1925	M. Campbell	Sunbeam	P	150.76/242.57
1926	H. O. D. Segrave	Sunbeam	S	152.33/245.09
	J. G. P. Thomas	Thomas Spec.	P	169.30/272.40
	J. G. P. Thomas	Thomas Spec.	P	171.02/275.17
1927	M. Campbell	Napier-Campbell	P	174.88/281.38
	H. O. D. Segrave	Sunbeam	Da	203.79/327.89
1928	M. Campbell	Napier-Campbell	Da	206.95/332.98
	R. Keech	White-Triplex	Da	207.55/333.95
1929	H. O. D. Segrave	Irving-Napier	Da	231.44/372.38
1931	M. Campbell	Napier-Campbell	Da	246.09/395.96
1932	Sir M. Campbell	Napier-Campbell	Da	253.97/408.64
1933	Sir M. Campbell	R-R Campbell	Da	272.46/438.39
1935	Sir M. Campbell	R-R Campbell	Da	276.82/445.40
	Sir M. Campbell	R-R Campbell	Bon	301.13/484.52
1937	G. E. T. Eyston	Thunderbolt	Bon	312.00/502.11
1938	G. E. T. Eyston	Thunderbolt	Bon	345.50/555.91
	J. R. Cobb	Railton-Mobil	Bon	350.20/563.47
	G. E. T. Eyston	Thunderbolt	Bon	357.50/575.22
1939	J. R. Cobb	Railton-Mobil	Bon	369.70/594.85
1947	J. R. Cobb	Railton-Mobil	Bon	394.20/634.27
1963	C. Breedlove	Spirit of America (3)	Bon	407.45/655.59*
1964	D. Campbell	Proteus-Bluebird (W-D)	E	403.10/648.59
	T. E. Green	Wingfoot Express	Bon	413.20/664.84
	A. Arfons	Green Monster	Bon	434.02/698.34
	C. Breedlove	Spirit of America (3)	Bon	468.72/754.17
	C. Breedlove	Spirit of America (3)	Bon	526.28/846.78
	A. Arfons	Green Monster	Bon	536.71/863.57
1965	C. Breedlove	Spirit of America Sonic 1	Bon	555.583/893.933
	A. Arfons	Green Monster	Bon	576.553/927.673
	R. Summers	Goldenrod (W-D)	Bon	409.277/658.526
	C. Breedlove	Spirit of America Sonic 1	Bon	600.601/966.367
1970	G. Gabelich	The Blue Flame	Bon	630.388/1014.294
1983	R. Noble	Thrust 2	BR	633.46/1019.237

* Not recognized by the AIACR (the international governing body).
** AIACR two-way runs requirement met.
Cars: (3), three-wheeler; (W-D), wheel-driven.
Courses: A, Achères (F); Ab, Ablis (F); A-S, Arles-Salon (F); Ar, Arpajon (F); B, Brooklands (GB); Bon, Bonneville (USA); BR, Black Rock (USA); D, Dourdan (F); Da, Daytona (USA); E, Lake Eyre (AUS); N, Nice (F); O, Ostend (B); P, Pendine (GB); S, Southport (GB); SC, Lake St Clair (USA).

1899

The *first successful attempt to climb the road up Mount Washington*, New Hampshire, was made by F. O. Stanley in a Stanley Steamer. It took him some 2 hours and 3 minutes. It was not until 25 July 1903 that the first petrol-engined car made the same trip to the 6288-ft/1918-metre summit. That was a 24 hp Toledo driven by Arthur C. Moses who took some 3 hours and 5 minutes. The following year, 1904, the hill climb became a proper event and was won by Harry Harkness in a 60 hp Mercedes with a time of 24 minutes 37.4 seconds and second fastest was F. E. Stanley (twin brother of F. O.) in a Stanley Steamer with a time of 28 minutes 19.4 seconds.

1900

The first circuit race, the *Course du Catalogue*, was run over two laps of a triangle of roads at Melun, and won by Girardot (Panhard).

The Gordon Bennett Trophy race series between teams representing nations was first run, from Paris to Lyons and contested by three French Panhards, a Belgian Bolide and a Winton (the first US car to compete in Europe). Two Panhards were the only finishers. For this event, national racing colours were first allotted – blue for France, yellow for Belgium, red for Italy. Others, such as white for Germany and, in 1901, green for Britain followed, and blue and white became the American colours. The requirement that cars be painted in the colours of their entrants, irrespective of the nationality of driver or country where the car was built, fell into disuse as sponsorship became widespread and today only Ferraris, predominantly red, are a reminder of that detail of Grand Prix past.

The Gordon Bennett Trophy lasted only until 1905, when French interests saw to it that it was superseded by the Grand Prix (q.v.). Meanwhile it has seen an international race victory for a British car: the Napier driven by Edge in 1902, triumph was rather hollow for Edge was 16th overall in the

Camille Jenatzy atop the bullet-shaped *La Jamais Contente* at Achères in 1899. This record car was powered by twin electric motors, each with direct drive to a rear wheel.

concurrent Paris–Vienna and there were no other Gordon Bennett finishers!

1901

The first race to carry the title 'Grand Prix' was run at Pau, as part of a motor sport week. The race, over 206 miles/331 km, was won by Farman (Panhard). It was a secondary event (the title Grand Prix had little motor racing significance before 1906) and on various Pau circuits second-line races were run intermittently through to the 1980s. From 1933 the title Pau Grand Prix was picked up, although the long break undermines claims that this is the oldest motor race. Since the 1970s the principal Pau race has been a Formula 2 (until 1984) or F 3000 championship event, on a street circuit used from 1933 (the Pau circuit used for the 1930 French GP was outside the town).

1902

The first race which could be considered a sponsored event in the modern sense was the *Circuit du Nord*, backed by the French Ministry of Agriculture to promote the use of alcohol fuel. Contemporary reports suggest that competitors used it as little as possible – challenging the scrutineers is by no means a modern pastime – and that curious odours lingered behind the cars. Winner of the 537-mile/864-km race was Panhard driver Maurice Farman. Full race sponsorship did not come to the Grand Prix world until 1971, when the British event was backed by the International Wool Secretariat, incorporating 'Woolmark' in its title.

Heroic figure of the Chevalier René de Knyff before the start of the 1902 Paris–Vienna race. Car is a Panhard 70, which had a 90 bhp 13.6 litre engine mounted directly to its wooden chassis.

Fernand Gabriel arrives at Bordeaux in the ill-fated Paris–Madrid race of 1903. In this Mors, with its 'wind-cutting' nose, he covered the 342 miles/550 km in 5 hours 14 min 13.2 sec.

This 650 kg Renault in the light car class of the 1903 Paris–Madrid contrasts sharply with cars such as the Mors. Louis Renault led the class at Bordeaux, and the strain of the drive shows on his face. His brother Marcel was killed in a similar car in this race.

The first circuit race to rank as a major international event, the 318-mile/512-km *Circuit des Ardennes*, was also the first significant race to be won by a British driver, Charles Jarrott (driving a Panhard).

1903

The Gordon Bennett Trophy was the first major race run in the British Isles, and an Act of Parliament was necessary before it could be organized on remote country roads near Ballyshannon in Ireland. Racing on public roads was assumed to have been impossible on the mainland of Great Britain, although legislative bodies in Ulster (as well as Eire), Jersey and the Isle of Man allowed it, even encouraging it as a tourist attraction. Then Birmingham City Council backed legislation to permit the Birmingham Super Prix (F/3000) to be organized on a street circuit in 1986. That 328-mile/528-km Gordon Bennett race was won by Mercedes driver Camille Jenatzy at 49.2mph/79.2kph.

Gobron-Brillié used *opposed-piston engines in competition cars*, persisting until 1907 with little success in racing, although one of these machines was the first piston-engined car to exceed 100 mph/161 km.

Clément Ader in France and Alexander Winton in the USA built *8-cylinder racing engines*; two years later Franklin built an *air-cooled racing straight-8*.

1904

Association Internationale des Automobile Clubs Reconnus (AIACR), the *first international governing body of motor sport*, formed after wrangles over French proposals to change the Gordon Bennett rules. It was reconstituted as the *Fédération Internationale de l'Automobile* in 1946. From 1922 until 1978 sporting matters were delegated to the *Commission Sportive Internationale* (CSI), which was succeeded by the *Fédération Internationale du Sport Automobile* (FISA).

Steam sprint car, Pelzer's Serpollet at the Gaillon hill climb in 1904.

First international race in the USA, the Vanderbilt Cup, run on a Long Island circuit and won by George Heath (Panhard). Five more Cup races were run on that circuit, then from 1911 until 1916 on circuits from Savannah to Santa Monica. The G. Vanderbilt Cup run at Roosevelt Field in 1936–7 attracted leading European teams (the winners were Nuvolari and Rosemeyer); then America turned its back on this style of racing until after World War II.

Louis Rigolly became the *first driver to achieve 100 mph/161 kph over an accurately measured distance*, a kilometre at Ostend, actually recording 103.56 mph/166.65 kph in a 16.7 litre Gobron-Brillié. In 1953 John Cooper reached the magic 100 mph in a Cooper with a 344-cc engine (at Montlhéry, when he was timed at 105.71 mph/170.11 kph).

1905

Walter Christie raced his *first front-wheel-drive racing car* in the eliminating trials for the Vanderbilt Cup. Two years later he won a Daytona Beach event in a front-wheel-drive car, and introduced this layout to Grand Prix racing.

The RAC Tourist Trophy first run, for standard touring cars on a 52-mile/84-km Isle of Man circuit (won by J. S. Napier driving an Arrol-Johnston, at 33.9 mph/54.54 kph). With occasional lapses the race has been run ever since, for the 50th time in 1986, and thus has a strong claim to be the longest-established motor race that is still run (*see also* Pau GP). The last Manx race was run in 1922; subsequent events have been run at Ards (9), Donington (2), Dundrod (5), Goodwood (7), Oulton Park (5) and Silverstone (16). For many years (1928–54) it was a sports car race, and a handicap event, but at Silverstone reverted to its origins in that it became a touring car (saloon) race and a round in the European Touring Car Championship in the 1970s and 80s.

First hill climb run at Shelsley Walsh, the oldest surviving hill climb venue in Europe. The 1905 event was won by E. M. C. Instone, driving a Daimler. Narrow and sinuous and by international standards ludicrously short at 1000 yards/914 metres, Shelsley Walsh has a firm place in the affections of many British enthusiasts.

Brighton Speed Trials first run, over a standing-start mile, on the lines of events at several British seaside towns including Bexhill and Blackpool; unlike those, the Brighton event is still run. Its history was fragmented, lapsing after that first running until 1923–4, then again until 1932–8. Since 1946 it has been run over a standing-start kilometre.

Frank Marriott poses in 'Rocket', the Stanley steam car he drove to a Land Speed Record in 1906. The streamlined bodywork was made of canvas, while the rear-mounted twin-cylinder engine was an enlarged Stanley production type.

The Hon. Charles Rolls with the 20 hp Rolls-Royce, competing in the 1906 Isle of Man Tourist Trophy which he won at 39 mph/63 kph.

1906

Targa Florio first run, over the 'Great Madonie' circuit of 92.48 miles/148.82 km of challenging Sicilian roads, and won by Itala driver Cagno, who averaged 29.07 mph/46.78 kph over the three laps. Jealously guarded by its patron, Vincenzo Florio, the event was occasionally run within the Tours of Sicily and from 1937 until 1940 was run on the relatively sophisticated Palermo circuit, but usually it was run on one of the Madonie circuits of roads climbing into the mountains, from 1932 on the 44.74-mile/72-km 'Short Madonie'. The 57th *Targa Florio*, in 1973, was the last to count in the sports car championship (World Championship of Makes by that time), although the title was carried by a national Italian rally after that, then as an historic quasi-race. The first race on the Short Madonie was won by Nuvolari in an Alfa Romeo at 49.27 mph/79.27 kph, the 1973 race by Gijs van Lennep and Herbert Müller in a Porsche RSR at 71.27 mph/115.39 kph.

The first French Grand Prix – the *Grand Prix de l'Automobile Club de France* and the first of all national Grands Prix – was run on two days and over 770 miles/1239 km at Le Mans, and won by Szisz (Renault) at 63 mph/101 kph. Until 1921 it remained unique; then an Italian Grand Prix was run. The event had a chequered history, usually being a Formula race but sometimes a sports car event. Winners of the world championship races: **1950** (R) Fangio (Alfa Romeo); **1951** (R) Fangio and Fagioli (Alfa Romeo); **1952** (Ro) Ascari (Ferrari); **1953** (R) Hawthorn (Ferrari); **1954** (R) Fangio (Mercedes-Benz); **1956** (R) Collins (Ferrari); **1957** (Ro) Fangio (Maserati); **1958** (R) Hawthorn (Ferrari); **1959** (R) Brooks (Ferrari); **1960** (R) Brabham (Cooper); **1961** (R) Baghetti (Ferrari); **1962** (Ro) Gurney (Porsche); **1963** (R) Clark (Lotus); **1964** (Ro) Gurney (Brabham); **1965** (C) Clark (Lotus); **1966** (R) Brabham (Brabham); **1967** (LM) Brabham (Brabham); **1968** (Ro) Ickx (Ferrari); **1969** (C) Stewart (Matra); **1970** (C) Rindt (Lotus);

First national Grand Prix was the 1906 French event. Eventual winner Ferenc Szisz (Renault) waits to start at Le Mans.

1971 (PR) Stewart (Tyrrell); **1972** (C) Stewart (Tyrrell); **1973** (PR) Peterson (Lotus); **1974** (D) Peterson (Lotus); **1975** (PR) Lauda (Ferrari); **1976** (PR) Hunt (McLaren); **1977** (D) Andretti (Lotus); **1978** (PR) Andretti (Lotus); **1979** (D) Jabouille (Renault); **1980** (PR) Jones (Williams); **1981** (D) Prost (Renault); **1982** (PR) Arnoux (Renault); **1983** (PR) Prost (Renault); **1984** (D) Lauda (McLaren); **1985** (PR) Piquet (Brabham); **1986** (PR) Mansell (Williams).

Circuits: C, Clermont-Ferrand; D, Dijon–Prenois; LM, Le Mans; PR, Paul Ricard (le Castellet); R, Reims; Ro, Rouen.

First purpose-built circuit in Australia opened at Aspendale (Victoria). A 1-mile/1.6-km gravel track, it was soon abandoned, then reopened with a concrete surface in 1923 and used spasmodically through to the 1930s.

Fastest steam car ever was the boat-shaped Stanley in which Fred Marriott broke the land speed record at Daytona, at 121.57 mph/195.606 kph.

1907

First British Grand Prix car, the Weigel straight-8, appeared. Two started in the French GP, both retired.

Brooklands Motor Course, the world's first purpose-built race track, opened at Weybridge. Built by Hugh Locke-King on his estate, it had a lap distance of 3¾ miles/6 km and featured two long banked curves; later variations were contrived. The fastest officially-recorded lap was set by John Cobb in the Napier-Railton in 1935, at 151.97 mph/244.52 kph. The Land Speed Record (q.v.) was broken at Brooklands before World War I, numerous class records were set at the track, and the first two RAC (British) Grands Prix were run on it. But although it was central to British motor sport for several years, the track was generally insignificant in international terms, and in the 1930s the most important races in Britain were being run on the road circuit at Donington. The last Brooklands meeting was held in August 1939, and in recent years sterling efforts have been made to preserve part of this monument to a long-past age of motor sport.

The Peking–Paris 'race' (in most respects it was more akin to a modern rally) was won by a crew captained by Prince Scipio Borghese. Using a 7.4 litre Itala, they completed the run in 44 days of driving. One more marathon international race, New York–Paris, was run in the following year and won by an American crew with a Thomas Flyer.

The St Petersburg–Moscow race, the only major

Felice Nazzaro's great season was 1907, when he won the three major races, Targa Florio, French Grand Prix and (here) the Kaiserpreis, for FIAT.

A trio of 7.7-litre 60 hp Napiers at the Brooklands Motor Course prior to the start of the 24-hour run in 1907 that was the first event on the track. S. F. Edge drove the car on the right single-handed to set a world record of 1581 miles/2544 km.

race ever run in Russia, was run for the first time and won by Arthur Duray (Lorraine-Dietrich). It was run again in 1908, when Hémery won in a Benz.

Largest engine ever to be raced in a Grand Prix was the 19,891 cc V4 in American Walter Christie's entry in the French GP. This was also the first GP car to have a V4 (mounted transversely) and the first to have front-wheel drive. Later that year a Christie was the first front-wheel drive car to win a major race (a 250-mile/402 kph event at Daytona Beach).

1908

A Chadwick run in the Vanderbilt Cup and American Grand Prize races had an *engine with forced induction*, by means of a centrifugal forerunner of the supercharger.

'Pit' became a racing term that has persisted in the face of inaccuracy – it owed its origin to the trench with a counter just above road level that was provided for team crews at the French GP. Ever since, a 'pit' has been a ground-level shelter, sometimes forming the ground floor of elaborate structures.

Only man ever to drive his very first race in the

Christian Lautenschlager ready for his first race, in the 1908 French Grand Prix at Dieppe. He won for Mercedes at 69.05 mph/111.129 kph.

premier event of the year, and win it, was Christian Lautenschlager, in a Mercedes in the French GP.

First American Grand Prize race run over 402 miles/647 km at Savannah and won by Wagner (Fiat). That forerunner of the American Grand Prix was run seven times, for the last time at Santa Monica in 1916, and the first US Grand Prix was run for sports cars at Riverside in 1958 (won by Chuck Daigh in a Scarab). In the following year it was a world championship Formula 1 race, Bruce McLaren becoming the youngest driver (at 22) ever to win a Grand Prix when he took the flag at Sebring. For two decades it seemed to find a permanent home at Watkins Glen, effectively becoming the US Grand Prix East as the Long Beach race became established from 1976. 'The Glen' was abandoned by the F1 circus after the 1980 GP, and from 1982 a race entitled United States Grand Prix (Detroit) effectively took its place. Winners of the world championship GPs: **1959** McLaren (Cooper); **1960** Moss (Lotus); **1961** Ireland (Lotus); **1962** Clark (Lotus); **1963** G. Hill (BRM); **1964** G. Hill (BRM); **1965** G. Hill (BRM); **1966** Clark (Lotus); **1967** Clark (Lotus); **1968** Stewart (Matra); **1969** Rindt (Lotus); **1970** Fittipaldi (Lotus); **1971** Cevert (Tyrrell); **1972** Stewart (Tyrrell); **1973**
Peterson (Lotus); **1974** Reutemann (Brabham); **1975** Lauda (Ferrari); **1976** Hunt (McLaren); **1977** Hunt (McLaren); **1978** Reutemann (Ferrari); **1979** Villeneuve (Ferrari); **1980** Jones (Williams); **1982** Watson (McLaren); **1983** Alboreto (Tyrrell); **1984** Piquet (Brabham); **1985** Rosberg (Williams); **1986** Senna (Lotus).

All took place at Watkins Glen, except 1959, Sebring, and 1960, Riverside; since 1982 races have been in Detroit.

1909

Indianapolis Speedway opened. Promoted by four local citizens, led by Carl G. Fisher, and designed by P. T. Andrews, this 2½-mile/4-km oval was to have a much longer life than any other main-line racing venue, despite its obvious limitations as speeds increased towards the 200-mph/321-kph-plus laps of the 1980s. At the first meeting the track surface broke up, so by the end of that first year it had been resurfaced with 3,200,000 bricks – hence 'The Brickyard'. The first race was a short sprint won by Louis Schwitzer (Stoddard-Dayton), and the first major event was a 250-mile/402-km race won by Bob Burman (Buick), but the opening meeting was marred by the first fatal accident at Indianapolis.

1910

First board track opened in the USA, at Playa del Rey. Steep bankings were a characteristic of these tracks (and a few similar concrete or asphalt tracks) and speeds were high. That first track had a lap of 1 mile/1.6 km, with later tracks tending to be of 1½ miles/2.4 km or 2 miles/3.2 km, and feature races of up to 500 miles/804 km were run on them. New tracks were built through to the mid-1920s, but maintenance costs were high so that by the end of that decade short-oval racing, on flat, loose-surfaced tracks, had taken over and survives to this day.

1911

First running of the 500-Mile Sweepstakes at Indianapolis. After a doubtful start at the track, Carl Fisher found a formula for success, and since then 'Indianapolis' has meant just one race, run on Memorial Day (30 May). It was run over 300 miles/483 km in 1916, outwardly as a gesture towards the war in Europe but in part because that meant few new machines (only 21 cars started, and the crowd was small), while it has occasionally been cut short by rain and in 1986 was postponed because of heavy rain on Memorial Day.

The first races were run to engine capacity regulations: 9.8 litres (600 cu. in.) in 1911–12; 7.4 litres (450 cu. in.) in 1913–14; and 4.9 litres (300 cu. in.) in 1915–19. The limit was 3 litres until 1922, then 2 litres until 1925 and 1.5 litres to the end of the decade; various capacity and fuel-related rules were applied until 1938 when the then-current GP capacities of 4.5 litres for unsupercharged engines and 3 litres for a supercharged unit were adopted. These lasted through to 1956 when the familiar 4.2/2.8 litre (256/170 cu. in.) rules for normally-aspirated or supercharged engines came in, with allowances for diesels and, in the 1960s, for steam engines, rotary engines and gas turbines (when the latter became competitive later in the decade the rules were changed to handicap them out of contention). In the 1970s up to nine capacity categories were applied in attempts to cover a range from pure racing to stock-block engines, two- and four-strokes, overhead, the rather quaintly-termed 'nonoverhead' camshaft types, and so on. Turbocharger boost pressures were to be limited.

The race has always been the pinnacle of US motor sport, and frequently the largest single-day sporting event in the world in terms of spectator attendances. Technical changes have not always been welcomed by an organization that has some-times been extraordinarily reactionary, and this has diluted international interest, although in the last two decades the most significant technical changes have been influenced by European practices, for example the swing to rear-engined designs after Lotus' victory in 1965 and the supremacy of Cosworth engines in the first half of the 1980s.

Winners of the 500: **1911** Harroun/Patschke (Marmon) 74.59 mph/120.01 kph; **1912** Dawson (National) 78.72/126.66; **1913** Goux (Peugeot) 75.92/122.17; **1914** Thomas (Delage) 82.47/132.69; **1915** de Palma (Mercedes) 89.84/144.55; **1916** Resta (Peugeot) 84.00/135.15; **1919** Wilcox (Peugeot) 88.05/141.67; **1920** Chevrolet (Monroe) 88.62/142.59; **1921** Milton (Frontenac) 89.62/144.19; **1922** Murphy (Murphy Special, i.e. Duesenberg-Miller) 94.48/152.02; **1923** Milton (Miller) 90.95/146.34; **1924** Corum/Boyer (Duesenberg) 98.23/158.05; **1925** de Paolo (Duesenberg) 101.13/162.72; **1926** Lockhart (Miller) 95.91/154.32; **1927** Sounders (Duesenberg) 97.55/156.96; **1928** Meyer (Miller) 99.48/160.06; **1929** Keech (Miller) 97.58/157.01; **1930** Arnold (Miller) 100.45/161.62; **1931** Schneider (Miller) 96.63/155.47; **1932** Frame (Miller) 104.14/167.56; **1933** Meyer (Miller) 104.16/167.59; **1934** Cummings (Miller) 104.86/168.72; **1935** Petillo (Miller) 106.24/170.94; **1936** Meyer (Miller) 109.07/175.49; **1937** Shaw (Gilmore) 113.58/182.75; **1938** Roberts (Miller) 117.20/188.57; **1939** Shaw (Maserati) 115.03/185.08; **1940** Shaw (Maserati) 114.27/183.86; **1941** Davis/Rose (Noc-Out Spl) 115.12/185.23; **1946** Robson (Thorne Spl) 114.82/184.74; **1947** Rose (Blue Crown Spl) 116.34/187.19; **1948** Rose (Blue Crown Spl) 119.81/192.77; **1949** Holland (Blue Crown Spl) 121.33/195.22; **1950** Parsons (Kurtis) 124.00/199.51; **1951** Wallard (Belanger Spl) 126.24/203.12; **1952** Ruttmann (Agajanian Spl) 128.92/207.43; **1953** Vukovich (Fuel Injection Spl) 128.74/207.14; **1954** Vukovich (Fuel Injection Spl) 130.84/210.52; **1955** Sweikert (John Zink Spl) 128.21/206.29; **1956** Flaherty (John Zink Spl) 128.49/206.74; **1957** Hanks (Belond Spl) 135.60/218.18; **1958** Bryan (Belond Spl) 133.79/215.27; **1959** Ward (Leader Card Spl) 135.86/218.59; **1960** Rathman (Ken-Paul Spl) 138.77/223.28; **1961** Foyt (Bowes Seal Fast Spl) 139.13/223.86; **1962** Ward (Leader Card Spl) 140.29/225.73; **1963** Jones (Agajanian Spl) 143.14/230.31; **1964** Foyt (Sheraton Thompson Spl) 147.35/237.08; **1965** Clark (Lotus) 150.69/242.46; **1966** G. Hill (Lola) 144.32/232.21; **1967** Foyt (Coyote) 151.21/243.29; **1968** B. Unser

Smoke-shrouded line up for the first Indianapolis 500, the field apparently waiting for the Stoddard-Dayton pace car (on the right) to be cranked into life. The front-row cars are (left to right) a National, an Interstate, a Simplex and a Case.

(Eagle) 152.88/245.98; **1969** Andretti (Hawk) 156.87/252.40; **1970** A. Unser (Colt) 155.75/250.60; **1971** A. Unser (Colt) 157.73/253.78; **1972** Donohue (McLaren) 162.96/262.20; **1973** Johncock (Eagle) 159.04/255.89; **1974** Rutherford (McLaren) 158.59/255.17; **1975** B. Unser (Eagle) 149.21/240.08; **1976** Rutherford (McLaren) 148.72/239.29; **1977** Foyt (Coyote) 161.33/259.58; **1978** A. Unser (Lola) 161.36/259.63; **1979** Mears (Penske) 158.69/255.33; **1980** Rutherford (Chaparral) 142.86/229.86; **1981** B. Unser (Penske) 139.08/223.78; **1982** Johncock (Wildcat) 162.02/260.69; **1983** Sneva (March) 162.11/260.83; **1984** Mears (March) 163.62/263.25; **1985** Sullivan (March) 152.982/246.200; **1986** Rahal (March) 170.722/274.691.

1912

Resumption of Grand Prix racing, after a three-year lapse due to factors as diverse as a recession in the infant car industry and French intransigence because 'their' race had been won by foreign teams. The age of giant cars – comprising large-capacity engines in rudimentary chassis – was passing. In the French race, still the only Grand Prix, new standards were set by Peugeot with a four-valves-per-cylinder twin-overhead camshaft engine of 7.6 litres. One of them, driven by Georges Boillot, won the race ahead of a traditional 14.1-litre Fiat.

Sunbeam scored the first team 1–2–3 in a major race, in the *Coupe de l'Auto*.

1913

Last Grand Prix cars fitted with chain drive were the Mercedes run in the *Grand Prix de France* at Le Mans (one placed third).

Isotta-Fraschini pioneered the use of brakes on all four wheels of racing cars, although these machines were not pure-bred but derived from sporting models. Cars with 10.6-litre engines were run, and a trio of 7.2-litre cars run in the Indianapolis 500, where all retired. In the following year Delage, Fiat, Peugeot and Piccard-Pictet built Grand Prix cars with four-wheel brakes.

The first Spanish Grand Prix was run, as a touring car race at Guadarrama (won by Salamanca in a Rolls-Royce). It was run as a Formula race in 1923 and 1927, then twice in the 1930s. It was revived on the Pedrables circuit at Barcelona in 1951, then lapsed until the late 1960s when it was run at the uninspiring Jarama autodrome. The Montjuich circuit, which was subsequently used, was a forerunner of the street circuits that sprang up a decade later, and ironically was discarded before such circuits became popular, following an acci-

Carefree days. J. A. Barber Lomax has three passengers in his Vauxhall during a 1913 hill climb at Shelsley Walsh. And a rear door is flying open.

Refuelling stop for Georges Boillot in the 1912 French GP. He won in this Peugeot, which set new standards with its fast-revving twin-ohc engine.

dent in which five spectators were killed in the 1975 GP. Financial uncertainties led to another interlude in the early 1980s, then there was another revival, the 1986 race at Jerez appropriately being sponsored by a sherry producer! Winners of the world championship races: **1951** (P) Fangio (Alfa Romeo); **1954** (P) Hawthorn (Ferrari); **1968** (J) G. Hill (Lotus); **1969** (M) Stewart (Matra); **1970** (J) Stewart (March); **1971** (M) Stewart (Tyrrell); **1972** (J) Fittipaldi (Lotus); **1973** (M) Fittipaldi (Lotus); **1974** (J) Lauda (Ferrari); **1975** (M) Mass (McLaren); **1976** (J) Hunt (McLaren); **1977** (J) Andretti (Lotus); **1978** (J) Andretti (Lotus); **1979** (J) Depailler (Ligier); **1981** (J) Villeneuve (Ferrari); **1986** (Je) Senna (Lotus).

Circuits: J, Jarama; Je, Jerez; M, Montjuich; P, Predrables.

1914

The first Grand Prix winner to construct a GP car bearing his own name was Felice Nazzaro (q.v.), who had won the 1907 French GP for Fiat. His Nazzaro cars appeared in the 1914 French GP (all three retiring), a year after he had driven a Nazzaro to win the *Targa Florio*. After World War I Nazzaro returned to Fiat, for whom he won the 1922 French GP.

The French Grand Prix over 468 miles/753 km of a circuit near Lyons was one of the great events of the first period of GP racing, contested by 37 cars representing six nations (France, Italy, Germany, Britain, Belgium and Switzerland). For the first time cars were started in pairs – hitherto, single cars had been started at intervals. The leading roles were played by Boillot, expected to win 'for France' in a Peugeot, and Mercedes drivers Sailer and Lautenschlager. Boillot and Sailer retired, Lautenschlager scored his second GP victory, and a month later Europe was at war.

The first racing car with a monocoque construction chassis/body was built by the Blood Brothers Machine Co., and named Cornelian. It also featured independent suspension front and rear. Powered by modest 1.7- and 1.9-litre engines, the Cornelian showed considerable promise (before retiring it ran 12th in the 1915 Indianapolis 500). The line was not developed after World War I.

1916

First Pike's Peak hill climb, on the 12.42-mile/20-km road rising 1500 metres/4918 ft above Colorado Springs. It was to become the only internationally-known climb in the USA. Fastest time at that first meeting was 20 min 55.6 sec, set by Rea Lentz in a Romano Eight Special; in the 63rd Pike's Peak Race to the Clouds (1985) a new record time of 11 min 25.39 sec was set by Michele Mouton in an Audi Sport Quattro. However, in the following year the record was back in the hands of Bobby Unser (q.v.), with an 11 min 9.22 sec climb in a 500 bhp Audi Sport Quattro S1. That was the 27th Pike's Peak victory for a member of the Unser family. Until 1970, Pike's Peak had been a points-scoring event in the USAC Championship Trail, which also included the Indianapolis 500!

1919

First of the classic races to be revived after the war was the Indianapolis 500, run one day after its traditional Memorial Day date to avoid accusations of insults to the dead. For the first time, 100-mph/161-kph laps were recorded in qualifying, seven drivers exceeding the magic figure. Howdy Wilcox won in a Peugeot – the last victory for a European car for 20 years – while among novelties there was a V12 Packard which Ralph de Palma placed sixth, having led the early laps (this car inspired Enzo Ferrari's long love affair with the V12 layout).

First European race of substance to be run after the war was the *Targa Florio*, late in November. André Boillot won in a Peugeot. First of the 25 starters was Enzo Ferrari, whose CMN lasted to the third lap.

1920

First Bugatti victory was scored by Ernst Friderich in a Type 13 in the international *voiturette* (light car) race at Le Mans.

Jimmy Murphy (and his riding mechanic Ernie Olsen) scored a notable first when they won the 1921 French GP in this Duesenberg – 41 years were to pass before another American won the race.

1921

French Grand Prix at Le Mans saw the first American victory in a major European race, Jimmy Murphy driving a Duesenberg to win the 322-mile/ 518-km event at 78.10 mph/125.69 kph. This Duesenberg was the first GP car to have hydraulic brakes, to the front wheels only (a 1933 Maserati was the first racing car to have them on all four wheels).

First Italian Grand Prix run, at Brescia. It was won by Jules Goux driving a Ballot, at 89.94 mph/ 144.71 kph. In the following year it was moved to Monza, where with few exceptions (Leghorn, 1937; Milan, 1949; Turin, 1948; Imola, 1980) it has been run ever since, although the circuits used at the *Autodromo Nazionale* outside Milan have varied. The first notable Italian GP was the 1923 race, *the first Grand Prix to be won by a supercharged car* (the Fiat 805 driven by Carlo Salamano); a combined road and banked track circuit at Monza was occasionally used in the 1950s, and for a Grand Prix for the last time in 1960 (when Phil Hill won in a Ferrari); the fastest race was run in 1971, Peter Gethin in a BRM winning in a four-car blanket finish at 150.72 mph/242.51 kph, before the road circuit was artificially slowed. Winners of the world championship GPs: **1950** Farina (Alfa Romeo); **1951** Ascari (Ferrari); **1952** Ascari (Ferrari); **1953** Fangio (Maserati); **1954** Fangio (Mercedes-Benz); **1955** Fangio (Mercedes–Benz); **1956** Moss (Maserati); **1957** Moss (Vanwall); **1958** Brooks (Vanwall); **1959** Moss (Cooper); **1960** P. Hill (Ferrari); **1961** P. Hill (Ferrari); **1962** G. Hill (BRM); **1963** Clark (Lotus); **1964** Surtees (Ferrari); **1965** Stewart (BRM); **1966** Scarfiotti (Ferrari); **1967** Surtees (Honda); **1968** Hulme (McLaren); **1969** Stewart (Matra); **1970** Regazzoni (Ferrari); **1971** Gethin (BRM); **1972** Fittipaldi (Lotus); **1973** Peterson (Lotus); **1974** Peterson (Lotus); **1975** Regazzoni (Ferrari); **1976** Peterson (March); **1977** Andretti (Lotus); **1978** Lauda (Brabham); **1979** Scheckter (Ferrari); **1980** Piquet (Brabham); **1981** Prost (Renault); **1982** Arnoux (Renault); **1983** Piquet (Brabham); **1984** Lauda (McLaren); **1985** Prost (McLaren); **1986** Piquet (Williams).

1922

The Monza autodrome opened, in a royal park north of Milan, comprising a high-speed banked track and a road circuit (the two could be used in combination). The original banked track was demolished in 1939, and a new track built in 1955;

Felice Nazzaro on his way to victory in the 1922 French GP, driving one of the neat little Fiat 804s which set new standards for designers.

neither was frequently used, whereas the road circuit has been the home of the Italian Grand Prix and other international events, notably for endurance and touring car championship races.

Sitges-Terramar banked track completed near Barcelona, with bankings too steep to be wholly practicable. It was soon abandoned.

First massed-start Grand Prix, and the first to have a rolling start, was the French GP at Strasbourg.

Vauxhall built a team of 3-litre Grand Prix cars – for the first season of racing under a 2-litre maximum capacity limit! The cars were raced only in the Tourist Trophy and national British events.

The first 24-hour road race to be run in Europe was the *Bol d'Or* at Saint Germain, won by André Morel in a 1.1-litre Amilcar at 37.54 mph/ 60.40 kph. The second race resulted in a tie between Salmson drivers Benoist and Desvaux. The race continued as a 1.1-litre event at Saint Germain until 1937 when it was run at Montlhéry, the first capacity increase (to 1.5 litres) coming in the following year. The race survived until 1955, and was a little odd in several ways, most notably in its regulation permitting only one driver, a rule which lasted until 1953. It was in any case a very different event from the earlier 24-hour races in the USA which were run on well-lit short-oval dirt and board tracks.

Mercedes introduced the supercharger to European racing, running a pair of 1.5-litre cars in the *Targa*

Florio, where one was placed a lowly 20th, overshadowed by Masetti's victory in an essentially pre-war Mercedes.

1923

Fiat introduced the supercharger to Grand Prix racing, on the 805. Fiat also scored the first race win for a supercharged racing car in Europe, with a car driven to victory in the *Gran Premio Vetturette* at Brescia.

Delage built the first V12-engined Grand Prix car. Designed by Planchon, it was built in only four months, although it was not fully race-worthy until 1924.

Voisin built Grand Prix cars on semi-monocoque lines, which were raced in the French GP. Lack of power from what were essentially production engines was a handicap, but in principle these cars anticipated the true monocoque in GP racing by 39 years.

Benz built the first Grand Prix car with its engine mounted behind the cockpit. The team achieved encouraging results in its only Grand Prix (the Italian race) but lack of funds hampered development. Two were run as sports cars in German national events in 1924–5, but the programme was abandoned as Benz and Mercedes amalgamated in 1926.

First British victory in a Grand Prix was scored by Henry Segrave, driving a Sunbeam in the French event at Tours.

The title 'European Grand Prix' first used for the Italian race at Monza. It was an additional title for one national Grand Prix each year through to the 1960s, adding nothing save supposed extra status. Then in 1983 the title was revived and applied to a second championship race in one country. Winners of the world championship European Grands Prix: **1983** (Brands Hatch) Piquet (Brabham); **1984** (Nürburgring) Prost (McLaren); **1985** (Brands Hatch) Mansell (Williams).

The first Le Mans 24-hour Race was run at the end of May. Conceived as a test for touring cars, it was the first international event to be run for such a duration and its 'inventors', Charles Faroux, Emile Coquille and Georges Durand, intended that the emphasis should be on endurance rather than speed. It was to become the pre-eminent sports car race – sometimes the most widely-publicized of all road races – and its fortunes have not necessarily reflected the ups and downs of sports car racing, for through the 24-hour race its organizers, the *Automobile Club de l'Ouest*, have been able to influence change in the category.

The race has survived several crises: the most sombre coming in the aftermath of racing's worst accident, at Le Mans in 1955 when 83 spectators and Mercedes driver 'Pierre Levegh' (Bouillon) were killed; the most worrying for its future as crowds fell sharply in the early 1980s.

Throughout, the race has been run on the same basic circuit, although this has several times been modified, most drastically after the 1931 race. The regulations have been complex, and contests such as fuel efficiency 'indexes' within the race have been very important; in recent years the regulations have generally followed world endurance championship and IMSA rules (incidentally, no driver may drive for more than four hours in a stint, or 14 hours in total).

Le Mans 24-hour Race winners (starters/finishers in parentheses):

10.726-mile/17.258-km circuit: **1923** (33/30) Lagache/Leonard (Chenard et Walcker) 57.205 mph/92.064 kph; **1924** (40/14) Duff/Clement (Bentley) 53.782 mph/86.555 kph; **1925** (49/16) de Courcelles/Rossignol (La Lorraine) 57.838 mph/93.082 kph; **1926** (41/13) Bloch/Rossignol (La Lorraine) 66.082 mph/106.350 kph; **1927** (22/7) Benjafield/Davis (Bentley) 61.354 mph/98.740 kph; **1928** (33/17) Barnato/Rubin (Bentley) 69.108 mph/111.219 kph.

10.153-mile/16.336-km circuit: **1929** (25/10) Barnato/Birkin (Bentley) 73.627 mph/118.492 kph; **1930** (17/9) Barnato/Kidston (Bentley) 75.876 mph/122.111 kph; **1931** (26/6) Howe/Birkin (Alfa Romeo) 78.127 mph/123.735 kph.

8.475-mile/13.636-km circuit: **1932** (26/9) Sommer/Chinetti (Alfa Romeo) 76.840 mph/123.084 kph; **1933** (29/13) Sommer/Nuvolari (Alfa Romeo) 81.400 mph/131.001 kph; **1934** (44/23) Chinetti/Etancelin (Alfa Romeo) 74.743 mph/120.289 kph; **1935** (58/28) Hindmarsh/Fontés (Lagonda) 77.847 mph/125.283 kph; **1937** (48/17) Wimille/Benoist (Bugatti) 85.125 mph/136.997 kph; **1938** (42/15) Chaboud/Trémoulet (Delahaye) 82.355 mph/132.539 kph; **1939** (42/20) Wimille/Veyron (Bugatti) 86.855 mph/139.781 kph; **1949** (49/19) Chinetti/Selsdon (Ferrari) 82.281 mph/132.420 kph; **1950** (60/29) Rosier/Rosier (Talbot) 89.713 mph/144.380 kph; **1951** (60/30) Walker/Whitehead (Jaguar) 93.495 mph/150.466 kph; **1952** (57/17) Lang/Riess (Mercedes-Benz) 96.669 mph/155.575 kph; **1953**

(60/26) Rolt/Hamilton (Jaguar) 105.841 mph/ 170.336 kph; **1954** (57/18) Gonzalez/Trintignant (Ferrari) 105.145 mph/169.215 kph; **1955** (60/21) Hawthorn/Bueb (Jaguar) 107.067 mph/ 172.308 kph.

8.364-mile/13.457-km circuit: **1956** (49/14) Flockhart/Sanderson (Jaguar) 104.465 mph/ 168.122 kph; **1957** (54/20) Flockhart/Bueb (Jaguar) 113.845 mph/183.217 kph; **1958** (55/20) Gendebien/Hill (Ferrari) 106.200 mph/ 170.914 kph; **1959** (53/13) Shelby/Salvadori (Aston Martin) 112.569 mph/181.163 kph; **1960** (55/20) Gendebien/Frère (Ferrari) 109.193 mph/ 175.730 kph; **1961** (55/22) Gendebien/Hill (Ferrari) 115.902 mph/186.527 kph; **1962** (55/18) Gendebien/Hill (Ferrari) 115.244 mph/ 185.469 kph; **1963** (49/12) Scarfiotti/Bandini (Ferrari) 118.104 mph/190.071 kph; **1964** (55/24) Guichet/Vaccarella (Ferrari) 121.563 mph/ 195.638 kph; **1965** (51/14) Rindt/Gregory (Ferrari) 121.092 mph/194.880 kph; **1966** (55/15) Amon/McLaren (Ford) 125.389 mph/210.795 kph; **1967** (54/16) Gurney/Foyt (Ford) 135.488 mph/ 218.038 kph.

8.369-mile/13.465-km circuit: **1968** (54/15) Rodriguez/Bianchi (Ford) 115.286 mph/ 185.536 kph; **1969** (45/14) Ickx/Oliver (Ford) 129.400 mph/208.250 kph; **1970** (51/7) Herrmann/ Attwood (Porsche) 119.298 mph/191.992 kph; **1971** (49/13) Marko/van Lennep (Porsche) 138.133 mph/222.304 kph.

8.475-mile/13.636-km circuit: **1972** (55/18) Pescarolo/G. Hill (Matra) 121.450 mph/195.472 kph; **1973** (55/21) Pescarolo/Larrousse (Matra) 126.670 mph/202.247 kph; **1974** (49/19) Pescarolo/ Larrousse (Matra) 119.265 mph/191.940 kph; **1975** (55/31) Ickx/Bell (Mirage) 118.981 mph/ 191.482 kph; **1976** (55/27) Ickx/van Lennep (Porsche) 123.494 mph/198.746 kph; **1977** (55/21) Ickx/Barth/Haywood (Porsche) 120.950 mph/ 194.651 kph; **1978** (55/17) Jaussaud/Pironi (Renault) 130.604 mph/210.188 kph.

8.467-mile/13.623-km circuit: **1979** (55/22) Ludwig/Whittington/Whittington (Porsche) 108.100 mph/173.913 kph; **1980** (55/25) Jaussaud/ Rondeau (Rondeau) 119.225 mph/192.000 kph; **1981** (55/21) Ickx/Bell (Porsche) 124.930 mph/ 201.056 kph; **1982** (55/18) Ickx/Bell (Porsche) 126.389 mph/204.128 kph; **1983** (55/21) Schuppan/Haywood/Holbert (Porsche) 130.699 mph/ 210.295 kph; **1984** (53/22) Ludwig/Pescarolo (Porsche) 126.880 mph/204.149 kph; **1985** (49/24) Ludwig/Barilla/'Winter' (Porsche) 131.749 mph/ 212.021 kph.

8.406-mile/13.528-km circuit: **1986** (52/19) Stuck/ Bell/Holbert (Porsche) 128.72 mph/207.197 kph.

1924

Montlhéry autodrome, longest-lived of European tracks, was opened. Designed by Raymond Jamin on an estate on the Orléans road some 15 miles/ 24 km south of Paris, it included a symmetrical banked *piste de vitesse* and roads which could be used to make up six circuits. It was extensively used for racing and record-breaking in the years up to, and following, World War II. Although still in use in the 1980s, it was no longer the venue of mainline events.

Spa-Francorchamps circuit inaugurated. A fast, demanding circuit, it was made up of roads linking Francorchamps, Malmédy and Stavelot in the Ardennes, and came to be regarded as a classic Grand Prix circuit. However, controversy about safety aspects led to the Belgian GP being run at other venues after 1970. The Grand Prix returned to a shorter Spa circuit, which cleverly incorpo-

Ettore Bugatti poses proudly with his Type 35 at Lyons, before the 1924 French Grand Prix. These elegant little cars were outclassed in racing by other major manufacturers' teams.

rated stretches of the original, in 1983 (lap length 4.318 miles/6.949 km).

The first Spa 24-hour Race was run in 1924, for touring cars (won by Springuel and Becquet in a Bignan at 48.70 mph/78.38 kph). It was run 11 more times before World War II, then occasionally as a sports car race, before it was positively revived as a touring car event in 1966. It has become established as one of the premier saloon races in Europe.

First Pescara Grand Prix (Coppa Acerbo) won by Enzo Ferrari, driving an Alfa Romeo. Races for Formula or sports cars were run on this long circuit of public roads for many years, and the 1957 event was a world championship race, won by Stirling Moss in a Vanwall.

Alfa Romeo introduced the first of their classic Grand Prix cars, the P2 designed by Vittorio Jano to take the place of the unsuccessful (and unraced) P1. Giuseppe Campari drove a P2 to a debut victory in the 1924 French GP at Lyon.

1925

First Belgian Grand Prix run at Spa, which was to be the venue for the 28 races run to 1970. After that the circuit in the Ardennes was abandoned by Formula 1 until the Belgian GP was once again run at Spa in 1983, albeit on a shorter circuit. The first race was won by Antonio Ascari (Alfa Romeo P2) at 74.56 mph/119.96 kph, while Pedro Rodriguez set a Grand Prix record speed by winning the 1970 race at 149.97 mph/241.30 kph in a BRM P153; Alain Prost's winning speed in a Renault RE40 on the revised circuit in 1983 was 119.14 mph/191.69 kph. Winners of the world championship Belgian GPs: **1950** Fangio (Alfa Romeo); **1951** Farina (Alfa Romeo); **1952** Alberto Ascari (Ferrari); **1953** Alberto Ascari (Ferrari); **1954** Fangio (Maserati); **1955** Fangio (Mercedes-Benz); **1956** Collins (Ferrari); **1958** Brooks (Vanwall); **1960** Brabham (Cooper); **1961** P. Hill (Ferrari); **1962** Clark (Lotus); **1963** Clark (Lotus); **1964** Clark (Lotus); **1965** Clark (Lotus); **1966** Surtees (Ferrari); **1967** Gurney (Eagle); **1968** McLaren (McLaren); **1970** Rodriguez (BRM); **1972** (N) Fittipaldi (Lotus); **1973** (Z) Stewart (Tyrrell); **1974** (N) Fittipaldi (McLaren); **1975** (Z) Lauda (Ferrari); **1976** (Z) Lauda (Ferrari); **1977** (Z) Nilsson (Lotus); **1978** (Z) Andretti (Lotus); **1979** (Z) Scheckter (Ferrari); **1980** (Z) Pironi (Ligier); **1981** (Z) Reutemann

Peter de Paolo (Duesenberg) was the first driver to win the Indianapolis 500 at over 100 mph/160 kph, in 1925.

(Williams); **1982** (Z) Watson (McLaren); **1983** Prost (Renault); **1984** (Z) Alboreto (Ferrari); **1985** Senna (Lotus); **1986** Mansell (Williams).

All races took place at Spa, except as noted: N, Nivelles-Baulers; Z, Zolder.

Tripoli Grand Prix, which was to become a significant race contested by the leading teams in the 1930s, *run for the first time*. The 132-mile/212-km race on the first Mellaha circuit was won by Balestrero, driving an OM.

First Moroccan Grand Prix run, as a touring car race at Casablanca, and won by de Vaugelas in a Delage. Run as a non-championship Formula 1 race on the Ain-Diab circuit in 1957 (won by Jean Behra in a Maserati), and for the only time as a championship race in 1958, when it was won by Stirling Moss in a Vanwall.

The 100-mph/160-kph barrier was broken at Indianapolis, Peter de Paolo winning the '500' at 101.13 mph/162.72 kph in a Duesenberg.

Riding mechanics, whose role had been reduced to that of heroic passengers in the 1920s, were barred from the Grands Prix (although cars still have to have two seats!).

Classic Reims-Gueux circuit on the sweeping roads of the Marne first used, with a lap length of 4.85 miles/7.815 km, revised in the 1950s to 5.18 miles/8.347 km. It was the scene of very fast and often memorable French GPs, such as the races that saw Mike Hawthorn's narrow victory over Fangio in 1953 or Jack Brabham's first GP win in a car bearing his name in 1966. Major sports car races were also run at the circuit. In the second half of the 1960s, the organizing club (the *AC de Champagne*) was in decline, and so was the circuit. By the end of the decade the last race had been run on it, although the gently mouldering facilities remained in the 1980s alongside a road turning off the Reims–Soisson *Route Nationale*.

1926

The British Grand Prix, or the RAC Grand Prix as it then was, run for the first time, on a pseudo-road circuit at Brooklands and won by Sénéchal and Wagner, sharing a Delage, at 71.61 mph/115.22 kph. It was the first race to count towards the newly-instituted world championship in 1950; and it is one of only two races that have counted towards every championship. The winners since 1950: **1950** (S) Farina (Alfa Romeo); **1951** (S) Gonzalez (Ferrari); **1952** (S) Ascari (Ferrari); **1953** (S)

In some of the Le Mans 24-hour races in the 1920s, early laps had to be completed with hoods erected (a 3-litre Bentley, No 7, and two 2-litre OMs lead the field away in 1926).

Ascari (Ferrari); **1954** (S) Gonzalez (Ferrari); **1955** (A) Moss (Mercedes-Benz); **1956** (S) Fangio (Ferrari); **1957** (A) Brooks/Moss (Vanwall); **1958** (S) Collins (Ferrari); **1959** (A) Brabham (Cooper); **1960** (S) Brabham (Cooper); **1961** (A) von Trips (Ferrari); **1962** (A) Clark (Lotus); **1963** (S) Clark (Lotus); **1964** (B) Clark (Lotus); **1965** (S) Clark (Lotus); **1966** (B) Brabham (Brabham); **1967** (S) Clark (Lotus); **1968** (B) Siffert (Lotus); **1969** (S) Stewart (Matra); **1970** (B) Rindt (Lotus); **1971** (S) Stewart (Tyrrell); **1972** (B) Fittipaldi (Lotus); **1973** (S) Revson (McLaren); **1974** (B) Scheckter (Tyrrell); **1975** (S) Fittipaldi (McLaren); **1976** (B) Lauda (Ferrari); **1977** (S) Hunt (McLaren); **1978** (B) Reutemann (Ferrari); **1979** (S) Regazzoni (Williams); **1980** (B) Jones (Williams); **1981** (S) Watson (McLaren); **1982** (B) Lauda (McLaren); **1983** (S) Prost (Renault); **1984** (B) Lauda (McLaren); **1985** (S) Prost (McLaren); **1986** (B) Mansell (Williams).

Circuits: A, Aintree; B, Brands Hatch; S, Silverstone.

First German Grand Prix run, as a sports car race at Avus (Berlin). The following year it was run over the full 17.58-mile/28.28-km Nürburgring, then from 1931 over the *Nordschleife* or North Nürburgring circuit, which was to become familiar as *the* Nürburgring. It was first run there as a world championship race in 1951, was run at Avus in 1959 and at Hockenheim in 1970 before finding a semi-permanent home at that featureless circuit from 1977. In 1985 the race was run at the Nürburgring again, albeit on the little-loved new autodrome-style circuit. Winners of the world championship German GPs: **1951** Alberto Ascari (Ferrari); **1952** Alberto Ascari (Ferrari); **1953** Farina (Ferrari); **1954** Fangio (Mercedes-Benz); **1956** Fangio (Ferrari); **1957** Fangio (Maserati); **1958** Brooks (Vanwall); **1959** Brooks (Ferrari); **1961** Moss (Lotus); **1962** G. Hill (BRM); **1963** Surtees (Ferrari); **1964** Surtees (Ferrari); **1965** Clark (Lotus); **1966** Brabham (Brabham); **1967** Hulme (Brabham); **1968** Stewart (Matra); **1969** Ickx (Brabham); **1970** Rindt (Lotus); **1971** Stewart (Tyrrell); **1972** Ickx (Ferrari); **1973** Stewart (Tyrrell); **1974** Regazzoni (Ferrari); **1975** Reutemann (Brabham); **1976** Hunt (McLaren); **1977** Lauda (Ferrari); **1978** Andretti (Lotus); **1979** Jones (Williams); **1980** Laffite (Ligier); **1981** Piquet (Brabham); **1982** Tambay (Ferrari); **1983** Arnoux (Ferrari); **1984** Prost (McLaren); **1985** Alboreto (Ferrari); **1986** Piquet (Williams).

Smallest Grand Prix field ever appeared for the French race – three Bugattis, of which one completed the full distance, one ran for 85 of the 100 laps, one retired. This was the first race of a new Formula, no other teams had cars ready, the organizers neglected to include a clause allowing for cancellation if a specified number of cars did not appear ...

The Miramas autodrome near Marseilles was completed in the same year and staged that farcical French GP. It also was a predictable failure. It was a dull, flat oval, venue for a few secondary races in the 1920s. An attempt to revive it in the mid-1930s failed.

The first Maserati Grand Prix car completed. A straight-8, it followed the lines of the 1925 GP Diatto, which had been designed by Alfieri and Ernest Maserati.

The first single-seater built for road racing in Europe was the Itala Type 11, which appeared 15 years after a single-seater had won at Indianapolis. The Itala never started in a race.

1927

First running of the Mille Miglia, the 1000-mile/1600-km road race from Brescia south to the outskirts of Rome, then looping back north over the Apennines to finish at Brescia (save in 1940, when it was run over a closed circuit at Brescia). It was to become one of the great sports car races, although it perhaps survived beyond its time into the 1950s; accidents in the 1957 race sealed its fate, but the spirit of the event has been recalled by commemorative runs in the 1980s. The first race was won by Minoia and Morandi in an OM at 47.99 mph/77.21 kph, the last by Taruffi in a Ferrari at 94.84 mph/152.59 kph, while the fastest race was driven by Moss and Jenkinson in a Mercedes in 1955 (97.96 mph/157.62 kph). Only one other non-Italian driver, Caracciola in 1931, won the full *Mille Miglia*.

The Nürburgring circuit in the Eifel mountains opened, some 20 years after the idea of a permanent German circuit in this region had been mooted. It was eventually built under the aegis of Konrad Adenauer, then mayor of Cologne, as a means of alleviating unemployment. The north circuit, best known of the variants, was 14.17 miles/22.799 km long, with 176 bends or corners and numerous changes of gradient. It changed little from 1927 until 1976 when the last Grand Prix was run on it. A bland new circuit utilizing a fraction of the old came into use in 1984, when it was the venue for the European GP.

Last Grand Prix Fiat, a very advanced 1.5-litre twin-6, was completed and raced just once, to win the Milan GP. This marked the end of a distinguished line, which as far as the Grands Prix were concerned stretched back to the first event and in the 1920s had produced some innovative cars. Fiats continued to be seen in other types of motor sport and from 1963, when the company took a controlling interest in Ferrari, it has underwritten the Ferrari GP programme (in the 1980s Ferrari GP cars carried the name 'Fiat' as they would for a sponsor).

Parry Thomas killed during an attempt on the Land Speed Record, when a driving chain broke on his car 'Babs' at Pendine Sands.

1928

The first Australian Grand Prix was run on a 6.46-mile/10.4-km circuit of loose-surfaced roads on Phillip Island off Victoria, as road racing was not permitted on the mainland. Winner was A. C. R. Waite (Austin 750). As the 1980s opened the race was run for Formula 1 cars, and won by Australian Alan Jones in a Williams; then for four years it was a Formula Pacific race. The 1981 and 1983–4 races fell to Roberto Moreno, the 1982 race to Alain Prost (the winning car was a Ralt RT4 in each race). In 1985 the Australian Grand Prix was the final event in the world championship, run on a 2.35-mile/3.78-km street circuit in Adelaide, which attracted universal praise. Winners of the world championship Australian GPs: **1985** Rosberg (Williams); **1986** Prost (McLaren).

The first Grand Prix accident involving a number of spectators occurred at Monza, when a Talbot driven by Materassi crashed into the crowd, killing 23 people.

Massive car, master driver – a Mercedes-Benz SSK driven by Rudolf Caracciola at Semmering in 1928.

1929

The first Monaco Grand Prix – the original 'round-the-houses' race – run and won by Bugatti driver 'Williams' at 49.83 mph/80.17 kph. The best-known circuit in the world remained virtually unchanged until 1972, when modifications to the stretch alongside the harbour extended the lap from 1.9 miles/3.06 km to 2.037 miles/3.28 km. Although this introduced more tight, slow corners, it did not greatly affect speeds; in dry conditions race speeds have been around, or just above, 80 mph/129 kph since the late 1960s (the first driver to exceed 80 mph/129 kph was Graham Hill in 1969, when he scored his fifth victory in the race). A new chicane extended the lap to 2.08 miles/3.35 km in 1986. Winners of the world championship Monaco GPs: **1950** Fangio (Alfa Romeo); **1955** Trintignant (Ferrari); **1956** Moss (Maserati); **1957** Fangio (Maserati); **1958** Trintignant (Cooper); **1959** Brabham (Cooper); **1960** Moss (Lotus); **1961** Moss (Lotus); **1962** McLaren (Cooper); **1963** G. Hill (BRM); **1964** G. Hill (BRM); **1965** G. Hill (BRM); **1966** Stewart (BRM); **1967** Hulme (Brabham); **1968** G. Hill (Lotus); **1969** G. Hill (Lotus); **1970** Rindt (Lotus); **1971** Stewart (Tyrrell); **1972** Beltoise (BRM); **1973** Stewart (Tyrrell); **1974** Peterson (Lotus); **1975** Lauda (Ferrari); **1976** Lauda (Ferrari); **1977** Scheckter (Wolf); **1978** Depailler (Tyrrell); **1979** Scheckter (Ferrari); **1980** Reutemann (Williams); **1981** Villeneuve (Ferrari); **1982** Patrese (Brabham); **1983** Rosberg (Williams); **1984** Prost (McLaren); **1985** Prost (McLaren); **1986** Prost (McLaren).

Maserati built the first twin-engined car to be run in road races. This *Sedici Cilindri* appeared conventional as its two-in-line engines were mounted side by side ahead of the driver.

First Irish Grand Prix, a handicap sports car race which took into account the results of the unlimited Eireann Cup and 1.5 litre Saorstat Cup. Venue was Dublin's Phoenix Park, where races were still run in the 1980s, albeit not for significant categories (it is doubtful if such events would have been sanctioned on a circuit that was primitive by contemporary standards). Winners of the three Irish GPs were: **1929** Ivanowski (Alfa Romeo); **1930** Caracciola (Mercedes-Benz); **1931** Black (MG).

JCC Double Twelve was a worthy attempt to run a 24-hour race at Brooklands, necessarily in two parts to circumvent track usage restrictions – night racing has seldom been possible on any

First classic street race. Bugatti drivers Etancelin, Dauvergne and Lehoux lead the Monaco field away in 1929, while eventual winner 'Williams' starts another Bugatti (12) from the middle of the second row.

British circuits, although recently a national-level 24-hour saloon race has become established at Snetterton. Winners of the three sports handicap Double Twelves were: **1929** Ramponi (Alfa Romeo); **1930** Barnato/Clement (Bentley); **1931** Earl of March/Staniland (MG).

1930

First Czech Grand Prix run on the 18-mile/30-km Masaryk circuit at Brno, von Morgen and Prince zu Leiningen sharing the winning Bugatti. The race was run six more times in the 1930s, and effectively once after World War II in 1947, when Whitehead won in a Ferrari. More recently a variant of this immensely challenging circuit has been used for European Touring Car championship races.

Woolf Barnato became the *first driver to win three successive Le Mans 24-hour Races*. Other drivers to achieve the 24-hour hat trick have been Olivier Gendebien (1960–2), Henry Pescarolo (1972–4) and Jacky Ickx (1975–7). Ickx came within 64 seconds of a second hat trick when he finished second in 1983.

Stutz Black Hawk at Le Mans, where a similar car placed second in 1929 – Stutz and Chrysler were the first American cars to bid for victory in the 24-hour race, albeit the cars usually had French crews.

Sir Henry Birkin, characteristic polka-dot scarf streaming behind him, in the Blower 4½ single-seater Bentley at Brooklands.

Small sports cars were a British speciality in the 1930s – here Norman Black finds something to smile about as he passes the pits at Ards on his way to a 1931 TT victory in a C-type MG Midget.

1932

As the Grand Prix regulation requiring two-seater bodywork was dropped, Alfa Romeo introduced the Type B (P3), *the first true monoposto Grand Prix car*. The Type B set new standards, which were not surpassed until Mercedes-Benz and Auto Union introduced a new generation of GP cars in 1934.

Bugatti introduced a four-wheel drive car, the T53, which was intended for Grands Prix but in fact appeared in practice for only one race. It was withdrawn, and thereafter was relegated to hill climbs. The first four-wheel drive car actually to compete against GP cars was a Miller driven by Peter de Paolo in the 1934 Tripoli GP.

1933

The first Grand Prix starting grid to be determined by lap times in practice formed up at Monaco.

Midget racing became formalized in the USA, leading to American Automobile Association control in the following year, although a national championship did not come until 1948.

A Citroën named La Petite Rosalie *droned round Montlhéry for 133 days* (with a break while the French Grand Prix was run) to cover 180,000 miles/289,600 km at an average speed of 58 mph/ 93.32 kph.

A one-year revival of the Elgin Trophy race, over 203 miles/327 km at Elgin (won by Frame in a

Tazio Nuvolari looking apprehensive as his Alfa Romeo is pushed to the start of the 1931 Mille Miglia.

Ford), and a 150-mile/241-km race on a circuit incorporating the Legion Ascot oval, proved to be a false dawn as far as the reintroduction of road racing in North America was concerned.

The Tripoli Grand Prix result was rigged, according to Piero Taruffi, the holders of the winning tickets in the State lottery run in conjunction with the race apparently sharing their profits with the leading drivers! After that the lottery arrangements were changed (and there have been no other known incidents of rigging).

1934

First Swiss Grand Prix run, on the challenging Bremgarten circuit at Berne, and won by Hans Stuck with an Auto Union. The race was run annually until 1939, and then from 1947 until 1954, when all racing was banned in Switzerland. The title was then applied to a non-championship race run at Dijon in 1975 (won by Clay Regazzoni in a Ferrari), then to a one-off championship event at this French circuit in 1982. Winners of the world championship Swiss GPs: **1950** Farina (Alfa Romeo); **1951** Fangio (Alfa Romeo); **1952** Taruffi (Ferrari); **1953** Ascari (Ferrari); **1954** Fangio (Mercedes-Benz); **1982** Rosberg (Williams).

First South African Grand Prix run, as a handicap

Contrasting with the neat little T35, the four-wheel drive Bugatti of 1932 appeared massive. It had some success in hill climbs.

The Citroën named *La Petite Rosalie* at Montlhéry after its duration record run in 1933.

The elegant Alfa Romeo Type B (P3), with Ferrari's prancing horse badge larger than it has been on recent Ferrari GP cars. His team poses at Montlhéry before the 1934 French GP. Drivers (left to right) are Varzi, race winner Chiron, and Trossi.

event at East London. After World War II it was revived as a *formule libre* race in 1960 and became a world championship race in 1962, being run three times at East London and, since 1967, at Kyalami. Winners of the world championship races: **1962** G. Hill (BRM); **1963** Clark (Lotus); **1965** Clark (Lotus); **1967** Rodriguez (Cooper); **1968** Clark (Lotus); **1969** Stewart (Matra); **1970** Brabham (Brabham); **1971** Andretti (Ferrari); **1972** Hulme (McLaren); **1973** Stewart (Tyrrell); **1974** Reutemann (Brabham); **1975** Scheckter (Tyrrell); **1976** Lauda (Ferrari); **1977** Lauda (Ferrari); **1978** Peterson (Lotus); **1979** Villeneuve (Ferrari); **1980** Arnoux (Renault); **1982** Prost (Renault); **1983** Patrese (Brabham); **1984** Lauda (McLaren); **1985** Mansell (Williams).

First year of the Grand Prix formula that became known by its principal stipulation, a maximum car weight of 750 kg/1653 lb, and which saw all cars following the then-established practice out-moded within the year. Two German teams, encouraged by rabid nationalism, introduced cars which set new technical and technological standards. Mercedes-Benz and Auto Union were to sweep all before them in the following years, their occasional defeats at the hands of the Italian teams coming completely against the trend.

The Mercedes-Benz W25 at least appeared conven-

Mercedes-Benz set new Grand Prix standards in 1934 with their W25, here driven by Caracciola in the French GP.

tional although, as it featured 'novelties' such as all-independent suspension, this was far from so. The Auto Union was designed by Dr Ferdinand Porsche for a team representing the combination of the Audi, DKW, Horch and Wanderer companies, and had its V16 engine mounted behind the cockpit.

The Mercedes won the Eifel race at the Nürburgring (thus becoming the first 'all-independent' Grand Prix car to win a race), while Hans Stuck's victory in the German GP was the first in a race of that stature for a rear-engined car.

ERA was in the forefront of second-level racing in the mid-1930s. This is the all-ERA front row for the 1935 Dieppe Grand Prix des Voiturettes (left to right, Seaman, Mays and race winner Fairfield).

A race meeting at Mines Field, California, has some claim to be the *forerunner of airfield-circuit road racing.*

1935

Tazio Nuvolari scored a remarkable victory for the old order in Grand Prix racing when he drove an Alfa Romeo P3 to defeat the mighty German teams in their 'home' Grand Prix at the Nürburgring.

For Scuderia Ferrari, Luigi Bazzi designed the bimotore *Alfa Romeo,* which had one P3 engine ahead of the cockpit, another behind it. The *bimotore* showed flashes of tremendous speed – it was intended to be a record-breaking car as well as a racing car – but it was never a practical proposition.

Top-flight driver Count Carlo Trossi built an experimental Grand Prix car with a supercharged two-stroke air-cooled radial engine mounted ahead of the front wheels, and driving through them. It was never raced.

Crash helmets became obligatory at Indianapolis.

First Donington Grand Prix run. The circuit in parkland between Nottingham and Derby was the first true road-racing venue on the British mainland, opened for motor-cycle racing in 1931 and made suitable for car racing in 1933. It closed in 1939, but was acquired by local builder and enthusiast Tom Wheatcroft in 1971; he built a new track, with lavish facilities, where racing started again in 1977 and where an extension to a length (2.5 miles/4 km) suitable for Grands Prix was opened in 1985. Winners of the Donington Grands Prix: **1935** Shuttleworth (Alfa Romeo); **1936** Ruesch/Seaman (Alfa Romeo); **1937** Rosemeyer (Auto Union); **1938** Nuvolari (Auto Union).

Outer circuit record at Brooklands broken by John Cobb in the Napier-Railton. His time of 1 min 0.41 sec (143.44 mph/230.79 kph) was never beaten.

Only Thai driver to make a mark in international racing, Prince Birabongse of Siam, started competing. In the second half of the 1930s he scored seven international race victories with ERAs. (Out of a total of 24 ERA victories in second-level single-seater racing his seven was the greatest number achieved by a single driver.) Bira com-

The Austin 750s were most unusual, in that they were raced as a team by a major British manufacturer, very successfully too, in the late 1930s. In the cockpits at this 1937 Brooklands team line up are Kay Petrie, Charles Goodacre and Bert Hadley.

Sir Malcolm Campbell during a trial run with the Rolls-Royce V-12-engined Bluebird at Daytona early in 1935. That year he twice broke the Land Speed Record with this car.

peted in Grands Prix after the war, in cars such as Gordinis and Connaughts. He died in London in 1985.

1936

Hungarian Grand Prix run at Budapest, and won by Tazio Nuvolari (Alfa Romeo). Save for some Formula Junior races in the early 1960s, the only postwar Hungarian events that could be regarded as 'international' were for East European championships. Then in 1985 the Formula 1 Constructors' Association signed a five-year deal for a championship Grand Prix to be run on the new 2.4-mile/3.8-km Hungaroring circuit 9 miles/15 km outside Budapest, with a first race in 1986. This was won by Nelson Piquet (Williams).

Another lap record destined to stand for all time was set by Auto Union driver Bernd Rosemeyer in the Swiss GP. He lapped Berne's Bremgarten circuit in 2 min 34.5 sec (105.40 mph/169.59 kph) and, although this was improved on in practice sessions, it was never broken in a race before the circuit closed in 1954.

The G. Vanderbilt Cup races at Roosevelt Field attracted mainline European teams to the USA for the only time in the 1930s. The 1936 race was won by Nuvolari (Alfa Romeo); the 1937 winner was Rosemeyer (Auto Union).

The first Brazilian races to attract front-rank European entrants were run on circuits at São Paulo and Rio de Janeiro (Gavea). Carlo Mario Pintacuda drove an Alfa Romeo to a rare victory over one of the dominant German teams (Auto Union) on the sinuous Gavea circuit in 1937.

The four-cylinder Offenhauser engine powered the winning car (Shaw's Gilmore Special) *at Indianapolis* for the first time. Based on a marine engine designed by Harry Miller in 1926, this strong beefy power unit was prominent in USAC racing until the second half of the 1970s, its position through almost 40 years being threatened only occasionally, for example by the Maserati victories at Indianapolis in 1939–40 or the Ford triumphs in the 1960s. In the next decade the Cosworth DFX decisively ended the reign of the Offy, which powered the Indianapolis 500 winner for the last time in 1976.

The 1937 Mercedes-Benz W125 was long regarded as the most powerful Grand Prix car ever built, its supercharged 5.66 litre straight-8 producing 600 bhp (646 bhp was recorded with a record-car 'sprint' version). Save for the ineffectual BRM

V16, this output was not approached in road-racing cars until the late 1960s, in CanAm sports-racing cars. The most powerful of these was the turbocharged Porsche 917-30 unit, a 5374 cc flat-12 engine which produced up to 1100 bhp. By the mid-1980s, 1.5 litre turbocharged Grand Prix engines had potential power outputs (in extreme 'qualifying' boost trim) equalling that of the Porsche, and exceeding that of the Mercedes in race trim.

Riding mechanics appeared for the last time at Indianapolis, the 500 thereafter falling into line with international racing practice. There was irony in this late adoption of a single-seater requirement, as the very first 500 had been won by a *monoposto* car ...

Crystal Palace circuit opened in south London, the only one in Britain controlled by a local authority and, until Donington was rebuilt, the only one to be used before and after World War II. Its major events were Formula 2 races. The circuit was closed in 1972.

1938

The only important Formula race to be run in Eire was the 1938 Cork Grand Prix, won by René Dreyfus in a Delahaye.

The first racing car to have disc brakes was a rear-engined Miller built for the Indianapolis 500. These were in effect pressure plates working on one face of a disc; the first racing cars to use the now-familiar disc-and-caliper type were BRMs and the Thinwall Special Ferrari in 1952.

Bathurst circuit first used, for the Australian Grand Prix (won by Peter Whitehead in an ERA at 66.1 mph/106.35 kph). This is a rare circuit on public roads, which survives into the 1980s and has become internationally known as the venue for an outstanding touring car race.

Nuvolari on his way to victory at Donington in a rear-engined Auto Union D-type in 1938, when few drivers challenged the Mercedes team.

Illustrating the Mercedes-Benz late-1930s supremacy, Lang and Caracciola put on a 'demonstration race' to enliven the French GP, which their team totally dominated with W154s.

Kurtis Kraft founded, on the basis of Frank Kurtis' existing race-car shop where short-track midget cars had been built since the mid-1930s. More than 1000 Kurtis midgets were to be sold (some in 'kit' form), and after World War II Kurtis twice started small-scale sports car production. However, the marque became best known for its Indianapolis roadsters – 58 were built, including five winners of the 500 and such famous cars as the Novis, before Kurtis turned away from race-car construction in the early 1960s.

Prescott hill climb first used, as a venue developed by the Bugatti Owners' Club. This is a typical British hill climb, in that it is very short and the atmosphere is very friendly. The original climb was only 880 yards/805 metres, lengthened to 1127 yards/1030 metres in 1960.

The sleek 27-litre Railton which John Cobb drove to break the Land Speed Record before and after the Second World War.

George Eyston twice took the Land Speed Record with the twin-engined 36.5-litre Thunderbolt in this form.

1939

Indianapolis 500 fell to a European car for the first time since 1919, Wilbur Shaw winning in a Maserati 8CTF ('Boyle Special'). This was Shaw's second 500 victory and in the following year he became the first driver to win three times at Indianapolis (he drove the same Maserati again in 1940). He became president and general manager of the Speedway after World War II.

The last races at Brooklands, on the Outer, Mountain and Campbell circuits, were run in August. Respective winners were Baker (Grahame-Paige), Cotton (ERA) and Mays (ERA). Recently non-competitive demonstrations have been run on the airfield and on a part of the banking that has been renovated by members of the Brooklands Society.

The first, and as it transpired only, *Yugoslav Grand Prix* was run on a circuit at Belgrade. It started six hours after Britain and France declared war on Germany, on September 3. Nuvolari won the race in an Auto Union, scoring the last victory for that marque.

1940

The last races in Europe before World War II became a widespread conflict were the *Mille Miglia* (run over a circuit of closed roads, Brescia–

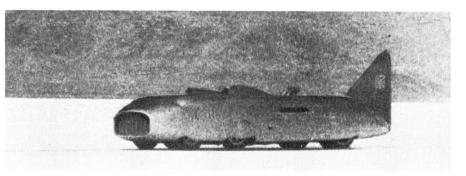

Cremona–Brescia, and won by von Hanstein and Baumer in a BMW) and the *Targa Florio*, which was also removed from its familiar setting and run on the Favorita circuit at Palermo (and won by Villoresi in a Maserati). Last of the 'European' races to be run was the last Tripoli Grand Prix, won by Farina in an Alfa Romeo 158.

First car to be built by Ferrari as an independent constructor appeared. It was built under the name Auto Avio Costruzioni, as Ferrari's agreement with Alfa Romeo then precluded the use of his own name. This Vettura 815 was a 1.5-litre straight-8 sports car, largely built around Fiat components. Two ran in the 1940 *Mille Miglia*; both led their class, both retired.

Alfa Romeo laid down the Type 512, in which designer Wilfredo Ricart followed Auto Union lines in mounting the engine (a supercharged flat-12) behind the cockpit. Two were built, and tested in 1942–3. One was destroyed in a fatal test accident; the other survives as a curiosity. Auto Union also prepared a car for the 1.5-litre formula that had been due to come into effect in 1941: it is intriguing to speculate that if races had been run to these regulations in the early 1940s, rear-engined Grand Prix cars might have become the norm some 15 years before they did. As it was Cooper set the trend in the second half of the 1950s.

1944

Sports Car Club of America (SCCA) formed. In its early years this was an amateur organization for amateur drivers, but early in the 1960s it took on

Racing resumed after the Second World War with a meeting in the Bois de Boulogne in September 1945. A Bugatti leads the way at the start of the Course Robert Benoist, named after a prominent driver who died in a German concentration camp in 1944.

the responsibility for running FIA championship events in the USA, and later such professional series as CanAm.

1945

The first postwar race meeting in Europe took place in the *Bois de Boulogne*, Paris, on 9 September 1945. The first race was won by Amédée Gordini, the 1.5-litre *Coupe de la Libération* was won by Louveau (Maserati), while the main event, the 74-mile/119-km *Coupe de Paris* was won by Jean-Pierre Wimille (Bugatti).

1946

A round-the-houses circuit at Geneva used for the first of three *Grands Prix des Nations*, this 1946 event marking the true revival of front-line racing (Farina won the 86-mile/138-km race in an Alfa Romeo at 64.10 mph/103.16 kph). Earlier Geneva races were insignificant, run on the Mayrin circuit outside the city.

There was a season of racing on the mainland of Europe in 1946, largely contested by Italian and French cars from the 1930s. Outstanding among these were the Alfa Romeo 158s, *voiturettes* before the war and destined to become outstanding Grand Prix cars under regulations which came into effect in 1948. These cars had been hidden through the war and were brought out to be raced four times in 1946. They failed at their first outing but in the *Grand Prix des Nations* at Geneva started a run of 31 victories.

First post-war race in Britain, the Ulster Trophy at Ballyclare, won by Bira (ERA).

First British airfield circuit opened at Gransden Lodge.

1947

NASCAR (National Association for Stock Car Racing) formed by Bill France, soon to become the most important organization in this field. France's immediate objective was to move Daytona racing away from its beach-and-road circuit to a proper track, and out of this ambition came the Darlington banked oval. This was followed by other banked tracks, above all of course at Daytona.

Four of the classic Grands Prix were revived, the Swiss, Belgian, Italian and French.

The first race for 500 cc cars was run at Gransden Lodge, and won by Eric Brandon in a Cooper. This was to provide the basis for the first international Formula 3, which was to be dominated by rear-engined Cooper cars, usually powered by Norton engines.

First Ferrari as such was the 125 sports-racing car, which made its competition debut in a sports car race at Piacenza in May (two were entered, one failed to start, the other retired in the race). In May Cortese drove one to score Ferrari's first victory, in a minor event at Rome's Caracella circuit. First significant victory for the marque was scored by Raymond Sommer at Turin's Valentine circuit in October 1947. The 125 was a stubby little car with a 1.5-litre V12 engine, run with cycle wings or fully-enveloping bodywork in 1947.

First Ferrari to race, a 125 driven by Cortese at Piacenza in May 1947, where he led but retired. Typically, crowd safety was not a major concern, and that was not to change until the mid-1950s.

1948

Silverstone circuit opened, on an airfield that had been used by an RAF Operational Training Unit. Initially it was leased by the RAC, and the first official meeting was the RAC Grand Prix. The circuit used the runways, and the erstwhile perimeter track layout for the Grand Prix circuit was adopted in 1949, remaining largely unchanged today although in 1987 an 'ess'-bend before the last corner was introduced.

Goodwood circuit opened, on another disused airfield (Westhampnett). This never achieved the status of Silverstone, although in the 1950s it was the venue for championship sports car races. Racing ended in 1966, although it has since been used for testing.

Zandvoort circuit opened, with a meeting organized by the British Racing Drivers Club. It too has changed little although, like Silverstone, the increase in its lap speeds has been curbed with an artificial corner. In 1987 a substantially redesigned track was proposed.

First postwar road race in the USA organized on a 6.6-mile/10.6-km circuit which ran through the main street of Watkins Glen, a tourist village near Lake Seneca. An accident in 1952 spelled the end for that 'European-style' circuit. An alternative outside the village was used 1953–5, then a 2.3-mile permanent circuit was built. This was the venue for 20 US Grands Prix (1961–80).

First drag strip opened at Goleta, California.

The first Formula 2 as such was introduced, although the idea of a secondary class was almost as old as racing, going back to the light cars that ran in the city-to-city races of the early 1900s. Throughout, a second category never meant 'second rate'; for example in the second half of the 1930s the leading cars included ERAs and the Alfa Romeo 158s that were to set the pace in the early world championship Grands Prix. The idea grew up that Formula 2 was a final stepping stone on a driver's path to Grand Prix racing, although to some it became an end in itself and in the 1980s drivers tended to move into Grand Prix seats from categories other than F2.

This 1935 Duesenberg was a supercharged version of the Model J with a short wheelbase chassis. Designated SSJ, it had about 320 bhp available from the 6.9-litre 8-cylinder engine and 120 mph/193 kph plus performance.

This 1900 Locomobile steam car was typical of those to be found in the USA at the turn of the century. The 2-cylinder engine was under the driving seat and there was tiller steering. Weather protection was non-existent and the boiler needed refilling with water every 20 miles/32 km.

In the 1930s Packard produced some very fine cars built to a standard equalling that of the contemporary Rolls-Royce. Like that marque they did not make annual model changes, though a vee radiator was introduced in 1932 and a vee windscreen in 1938. The car shown here has both those features and an elegant cabriolet body, seen here in the De Ville position with the driving compartment open.

The Cord was America's first front-wheel-drive production car in 1929, but the 810 model that followed in 1935 was also noted for its advanced streamlined appearance. Shown here is the later 1937

Model 812 with a longer wheelbase and the option of a supercharger for the 4.7-litre V8 engine.

This 1929 Mercedes-Benz 38/ 250 with massive 7-litre engine was about the fastest touring car available at the time and featured a supercharger to give even more performance for overtaking. Appropriately this car was originally owned by Sir Malcolm Campbell of Land Speed Record fame.

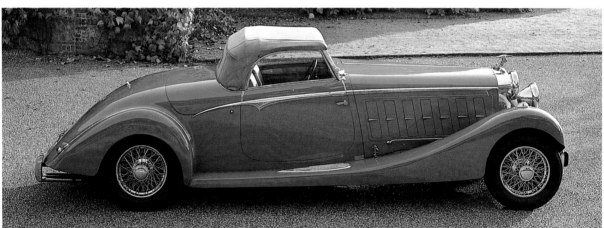

The French-built Type 68 Hispano-Suiza was one of *the* luxury touring cars of the 1930s. Its 9425 cc V12 engine made over 100 mph/161 kph possible with ease. This 1934 example has a Saoutchik-style body with elegant sloping tail and seating for two. Atop the radiator is the Hispano-Suiza stork mascot.

Touring of Milan built the elegant two-seater body on this 1932 Alfa Romeo, which looks every inch the sports car it is. Under the bonnet of this 8C 2300 is a straight-8 alloy engine with twin overhead camshafts and a supercharger.

This 1928 Bentley 4½-litre was pictured on its return to Le Mans in 1979, 50 years after it had been one of the team cars that gave Bentley the first four places in the 24-hour race. On that occasion (in 1929) this car finished fourth, driven by Frank Clement and Jean Chassagne. The 4½-litre 4-cylinder Bentley was also at home on the road as a fast touring car and in those days even the Le Mans works cars were driven across France to the race and driven back afterwards.

The post-war MG TC and TD introduced many Americans to the concept of a European sports car. This is the later TF 1500 with sloping radiator, faired-in headlamps and a 63 bhp 1466 cc engine. The octagonal instruments were an MG feature.

The 1969 Triumph TR6 was styled by Karmann and the interior met American safety requirements. It was powered by a 6-cylinder 2498 cc engine with fuel injection giving 142 bhp, though American market versions used carburettors.

Last of the traditional British sports cars, the Morgan is still made at Malvern using methods that have hardly changed since the 1930s. This 4/4 model with 1599 cc engine and the distinctive Morgan sliding pillar independent front suspension dates from 1972, but current models look hardly any different.

The Rolls-Royce Silver Spirit in the foreground replaced the Silver Shadow II (behind) in 1980 and is the current Rolls-Royce 4-door saloon. The Silver Shadow was the most successful model ever produced by Rolls-Royce with 30,053 saloon and long wheelbase versions built between 1966 and 1980, plus 2280 Bentley-badged models.

Typical of the American performance model of 1987 is this Pontiac Firebird TransAm with 5-litre (305 cu. in) V8 engine pumping out 165 bhp and the option of a new 5.7-litre (350 cu. in) V8 producing 210 bhp.

Until 1975 all Porsches were rear-engined and drove the rear wheels, then with the arrival of the 924 there was a front-engined model for the first time. In 1986 Porsche went further still and produced the 959 supercar with 450 bhp from 2850 cc and drive to all four wheels as this cutaway version shows.

The world's fastest authentically tested road cars are both Italian, and both capable of around 180 mph/289 kph. The Lamborghini Countach, pictured above with the optional rear aerofoil wing, is a mid-engined 2-seater coupé with lift-up front-hinged doors and a 5167 cc V12 engine producing 455 bhp. The Pininfarina-styled Ferrari Testarossa, appropriately shown in this picture with red paintwork, is also a mid-engined 2-seater coupé but with conventional doors. The Ferrari flat-12 4942 cc engine uses Bosch fuel injection, instead of the Lamborghini's six carburettors, to produce 390 bhp.

Above Timo Makinen's Mini Cooper in the 1966 Monte Carlo Rally, which he clearly led at the finish, only to be disqualified on a filmsy pretext.

Roger Clark, leading British rally driver of the 1970s, on the 1976 Scottish Rally in the well-developed Ford Escort RS1800.

Peugeot's 205T16 was the championship car of 1985–6, and when such 'supercars' were ruled out of world championship events Peugeot used them with just as much success in the Paris–Dakar.

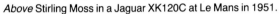

Above Stirling Moss in a Jaguar XK120C at Le Mans in 1951.

Top right An outstanding GT40, the JWA car that won the Le Mans 24-hour Race in 1968–9.

Right Victory in the 24-hour classic fell to Renault in 1978, with this A442B.

Above One of the last open sports-racers, a Lancia Group 6 car and the controlled frenzy of a pit stop at the Nürburgring in 1982.

Above right Winner of the 1970 Le Mans race was this Porsche 917.

Right Jaguar's return to racing was widely welcomed, although the sponsor's colours on their XJR-6s were rather lurid. This car is at Brands Hatch in 1986.

Above Last main-line front-engined Grand Prix car was Ferrari's Dino 246, here driven by Phil Hill in the 1960 French GP.

Right The DFV-engined Matras run by Tyrrell's team and driven by Stewart were very successful in 1968–9. This MS10 with high aerofoil is in the 1968 Italian GP.

Below Lauda and Hunt, Ferrari and McLaren, in a moment of their season-long battle for the 1976 world championship.

Right Outstanding combination of the mid-1980s, Alain Prost in a McLaren MP4 (here an MP4/2C in the 1986 Detroit GP).

Below Great breakthrough for Renault, and turbo engines, came when Jabouille won the 1979 French GP in this RS10.

Bottom Neat lines of the Williams FW07, driven by Alan Jones in the 1979 British Grand Prix.

The Grand Prix Rules

World championship Grands Prix have been run under Formula 1 regulations for all but two years, 1952–3, when negligible support from teams promised poor racing and organizers turned to Formula 2. There were of course rules for the first national event to carry the title Grand Prix, the French race of 1906, but the term 'formula' which is now part of the everyday language of motor sport did not come into wide use until the late 1940s.

The regulations have not always been acceptable to race organizers, or to entrants, and sometimes they have not worked as the sport's administrators intended, for they have often ignored a golden rule of thumb – many designers are infinitely more talented than bureaucrats, especially bureaucrats with oblique motivations, and those designers will be adept in the art of exploiting loopholes. Thus the CSI devised a 750-kg maximum weight formula in the expectation that it would constrain GP speeds at a gently rising level from 1934; it failed, because German constructors applied unprecedented technical resources to racing, building cars which the administrators could not have envisaged when they drew up the rules. The FISA worked hard towards a goal of all-turbo Grands Prix in the mid-1980s, only to find, as it was achieved, that costs and performance potential were soaring out of control; the goal was therefore changed, to ensure that turbos were outlawed ...

Since 1938 the principal restriction has always been the most sensible one, on engine capacities, although attempts to lay down equivalences between normally-aspirated power units and forced induction types have generally failed. Other requirements have been subsidiary; for example concerning race distances or duration, types of fuel, or in parts of the car such as aerodynamic devices, where once again the rule-makers were caught flat-footed by designers. Many changes have been made in the interests of safety during the lives of formulae since 1960.

The principal regulations governing Grands Prix since 1906:

1906 Maximum car weight 1000 kg/2204 lb

1907 Fuel allowance of 231 litres/51 Imp. gallons (equivalent to 9.4 mpg)

1908 Minimum weight 1100 kg/2425 lb; cylinder bores restricted to 155 mm (four-cylinder engines) or 127 mm (six-cylinder engines)

1912 Maximum body width of car 175 cm (69 in)

1913 Weight limits 800–1100 kg/1763–2425 lb, without fuel. Fuel allowance 20 litres/100 km (equivalent to 14.12 mpg)

1914 Maximum engine capacity 4.5 litres; weight 1100 kg/2425 lb

1921 Maximum capacity 3 litres; minimum weight 800 kg/1763 lb

1922–5 Maximum capacity 2 litres; minimum weight 650 kg/1433 lb. Riding mechanic not required after 1924

1926–7 Maximum capacity 1.5 litres; minimum weight 700 kg/1543 lb

1928 Car weight between 550 kg and 750 kg/1212 lb and 1653 lb

1929–30 Minimum weight 900 kg/1980 lb. Fuel allowance 14 kg/100 km (approximating to 14.5 mpg)

1931 Minimum race duration 10 hours

1932 Race duration 5–10 hours. Single-seater bodies permitted

1933 Minimum race distance 500 km/312 miles

1934–7 Maximum weight 750 kg/1653 lb

1938–9 Maximum engine capacities 3 litres (supercharged) or 4.5 litres (normally aspirated). Minimum weight of cars with engines at upper capacity limits 850 kg/1874 lb

1948–51 Maximum engine capacities 1.5 litres (supercharged) or 4.5 litres (normally aspirated)

1952–3 Formula 2 regulations applied – maximum engine capacities 500 cc (supercharged) or 2 litres (normally aspirated)

1954–60 Maximum engine capacities 750 cc (supercharged) or 2.5 litres (normally aspirated). 'Commercial' fuel obligatory from 1958

1961–5 Maximum capacity 1.5 litres (minimum 1.3 litres); minimum weight 450 kg/990 lb

1966–85 Maximum engine capacities 3 litres (normally aspirated) or 1.5 litres (with forced induction – originally intended to admit supercharged engines, but applied to turbocharged units). Initial minimum weight 500 kg/1102 lb, increased to 585 kg/1287 lb by 1981, then reduced to 540 kg/1188 lb in 1983. Many subsidiary regulations introduced: for example to ban engines with more than 12 cylinders from 1971; to ban excessive aerofoils ('wings') and high engine air intake airboxes; to rule out space frames (by banning bag fuel tanks), ground effects (including sliding 'skirts') and the lowering of suspension systems by stipulating flat-bottom cars; to ban more than four wheels; and so on. Among positive requirements with safety in mind, culminating in 'survival cell cockpit' (1982), were on-board fire extinguisher systems, deformable fuel tanks, then single fuel cells. Fuel consumption was effectively introduced in 1984 as the allowance per car for a race was cut from 250 litres to 220 litres/55 imp. gallons to 48 Imp. gallons

1986 Turbocharged engines only (capacity 1.5 litres), with chassis requirements following preceding years, and fuel allowance 195 litres/43 imp. gallons

1987–9 Maximum capacities 3.5 litres (normally aspirated) or 1.5 litres (turbocharged). Multi-stage and liquid-cooled intercoolers banned, along with other turbo refinements; turbo boost restricted by 'pop-off' valves; and a weight penalty (540 kg to 500 kg/1188 lb to 1102 lb) in favour of cars with normally-aspirated engines. These regulations were intended to achieve power equality over two seasons, as a lead-in to Formula 1 being reserved to cars with normally-aspirated engines in 1989

The 1948 regulations allowed for cars with engines up to 2 litres or 500 cc supercharged; it ran until 1953 and, as Formula 1 virtually collapsed when Alfa Romeo withdrew at the end of 1951, the world championship races were run for Formula 2 cars in 1952–3 (Ferrari winning all save one of the championship races). A 1.5-litre Formula 2 was current from 1957 until 1960, when, to all intents and purposes, it became the Grand Prix formula. A 1000 cc Formula 2 ran from 1964 until 1966, and for 1967 it was succeeded by 1.6-litre rules. In 1972 the capacity limit was raised to 2 litres, for production-based engines, and this limit applied when 'pure' racing engines were admitted in 1976. The European Formula 2 championship was run until 1984 (the last F2 race being run at Brands Hatch), when it was succeeded by Formula 3000. While F2 withered in Europe, its flourishing equivalent in Japan had become that country's premier racing class by the mid-1980s.

Maybach Special completed as a hill-climb car, subsequently raced by Stan Jones with considerable success – it was the first Australian car to match European cars such as the V16 BRM.

1949

Ferrari's first Grand Prix victory scored by Alberto Ascari in the Swiss GP, driving a single-stage supercharged 125. Late in the year Peter Whitehead drove a single-stage car to win the Czechoslovak GP, the first British driver to win an event of such status since World War II.

Extraordinarily advanced Cisitalia GP car (Porsche Type 360) *completed*, with a horizontally-opposed 12-cylinder supercharged engine mounted behind the cockpit, four-wheel drive, a space frame chassis and all-independent suspension. This car was never seriously raced (its only

New names in 1949 – Colin Chapman driving a Lotus 2 on a trials event.

competitive appearance was in Argentina, as the Autoar) as the Cisitalia company failed. Had it been developed to raceworthiness, the history of motor racing since 1949 would have been vastly different ...

Silverstone International Trophy race first run (and won by Alberto Ascari in a Ferrari). This was eventually to have the longest history of all non-championship Formula 1 races, through to 1978 as a 'mainline' F1 race. Then it was run for Formula 2 cars until, in 1985, it became the first race for the new Formula 3000 category (won by Mike Thackwell driving a Ralt).

1950

World Championship for Drivers instituted. Overall placings are decided on a points basis, cumulating as a season progresses and awarded to the first six in a race: first, 9 points; second, 6; third, 4; fourth, 3; fifth, 2; sixth, 1. (Until 1960 a victory scored only 8 points; until 1959 a point was awarded for the fastest lap in a race, but only the first five places scored.) Throughout, only the points scored in a specified number of races have counted, although drivers' gross and net totals have recently been the same (exceptions have been the 1979 and 1980 champions). Twenty-four races have been scoring events, including the Indianapolis 500 until 1960, but only the British and Italian Grands Prix have been run in every world championship season.

World Champion Drivers (the number of championship races in a season is given in brackets after the date, and the champions' net/gross points scores after their names): **1950** (7) Giuseppe Farina (I), Alfa Romeo (30); **1951** (8) Juan Manuel Fangio (RA), Alfa Romeo (31/37); **1952** (8) Alberto Ascari (I), Ferrari (36/52½); **1953** (9) Alberto Ascari (I), Ferrari (34½/46½); **1954** (9) Juan Manuel Fangio (RA), Maserati and Mercedes-Benz (42/57); **1955** (7) Juan Manuel Fangio (RA), Mercedes-Benz (40/41); **1956** (8) Juan Manuel Fangio (RA), Ferrari (30/33); **1957** (8) Juan Manuel Fangio (RA), Maserati (40/46); **1958** (11) Mike Hawthorn (GB), Ferrari (42/49); **1959** (9) Jack Brabham (AUS), Cooper (31/34); **1960** (10) Jack Brabham (AUS), Cooper (43); **1961** (8) Phil Hill (USA), Ferrari (34/38); **1962** (9) Graham Hill (GB), BRM (42/52); **1963** (10) Jim Clark (GB), Lotus (54/73); **1964** (10) John Surtees (GB), Ferrari (40); **1965** (10) Jim Clark (GB), Lotus (54); **1966** (9) Jack Brabham (AUS), Brabham (42/45); **1967** (11) Denis Hulme (NZ), Brabham (51); **1968**

(12) Graham Hill (GB), Lotus (48); **1969** (11) Jackie Stewart (GB), Matra (63); **1970** (13) Jochen Rindt (A), Lotus (45); **1971** (11) Jackie Stewart (GB), Tyrrell (62); **1972** (12) Emerson Fittipaldi (BR), Lotus (61); **1973** (15) Jackie Stewart (GB), Tyrrell (71); **1974** (15) Emerson Fittipaldi (BR), McLaren (55); **1975** (14) Niki Lauda (A), Ferrari (64½); **1976** (16) James Hunt (GB), McLaren (69); **1977** (17) Niki Lauda (A), Ferrari (72); **1978** (16) Mario Andretti (USA), Lotus (64); **1979** (15) Jody Scheckter (ZA), Ferrari (51/60); **1980** (14) Alan Jones (AUS), Williams (67/71); **1981** (15) Nelson Piquet (BR), Brabham (50); **1982** (16) Keke Rosberg (SF), Williams (44); **1983** (15) Nelson Piquet (BR), Brabham (59); **1984** (16) Niki Lauda (A), McLaren (72); **1985** (16) Alain Prost (F), McLaren (73/76); **1986** (16) Alain Prost (F), McLaren (72).

Formula 3 was adopted as the third-level international racing category, for cars with unsupercharged 500 cc engines. It was in force until 1960 and, although its effectiveness was diluted by Cooper domination, it provided an excellent schooling category for many drivers. After a five-year period of Formula Junior racing at this level, a 1-litre Formula 3 ran from 1964 until 1970, and this was followed by regulations admitting cars with 1.6-litre engines which had their power outputs restricted by a limit on air supply. The capacity limit was raised to 2 litres from 1974, and in the early 1980s the most prominent power units were Toyota, Alfa Romeo and Volkswagen units, race-prepared by specialists such as Novamotor and Judd. In 1985 'flat-bottom' cars were required,

the most successful chassis being built by Ralt, Reynard, Martini and Dallara.

Brands Hatch car racing circuit opened, with a lap of 1 mile/1.6 km. It followed the lines of a slightly shorter motor-cycle grass track that had been in use since 1928 (which in turn followed the lines of a 1926 cycle racing track). It was extended to 1.24 miles/2 km in 1954, and the 2.69-mile/4.33-km Grand Prix circuit was opened in 1960. The lines of the circuit have changed little since 1960, but the facilities have become ever more sophisticated as it was accepted as the alternate venue for the British Grand Prix.

First BRM started in a race. This was an extremely complex Grand Prix car, with a 1.5-litre supercharged V16 engine, which stretched the resources of the small BRM team to the limit. The car had a very long gestation period, was never developed to raceworthiness as a Grand Prix contender (its only placings in championship races were a fifth and a seventh in the 1951 British race) but lingered in second-line racing until 1955. Power output of its V16 was claimed to be 485 bhp at 12,000 rpm, although this has been questioned. 'Respectability' came to BRM much later, with a first Grand Prix victory in Holland in 1959, and when Graham Hill gained the world championship with the team in 1962. The team was in decline in the mid-1970s and was wound up in

The first Formula 3, for 500 cc cars, was enormously popular in Britain, and like this early-1950s grid at Brands Hatch was dominated by Cooper cars.

1979. BRMs started in 197 Grands Prix and won 17.

AFM was the first new German racing car to appear after World War II, built by Alex von Falkenhausen Motorenbau. In the hands of Hans Stuck it showed considerable promise in Formula 2 racing, but was also exceedingly unreliable.

Sebring circuit first used, showing fast-growing interest in road racing in the USA. This Florida track had considerable shortcomings (the airfield on which it was contrived remained operational), but it became the venue for the sports car championship 12-hour race, first run in 1952, and for the first US Grand Prix to be a world championship event, in 1959.

First Carrera Panamericana run, over 2178 miles/3504 km across Mexico, and won by Hershel McGriff in an Oldsmobile at 77.43 mph/124.58 kph. The next four races attracted top European teams, to race over a 1934-mile/3112-km course on normal roads. Ferrari won in 1951 and 1954, Mercedes-Benz in 1952 and Lancia in 1953. The race was an anachronism in the 1950s and, inevitably, was discontinued.

Alfa Romeo won the first world championship race in which its team competed, although this was on a technicality as its 158s had been raced before that 1950 British GP. Only two other marques have achieved such a notable 'first'; Mercedes-Benz in 1954 (French GP) and Wolf in 1977 (Argentine GP). The Alfa Romeo team's record of six successive victories in that season has been bettered only three times, in years when there were more championship races on the calendar (by Ferrari in 1952–3 and McLaren in 1984).

First Netherlands Grand Prix run, on the challenging circuit among the seaside dunes at Zandvoort that was used for all subsequent Dutch GPs. The race became a world championship round in 1952, was run fairly regularly until 1985, then was dropped from the calendar in 1986. Winners of the world championship races: **1952** Ascari (Ferrari); **1953** Ascari (Ferrari); **1955** Fangio (Mercedes-Benz); **1958** Moss (Vanwall); **1959** Bonnier (BRM); **1960** Brabham (Cooper); **1961** von Trips (Ferrari); **1962** G. Hill (BRM); **1963** Clark (Lotus); **1964** Clark (Lotus); **1965** Clark (Lotus); **1966** Brabham (Brabham); **1967** Clark (Lotus); **1968** Stewart (Matra); **1969** Stewart (Matra); **1970** Rindt (Lotus); **1971** Ickx (Ferrari); **1973** Stewart (Tyrrell); **1974** Lauda (Ferrari); **1975** Hunt (Hesketh); **1976** Hunt (McLaren); **1977** Lauda (Ferrari); **1978** Andretti (Lotus); **1979** Jones (Williams); **1980** Piquet (Brabham); **1981** Prost (Renault); **1982** Pironi (Ferrari); **1983** Arnoux (Ferrari); **1984** Prost (McLaren); **1985** Lauda (McLaren).

Louis and Jean-Louis Rosier in a Lago-Talbot became the only father-and-son team to win the Le Mans 24-hour race. Mario Andretti, cherishing an ambition to emulate the French pair, was third with his son Michael in 1983, although Alliot shared their Porsche 956.

1951

Alfa Romeo withdrew their Type 158/159 from racing, where it had dominated the Grands Prix in 1946–8 and 1950–1, gaining 31 victories from 35 starts. This car had been designed for prewar *voiturette* racing, and turned out to be the last effective Grand Prix car with a supercharged engine.

Longest Grand Prix ever to count for the world championship was the French event, run at Reims over 77 laps of the classic circuit running through the hamlet of Gueux (total distance was 374 miles/601.8 km).

Jaguar won the Le Mans 24-hour Race for the first time, with the XK120C ('C-type') derivative of the XK120. In 1953 a 'C' won again, then its D-type successor won three successive Le Mans races, 1955–7.

National Hot Rod Association formed in Los Angeles by Wally Parks, in parallel with the American Hot Rod Association, to control the fast-expanding but then irresponsible sport of drag racing. It was quickly moved off the highways and onto disused airstrips, and towards its development as one of the most important of all motor sports. At that time 17 seconds was a good time for the 1/4-mile/402 metres acceleration contest that is the heart of the sport; three decades later the record for a Top Fuel car was down to 5.26 sec (set by Darrell Gwynn at Dallas in 1986).

First Portuguese Grand Prix run, as a sports car race at Oporto. It was first run for Formula 1 cars in 1958, over a street circuit at Oporto. After 1960 it lapsed, to be revived in 1984 at the Estoril autodrome. Winners of the F1 races: **1958** (O) Moss (Vanwall); **1959** (L) Moss (Cooper); **1960** (O) Brabham (Cooper); **1984** (E) Prost (McLaren); **1985** (E) Senna (Lotus); **1986** (E) Mansell (Williams).

Circuits: E, Estoril; L, Lisbon; O, Oporto.

Crash helmets became compulsory in FIA-governed events, road racing thus falling into line with Indianapolis.

The first Cunningham, the C2, made its debut at Le Mans. This American team gained third place in the 24-hour race in 1953 and 1954.

1952

Disc brakes fitted on formula and sports cars, the BRMs and Thinwall Special Ferrari, which complied with Formula 1 regulations but were raced only in *formule libre* races, and the C-type Jaguar.

The world championship Grands Prix were run to the 2-litre Formula 2 regulations in 1952–3, and in both seasons Ferrari achieved unbroken runs of seven successive victories. This remained unequalled until 1984, when the dominant McLaren team scored seven successive victories. A score of six has been reached only once (by Alfa Romeo in 1950) and two teams have achieved five successive victories, Cooper in 1960 and Lotus in 1965. Ferrari's number one driver in 1952, Alberto Ascari, won six races in succession (Farina won the seventh for the team in that season) and his run was extended into 1953, when he won the first three Grands Prix. Brabham and Clark both enjoyed runs of five successive victories, in 1960 and 1965 respectively.

'Pierre Levegh' was the last driver to attempt to drive single-handed through the Le Mans 24-hour Race. He was leading with 1½ hours to go when the engine of his Talbot failed. Thereafter such efforts were ruled out.

Ferrari adapted the 4.5 litre Grand Prix design for Indianapolis, where the 500 was by then a happy hunting ground for roadsters with Meyer-Drake Offenhauser engines. Two of the four Ferraris built qualified, but were hardly competitive. Ascari drove the works entry – the first from Europe for a quarter of a century – retiring when a wire-spoked wheel failed. A new Ferrari commissioned for the 1953 race by Luigi Chinetti did not qualify. The factory then lost interest in the race, until the mid-1980s.

The first Cooper to race in Grands Prix was the Bristol-engined 2-litre T20 in 1952–3. Ironically, in view of the contemporary success of rear-engined Formula 3 Coopers and the imminence of the reintroduction of this layout to Grand Prix racing by Cooper, these T20s were front-engined. The first rear-engined Cooper to appear in Grands Prix was the T40 raced by Brabham in 1955.

Confederation of Australian Motor Sport (CAMS) took over control of motor sport from the Australian Automobile Association.

1953

First Argentine Grand Prix run, at the Buenos Aires autodrome where, spasmodically, all subsequent races counting for the world championship were held. Winners: **1953** Ascari (Ferrari); **1954** Fangio (Maserati); **1955** Fangio (Mercedes-Benz); **1956** Musso and Fangio (Ferrari); **1957** Fangio (Maserati); **1958** Moss (Cooper); **1960** McLaren (Cooper); **1972** Stewart (Tyrrell); **1973** Fittipaldi (Lotus); **1974** Hulme (McLaren); **1975** Fittipaldi (McLaren); **1977** Scheckter (Wolf); **1978** Andretti (Lotus); **1979** Laffite (Ligier); **1980** Jones (Williams); **1981** Piquet (Brabham).

Nürburgring 1000-km race first run, and won by Ascari/Farina in a Ferrari. It became one of the constants of the world sports car and endurance championships.

Oulton Park circuit opened in attractive parkland near Chester. As another indication of the spread of British interest in racing, this circuit seemed to have a bright future and for many years front-line teams were attracted to its non-championship Formula 1 events, and the Gold Cup attained considerable status. This withered in the 1970s when, for car racing, the long circuit was abandoned; its revival in the 1980s did not bring an increase to the stature of Oulton Park, or its races.

World Sports Car Championship inaugurated. In effect this has continued through to the 1980s, although it has lacked the continuity – and indeed the popular appeal – of the Grand Prix championships for drivers and constructors, in part because it has been subject to the whims of the sport's administrators and politicians.

The original championship ran until 1961, when it was superseded by parallel 'GT' and 'Prototype' championships. The first reflected a move to kill off sports-racing cars, the second the failure of that move! In 1968 a Manufacturers' Championship – a sports car championship in all but title – was introduced, the title 'World Championship of Makes' being used through the 1970s. Then in 1981 came the World Endurance Championship of Makes and the World Endurance Championship for Drivers; confusingly, these were not parallel, there being more races counting for the drivers' title than for the constructors! This partly came about because there were more American races in the drivers' championship, as the administrators were incapable of closing the very narrow gap between the regulations for 'European-style' sports car racing and the increasingly important IMSA series in the USA. Moreover, the two capacity classes in the constructors' championship scored equally, so the overall champion marque could – and did in the early 1980s – come from the ranks of the small-engine category; there was no instant attraction for the public when consistent race winners failed to gain the championship...

World Sports Car Championship winners: **1953** Ferrari; **1954** Ferrari; **1955** Mercedes-Benz; **1956** Ferrari; **1957** Ferrari; **1958** Ferrari; **1959** Aston Martin; **1960** Ferrari; **1961** Ferrari.

GT Championship winners: **1962** Ferrari; **1963** Ferrari; **1964** Porsche; **1965** Ferrari; **1966** Porsche; **1967** Ferrari.

Prototype Championship winners: **1962** Ferrari; **1963** Ferrari; **1964** Ferrari; **1965** Shelby; **1966** Porsche; **1967** Porsche.

World Championship of Makes winners: **1968** Ford; **1969** Porsche; **1970** Porsche; **1971** Porsche; **1972** Ferrari; **1973** Matra; **1974** Matra; **1975** Alfa Romeo; **1976** Porsche; **1977** Porsche; **1978** Porsche; **1979** Porsche; **1980** Lancia.

World Endurance Championship of Makes winners: **1981** Lancia; **1982** Porsche; **1983** Porsche; **1984** Porsche; **1985** Porsche; **1986** Porsche (Brun Motorsport).

Mike Hawthorn became the first British driver to win a world championship Grand Prix, when he beat Fangio by the narrowest of margins in the French GP at Reims, driving a Ferrari. Previous world championship races (except the Indianapolis 500) had all been won by Italian or Argentine drivers; Maurice Trintignant was to be the *first Frenchman to win a championship GP* (at Monaco in 1955), and the next 'national firsts' were: Australia (Jack Brabham at Monaco in 1959); Sweden (Jo Bonnier in Holland in 1959); New Zealand (Bruce McLaren in the 1959 US Grand Prix); and the USA (Phil Hill in Italy in 1960).

First World championship race accident involving spectators occurred in Argentina, nine being killed when Farina crashed in a Ferrari.

1954

New Zealand Grand Prix first run, as a *formule libre* race at Ardmore (where it was to be run until 1962, when it was moved to Pukekohe). Stan Jones

Alberto Ascari (Lancia D4) on his way to victory in the 1954 Mille Miglia.

won that first race in a Maybach Special; Moss won three of the Ardmore GPs, as did Brabham.

Buenos Aires 1000-km race was the first sports car championship event to be run in South America, won by Farina/Maglioli driving a Ferrari. It was run at the Buenos Aires autodrome, which became the usual venue for the event (in 1957 it was run at Costanera). However, the race had an erratic history and was run for the last time in 1972.

Aintree circuit inaugurated, using the facilities of a horse-race course; consequently it was fairly flat and dull and, initially, a rare 'anti-clockwise' circuit. It was the venue for five British Grands Prix (the first in 1955, the last in 1962), and secondary Formula 1 events were also run on the 3-mile/4.8-km Grand Prix circuit. This fell into disuse, but valiant local efforts kept the shorter club circuit in being into the early 1980s.

Mercedes-Benz returned to Grand Prix racing with the W196. This car had a straight-8 engine with desmodromic (mechanical) valve gear, which had been seen in a Grand Prix car as early as 1914 on a Delage, was first successfully applied in this Mercedes, yet has not featured subsequently. It also had inboard, shaft-driven front brakes (featured again in 1970 on a Lotus) and full-width bodywork. This was soon abandoned in favour of conventional open-wheel bodies. Much of the team's 1954 success was owed to Juan Manuel Fangio, but its superiority in 1955 was more clear cut as Stirling Moss backed up the great Argentine driver.

Lancia entered the Grand Prix lists with a highly original car designed by Vittorio Jano. It had a tubular frame and the engine was used as a load-

Stirling Moss in a Mercedes-Benz W196 at Monaco in 1955, followed by Ascari in a Lancia D50. Both led the race, both retired.

Russia showed signs of interest in international motor sport in the mid-1950s with cars such as this Kharkov 6, which one V. Nikitin drove to break 1.5- and 2-litre class records in 1954.

bearing member, more than a dozen years before this practice became widespread. Its appearance was unusual, too, with outrigged sponsons carrying fuel and oil (the intention was to concentrate these variable loads within the wheelbase, when the general practice had been to carry fuel in the tails of cars). It showed great promise, but as a Lancia this D50 design was never developed to full raceworthiness – the company was in serious financial trouble, and part of the Fiat-underwritten cost of survival was to hand over the GP equipment to Ferrari...

First Vanwall appeared, with a 2-litre engine as it had been intended for the Formula 2 GPs of 1953. Larger engines were developed, and the team survived a difficult period, which continued as a striking low-drag bodywork was introduced in 1956. That year Moss drove a Vanwall to win the International Trophy at Silverstone, and in the following year the team won Grands Prix – the Vanwall driven to victory in the British race by Tony Brooks and Stirling Moss was *the first British car ever to win a world championship race.*

The name Coventry Climax reappeared in racing, in the form of a 1097 cc FWA engine in a Kieft run at Le Mans.

Argentine driver Onofre Marimon was the first driver to be killed in an accident at a world championship meeting, in practice for the German GP. *First driver to be killed during a championship race* was Bill Vukovich, at Indianapolis in 1955 (the 500 was then a championship event). In the next 30 seasons, 19 drivers were fatally injured in accidents at GP meetings.

1955

The worst accident in racing history occurred towards the end of the third hour of the Le Mans 24-hour race, when a Mercedes-Benz 300SLR driven by 'Pierre Levegh' (Bouillon) touched an Austin Healey and was deflected into a public enclosure, a safety bank failing to contain it. Levegh and 83 spectators were killed.

Mike Hawthorn (Jaguar D-type) leading Fangio (Mercedes-Benz 300 SLR) during their duel for the lead in the opening phase of the 1955 Le Mans 24-hour Race.

DB built a Grand Prix car using the power unit alternative to a 2.5-litre normally aspirated engine permitted by the Formula – a 750-cc supercharged engine, using it to drive the front wheels. The car was quite uncompetitive at its only race appearance.

A Connaught driven by Tony Brooks won the non-championship Syracuse GP in Sicily – the *first British car to win a Grand Prix* since 1924. This led to the B-type Connaught being named 'Syracuse'. The Connaught team scored some good GP placings with their 2.5-litre cars, but it was sadly under-financed and ceased operating in 1957.

1956

The United States Auto Club (USAC) formed to take over the control of the four premier categories of racing in the USA, as the American Automobile Association withdrew from its sporting role. At the time the Indianapolis-based USAC seemed forward-looking; little more than a decade later its resistance to overseas influences and technical advances made it appear reactionary and led to conflict with organizations such as CART in the 1970s.

The Soviet Union became a member of the FIA. As some class speed records had been broken by Russian cars in 1954, and racing cars conforming to the 500-cc Formula 3 had been built, there were hopes that Russia might become involved in international motor sport. However, racing tended to be confined to national meetings, save for participation in series such as the East European Peace Cup championship.

The first Lola car was built by Eric Broadley, an 1172-cc Formula sports-racing car, for club events.

Two years later the Mk 1 became the first Lola to be produced in some numbers (35 were built) and win at an international level. Lola subsequently built cars for most single-seater and sports-racing categories, producing their 1000th car in 1975.

Last Bugatti was the highly unconventional T251 Grand Prix car. Designed by Colombo, it had an 8-cylinder engine mounted transversely behind the driver in a space-frame chassis. It appeared only once, at the French GP, where it was not competitive and soon retired.

First Lotus single-seater was the Type 12 Formula 2 car, with a front-mounted Coventry Climax engine. It made its debut in the Easter Monday meeting at Goodwood. Driven by Cliff Allison, it retired, thus accurately foreshadowing the performances of Colin Chapman's clever little front-engined single-seaters.

Tiny Roskilde circuit opened in Denmark, with a lap of only 0.65 km/0.4 miles. Despite this, it was used for formula car races (in 1961–2 even Formula 1 cars). It lasted for a decade, being superseded by the Jyllandsring, which boasted a lap of just over 1 mile/1.6 km.

1957

The Cuban Grand Prix inaugurated at Havana, where it enjoyed a brief life as a sports car championship race. First winner was Fangio, Moss won the next two events (one very short, as it was stopped after a fifth-lap accident), then such frivolous entertainments became alien to the island.

Race of the Two Worlds, run over the banked track at Monza, was billed as a confrontation between the then very different worlds of European and US track racing. It failed to live up to its billing primarily because it received little support from European entrants, the principal opposition to the track roadsters coming from Ecurie Ecosse Jaguar sports cars. In 1958 the European response was stronger, and a Ferrari was placed third. That was not enough encouragement for the organizers to repeat the event, and Indianapolis cars were not seriously raced in Europe again until 1978, when USAC National Championship races were run at Silverstone and Brands Hatch. Winners of the 1957–8 Monza races (each over 499 miles/803 km) were Jimmy Bryan (160.06 mph/257.53 kph) and Jim Rathmann (166.72 mph/268.25 kph).

Classic shot of a master –
Juan Manuel Fangio in full
flight in a Maserati 250F in the
French Grand Prix in 1957.

Moss acknowledges the
chequered flag at the end of
the 1957 British Grand Prix at
Aintree. Although Roy
Salvadori is pushing his
Cooper to the line (for fifth
place!) this rear-engined car is
a truer sign of things to come . . .

The last European race in the spirit of the old city-to-city events, the Mille Miglia, run – a crash which cost the lives of Ferrari driver the Marquis de Portago, his co-driver and 12 spectators led the Italian government to restrict racing. The title was used by a rally, and in the 1980s the 'retrospective' *Mille Miglia* was a popular and successful historic event.

Riverside International Raceway opened, in the mountains some 60 miles/95 km from Los Angeles. It offered alternative circuits, and was the venue for races as diverse as a United States Grand Prix (in 1960) and NASCAR events. The circuit flourished through to the end of the 1960s, then slipped into a decline.

First Crosslé built, an 1172 Formula one-off. The first Crosslé single-seater, the 3F for the same category, came three years later, to be followed by the first formula car (the 4F for F junior) in 1960. Since then John Crosslé's company has been far and away the leading Irish racing car constructor, type numbers reaching 60 in 1985, with F Ford cars being sold in significant numbers.

The first permanent racing drivers' school (as distinct from occasional, short-lived courses) was established by Jim Russell at Snetterton, where it still is.

The first British car to win a world championship race was a Vanwall, driven by Tony Brooks and Stirling Moss in the British Grand Prix at Aintree.

European Hill-Climb Championship revived, in effect as a successor to the Mountain Championship of the 1930s. It was made up of between six and twelve rounds, sometimes including an international motor sport event in Andorra (the *Col de la Botella* climb) as well as the only one in

Switzerland since 1955 (the St Ursanne–Les Rangiers climb). The series was normally open to 2-litre sports cars, saloons and GT cars, but interest waned in the second half of the 1970s.

1958

FORMULA 1 CONSTRUCTORS' CHAMPIONSHIP INSTITUTED (later generally known as the Constructors' Cup). Save that initially only the highest-placed car of a marque in the first six finishers scored, the points system followed that of the Drivers Championship – 9, 6, 4, 3, 2, 1 points being awarded for placings from first down to sixth. Recently all points scored by a team have counted.

Winners of the Constructors' Championships: **1958** Vanwall (GB); **1959** Cooper (GB); **1960** Cooper (GB); **1961** Ferrari (I); **1962** BRM (GB); **1963** Lotus (GB); **1964** Ferrari (I); **1965** Lotus (GB); **1966** Brabham (GB); **1967** Brabham (GB); **1968** Lotus (GB); **1969** Matra (F); **1970** Lotus (GB); **1971** Tyrrell (GB); **1972** Tyrrell (GB); **1973** Lotus (GB); **1974** McLaren (GB); **1975** Ferrari (I); **1976** Ferrari (I); **1977** Ferrari (I); **1978** Lotus (GB); **1979** Ferrari (I); **1980** Williams (GB); **1981** Williams (GB); **1982** Ferrari (I); **1983** Ferrari (I); **1984** McLaren (GB); **1985** McLaren (GB); **1986** Williams (GB).

Constructors' Championship race victories. Although Ferrari heads a listing over the years of both world championships, with 91 wins 1951–86, Lotus claimed more races over the Constructors' Championship years, 1958–86. The top-scoring teams during that period were: Lotus, 77; Ferrari, 66; McLaren, 52; Brabham, 35; Williams, 31; Tyrrell, 23; BRM, 17; Cooper, 16; Renault, 15.

The first victory for a rear-engined car in a world championship race was scored by Stirling Moss, driving Rob Walker's Cooper Climax in the Argentine Grand Prix. The first championship race in Europe to fall to a rear-engined car was the Monaco GP, won by Maurice Trintignant in Walker's Cooper.

First Lotus Grand Prix car was the slim front-engined 16, complicated and unreliable, and consequently unsuccessful.

Elfin Sports Cars founded, soon to become Australia's leading competition car constructor, completing 300 racing cars in the next 15 years. In the mid-1980s Elfin was building cars for the Australian Formula 2 and Formula Ford.

Formula Junior introduced in Italy, as a national class. In the following year it became an international formula, effectively taking the place of Formula 3 for a period and also attracting entrants from the small-capacity sports car classes. It admitted single-seaters with production-based engines up to 1000 cc or 1100 cc, according to the weight of the car. Within a year of its upgrading to an international category, the front-engined cars on 'traditional' lines had been swept away by rear-engined British cars, above all by Cooper and Lotus, while the dominant power units were basically BMC and Ford engines. Formula Junior proved to be an excellent *ab initio* class, drivers of the calibre of Clark, Stewart and Surtees cutting their single-seater teeth on it.

First Zeltweg circuit came into use, and was to be the venue for the early Austrian GPs, from 1963. It was extemporized on an operational airfield and, for a long-term future, motor racing enthusiasts in the area had to look to the promise of a new purpose-built circuit. This took shape nearby as the *Österreichring, opened in 1969,* which has become established as one of the outstanding championship circuits of Europe, fast and demanding for drivers, set in a bowl in the hills to give spectators first-class viewing (lap length 3.692 miles/5.942 km).

British Touring Car Championship run for the first time, inspired by the success of saloon car events at race meetings through the decade. In time it became the RAC Touring Car Championship, still crowd-pleasing but not without problems as haggles over the *minutiae* of regulations became as intense as the races.

1959

Daytona International Speedway opened, 4 miles/6.4 km from the historic Daytona Beach site. Initially the emphasis was on stock car racing on the banked tri-oval; then, with a road circuit combining infield roads with the bankings, it became a

Jack Brabham in a characteristically crouched driving position in a Cooper at Monaco in 1961.

venue for international sports-car championship events, including the only 24-hour race in the USA.

Bruce McLaren (q.v.) became *the youngest driver to win a world championship race* when he took the flag at the end of the United States Grand Prix at Sebring. He was 22 years of age.

1960

The great period of transition in single-seater racing was almost completed but, aside from the American tracks, there was one last victory for a front-engined car on classic lines when Phil Hill won the Italian Grand Prix in a Ferrari Dino 246. To the partisan Monza crowd it was of little account that this Ferrari victory was achieved against negligible opposition, as British teams chose to boycott the race.

The last front-engined car on conventional lines had made its appearance in the Grands Prix of that year, the Scarab built by Lance Reventlow's *equipe*, which had cut its teeth on sports-racing cars in the USA. Lessons could have been learned from the failure of the front-engined Aston Martin DBR4/250 in 1959, and the Scarab was so outclassed that the team was withdrawn in mid-season.

1961

First Canadian Grand Prix, run as a sports car race at Mosport Park. Became a Formula race, and a world championship event in 1967, and since 1978 has been run at Montreal's *Île Notre Dame* circuit, now named after Gilles Villeneuve, Canada's greatest driver. Winners of the world championship races: **1967** (M) Brabham (Brabham); **1968** (J) Hulme (McLaren); **1969** (M) Ickx (Brabham); **1970** (J) Ickx (Ferrari); **1971** (M) Stewart (Tyrrell); **1972** (M) Stewart (Tyrrell); **1973** (M) Revson (McLaren); **1974** (M) Fittipaldi (McLaren); **1975** (M) Hunt (McLaren); **1976** (M) Scheckter (Wolf); **1978** (ND) Villeneuve (Ferrari); **1979** (ND) Jones (Williams); **1980** (ND) Jones (Williams); **1981** (ND) Laffite (Ligier); **1982** (ND) Piquet (Brabham); **1983** (ND) Arnoux (Ferrari); **1984** (ND) Piquet (Brabham); **1985** (ND) Alboreto (Ferrari); **1986** (ND) Mansell (Williams). Circuits: J, St Jovite; M, Mosport Park; ND, *Île Notre Dame*.

Intercontinental Formula devised, for single-seater with unsupercharged engines of 2–3 litres. This was an attempt by the British establishment to extend the life of the 2.5-litre Grand Prix formula, in a reaction against the new 1.5-litre GP reg-ulations. The intent was misguided, the Intercontinental Formula short-lived.

Kyalami circuit opened on a plateau 15 miles/24 km outside Johannesburg, some 5000 ft/1525 metres above sea level and the highest circuit used for top-line racing since the Mexico City Autodrome fell from grace. It has a lap distance of 2.54 miles/4.08 km, with one long straight. Kyalami has been the venue of the South African Grand Prix since 1967, and was favoured by teams for winter testing. The principal Kyalami sports car race, the main event in the Springbok series, later became a world endurance championship round but attracted derision with its pitiful entry in 1984.

Mosport Park circuit opened, some 60 miles/100 km east of Toronto. In the 1960s this 2.46-mile/3.96-km circuit was considered more than adequate, but in the second half of the 1970s it fell out of favour. The Canadian Grand Prix was run at Mosport eight times between 1967 and 1976, and throughout its history it has been used for sports-car races.

The Dutch Grand Prix was the only world championship race in which no drivers retired and none made pit stops (15 cars started, eight of the 15 finishers were on the same lap as von Trips' winning Ferrari).

The Cooper team ran a T54 in the Indianapolis 500, following tests with an unmodified T53 Grand Prix car the previous year. The T54 had a Coventry Climax FPF engine of 2.7 litres producing 270 bhp, which on paper was far from adequate, yet Jack Brabham drove it to ninth place in the 500. That was too easily dismissed by some observers, but the 'funny little car' signalled the end of the long reign of 'roadsters' in US track racing.

The Ferguson P99 was the first four-wheel drive car to win a Formula 1 race and, incidentally, the last front-engined car to be built to Formula 1 regulations (it also served as a test vehicle for Ferguson Research). The race victory came in the Oulton Park Gold Cup, when it was driven by Stirling Moss. Its only Grand Prix appearance was in the 1961 British race, when it was disqualified. The P99 was later run in Tasman races, and Peter Westbury used it to win the 1964 British Hill Climb Championship.

The first Brabham car made its debut, as an MRD – initials which combine unfortunately in French and were therefore discarded in favour of Brabham's name coupled with that of his partner

Ron Tauranac in the model designation 'BT'. The name and designation sequence have been carried through the modern cars, although Brabham and Tauranac have long since ceased to have any connection with the company. The MRD was a Formula Junior car, and the *first Grand Prix Brabham (BT3) appeared in 1962*.

First Chaparral appeared, a conventional sports-racing car, unlike the innovative Chaparrals that were to follow it. The name derives from that of a ground-runner bird common in the south-west States of the USA.

Wolfgang von Trips, first German driver to win a world championship race (the 1961 Dutch GP), *crashed* after colliding with Clark's Lotus in the Italian GP at Monza. Von Trips and 13 spectators were killed as his Ferrari left the track.

Grand Prix Drivers' Association formed. After occasional and largely inconsequential conflict with the constructors and some organizers it was merged with the Formula 1 Constructors' Association in 1976, then re-formed independently in 1979. In 1982 most of the Formula 1 drivers at Kyalami for the South African GP 'withdrew their labour' on the first day of practice, in protest against a licence system.

1962

The first Mexican Grand Prix was run at Mexico City, at 7300 feet/2225 metres above sea level the highest circuit ever used for championship racing. In the following year it became a championship race; undisciplined crowds were a major factor leading to the event being dropped eight years later. The race was revived on the Ricardo Rodri-guez circuit in 1986. Winners of the world championship GPs: **1963** Clark (Lotus); **1964** Gurney (Brabham); **1965** Ginther (Honda); **1966** Surtees (Cooper); **1967** Clark (Lotus); **1968** G. Hill (Lotus); **1969** Hulme (McLaren); **1970** Ickx (Ferrari); **1986** Berger (Benetton).

The Tasman series of races in Australia and New Zealand originated, with regulations that were virtually carried over from the 2.5-litre GP formula. It thus extended the life of erstwhile GP cars, and made for a cohesive summer season in the southern hemisphere. It was later run for F5000 cars, but then the two countries went their own ways (in motor sporting matters).

Formula Vee born in Florida, the first single-seater class built around standard components from one range of cars to gain international acceptance. It performed its *ab initio* role admirably for several years, until generally overshadowed by classes such as Formula Ford, which in part was more attractive as its regulations made for cars more like 'proper' racers in their characteristics.

The 150-mph/241-kph barrier broken at Indianapolis, when Parnelli Jones qualified at 150.370 mph/241.945 kph in an Offenhauser-engined Watson. Rodger Ward won the race at 140.293 mph/225.731 kph, also a record. This race also saw the entry of a gas turbine-powered car by John Zink and, more significantly, the *first car with a stock-block engine* to qualify for the '500' since 1947 – and the Buick engine in that car, built by Mickey Thompson, was mounted behind the cockpit. Dan Gurney qualified it for the third row, and failed to finish the race, but he was to be

In the Lotus 25, Colin Chapman brought monocoque design to modern racing, and sooner or later every other designer had to follow his lead. Here Jim Clark shows off the clean lines and minimal frontal area of a 25 in the 1963 International Trophy at Silverstone.

Porsche had little success with their first Grand Prix ventures, a solitary championship victory being scored by Dan Gurney in the 1962 French race.

instrumental in clinching the 'rear-engined revolution' on US tracks.

1963

First Austrian Grand Prix run, as a non-championship race at Zeltweg airfield circuit, which had been in use for sports car, F2 and F1 races since 1958. After its second running it became a sports race until 1970, when it was run at the splendid Österreichring circuit which has been used ever since. Winners of world championship Austrian GPs: **1964** Bandini (Ferrari); **1970** Ickx (Ferrari); **1971** Siffert (BRM); **1972** Fittipaldi (Lotus); **1973** Peterson (Lotus); **1974** Reutemann (Brabham); **1975** Brambilla (March); **1976** Watson (Penske); **1977** Jones (Shadow); **1978** Peterson (Lotus); **1979** Jones (Williams); **1980** Jabouille (Renault); **1981** Laffite (Ligier); **1982** de Angelis (Lotus); **1983** Prost (Renault); **1984** Lauda (McLaren); **1985** Prost (McLaren); **1986** Prost (McLaren).

Dragsters run by leading drivers such as Don Garlits appeared with 'wings', the first cars actually to compete with such aerodynamic aids – surprisingly, in view of the demonstrated value of stub wings

The old and new orders at Indianapolis – Eddie Sachs in a traditional Offenhauser-engined roadster in 1963 and Jim Clark driving towards victory in a Ford-engined Lotus in 1965.

on devices like the Opel rocket car three decades earlier. The Swiss designer-engineer Michael May had fitted a very large wing to a Porsche 550 in 1956; this car was run in practice for two races, but was not permitted to race with a device that seemed potentially dangerous (it appeared only a year after the Mercedes-Benz 300SLR was run with its air brake at the rear). The first race use of high-mounted wing aerofoils, to provide downforce as an aid to road-holding, was on the Chaparral 2F sports-racing car in 1967. In 1968 high wings came into general use on road-racing single seaters, only to be precipitately restricted by regulations after dramatic accidents in 1969.

The first gas turbine-engined car to run in a classic road race was the Rover-BRM driven by Graham Hill and Richie Ginther in the Le Mans 24-hour Race. As a formula equating its power unit with a piston engine could not be agreed, it ran a 'time trial', covering a distance which would have classified it eighth overall. In 1965 it was run at Le Mans again, with a sleek coupé body, Hill and Jackie Stewart placing it tenth overall.

Suzuka circuit opened in Japan with the first international race meeting in that country. This was dominated by invited drivers from overseas, Peter Warr winning in a Lotus 23. This 3.73-mile/6-km circuit had been constructed primarily as a Honda test facility, and Fuji was to take its place as Japan's premier circuit.

The first victory for a car powered by an American engine in an FIA championship, in this case the GT championship, came in the Bridgehampton Double 500, which Gurney won in a Ford-powered Shelby AC Cobra. In 1965 the Cobras won the GT championship in the names of Ford and Shelby (the British origins of the chassis being conveniently forgotten).

First gas turbine car to run in a classic road race, the Rover-BRM driven by Hill and Ginther at Le Mans in 1963.

1964

Ford unveiled their challenge for international sports car honours, the GT40, a sleek GT coupé following 'European' lines, and indeed built in England. In some respects the venture was overelaborate, but a MkII derivative did win at Le Mans in 1966, thus achieving the primary objective of the Ford programme, while a MkIV won in 1967. Remarkably, a GT40 run by the Gulf-JWA team then won the 24-hour race twice.

St Jovite (Mont Tremblant) circuit opened in French Canada. Picturesque, but less than adequate in some respects, this 2.65-mile/4.265-km circuit was used for the Canadian Grand Prix in 1968 and 1970.

First Honda Grand Prix car appeared and in the following year won its first race (and the last of the 1.5 litre GP formula), the Mexican GP. This was also the *first GP car with a transversely mounted 12-cylinder engine.*

First McLaren racing car completed, a space-frame sports-racing car. *The first GP McLaren*, the M2B, which had a novel stressed-skin hull formed of an aluminium-balsa wood-aluminium sandwich material, came in 1966.

Watson provided the chassis for the Indianapolis winner for the fourth successive year (and for the last roadster to win the 500). The only other constructor to score four successive victories was March, 1983–6.

First British drag race meeting held at Blackbushe Airport, as one of a series of five events organized by Sydney Allard. It saw American Don Garlits record 8.28 sec over the ¼ mile/402 metres. (In a 1963 demonstration, Dean Moon and Mickey Thompson had recorded 8.84 quarters, then the fastest standing-start ¼ miles run in Europe.)

1965

Zolder circuit first used for an international meeting. With a lap distance of 2.6 miles/4.18 km it conformed to modern ideas of an artificial road circuit, almost flat but with an acceptable mix of corners and bends among the pine trees. It was first used for the Belgian GP in 1973, then for an unbroken sequence of Grands Prix, 1975–82. Practice for that 1982 race was marred by Gilles Villeneuve's fatal accident.

First Matra racing cars appeared. The aerospace company entered racing almost accidentally, for, as a principal creditor, it acquired the assets of the small specialist constructor René Bonnet when

Goldenrod, the fastest piston-engined car, in which Robert Summers achieved 418.50 mph/637.36 kph in 1965. It had four Chrysler engines with a total capacity of 28 litres.

that company failed. The first Matra (MS1) was a Formula 3 car, which won one of the main F3 races of the year at Reims. This was immensely encouraging to an *équipe* which naturally adopted a leading role in the resurgence of French racing. Formula 2 cars followed, leading to a close association with Ken Tyrrell and Jackie Stewart, and to substantial backing for a French Grand Prix effort. In partnership with Tyrrell and Stewart this was successful, albeit with Ford-DFV engines (nine races fell to the team in 1968–9). From 1970 Matra pressed on with an all-French effort, less successfully ...

Jim Clark won the Indianapolis 500 in a Lotus 38 with a 500-plus bhp Ford V8, the first win in the 500 for a British constructor and a British driver and, incidentally, the first at over 150 mph (150.686 mph/242.454 kph). This was the high point of a Ford-backed assault on the race, which had come close to success at the first attempt, in which Clark drove a Lotus 29 into second place in 1963.

Exhuberant and crowd-pleasing saloon racing – Jim Clark in a Lotus-Cortina at Oulton Park in 1966.

1966

Fuji International Speedway was the venue for the first major international single-seater race to be run in Japan. The event was for USAC cars, and was won by Jackie Stewart in a Lola. Alternative circuits were available within the Speedway, which became the country's principal racing venue. The two world championship Japanese Grands Prix were run at Fuji in 1976–7.

The new Hockenheim circuit was opened. Built with compensation funds received when an *autobahn* was cut across the old circuit, which had been used for minor races before and after World War II, it comprised a twisting stadium section with two long fast legs linked by a fast and demanding curve. Chicanes were to be constructed on the fastest stretch. Hockenheim gained notoriety as the circuit where Jim Clark had his fatal accident in a 1968 Formula 2 race. It was first used for the German Grand Prix in 1970, then from 1977 until 1984 while the new Nürburgring was built.

Canadian-American Challenge Cup (CanAm) series first run, for sport-racing cars. John Surtees won the first short series in a Lola, then came a period of McLaren domination with the classic M8s (McLarens won 31 races), followed in 1972 by Porsche invincibility with turbocharged 5- and 5.4-litre 917 *Spyders*. That in turn led to the adoption of F5000 until 1976. In the next season there was a reversion to sports-racing cars, or pseudo sports-racing cars as many were single seaters with full-width bodywork. In that form CanAm lost much of the significance it once had.

Claude Ballot-Léna co-drove a Marcos into 15th place at Le Mans; in 1985 he became the *first driver to contest 20 consecutive 24-hour races at the Sarthe circuit.* He usually drove Porsches, placing as high as third (1977), or Ferraris, placing in the top six with the by-then rare Italian cars in 1972, 1973 and 1981.

First lady to compete in an NHRA A-class dragster was Shirley Muldowney, who broke the local record on her debut at Englishtown. She became a leading Top Fuel competitor, winning three championships, and survived a very serious accident in 1984 to return to the sport in 1986.

1967

Jarama circuit opened, near Madrid, with a 2.1-mile/3.4-km sinuous lap that included only one straight. It was used for nine Spanish GPs between 1968 and 1981.

The BOAC 500 at Brands Hatch became the British round in the sports-car championship. The first race was won by Phil Hill and Mike Spence in a Chaparral 2F. The event became the BOAC 1000 in 1970, and then the British Airways 1000 in 1974. It was then abandoned, and the next endurance championship race (for the drivers' championship that had by then come into existence) to be run at Brands Hatch was the Flying Tigers 1000 in 1981 (won by Guy Edwards and Emilio de Villota in a Lola). This race became the Shell Oils 1000, then the Grand Prix International 1000 km, and in 1984 the British Aerospace 1000 km, before Shell resumed their sponsorship. Meanwhile, the British round in the principal championship, for Makes, was the Silverstone Six Hours (later a 1000-km event).

the Cosworth plant in Northampton, the DFX, had started to make an impression on USAC/CART racing in North America in 1976, when Al Unser won three races in a Cosworth-powered Parnelli. Two years later the DFX was totally dominant in this form of racing, and was still firmly on top in its tenth anniversary season.

Changes in the Grand Prix regulations led to the development of the normally-aspirated 3.5 litre Ford-Cosworth DFZ for 1987.

The only Formula single-seater to have a chassis made largely of wood was the F2 Protos, which had a stressed-skin hull of laminated plywood designed by Frank Costin. Its best race placing was a second at Hockenheim.

First Formula Ford race took place at Brands Hatch. This soon proved to be an ideal low-budget category in which aspiring drivers could develop

John Surtees at the wheel of a Honda in the 1967 Monaco Grand Prix.

The most significant engine in recent front-rank racing appeared, the Ford-Cosworth DFV 3-litre Grand Prix V8. Designed by Keith Duckworth to fulfil the second part of a commission from Ford (the first had been for a Formula 2 engine), the DFV (Double Four Valve) was exclusive to Team Lotus in 1967, when it powered the winning car in four Grands Prix.

It then became generally available, and was in the forefront through to 1983, powering 155 Grand Prix-winning cars of 12 different teams, as well as the winners of many non-championship and Aurora races, and endurance events. From 1985 it was the mainstay power unit of Formula 3000 (the 400th DFV was delivered to an F3000 team in 1986). A variant, the DFY, came as the turbo era was firmly established, and that 155th victory was scored by Michele Alboreto in a Tyrrell in the 1983 Detroit GP.

Meanwhile, a turbocharged derivative built at

driving skills and gain racing experience, and by the 1980s was the most widely-subscribed racing formula of all time, by which time it had also given rise to another successful category, Formula Ford 2000. Originally F Ford was built around the Ford Cortina 1.5 litre engine; later the same company's 1.6 litre Kent engine was specified. Tight chassis regulations were aimed at simplicity, again to help keep costs low and exemplified in the first batch of Lotus 51 cars built in response to John Webb's order for 50 cars to get F Ford off the ground. Inevitably, cars became more sophisticated.

A Lotus 56 came within 8 miles/12.9 km of victory in the Indianapolis – the nearest a gas turbine-powered four-wheel-drive car has ever come to winning a race of such importance. Driven by Parnelli Jones, the dayglow-red car had dominated the race, leading 171 laps and was well ahead of the field with three laps to go when a gearbox bearing with an estimated value of $6 failed ... That race was also the *first '500' to be run over two days*, being stopped by heavy rain after only 17 laps and restarted on May 31. It had also attracted *the largest-ever entry*, of 90 cars.

National Off-Road Racing Association (NORRA) formed, primarily to run the first organized Mexican 1000 Rally, in effect the Baja desert race down the length of the lower California peninsula.

1968

John Surtees joined the ranks of the driver-constructors, building his first car at the end of the year, the TS5 for Formula 5000 in 1969. His first GP car, the TS7, came in 1970. That year Surtees drove one to win the Oulton Park Gold Cup, but Grand Prix success proved elusive although the neat Surtees cars sometimes came close to victory (Mike Hailwood's second in the 1973 Italian GP in a TS9 was the best placing). Surtees abandoned racing car construction, and his team, in 1979.

Sponsorship came to Grand Prix racing, in the form of Lotus 49s painted in the colours of Players' Gold Leaf brand of cigarettes, and the entrant became Gold Leaf Team Lotus. Although the cost of racing was obviously increasing – albeit not then spiralling as it would a decade later – the governing bodies had tried to prevent this. Earlier efforts such as Jack Brabham's 'Redex Special' Cooper in the mid-1950s had been ruled out, but by the late 1960s attempts to restrain commercial decals within specified areas on cars were obviously pointless, and Formula racing inevitably followed the US track racing example. In the 1980s anti-smoking lobbies began to influence TV producers, and hence race organizers mindful of a major source of income, and while cars continued to be painted in the colours of cigarette packets actual brand names were removed in some countries. Oddly, the 1968 Lotus initiative was not imitated until 1970, when Yardley sponsored the BRM team.

A championship Grand Prix fell to an independent entrant for the last time, when Jo Siffert drove R. R. C. Walker's Lotus 49 to victory in the British race, at Brands Hatch.

The sports car championship was gained for Ford, ironically after the company had withdrawn its official teams. With Gulf sponsorship, the JWA team campaigned GT40s, 'obsolescent' according to Ford, but uprated under the direction of John

Wyer to remain effective contenders. His JWA team clinched the championship in the last race of the series, at Le Mans.

Electric-powered vehicle speed record raised to 138.862 mph/223.503 kph by Jerry Kugel, driving the Ford-Autolite 'Lead Wedge' at Bonneville.

Santa Pod, Britain's only permanent drag strip, established at the disused Poddington airfield.

1969

Four-wheel drive enjoyed fleeting popularity among Grand Prix teams – the British race was the first GP in which more than one such car started, no fewer than four coming to the grid. These were built by Matra, Lotus and McLaren. Significantly, BRM did not follow this 1969 trend, for they had experience which proved that weight and complexity outweighed the traction advantages (and these were in fact diminishing because of tyre improvements). Four-wheel drive reappeared only briefly, in 1971 as Lotus ran the 56B gas turbine car in a few Grands Prix.

A Ford GT40 (1075) run by the JWA team became the first car to win the Le Mans 24-hour Race in successive years. This was next achieved by the Joest team with a Porsche 956 (117) in 1985–6.

1970

First March Grand Prix cars built, by a company which had produced its very first racing car in the second half of the previous year. The 701 was a straightforward car, used by independent entrants as well as the works team, and in one of these Jackie Stewart scored the marque's first Grand Prix victory, in the 1970 Spanish GP. Only two more world championship races fell to March, in the 137 contested through to 1983. By that time the major March successes were being gained on American tracks, although the supply of customer cars for F2 and later F3000 continued. In 1987 March returned to the Grand Prix.

First Tyrrell Grand Prix car built, in great secrecy. It appeared in time for the autumn races, showing potential in the hands of Stewart but failing to finish in four starts. Thereafter the Tyrrell team was enormously successful for three seasons, and reasonably successful for another ten, winning 23 championship events between 1971 and 1983. Ken Tyrrell was the last constructor to use the Ford-Cosworth DFV engine, turning to turbocharged units (Renault) only in 1985, and he was the first to take up the normally-aspirated option in 1987 with Ford-Cosworth DFZ engines.

Road racing in the traditional manner – 1970 Targa Florio winner Brian Redman blasts his Porsche 908/3 through Campofelice.

The first road racing car in which 'negative lift' was generated by means other than external aerodynamic devices was the Chaparral 2J sports-racing car, which used an auxiliary engine to exhaust underbody air and thus 'suck' it down onto the road. Flexible skirts partly sealed the underbody area. This car failed to win a CanAm race, but demonstrated potential (and drew designers' attention to the undersides of cars) before it was banned.

Bruce McLaren (q.v.), a quiet New Zealander, winner of four Grands Prix, winner at Le Mans, twice CanAm champion, founder and inspiration of the racing car company that bears his name, *killed while testing a CanAm car at Goodwood.*

Jochen Rindt became the first driver to be awarded the world championship posthumously. He died after an accident in practice for the Italian Grand Prix, but in the last three races of the season no other driver equalled the score of 45 points he had built up before the Italian race. Austrian Rindt was enormously successful in Formula 2 in the second half of the 1960s, won at Le Mans in 1965, contested 60 Grands Prix and won six.

1971

Lotus raced the gas turbine-engined 56B in Grands Prix, achieving little with this modified version of a design for the Indianapolis 500.

Two Formula 2 races were run at Bogota, at 8000 ft/2440 metres above sea level the highest circuit ever used for formula events (winners of the races were Siffert and Rollinson).

British Grand Prix was the first world championship race to incorporate the name of a sponsor ('Woolmark') in its title.

The Fittipaldi brothers, Emerson and Wilson, started in Gold Leaf Team Lotus cars in the Argentine GP, the first time brothers had raced together in a Formula 1 team.

IMSA Camel GT championship inaugurated. For the next 14 years it was dominated by Porsche cars. In 1984 the overall championship fell to March-Chevrolet, but in 1985 Porsche 962s won 16 of the 17 races in the series, the odd one falling to Jaguar. In the second half of the 1980s this championship attracted larger and more varied entries than world series races, and turbocharged US engines (in British chassis) proved highly competitive.

Denny Hulme in a McLaren M8D in 1970, when the McLaren team dominated CanAm racing.

The combination of Jackie Stewart and Ken Tyrrell's team set the pace in early-1970s Grand Prix racing (Tyrrell 003 in practice for the 1971 British GP).

The fashionable 'wedge' shape shown off by the Eagle which Gordon Johncock drove to win the 1973 Indianapolis 500.

1972

First Williams Grand Prix car appeared, albeit named 'Politoys' for its principal sponsor. A limited budget meant that it appeared late and ran only twice. Williams cars named Iso started 30 times in 1973–4, then in 1975 Frank Williams' cars were at last run as Williams. They were promising, and that promise was fulfilled in 1979 and the early 1980s (the Constructors' Championship fell to Williams in 1980–1). Frank Williams held out against turbocharging until 1983, when he brought Honda back into Grand Prix racing in a partnership that was slow to mature but eventually gave GP victories to Rosberg, Mansell and Piquet, and the Constructors' Championship again in 1986.

First 200 mph/322 kph qualifying lap for a USAC race, set by Bobby Unser in an Eagle during practice for the California 500.

1973

First Brazilian Grand Prix ranking as a world championship event was run at the Interlagos autodrome, although races for Grand Prix cars had

been run at Rio de Janeiro and São Paulo in the 1930s. Winners of the world championship races: **1973** (I) Fittipaldi (Lotus); **1974** (I) Fittipaldi (McLaren); **1975** (I) Pace (Brabham); **1976** (I) Lauda (Ferrari); **1977** (I) Reutemann (Ferrari); **1978** (J) Reutemann (Ferrari); **1979** (I) Laffite (Ligier); **1980** (I) Arnoux (Renault); **1981** (J) Reutemann (Williams); **1982** (J) Prost (Renault); **1983** (J) Piquet (Brabham); **1984** (J) Prost (McLaren); **1985** (J) Prost (McLaren); **1986** (J) Piquet (Williams).

Circuits: I, Interlagos; J, Jacarepagua (Rio de Janeiro).

Ensign team appeared and, through the dogged persistence of Mo Nunn, was to last longer than several other independent (and generally underfinanced) Formula 1 ventures in the 1970s. Ensign contested 98 Grands Prix between 1973 and 1982, scoring just 19 championship points.

Shadow team appeared, the UOP-backed DN1 cars showing considerable promise. This was sustained through to the second half of the decade – Alan Jones scored the team's only championship win in 104 starts in Austria in 1977. Then as key members of the team left in acrimonious circumstances to form the Arrows team, Shadow's fortunes went into a decline and 1979 was the team's last full season.

1974

First Hesketh F1 car built, following Lord Hesketh's extrovert little team's success with a March driven by James Hunt in 1973. Hunt drove the conventional 308B to victory in the Silverstone International Trophy, and in the following year won the Dutch GP. In the autumn of that year the original team collapsed, although an element of it remained to run cars for drivers with their own financial backing. Meanwhile the Hesketh 308C had been sold to Walter Wolf, to become the first Wolf-Williams. Hesketh cars ran in 52 Grands Prix.

Roger Penske, successful racing driver and, towards the end of the 1960s, an entrant (in track and road racing), *became a constructor*, setting up a base at Poole. First car was the straightforward Cosworth-engined PC1 which made its debut in the 1974 Canadian GP. Two years later John Watson scored the team's only Grand Prix victory, in Austria. At the end of the 1976 season, after contesting 30 Grands Prix, the team concentrated on US racing, where Penske was a leading figure in the formation of CART. The Indianapolis 500 fell to a PC6 in 1979 and a PC10 in 1982.

In a season when several valiant efforts, such as the Amon, the Lyncar and the Token, flitted across the Grand Prix stage, *the Maki F101 stood out, simply because of its Japanese origins*. It was in fact a 'Cosworth kit car' using such staple items as the DFV engine and Hewland gearbox and in its

only circuit appearances was dismally uncompetitive.

Electric car records set over two-way flying start kilometre and mile at Bonneville by Roger Hedlund in 'Battery Box', at 175.061 mph/ 281.673 kph.

1975

First major race run on a street circuit at Long Beach, for F5000 cars (won by Brian Redman in a Lola T332). This 'proved' the circuit, created (and dismantled) very quickly with concrete walls, tyre walls, debris catch fencing, etc., and in 1976 the race was a world championship event. As such it was run until 1983, when a CART event took its place and title. Winners of the world championship Grands Prix of the United States (West): **1976** Regazzoni (Ferrari); **1977** Andretti (Lotus); **1978** Reutemann (Ferrari); **1979** Villeneuve (Ferrari); **1980** Piquet (Brabham); **1981** Jones (Williams); **1982** Lauda (McLaren); **1983** Watson (McLaren).

Renault introduced a turbocharged version of the V6 engine used in their sports-racing car programme, the Garrett AiResearch turbocharged CHS unit producing around 500 bhp. In the A442 it won its first race, but the Renault team did not win another race until Le Mans in 1978, which was their last sports car event. By that time Renault had introduced the turbocharger to GP racing.

Graham Hill's team moved forward with their own car, the GH1, which was followed by the neat, low GH2 designed by Andy Smallman.

The Copersucar appeared, as *the first Brazilian GP car*, although Richard Divila's design was a 'Cosworth kit car' under its striking skin. The team

Right Only lady driver to score in the world championship, Lella Lombardi. She contested 12 Grands Prix in 1975–6, then settled to a successful career as a sports car and saloon driver.

Battery Box, which Roger Hedlund (behind cockpit) drove to electric car records in 1974.

entered 72 GPs under this name between 1975 and 1979, then its name was changed to Fittipaldi. Despite the work of Emerson Fittipaldi in the later years, it was a forlorn effort and after contesting a total of 104 GPs with little to show but 44 points, it was wound up.

Lella Lombardi became the first lady driver to score a world championship point, or more correctly a half point as she was sixth in the Spanish GP which was stopped prematurely because of an accident. Lombardi contested 12 GPs, but was more successful in small sports cars and touring cars.

A Top Fuel dragster driven by Don Garlits ('Big Daddy', a pacesetter in the sport since the mid-1950s) *broke the 250 mph/402 kph barrier*. In 1984 Joe Amato achieved 260 mph/418 kph, and then in 1986 Garlits recorded a terminal speed over 270 mph/434 kph at the end of the standing-start ¼-mile/402 metres. That record was shattered in the same year at Motorplex (Dallas) by Darrell Gwynn, who recorded 5.26 sec (278 mph/447 kph).

1976

First Ligier Grand Prix car, the Matra-engined JS5, *made its debut* in the Brazilian GP. First championship victory came in the 1977 Swedish GP, but the team's most successful seasons were 1979–80 when the JS11 was DFV-powered. A change of name to Talbot-Ligier meant a return to the Matra engine; a reversion to Ligier meant another spell with DFVs; then from 1984 the team used Renault turbo engines.

Tyrrell caused a sensation with the six-wheeled Project 34 Grand Prix car. Its four 10-in/25-cm front wheels were intended to reduce drag and give improved cornering and braking through the larger tyre 'contact patch'. It won only one race, driven by Scheckter in the 1976 Swedish GP. Partly because tyre development for the small wheels lagged behind that for conventional wheels, this striking car was less competitive in 1977 and was then abandoned. Later March and Williams tested cars with tandem rear wheels; neither was raced (although the March did appear in some hill

James Hunt's 1976 world championship was gained in dramatic circumstances, in the McLaren M23 which was a very straightforward and undramatic car (Canadian GP, 1976).

Alastair Douglas-Osborn's Pilbeam R22 storms up Shelsley Walsh hillclimb. In 1976/77 he achieved six F.T.Ds in eight Shelsley meetings.

climbs) and in 1983 cars were restricted to four wheels by the regulations.

The name Alfa Romeo returned to Grand Prix racing, as suppliers of sports-unit-based engines to the Brabham team.

Janet Guthrie was admitted to Indianapolis qualifying, passing the rookie driving test (and having been placed 15th in the Trenton 200). She failed to qualify, although by lapping at over 180 mph/290 kph in a loaned Coyote she showed that her car was more at fault than her abilities. She qualified for the 500 in 1977, then turned to NASCAR racing.

1977

Renault brought the turbocharged engine into Grand Prix racing, in the RSO1 which made its debut at Silverstone. The team scored its first points at the end of the next season, and in 1979 was fully competitive with the RS11 – that year a Renault won the French GP. More victories followed – three in each of the next two years, four in 1982 and 1983 – but the championships that were so important to Renault never came. The turbo engine was made available to other teams, and this policy was continued after Renault's own GP team was wound up at the end of 1985. By then it had contested 123 Grands Prix and won 15, amassing 312 Constructors' Championship points.

The first Wolf Grand Prix car, WR1 designed by Harvey Postlethwaite, *was driven to a debut race victory* by Jody Scheckter in Argentina. Scheckter won two more GPs for Walter Wolf's team in 1977, but there were no victories after that year and Wolf gave up at the end of 1979 when the team's assets were acquired by the Fittipaldi brothers.

Lotus introduced 'ground effects' aerodynamics to single-seater racing, in the 78. This utilized the airflow passing under a car, funnelling it through the sidepods to venturi to generate downforce. 'Skirts' beneath the outer edges of the sidepods sealed most of the airflow under the car. A refined derivative of the 78, the Lotus 79, dominated the world championship in 1978 when the black and gold cars won eight GPs.

A CanAm 'sports car' series was reintroduced, and contested by a curious assortment of cars, many of them centre-cockpit single-seaters (e.g. erstwhile F5000 cars) with full-width bodywork. Champion was French driver Patrick Tambay, driving Carl Haas' Lolas – an association between entrant and driver that was to be picked up in Grands Prix in 1986.

A. J. Foyt became the first driver to win the Indianapolis 500 four times.

British Grand Prix organizers had to arrange an extra day of practice, for an entry of 41 cars meant that some drivers had to qualify to go ahead to the formal grid qualification sessions (among them was Gilles Villeneuve, showing his talent in a GP car for the first time).

Goodyear scored their 100th Grand Prix victory.

1978

Arrows was the newcomer of the year, with the A1. The team was formed by four ex-Shadow personnel in November 1977, and the A1 was completed in January 1978. In a High Court action in the summer of that year it was shown that the car had more than coincidental similarities to a Shadow design, and it had to be withdrawn. By that time the A2 was ready. Arrows' highest placing in the Constructors' Championship was seventh, in 1980.

Brabham essayed a ground-effects system in which a large fan drew air from beneath the car, which was 'sealed' at the sides with 'skirts'. This BT46 was raced only once, in the Swedish GP, when Lauda drove it to a clear victory. That result had to stand, as it could not clearly be shown that the car breached the regulations. But these were re-written and the BT46 was effectively banned.

Michelin introduced radial tyres into Grand Prix racing, and the first victory for a car fitted with them fell to Ferrari when Reutemann won the Brazilian GP.

First races to count as scoring events in the USAC national championship to be run outside North

The Lotus 79 was an advanced 'ground effects' car, with well-balanced lines, which Mario Andretti drove to win the 1978 world championship (here in the Italian Grand Prix).

America were held at Silverstone and Brands Hatch, being won by A. J. Foyt (Coyote) and Rick Mears (Penske) respectively.

Bruno Giacomelli enjoyed the most successful season of any driver in Formula 2, 1967–84, winning eight races in March cars and scoring 82 points.

Sports 2000 category introduced, with a first race at Oulton Park. In effect it derived from Formula Ford 2000, the cars being mechanically similar but with full-width sports-racing bodywork. In a difficult economic period Sports 2000 caught on slowly, but by the early 1980s was well established in several countries.

1979

Alfa Romeo returned to Grand Prix racing in their own right (they continued to supply engines to Brabham, although at the end of the year that team returned to DFV engines). The Alfa Romeo raced was the 177, effectively a development car. In the following year the 179 was introduced for a serious effort. The results were disappointing, and were to be so through succeeding seasons. From 1983 until 1985 the Euroracing team ran the Alfa Romeos in Grands Prix, then Alfa Romeo withdrew their cars from racing, although engine development continued (in the 1986 season only the modest Osella team used Alfa's turbo engines). Alfa Romeo withdrew from Formula 1 racing in 1987 to concentrate on saloon racing.

Championship Auto Racing Teams (CART), which had been formed in the previous year, *ran its own race series* in direct opposition to the established USAC championship trail, thus bringing to the boil a conflict that had been simmering in top-flight American racing. There was no immediate victor, but in the following seasons the CART Indycar series became dominant.

First driver to exceed 300 mph/483 kph on British soil was Sammy Miller, in a dragster at Santa Pod (his terminal velocity was 307 mph/494 kph).

The rocket-powered Budweiser in which Stan Barrett broke through the 'sound barrier' on land, in 1979.

1980

Ferrari's turbocharged engine made its debut late in the season, the 126C V6 that was to be preferred to a supercharged alternative. Nevertheless, the year which many pundits expected would see turbocharged engines dominant in fact saw the Cosworth DFV normally-aspirated V8 power the winning cars in 11 of the 14 championship races.

USAC introduced a sudden change in Indycar regulations, substantially reducing the turbo boost pressure permitted for 6-cylinder racing engines. This seemed blatantly aimed at Porsche, the only company developing a turbo-6 for this class of racing – their engine, which was being track-tested as the change was announced, was rendered obsolete overnight. Effectively this seemed to rule out the entry of a European-style works team into USAC (and CART) racing, but Lotus did build the 96 for 1985 (financial arrangements fell through and the car never raced). Ferrari was then tempted by the lure of the 500 and Porsche developed an Indycar V8. Porsche adapted their 1980 engine for endurance racing, and it was used in the 936 that scored a stunning debut victory at Le Mans in 1981.

Stan Barrett claimed to be the first man to exceed the speed of sound on land, driving the Budweiser Rocket tricycle at Rogers Dry Lake (formerly Muroc Dry Lake). US Air Force readings showed the device reached Mach 1.0106, or 739.666 mph/1190.12 kph, on its single run. The simple fact that Barrett did not make a second, return, run meant that he could not claim an official speed record.

Youngest driver ever to qualify to start in a Grand Prix was New Zealander Mike Thackwell (born 1961), at the Canadian GP. An accident led to a restart, for which Thackwell had to hand over his car to Tyrrell team-mate Jean-Pierre Jarier, and as the restarted race was run for the full distance Thackwell was technically not the youngest man to race in a Grand Prix. That distinction still belongs to another New Zealand driver, Chris Amon.

Jean Rondeau became the first man to win the Le Mans 24-hour Race in a car bearing his name, co-driving a Rondeau M379 to victory with Jean-Pierre Jaussaud. The first Rondeau sports car had been built in 1976. The M379 was the most successful type, some replicas being sold to other entrants. Its sports-racing successors were failures, and in 1984 Rondeau turned to building Reynard Formula Ford cars under licence, as the category was introduced into France and heavily promoted by Ford. In 1986 an original Rondeau F Ford design was laid down, but early that year Jean Rondeau was killed in a road accident.

The first 24-hour race to be run in Britain was organized at Snetterton – the one circuit sufficiently remote from built-up areas to allow night racing (for that reason an earlier '24-hour' race had been split into two parts, as the Brooklands Double Twelve, run 1929–31). The Snetterton saloon event was a modest venture at national level, and as such it was a success.

Diesel car records set at the Nardo track in Italy by the ARVW (Aerodynamic Research Volkswagen), which had a 2.4-litre turbocharged engine. It achieved 215.405 mph/330.496 kph for the standing-start mile and averaged 219.89 mph/353.80 kph for an hour from a standing start.

1981

Toleman entered Grand Prix racing with the TG181, designed by Rory Byrne to follow his 1980 Formula 2 championship-winning TG280 and powered by a Hart turbo engine. The team did not qualify to start in their first nine attempts in Formula 1, but in the following seasons the Tolemans became more competitive, Senna placing one second at Monaco (and within an ace of victory) in 1984. In 1985 the team seemed to be excluded from racing because of tyre-supply machinations, but eventually took over the ailing Spirit team's tyre contract. For the 1986 season the team was taken over by its principal sponsor, Benetton. The Benetton B186 used BMW engines in place of the Hart turbo units. The team's first GP victory was scored by Gerhard Berger in Mexico in 1986.

Theodore was a revived name, adopted for Teddy Yip's team, which used erstwhile Shadow cars while its TR3 was completed for a mid-season debut. A Theodore TR1 had run in one 1978 GP; its

1980s successors were to contest 33 GPs in three seasons, and score just two championship points.

McLaren International introduced the MP4. Designed by John Barnard, this was to become the outstanding Grand Prix car of the first half of the 1980s, winning 24 races in its first five seasons, driven by Lauda and Prost – who both gained world championships with it – and Watson. Initially the MP4 was powered by Cosworth DFV engines, but it had been laid down in anticipation of the TAG Porsche turbo engine becoming exclusively available to the resurgent McLaren team, and was most successful with this sophisticated engine.

Lotus introduced the 'twin-chassis' 88, in which the outer chassis (primarily the bodywork) absorbed aerodynamic loadings, while the inner chassis (comprising monocoque, engine, gearbox and fuel tank) took loadings from the suspension. Through the first half of the season the innovative 88 was the subject of protests and intense study of the regulations by baffled race stewards. Eventually it was ruled out.

Brabham designer Gordon Murray produced a less complex response to a ban on sliding skirts – a ban that was ineptly drafted, inviting clever designers to find loopholes. Brabham introduced a hydro-pneumatic suspension system whereby the fixed skirts were at the required height of 6 cm/2.36 in above the road surface while the car was at rest, the car then being allowed to sink so that the skirts were almost in contact with the road when it was moving. This gave the BT49 a great advantage, and the authorities could not rule it out ... All other teams had to follow this lamentable example later in the season. It led to a period when cars had rock-hard suspension systems, were fast but inherently dangerous.

New turbocharged engines were introduced by BMW, initially exclusively for Brabham (and then only usable in racing after many test and development failures, although eventually they were to be successful), and later in the year by Alfa Romeo.

Ralt cars started on a sequence of victories in British F3 racing that was to run unbroken from May until the opening race of the 1985 season, when a Reynard won at Silverstone.

First San Marino Grand Prix run at the superbly equipped Dino Ferrari autodrome near Imola. Initially the Italian Grand Prix was successfully run at this circuit in 1980, and the Imola organizers followed up its success by naming their race after the nearby independent republic in order to avoid the rule that two national Grands Prix should not be held in a season – this was thus deemed not to be a second Italian GP, at least in its title! Winners of world championship San Marino GPs: **1981** Piquet (Brabham); **1982** Pironi (Ferrari); **1983** Tambay (Ferrari); **1984** Prost (McLaren); **1985** de Angelis (Lotus); **1986** Prost (McLaren).

First Caesar's Palace Grand Prix run on a sinuous circuit contrived on the car park of a Las Vegas hotel. It was a world championship event twice, its place then being taken by a CART event. World championship GP winners: **1981** Jones (Williams); **1982** Alboreto (Tyrrell).

Bobby Unser took pole for the Indianapolis 500 at 200.545 mph/322.677 kph in a Penske PC9.

Carlos Reutemann completed a run of 11 points-scoring Grand Prix drives in the Long Beach race, in which he was runner-up to his Williams teammate Alan Jones for the third consecutive race.

World Endurance Championship for Drivers took in a confusing number of races (seven of the scoring events were run in North America) and was open to drivers in a confusing number of categories – the imbalance in both respects being intended to attract US interest in sports-car racing. Winner was American Bob Garretson. Under changed regulations subsequent champion sports car drivers were: **1982–3** Jacky Ickx (B); **1984** Stefan Bellof (D); **1985** Hans Stuck (D) and Derek Bell (GB); **1986** Derek Bell (GB).

Driver Cooling System devised by Denis Carlson first used in racing (in Trans-Am events), then adopted by Indycar drivers in 1983, by some GP teams in 1984 after Williams drivers had proved its worth in the extremely hot Dallas GP, and by NASCAR drivers in the following year. System involved a hood with many 'capillary tubes' through which cooling gel was pumped from a refrigerated cartridge. Later vests were developed on the same lines.

1982

First United States Grand Prix (Detroit) run on a 2.50-mile/4.023-km street circuit at Detroit. This was bumpy, very hard on transmissions and ran between walls or guard rails for much of the lap, allowing little margin for driver error. Winners of the world championship GPs at Detroit: **1982** Watson (McLaren); **1983** Alboreto (Tyrrell); **1984** Pi-

quet (Brabham); **1985** Rosberg (Williams); **1986** Senna (Lotus).

McLaren and TAG (Techniques d'Avant Garde, then one of Williams' sponsors) *announced their funding of a Porsche-designed Grand Prix engine* – a plan that was to bring to the Porsche name Grand Prix success in an abundance denied the German company in their 1960s ventures.

Jaguar's return to major endurance races was foreshadowed when the XJR-5 coupé, built and raced by Group 44, made its debut at Elkhart Lake.

Grand Prix drivers staged a strike in protest against a new 'super-licence' form; in particular against clauses regarding their contracts with teams which they were expected to sign. This action threatened the South African GP, but in the event final practice sessions and the race took place.

Most teams which were members of the Formula 1 Constructors' Association – which meant most Grand Prix teams – *decided to boycott the San Marino GP,* in protest against a ban on topping up the tanks for water-cooled brakes after a race. This practice exploited a possible loophole in the minimum weight regulations, especially welcomed by the teams running normally-aspirated engines, for any form of weight reduction helped them remain competitive with the turbo cars. Fourteen cars raced (smallest GP field since there were 13 starters in the 1969 French and German GPs). Pressure from sponsors helped to ensure that there was no repetition of this incident.

Professional Racing Drivers Association formed out of membership of the Grand Prix Drivers' Association, but fortunately the 'political' strife of that unfortunate season was fading and there was no call for any of the trade union activity that might be implicit in either title.

Monaco GP saw bewildering changes of fortune in its last two laps. Prost led in a Renault, but crashed; Patrese then led, and spun to a standstill just off the racing line on the damp track; Pironi took over the lead in a Ferrari, but coasted to a halt as his engine died because of an electrical fault; de Cesaris then led in an Alfa Romeo, which stopped as it ran out of fuel; Daly might have taken the lead in a Williams, but a little earlier he had smashed the gearbox casing and as the oil ran out it ceased to function. Meanwhile Patrese's Brabham had been pushed to a place of safety by a marshal, and that happened to get it into a position where it could run down hill; Patrese let it roll, the engine fired, he completed the lap ... to win.

At Indianapolis the Wildcat-Cosworth driven by Gordon Johncock *and the Penske-Cosworth* driven by Rick Mears *were side by side at the end* of the 500. Johncock won by 16-hundredths of a second.

Jacky Ickx won the Le Mans 24-hour Race for the sixth time. His co-driver Derek Bell scored his third Le Mans victory in the same race. The pair headed a works Porsche team 1–2–3 in their Rothmans 956.

The pit stop reintroduced to Grand Prix racing as a strategy (rather than as a response to a mishap or mechanical failure) by the Brabham team. The advantages to be gained by running half a race on half a tank of fuel and relatively soft tyres, with a stop to refuel and change wheels, were such that other teams had to follow the example. Refuelling was to be banned, but wheel-change stops remained a feature of GP racing into the second half of the 1980s, and in the better-drilled stops during 1985 cars were at a standstill for less than 10 seconds while all wheels were changed.

1983

Grand Prix cars were subject to a 'flat-bottom' rule, and most pundits agreed that sense prevailed as the ground-effects era ended. By 1985 flat bottoms were required in all international single-seater categories (Formula 3 races being run to these regulations in 1985). However Indycar regulations for 1984–7 allowed for side-pod ground effects, albeit with ground clearance stipulated.

Honda returned to GP racing, supplying the turbocharged RA 163-E for the Spirit team's soli-

Thrust 2, piloted to a Land Speed Record by Richard Noble in 1983. The driver sat alongside the Rolls-Royce Avon jet engine, with a spare cockpit available on the opposite side of the car!

tary car – an arrangement whereby the V6 was race-tested in a conversion of a Formula 2 car in preparation for a full season with Williams in 1984 (when the Spirit team had to use Hart or Cosworth engines).

Team Lotus raced a Grand Prix car within five weeks of the decision to start design work. Early in the season it became only too obvious that the 93T was uncompetitive, so JPS Lotus team manager determined to lay down a successor rather than spend further development time on it. The 94T was designed by Gerard Ducourage, two were built and performed well in their first race, the British GP, in those five weeks in June and July.

March Engineering completed their 1000th racing car, an 83C for Indycar racing. This landmark was reached in 13 years, when March production included more than 200 cars for each of Formula 2, Formula 3, and the closely-related Atlantic/B/Pacific categories.

A Jaguar team contested the European Touring Car (saloon) series, which was in its 21st season. The team won five races, compared to the six which fell to their principal rival BMW. The 1984 Jaguar team, which enjoyed fuller works status, then won seven to BMW's four, while a single race fell to a turbocharged Volvo.

The 128 dragsters in the Super Gas field at the US Nationals at Indy Raceway Park were covered by 0.068 seconds after qualifying.

Richard Noble broke the 21-year US stranglehold on the Land Speed Record, when his Thrust 2 reached 633.46 mph/1019.237 kph at the hitherto-unused Black Rock Desert Venue, USA.

1984

First United States Grand Prix (Dallas) run on a contrived 2.424-mile/3.901-km circuit which fell

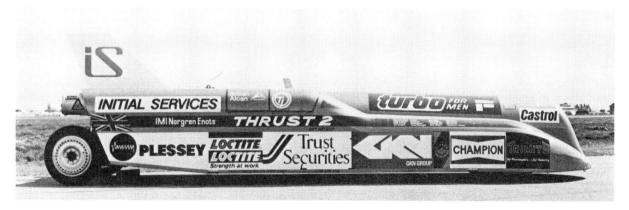

far short of the standards which should have been stipulated – even the requirement that an international race be run to 'prove' a circuit before a Grand Prix could be sanctioned was overlooked ... However, the financial requirements were met. At the first meeting the track surface broke up, but the race was run. Winner was Keke Rosberg in a Williams.

The Tyrrell team was excluded from the world championship following allegations that an analysis of water taken from one of the cars after the Detroit race showed that the regulations had been infringed. Points scored before that race were 'cancelled'. Tyrrell took legal action which enabled him to enter events later in the season.

Austrian GP was an 'all-turbo' race, as the two cars with normally aspirated engines which practised did not qualify to start. *First race with an all-turbo entry* was the 1985 Dutch Grand Prix.

The fuel allowance of 220 litres (48.4 Imp. gallons) for a Grand Prix led to the spectacle of 'economy runs' and to side effects, ranging from pre-chilling of fuel (which contracts as its temperature falls) to turbo engines burning pistons as mixtures were too lean. Refuelling during races was also banned.

McLaren won 12 Grands Prix, handsomely surpassing the previous best score of eight victories set by Lotus in 1978. Ferrari, Lotus and Tyrrell had earlier scored seven victories in single seasons. Ironically, in 1984 McLaren driver Alain Prost equalled Jim Clark's 1963 record of seven victories in a season, yet, unlike the Scot, Prost did not win the world championship.

The nine points which Niki Lauda scored in the South African Grand Prix in April *lifted his overall points score above 400*. At that time only two other drivers, Stewart and Reutemann, had ever scored more than 300 points in their careers.

March enjoyed an astonishing numerical superiority at Indianapolis; 30 of the 33 cars which qualified for the start were built by March, 27 84Cs and three 83Cs. Moreover, every one of the 14 cars which finished in the 500 was a March – 13 84Cs and an 83C. The slowest qualifying speed had been 201.217 mph/323.758 kph, the fastest was 210.029 mph/337.937 kph, and the race was won by Rick Mears in a Cosworth-engined 84C at a record speed of 163.612 mph/263.252 kph.

Zakspeed moved into Grand Prix racing with their own 841 car which, unusually for a minor constructor, was powered by their own engine, a 4-cylinder turbo unit. Zakowski's Zakspeed Racing

had been established in the late 1960s, and from 1969 worked closely with Ford. In 1978 Zakspeed developed a turbo Capri, and in the early 1980s moved into the sports-racing class with the Ford C100 (continuing with this as a Zakspeed when Ford closed down the programme). The Formula 1 car which was announced in the autumn of 1984 was raced in European events in 1985, without notable success.

Six weeks before the first race of the endurance championship the regulations were changed, the promulgated 15 per cent cut in the fuel allowance being abandoned as FISA endeavoured to bring the world championship into line with the flourishing American IMSA series. One outcome was that Porsche withdrew their works team from Le Mans, where it had contested the 24-hour race every year since 1951 (except 1975). An independent Porsche won at Le Mans (heading six others), and a month later the governing body decided that the fuel allowance cut would be implemented in 1985.

A new 2.82 mile/4.54 km Nürburgring circuit was opened in the summer and was the venue for the European GP in the autumn. Replacing the old 'Ring (see 1927), it had a succession of constant-radius corners – safe but utterly bland.

Initial judgment found for the estate of Mark Donohue in a case brought against the Penske corporation and Goodyear, with the complication of a cross case by Penske against the tyre company. This arose out of Donohue's fatal accident in a Penske March during warm-up for the 1975 Austrian GP. There was an immediate fear that the award of damages totalling almost £20 million against Goodyear could profoundly jeopardize racing in the USA, but, as is the way of these matters, these worries faded as the appeal proceeded.

Last international championship Formula 2 race was run at Brands Hatch, won by Philippe Streiff in an AGS. Between 1967 and 1984, 209 F2 championship races were run. The most successful chassis constructor was March (78 victories), followed by Ralt (22) and Brabham (18), while BMW engines powered 95 race-winning cars. Jochen Rindt won most races (12), closely followed by Bruno Giacomelli (11), Mike Thackwell and Jacques Laffite (8 each); Thackwell scored the highest number of points (164 in four seasons), followed by Brian Henton (126) and Patrick Depailler (119). Local F2 series continued until 1986 in Japan and in South America.

1985

Lola returned to Grand Prix racing, albeit the car carrying the name of Beatrice as the team was underwritten by the US-based multinational conglomerate as part of a race programme that also took in CART (where Lola had been active for some time). Team director was Carl Haas, while ex-McLaren pair Teddy Mayer and Tyler Alexander ran the GP team. The car made its debut with a Hart engine, but in the 1986 San Marino GP Alan Jones gave the Duckworth-designed Ford-labelled turbo engine its first race in a Lola. By that time the Beatrice part of the team title had diminished and was soon to disappear because of changed company personnel and policies, although enough of the contracted finance remained to sustain Team Haas through to the summer. In 1986 the team scored just six points; as the season ended it was folded, although Lola was to continue.

Renault Sport developed a version of the EF15 GP engine with a pneumatic valve operation system, in which springs were replaced by pistons operated by compressed air. This obviated the age-old problem of 'valve-bounce', and raised the effective rev. limit of the engine by around 1500 rpm to 13,000 rpm. This version of the engine was available to Renault's 'customer teams' (Lotus, Ligier and Tyrrell) until Renault withdrew at the end of 1986. Renault also developed a substitute for the traditional distributor, comprising a low-tension electrical system distributed to cylinders by computer.

Formula 3000 introduced, to take the place of Formula 2 and the European Formula 3 championship. Regulations stipulated normally-aspirated 3-litre engines with an approved electronic rev. limiter which imposed a 9000 rpm rev. limit. Together with restrictions on tyres and other regulations, this was intended to contain car performances at a level roughly midway between Formula 3 and Formula 1. Grids were modest in 1985 but full in 1986, although racing for this category was confined to Europe as the hoped-for South American 'mini series' did not materialize. In 1987, however, it took the place of F2 in Japan.

Bill Elliott won the Winston 500 NASCAR Grand National race at Talladega (Alabama) at 186.288 mph/299.801 kph in a Ford Thunderbird. This was the fastest 500-mile race ever run.

Australian GP winner Keke Rosberg made three pit stops, all for tyre changes. This had not happened in the modern era of championship racing, and had seldom occurred throughout the years of the 2.5-litre formula (although the winning Vanwall shared by Brooks and Moss in the 1957 British GP did stop three times). It had hardly even been customary in the earliest years of the championship, the outstanding exception being the 1951 French GP, when Fangio made three stops in the Alfa Romeo in which he started the race, then two in team-mate Fagioli's car which he took over.

Porsche claimed its tenth Le Mans victory, 'by proxy', as the winning 956B was run by the independent Joest New Man team.

A second international championship was introduced into the endurance series, for Group C2 cars (700-kg/1540-lb minimum weight), which had been inaugurated two years earlier as a Junior class to fill grids. The first C2 championship fell to Spice Engineering's Tiga GC85 and its drivers Gordon Spice and Ray Bellm. Ecurie Ecosse won the title in 1986 with their MG Metro 6R4-engined car, Ray Mallock and Marc Duez driving it to clinch the championship at Fuji.

By the early 1980s Renault had high championship hopes, but these were never quite fulfilled, despite the efforts of the team with their turbo cars and drivers such as Patrick Tambay, here on his way to third place in the 1985 Portuguese Grand Prix.

This Joest team Porsche 956 gained the 10th Le Mans victory for the German marque in 1985, and that was the second victory for this car, equalling the achievement of a JWA Ford GT40 in 1968–9.

First Malaysian race to be an international championship event was the Selanger 800 at Shah Alam, final race in the World Endurance Championship, won by Mass and Ickx in a works Porsche 962C from a Jaguar XJR-6.

First team championship in the endurance series was won by Rothmans-Porsche, the works team which took six of the nine '1000-km' races (in fact only three of those events reached 1000 km, the three others being stopped short of their scheduled distances).

Christian Danner became the first German driver to win an international single-seater championship since World War II when he clinched the European F3000 title in the final race of the series at Donington Park.

The Estonian constructor TARK completed its 1000th racing car, an Estonia 20M for the East European 1.3-litre Formula Vostok. The first Estonia, an F3 car on Cooper lines, was built in 1958, and succeeding models followed West European patterns, although through to the second half of the 1980s all were space-frame designs.

Van Diemen became the first constructor to complete 1000 cars for a single road-racing category, Formula Ford. Ralph Firman had formed Van Die-

Nelson Piquet's Williams-Honda in the Mexican Grand Prix, a race revived in 1986 after a long lapse.

Brilliant Brazilian driver Ayrton Senna driving a Lotus-Renault in the 1986 German Grand Prix. For the next season this team turned to Honda engines and substituted bright yellow Camel colours for Player's black and gold.

men in 1973, and through the next ten years his F Ford cars were consistently successful, a lapse in 1983 being followed by a rapid recovery.

1986

The Ferrari team contested its 400th championship Grand Prix in the French race, when Alboreto and Johansson failed to score in the F186 turbo cars. Ferrari had won 91 championship GPs to that time, and a Ferrari had started from pole in 103 races.

Closest-ever Grand Prix finish came at the end of the revived Spanish event at Jerez, when Ayrton Senna in a Lotus won from Nigel Mansell in a Williams by an official 0.014 seconds, or 93 centimetres/36.6 inches.

Italian Grand Prix was started with neither of the fastest drivers in qualifying at the front of the grid. Teo Fabi (Benetton), who should have been on pole, started from the back after his engine 'died' before the parade lap, while Alain Prost abandoned his McLaren as its engine refused to fire and started in the spare car after the rest.

American Racing Series ('Mini-Indy') launched under an SCCA sanction to fill the wide gap between F Ford and CART racing, with a ten-race series run as supporting events at CART oval-, road- and street-circuit meetings. In many respects this category was a parallel to the European F3000, but ARS was inaugurated as a one-model series, March building 25 86A cars for it. Derived from the F3000 85B, the 86A was powered by a Buick 4.2 litre V8, and was known as a Wildcat for US promotional purposes.

Rick Mears set a closed-circuit record at 233.934 mph/376.399 kph in a Penske Racing March 86C at the Michigan International Speedway, thus breaking Mark Donohue's 1975 record of 221.160 mph/355.846 kph set in a Porsche 917-30K at Talladega Speedway. These were both specially set-up attempts, but earlier in 1986 Mears had turned in a 217.581 mph/350.088 kph qualifying lap at Indianapolis.

Last-ever Formula 2 race was the final event in the All-Japan championship, run at Suzuka and won by Kazuyoshi Hoshino in a March-Honda.

First street-circuit meeting on the British mainland had the Halfords Birmingham Super Prix as its principal race, unhappily ruined by a downpour. It was won by Luis Sala, in an F3000 Ralt-Cosworth.

Jaguar won their first victory in a world sports car championship race since 1957, when Derek Warwick and Eddie Cheever drove a factory-backed XJR-6 (built and run by Tom Walkinshaw Racing) to win the Silverstone 1000-km race at 129.08 mph/207.69 kph.

A specially prepared 650-bhp 5-cylinder turbocharged Audi 200 quattro of 2144 cc set *a closed-circuit speed record for four-wheel drive vehicles* of 206.825 mph/332.781 kph at the Alabama International Motor Speedway at Talladega, USA, driven by Bobby Unser (q.v.).

After several years developing an 'active suspension' system, on road cars as well as racing cars, Lotus were confident enough to use it on the circuits in 1987. Here Ayrton Senna tests an 'active suspension' Lotus-Honda 99T at Imola before its debut race in Brazil, where he led the GP before retiring.

Rear-engined trials. The 1923 Benz Tropfenwagen (top) showed promise, but it was never properly developed. However, it did point the way for the successful Auto Unions of the 1930s, and those cars were echoed in the Gulf Miller at the end of that decade, which also boasted four-wheel drive. It was not a success on the US tracks.

Aerodynamic experiments. In 1923 Bugatti (top) and Voisin tried these streamlined devices; neither was successful, the former in part because of its odd wheelbase dimensions, the Voisin because it was under-powered.

Six wheels were seen as a way to improve aerodynamics by Tyrrell on the P34, here being driven to its only race victory by Scheckter in Sweden in 1976. Six wheels at the other end of a car were expected to give improved traction, but this 1982 Williams (driven on test by Rosberg) was never raced, and soon only four wheels were permitted.

Below Brabham's approach to 'ground effects' was to use an engine-driven fan to 'suck' the car onto the track. The BT46B raced only once, when Niki Lauda drove it to victory in the Swedish GP of 1978.

RALLIES

1878

Arguably the *first competition to take place on public roads between mechanically-propelled vehicles* was an event held in Wisconsin, USA in July 1878. It received six entries from various steam-propelled vehicles but eventually only two took the start. In the course of the event they had to tackle special tests which comprised for the most part ploughing and weight hauling. The winners were Messrs Shomer and Farrand at the helm of an Oshkosh locomotive which averaged 6 mph/ 9.7 kph and took just over 33 hours to reach the finish in Madison and collect the $5000 first prize.

1887

The *first road competition held in Europe* was the race sponsored by the *Velocipede* and organized by its editor, M. Fossier. It was held over a short course near Paris. To great surprise, it received only one entry, that of a steam quadricycle driven by the Comte de Dion. Not surprisingly, he won.

In November *an event took place in the USA which modelled itself on the original Paris–Rouen.* This was largely due to the reports of that event in the *New York Herald* from an intrepid young reporter who had followed part of that event on a bicycle. The American event was sponsored by the *Chicago Times-Herald* and ran over a 94-mile/151-km course between Chicago and Waukegan. Like its European predecessor, it received over 100 entrants but on the start day, 2 November, only two turned up. The Duryea broke down and the Benz driven by Muller won the reduced first prize of $500 for finishing. The event was rescheduled for 28 November when six cars, four petrol and two electric, turned up. Because of snow, the route was shortened to 54 miles/87 km and the only two cars to get through to Evanston were Frank Duryea

and the aforementioned Mr Muller. Duryea had covered the distance in 8 hours 23 minutes to average 7 mph/11.3 kph. Perhaps the most remarkable aspect of his win was that he was serviced by his brother Charles who used a horse-drawn sleigh, surely the first example of a factory service car in rallying.

At the house of the Comte de Dion in the *Quai d'Orsay*, Paris, the *Automobile Club de France was founded* on 12 November.

1896

To celebrate the fact that motor vehicles in Great Britain no longer had to be preceded by a man carrying a red flag, an entrepreneur called Harry Lawson organized an *Emancipation Run from London to Brighton.* The purpose of the event was in fact to publicize his own wares and the outcome was rather chaotic, but this event was later taken up by the Royal Automobile Club and survives today in a much better organized form.

1897

In the same year that saw the *foundation of the Automobile Club of Great Britain and Ireland* (which was to become the Royal Automobile Club under Edward VII in 1907) the journal *The Engineer* organized *a trial for motor vehicles* to be held on 27–8 May. It had 70 entrants but on the day only six appeared to tackle the 200 miles/ 320 km and diverse tests. Regrettably, the judges saw fit to stop the contest in mid-song since none of the vehicles seemed to fulfil the conditions specified in the regulations.

1898

Inter-city competitions were spreading. Berlin–Potsdam brought the sport to Germany, while an event from Brussels to Spa ensured that the Belgians were in on the act. Even the Swiss ran an event from Geneva to Meillerie and back. But it was the Paris–Amsterdam–Paris, held between 7 and 13 July that became the *first such event to cross international borders.*

The *first one-marque event* ever held was for Mors cars and was held over 79 miles/127 km between Saint Germain and Vernon and back to Saint Germain. Run on 20 October, it was won by Levegh.

1899

The *first Tour de France Automobile was held* between 16 and 24 July in seven daily stages amounting to 1350 miles/2172 km. It saw the *first appearance of the parc fermé* that is so well known in modern rallying. Each night, the cars were put in a park where the driver had one hour to service his vehicle before withdrawing. He had another hour in the morning before the re-start. Anyone arriving at the re-start after they were due to leave – a common occurrence – was given 2 hours to work on his car. The event was won by the Chevalier René de Knyff in a 16 hp Panhard. His average speed for the whole event was just over 30 mph/48 kph.

1900

The *first 1000-Miles Trial was held in Britain.* This precursor of the RAC Rally was organized by the Automobile Club of Great Britain and started from Hyde Park Corner in London on 23 April. It lasted 11 days and was tough enough with its special sections and a speed test on a private road to reduce the 65 starters to 23 at the finish. Best of these was the Hon. C. S. Rolls driving a Panhard, but it was the British team of Daimlers that won the team prize. The event was perhaps a little too fast for public acceptance and later versions had to accept lower average speeds.

1901

The Automobile Club of America held a trial from New York to Buffalo which distinguished itself by *having to be stopped when the news broke that President McKinley had been assassinated.* Some 42 of the 80 starters were still running at Rochester when proceedings were halted.

1902

The *most successful of all the inter-city races* of the early era, which were to be reincarnated as rallies

in the 1930s, was the Paris–Vienna. It was won by Marcel Renault in his 16 hp Renault. Because of problems encountered with recce-ing and practising of the route on the cancelled Nice–Abbazia race in April of the same year, recce-ing was forbidden on the Paris–Vienna to make the route authorizations easier to obtain.

The *Scottish Automobile Club held its first trial* which ran from Glasgow to London with a night halt in York. It attracted five entries and the winners were Stocks/Talbot-Crosbie in a de Dion.

1903

The *twin tragedies of the Nice Speed Week*, when Count Zborowski was killed at the wheel of his new 60 hp Mercedes, and of *the Paris–Madrid race*, when Marcel Renault was killed together with competitors and spectators in other unrelated accidents, meant that *racing on the public road was virtually dead.* It was no coincidence that the same year the Gordon Bennett race took place on a closed – and specially prepared – circuit in Ireland. Any competition that took place hereafter on public roads would need to pass itself off as a 'reliability' event.

The second 1000-Miles Trial was held in Britain. Centred on the Crystal Palace in South London, it comprised eight daily loops and the principal requirement was that the cars should not at any time stop during the day's run. A hundred of the starters failed to do that: only four managed to comply.

1904

The first recorded motoring event to take place in India was organized by the Motor Union of West India to coincide with the Christmas holidays. It started from Delhi and finished in Bombay but was more of a treasure hunt than a serious motoring event. It was not for some 64 years that India was to see a major international rally, the 1968 London–Sydney, and another 10 after that before creating its own very tough Himalayan Rally.

1905

The first Herkomer Trophy was held in southern Germany and was organized by the portrait painter Hubert von Herkomer, whose second love was the motor-car. The event started and finished in Munich and visited Baden-Baden, Regensburg and Nuremburg, lasting well over a week. Com-

Forerunner. Prince Heinrich at the wheel of his Benz during the 1906 Herkomer Fahrt.

petitors had to keep to set average speeds which varied over the sections and there were numerous time controls. In those respects it resembled a modern rally. Despite its confusing calculations, it proved socially and internationally popular and a second event was held in 1906 in which there was a Royal participant, Prince Heinrich of Prussia, driving a 40 hp Benz. He liked the driving but he did not like the regulations or the wild cheating that went on. The event died on its feet when it was held for the final time in 1907 as a purely German event with no overseas entries.

1908

Prince Heinrich lent his name and authority to *the first Prinz Heinrich Fahrt* and insisted that observers be carried in the cars to prevent rules going unobserved. The event was successful and attracted 130 starters who covered a route between Berlin and Frankfurt in just over a week. It was an event dominated by factory entries and won by Fritz Erle in a works 50 hp Benz.

1910

In the year that the third *Prinz Heinrich Fahrt* was won by a chap called Ferdinand Porsche driving a Daimler, the Austrian Automobile Club organized its *first International Alpenfahrt* where much emphasis was placed on ascent of various passes. There was no outright winner but cups were given for good performances. By 1912 it had expanded considerably and now took seven days instead of the original three. Rolls-Royce entered and were defeated by the severity of the Austrian roads. They returned in 1913 and one of their team finished unpenalized in what was an unremarkable event. But in the 1914 *Alpenfahrt*, James Radley returned with a specially prepared Rolls-Royce and he had the distinction of gaining one of the 16 cups awarded for finishing with no penalties. World War I intervened or this purely

Austrian event might have gone from strength to strength to judge by its success in 1914. But the Austrians could not get it started again after the war, and it was not until 1926 that they got a jointly organized rally going that later spawned the largely French Alpine Rally. There was a revival of the Austrian *Alpenfahrt* as a rally but this came after World War II. For a time it was in the European Rally Championship – it was won by Paddy Hopkirk in an Austin Healey 3000 in 1964 – and eventually grew to be one of the rallies in the first year of the World Rally Championship. But that 1973 event was marred by controversy and protest over a road blocked by the Alpine Renault team manager. The rally was not held in 1974 because of these problems, plus those of the petrol 'crisis', and has not been held since.

1911

MONTE CARLO RALLY. To publicize how pleasant it was to spend time in Monte Carlo out of season in January, a man called Antony Noghes proposed that the *Société des Bains et Mer de Monaco* should sponsor an automobile event starting from all the winter-bound capitals of Europe and converging on the Principality. The first event was held in 1911 and was a great success, inspiring emulators 40 and 50 years later. The early Monte Carlo rallies had relatively undemanding road sections from the starting town to Monaco, where final points were gained for *Concours d'Élégance*. But the winter weather encountered was often severe enough to select out the better crews. In 1928, only 24 of the 65 starters were classified. In its heyday in the early 1950s, over 300 would start and there would be 250–70 at the finish. But even then, bad weather could play havoc, as it did in 1965 when only 22 finished from 237 – the night of the blizzard.

Interrupted by World War I, the Monte started again in 1924 and ran without break until World

Donald Healey in the Invicta 4½ after winning the 1931 Monte Carlo Rally.

Below Erik Carlsson exuberant in a Saab – a familiar combination in the 1960s. Here he is on his way to victory in the Monte Carlo Rally.

War II. It did evolve somewhat in those years but mainly in the field of formulae to try and equalize the different routes and the different cars. Some people built special cars to try and win, and there were always the eccentrics with cars on skis.

The main thing is that the Monte preserved its reputation and its multi-start format to spring anew in 1949 to lead the postwar European love affair with cars and rallying. The formulae were still around which gave Maurice Martin his win in 1961 with a Panhard, ahead of two similar cars – the only winner of whom almost no-one had a photograph. In 1956 a common route was in-stigated between, on this occasion, Paris and Monaco, while in 1960 this was much shortened (Chambery–Monaco) and a final mountain circuit held in the hills behind Monaco for the 90 best classified cars. That has dropped to 60 but is still held today. In the same year special stages were introduced, but still formulae were applied and it was not until 1964 that they disappeared for good.

But in 1966 the FIA introduced new technical regulations for Group 1 cars and the Monte was the first event. The Minis, Ford Cortinas and Imps were excluded for allegedly contravening the lighting regulations and the Monte led the way again – this time in scandal. It says something for the strength of the event that it has survived this, a petrol crisis in 1974 and the attempts of FISA to stop it in 1985.

The most successful drivers on the Monte are Sandro Munari with wins in 1972 (Lancia Fulvia), 1975–7 (Lancia Stratos) and Walter Röhrl 1980 (Fiat Abarth), 1982 (Opel Ascona), 1983 (Lancia 037) and 1984 (Audi Quattro). Röhrl must have the edge having won it in four very dissimilar cars.

Monte Carlo Rally overall winners

Year	Crew	Car
1911	Rougier	Turcat-Méry 25 hp
1912	Beutler	Berliet 16 hp
1924	Ledure	Bignan 2 litre
1925	Repusseau	Renault 40 hp
1926	Hon V. Bruce/Brunell	A.C. Six
1927	Lefévre/Despeaux	Amilcar 1098 cc
1928	Bignan	Fiat 509A 990 cc
1929	Dr Van Eijk	Graham-Paige 4.7 litre

1930	Petit	La Licorne 905 cc
1931	Healey	Invicta 4.5 litre
1932	Vasselle	Hotchkiss AM 2.5 litre
1933	Vasselle	Hotchkiss 620 3.5 litre
1934	Gas/Trevoux	Hotchkiss 620 3.5 litre
1935	Lahaye/Quatresous	Renault Nervasport
1936	Zamfirescu/Cristea	Ford V8 3.6 litre
1937	Le Begue/Quinlin	Delahaye 135 3.5 litre
1938	Bakker Schut/Karel Ton	Ford V8 3.6 litre
1939	Trevoux/Lesurque	Hotchkiss 686 3.5 litre
	Paul/Contet	Delahaye 135 3.5 litre
1949	Trevoux/Lesurque	Hotchkiss 686 3.5 litre
1950	Becquart/Secret	Hotchkiss 686 3.5 litre
1951	Trevoux/Crovetto	Delahaye 175 4.5 litre
1952	Allard/Warburton	Allard P 4.3 litre
1953	Gatsonides/Worledge	Ford Zephyr 2.3 litre
1954	Chiron/Basadonna	Lancia Aurelia GT
1955	Malling/Fadum	Sunbeam MkIII 2.3 litre
1956	Adams/Bigger	Jaguar MkVII 3.4 litre
1957	No rally due to the Suez crisis	
1958	Monraisse/Feret	Renault Dauphine
1959	Coltelloni/Alexandre	Citroën ID 19
1960	Schock/Möll	Mercedes-Benz 220 SE
1961	Martin/Bateau	Panhard PL 17
1962	Carlsson/Haggbom	Saab 96
1963	Carlsson/Palm	Saab 96
1964	Hopkirk/Liddon	Cooper S 1071 cc
1965	Makinen/Easter	Cooper S 1275 cc
1966	Toivonen/Mikander	Citroën DS 21
1967	Aaltonen/Liddon	Cooper S 1275 cc
1968	Elford/Stone	Porsche 911 T
1969	Waldegaard/Helmer	Porsche 911
1970	Waldegaard/Helmer	Porsche 911 S
1971	Andersson/Stone	Alpine Renault 110
1972	Munari/Manucci	Lancia Fulvia 1600 cc
1973	Andruet/'Biche'	Alpine Renault 110
1974	No rally thanks to 'petrol crisis'	
1975	Munari/Sodano	Lancia Stratos
1976	Munari/Maiga	Lancia Stratos
1977	Munari/Maiga	Lancia Stratos
1978	Nicolas/Laverne	Porsche Carrera 3 litre
1979	Darniche/Mahe	Lancia Stratos
1980	Röhrl/Geistdorfer	Fiat Abarth 131
1981	Ragnotti/Andrie	Renault 5 Turbo
1982	Röhrl/Geistdorfer	Opel Ascona 400
1983	Röhrl/Geistdorfer	Lancia Rallye 037
1984	Röhrl/Geistdorfer	Audi Quattro
1985	Vatanen/Harryman	Peugeot 205 Turbo 16
1986	Henri Toivonen/Cresto	Lancia Delta S4
1987	Biasion/Siviero	Lancia Delta HF

1925

While rallies were reviving strongly in Europe after World War I, things in Britain were more oriented to the race track. The _Scottish Six Days Trial had to be cancelled_ while the SMMT saw fit to ban 'trade' involvement in UK trials and rallies.

1926

A collaboration between the Austrians, Swiss, Italians and French resulted in _a revival of the Alpine Rally_. This 1926 event started and finished in Milan and stuck to the idea of giving out cups for unpenalized runs. Every finisher got one that first year but it gradually expanded and got more difficult. The Germans joined in in 1928 and by 1931, when Donald Healey won one of seven _Coupes_ in his Invicta, it was a full six days of hard motoring in the Alps starting from Munich and finishing in Berne.

At this stage, individual entries could win Glacier Cups for their individual unpenalized performances while Alpine Cups were awarded to teams of unpenalized cars. For example, when the 1932 rally terminated in San Remo, the Talbot 105 team won an Alpine Cup, a performance repeated in 1934. This was the heyday of British drivers such as H. J. Aldington (Frazer Nash), Tommy Wisdom (MG Magnette and Talbot 105), Sammy Davis (Armstrong Siddeley) and the Rileys in cars of their own make.

The Alpine Rally was not held in 1935. Indeed it was cancelled because the German drivers were not allowed to send money to the French organizers! But in 1936 it went ahead under Swiss organization and both Donald Healey (Triumph Vitesse) and Tommy Wisdom (SS 100) won Glacier Cups. German domination in the event was otherwise almost total and the remaining events preceding World War II were not well supported by other nationals.

After the war it fell to the French connection to revive the event. The _Association Sportive de l'Automobile Club de Marseille Provence_ stepped

Classic rally car of the 1970s, the Lancia Stratos. This is Munari on a dry and snow-free Monte Carlo Rally in 1977, heading for victory.

Below, right The 1981 Monte Carlo winning Renault 5 Turbo, driven by Jean Ragnotti.

The Talbot team lined up at Nice before the start of the 1934 Alpine Rally.

in and in July 1947 organized the first of a series of events that were known as the *Coupe des Alpes*, or just the Alpine Rally. The *Coupe* or Cup was not just an Alpine one and awarded for individual performances. A later innovation was to give a silver *Coupe* to someone who had won three *Coupes* non-consecutively, and a gold *Coupe* to a person who won three *Coupes* in consecutive years. There were only four drivers who ever won silver *Coupes*: they were Don Morley (Healey 3000) 1961, 1962 and 1964; René Trautmann (Citroën DS) 1960, 1962 and 1963; Paddy Hopkirk (Sunbeam Rapier and Mini Cooper) 1956, 1959 and 1965; and Jean Rolland (Alfa Romeo) 1963, 1964 and 1966. Three drivers won golden *Coupes*: Ian Appleyard (Jaguar XK) 1951, 1952 and 1953; Stirling Moss (Sunbeam Talbot) 1952, 1953 and 1954; and Jean Vinatier (Alpine Renault) 1968, 1969 and 1971 – the 1971 result was allowed to

The immortal 'Big Healey' Peter Riley and Tony Ambrose on the 1961 Alpine Rally, in the heyday of the Austin-Healey 3000.

count as there was no rally in 1970. In any case, Vinatier qualified for a silver *Coupe* with an additional Alpine *Coupe* in an R8 Renault won in 1965.

The *Coupe des Alpes* flourished and became one of the top three rallies in the world during the early 1960s. However, because it needed the high *cols* free of snow, it had to run in mid-summer and the costs of closing roads and the disruption to tourism caused by professional crews recce-ing for weeks on end brought it into difficulties that only increasing sums of money could cure. In 1970 it could not obtain permission to run and was cancelled. In 1971 the last *Coupe des Alpes* had 35 starters – not enough to qualify for the FIA Championship.

It remains, however, as a symbol of experience and fortitude, of the ability of man to pace his own efforts and that of his machine against some of the most challenging tarmac roads in Europe.

1927

MARATHON DE LA ROUTE. After organizing several car and motor-cycle events of a fairly short nature, the Royal Motor Union of Liège decided in 1927 that they needed longer events to test fully the endurance of both car and driver. Their first such event, held under the title of *Marathon de la Route*, went from Liège to Biarritz and back. All six cars that finished were equal on zero penalties and the club decided to make things harder.

So well did they succeed in that aim that, under the direction of Maurice Garot, they produced a rally that normally had few finishers and none of them unpenalized. Only on one famous occasion in 1951, when the bandleader, Johnny Claes, partnered by the father of Jacky Ickx, drove to victory in a Jaguar XK120, did the winner finish with no

133

penalty points. Claes distinguished himself further two years later when he won again in a Lancia Aurelia, but this time it was for driving almost all of the non-stop event single-handed after his co-driver fell ill. It was said of M. Garot that his ideal rally would be one with just one finisher. He never achieved that but he did get it down to single figures twice.

The big problem with this grandest and toughest of rallies was in finding countries hospitable to its open-road, endurance format. In the early 1960s Yugoslavia and Bulgaria provided a *laissez-faire* use of their roads but, with the gradual increase in tourism, even they could not allow fast cars freedom of movement in August and September. The last *Marathon* to be held on the open road was the rally to Sofia in 1964. The event name survived a further five years attached to an endurance event held at the Nürburgring, only finally to die, mourned by the rally fraternity, after the 1969 event.

Winners of the Marathon de la Route

Year	Crew	Car
Liège–Biarritz–Liège		
1927	Six cars equal on zero penalties	
Liège–Madrid–Liège		
1928	Minsart/Havelange	Bugatti 44 3000 cc
1929	Nine cars equal on zero penalties	
1930	Minsart/Reynaertz	Bugatti
Liège–Rome–Liège		
1931	Toussaint/Evrard	Bugatti 49 3300 cc
1932	Orban/Havelange	Bugatti 46 5300 cc
1933	Georges/Collon	FN 3.2 litre
	Von Guillaume/Bahr	Adler 2 litre
1934	Evrard/Trasenster	Bugatti
	Peeters/Collon	Bugatti
	Lahaye/Quatresous	Renault
	Bahr/Von Guillaume	Imperia
	Van Naemen/Canciani	Lancia
	Thirion/Bouriano	Bugatti
	Bernet/Sailer	Mercedes-Benz
1935	Trasenster/Breyre	Bugatti
	Lahaye/Quatresouse	Renault

A Triumph TR3 on the 1958 Liège–Rome–Liège, looking every inch a production sports car in the truest sense . . .

1936	Rally not held due to date dispute with Belgian authorities	
1937	Haeberle/Glockler	Hanomag
1938	Trasenster/Breyre	Bugatti
1939	Trasenster/Breyre	Bugatti
	Trevoux/Lesurque	Hotchkiss

Rally not held between 1940 and 1949 thanks to World War II

1950	Dubois/De Cortanze	Peugeot Special 1490 cc
1951	Claes/Ickx	Jaguar XK120 3442 cc
1952	Polensky/Schlutter	Porsche 356 1486 cc
1953	Claes/Trasenster	Lancia Aurelia GT 2500 cc
1954	Polensky/Linge	Porsche 356 1486 cc
1955	Gendebien/Stasse	Mercedes-Benz 300 SL
1956	Mairesse/Genin	Mercedes-Benz 300 SL
1957	Storez/Buchet	Porsche 356 1498 cc
1958	Hebert/Consten	Alfa Romeo Giuletta 1300 cc
1959	Buchet/Strahle	Porsche Carrera 1598 cc
1960	Moss P./Wisdom A.	Austin-Healey 3000

Liège–Sofia–Liège

1961	Bianchi/Harris	Citroën DS 19
1962	Böhringer/Eger	Mercedes-Benz 220 SEB
1963	Böhringer/Kaiser	Mercedes-Benz 230 SL
1964	Aaltonen/Ambrose	Austin-Healey 3000

The name **Marathon de la Route** was then applied to an event held at the Nürburgring and run for a period of 84 hours

1965	Greder/Rives	Ford Mustang 4.7 litre
1966	Vernaeve/Hedges	MGB GT 1798 cc
1967	Herrmann/Neerpasch/ Elford	Porsche 911 2 litre
1968	Linge/Glemser/ Kauhsen	Porsche 911 2 litre
1969	Kallstrom/Barbasio/ Fall	Lancia Fulvia HF 1600 cc

No further events held

1932

This was *the first year that H. J. Aldington took one of his legendary TT Replica Frazer Nash cars to the Alpine Trial* and he was rewarded with a *Coupe des Glaciers* for a penalty-free performance. He repeated that success in 1933 and 1934 which would have entitled him to a postwar *Coupe d'Or*.

1936

The Monte Carlo was won by a most extraordinary car, the Ford V8 special of the Rumanians Zamfirescu and Cristea. Based on a standard car, it had the doors and most of the rear body cut away and replaced with canvas and the spare wheels were mounted inside the wheelbase ahead of the rear wheels. There was also a device like a 'fiddle brake' used on trials cars to lock individual wheels. Cristea had practised the final driving test to perfection and, using the unique braking system with great skill, won the final test and the rally by 1.5 seconds.

1950

THE SWEDISH RALLY. The Swedish Rally started life as a Monte Carlo clone in the summer of 1950 as an event known as the Rally to the Midnight Sun. It had three starting points in the south and finished in Kiruna towards the Arctic Circle. It stayed a summer rally until 1965, having first immortalized itself by holding a special stage down a mine in Kiruna during the 1963 event.

The 1965 winter event was called the Swedish Rally, started at Orebro and finished in Stockholm. From 1966 until today the rally has been based in Karlstad, except for the start in 1971 which went to Gothenberg to honour its 350th anniversary. One notable experiment was carried out in 1973 when studded tyres were banned; it has not been repeated, though the continued use of studded tyres on the snow-ploughed forest roads often breaks through the ice and the rally runs virtually on gravel.

It has been won by Swedes from its inception until 1981, when Hannu Mikkola gave Audi its first World Championship win and the first win for four-wheel drive. The most successful driver is Stig Blomqvist who scooped a hat-trick of victories for Saab in 1971–3, won it again for them in 1977 and 1979 and then added two victories for Audi in 1982 and 1984.

Early RAC Rallies were gentle affairs, with no hard forest stages, but pylon tests at seaside resorts determined results. (Kathleen, Countess of Drogheda, driving an SS1 in braking tests in 1932.)

Winners of the Swedish Rally

Year	Crew	Car
1950	Cederbaum/Sohlberg	BMW 328
1951	Bengtsson/Zetterberg	Talbot Lago
1952	Persson/Norrby	Porsche 1500
1953	Nottorp/Jonsson	Porsche 1500
1954	Hammarlund/Petterson	Porsche 1500
1955	Borgefors/Gustavsson	Porsche 1500
1956	Bengtsson/Righard	VW 1200
1957	Jansson/Jansson	Volvo PV444
1958	Andersson/Jacobson	Volvo PV444
1959	Carlsson/Pavoni	Saab 93
1960	Skogh/Skogh	Saab 96
1961	Skogh/Skogh	Saab 96
1962	Soderstrom/Olsson	Mini Cooper S
1963	Jansson/Peterson	Porsche Carrera
1964	Trana/Thermaenius	Volvo PV544
1965	Trana/Thermaenius	Volvo PV544
1966	Andersson/Svedberg	Saab 96
1967	Soderstrom/Palm	Lotus-Cortina
1968	Waldegaard/Helmer	Porsche 911T
1969	Waldegaard/Helmer	Porsche 911S
1970	Waldegaard/Helmer	Porsche 911S
1971	Blomqvist/Hertz	Saab 96 V4
1972	Blomqvist/Hertz	Saab 96 V4
1973	Blomqvist/Hertz	Saab 96 V4
1974	Rally cancelled due to fuel crisis	
1975	Waldegaard/Thorselius	Lancia Stratos
1976	Eklund/Cederberg	Saab 96 V4
1977	Blomqvist/Sylvan	Saab 99 EMS
1978	Waldegaard/Thorselius	Ford Escort RS
1979	Blomqvist/Cederberg	Saab 99 Turbo
1980	Kullang/Berglund	Opel Ascona 400
1981	Mikkola/Hertz	Audi Quattro A1
1982	Blomqvist/Cederberg	Audi Quattro A1
1983	Mikkola/Hertz	Audi Quattro A2
1984	Blomqvist/Cederberg	Audi Quattro A2
1985	Vatanen/Harryman	Peugeot 205 T16
1986	Kankkunen/Piironen	Peugeot 205 T16
1987	Salonen/Harjanne	Mazda 323 4WD

1951

THE RAC RALLY. From 1932 until 1939 the RAC held a national rally called the RAC Rally. This was the successor to the old 1000 Miles Trial. It had no overall classification and the event did not feature hard motoring on public roads but was settled by 'tests' held normally at the finish. After World War II it was revived in 1951 as an international rally, but was still decided by what were really manoeuvrability tests. As it progressed through the 1950s, hill climbs and difficult navigation sections were added. In 1957 the rally missed a year, thanks to Suez, while in 1958 snow in March led the organizers to shift the date to November for 1959, when snow drifts in Scotland led to protests and problems for the organizers.

It was that same year that Jack Kemsley took up the organization and by 1961 he had moved the event into the forests, where it has largely stayed ever since. It was won by Scandinavian drivers for 11 straight years until Roger Clark took a home win in 1972; his second win, in 1976, has been the only other one by a non-Scandinavian. In recent years, Hannu Mikkola has been the most successful driver on the event, winning it four times (1978, 1979, 1981 and 1982) and finishing second four times (1977, 1980, 1983 and 1984).

The rally has chosen a host of starting places around Britain, including London, to satisfy commercial and regional pressures, but most recently has favoured York, Chester, Bath and Harrogate.

Winners of the RAC Rally

Year	Crew	Car
1951	Appleyard/Mrs Appleyard	Jaguar XJ120
1952	Imhof/Mrs Frayling	Allard Cadillac J2
1953	Appleyard/Mrs Appleyard	Jaguar XJ120
1954	Wallwark/Brookes	Triumph TR2
1955	Ray/Horrocks	Standard 10
1956	Sims/Ambrose	Aston Martin DB2
1957	Cancelled due to Suez crisis	
1958	Harper/Deane	Sunbeam Rapier Mk1
1959	Burgess/Croft-Pearson	Ford Zephyr Mk2
1960	Carlsson/Turner	Saab 96
1961	Carlsson/Brown	Saab 96
1962	Carlsson/Stone	Saab 96
1963	Trana/Lindstrom	Volvo PV544
1964	Trana/Thermaenius	Volvo PV544
1965	Aaltonen/Ambrose	Mini Cooper S 1275 cc
1966	Soderstrom/Palm	Lotus-Cortina Mk1
1967	Cancelled due to foot-and-mouth disease	
1968	Lampinen/Davenport	Saab 96 V4
1969	Kallstrom/Haggbom	Lancia Fulvia 1.6 litre
1970	Kallstrom/Haggbom	Lancia Fulvia 1.6 litre
1971	Blomqvist/Hertz	Saab 96 V4
1972	Clark/Mason	Ford Escort RS
1973	Makinen/Liddon	Ford Escort RS
1974	Makinen/Liddon	Ford Escort RS
1975	Makinen/Liddon	Ford Escort RS

Salonen's winning Peugeot 205T16 on the 1986 Lombard RAC Rally is far removed from the cars (and scenery) of half a century earlier.

1976	Clark/Pegg	Ford Escort RS
1977	Waldegaard/Thorselius	Ford Escort RS
1978	Mikkola/Hertz	Ford Escort RS
1979	Mikkola/Hertz	Ford Escort RS
1980	Henri Toivonen/White	Sunbeam Talbot Lotus
1981	Mikkola/Hertz	Audi Quattro
1982	Mikkola/Hertz	Audi Quattro
1983	Blomqvist/Cederberg	Audi Quattro A1
1984	Vatanen/Harryman	Peugeot 205 T16
1985	Henri Toivonen/Wilson	Lancia Delta S4
1986	Salonen/Harjanne	Peugeot 205 T16

THE 1000 LAKES RALLY. The first international 1000 Lakes Rally was the brainchild of those Finns who had been to the postwar Monte Carlo rallies. They called their event the *Jyvaskylan Suurajot* (Grand Prix of Jyvaskyla), since it was centred on the town of Jyvaskyla in central Finland where it is still based. It was always a summer event and within two years it was using special stages over the famous jumping dirt roads for which the area is famous.

In the late 1950s works teams started to come from abroad and won the event a couple of times, but the Finns soon re-established their grip on it and only Stig Blomqvist (1971) has managed to wrest it from them. Certainly there is a special skill in negotiating the roller-coaster roads and committing to memory or to paper the way each crest and bend follows the other. Simo Lampinen, Timo Makinen, Hannu Mikkola, Markku Alen and now Timo Salonen have won the rally 20 times between them since 1960. The only encroachment on the Finnish domination has been in their occasional use of British or Swedish co-drivers.

Winners of the 1000 Lakes Rally

Year	Crew	Car
1951	Karlsson/Mattila	Austin Atlantic
1952	Elo/Nuortila	Peugeot 203
1953	Hietanen/Hixen	Allard
1954	Kalpala/Kalpala	Dyna Panhard
1955	Elo/Nuortila	Peugeot 403
1956	Kalpala/Kalpala	Donau
1957	Carlsson/Pavoni	Saab 93
1958	Kalpala/Kalpala	Alfa Romeo
1959	Callbo/Nurmimaa	Volvo
1960	Bremer/Lampi	Saab 96
1961	Aaltonen/Nurmimaa	Mercedes-Benz 220SE
1962	Toivonen/Kallio	Citroën DS 19
1963	Lampinen/Ahava	Saab 96
1964	Lampinen/Ahava	Saab 96
1965	Makinen/Keskitalo	Mini Cooper S
1966	Makinen/Keskitalo	Mini Cooper S
1967	Makinen/Keskitalo	Mini Cooper S
1968	Mikkola/Jarvi	Ford Escort TC
1969	Mikkola/Jarvi	Ford Escort TC
1970	Mikkola/Palm	Ford Escort TC
1971	Blomqvist/Hertz	Saab 96 V4
1972	Lampinen/Sohlberg	Saab 96 V4
1973	Makinen/Liddon	Ford Escort RS
1974	Mikkola/Davenport	Ford Escort RS
1975	Mikkola/Aho	Toyota Corolla
1976	Alen/Kivimaki	Fiat Abarth 131
1977	Hamalainen/Tiukkanen	Ford Escort RS
1978	Alen/Kivimaki	Fiat Abarth 131
1979	Alen/Kivimaki	Fiat Abarth 131
1980	Alen/Kivimaki	Fiat Abarth 131
1981	Vatanen/Richards	Ford Escort RS
1982	Mikkola/Hertz	Audi Quattro
1983	Mikkola/Hertz	Audi Quattro
1984	Vatanen/Harryman	Peugeot 205 Turbo 16
1985	Salonen/Harjanne	Peugeot 205 Turbo 16
1986	Salonen/Harjanne	Peugeot 205 Turbo 16

1952

British rally fans had plenty to shout about when *Sydney Allard won the Monte Carlo Rally* in a P-type saloon bearing his own name and powered by a 4.3 litre American V8. After that, big engines, and V8s in particular, went out of fashion as rally winners, partly due to the Monte formulae. In 1964 Ford America came with V8 Falcons and one, driven by Bo Ljungfeldt, came second overall. In 1965 Peter Harper survived the blizzard to put a V8 Sunbeam Tiger in fourth place, but since then the largest engine to win a Monte Carlo has been the 3-litre Porsche of Jean-Pierre Nicolas in 1978. Henri Greder used one of the Falcons from the Monte Carlo to win the Geneva Rally in 1964.

1953

THE SAFARI RALLY. To commemorate the coronation of Queen Elizabeth II, rally enthusiasts in Nairobi secured the sponsorship of a Kenyan newspaper and ran an event called the Coronation Safari. There were starting points in Kenya, Uganda and Tanzania along Monte Carlo lines, but the classes for the cars were based on East African price rather than cubic capacity. There were no special stages, since the African roads were enough, and so it has remained until today.

In 1955 it was sanctioned by the RAC as Kenya had no motor sport body, and finally went international in 1957, the same year that it moved its date to Easter so that volunteer workers on the rally could run it during the holiday. It changed its name to the East African Safari in 1960 and adopted the international cubic capacity class system. Already it was on the calendar for European manufacturers keen to sell cars in Africa and establish at home a reputation for solid, rugged reliability. Ford, Rootes and Renault were first amongst these, to be followed by Saab, BMC and Citroën. The one thing that they all discovered was that, every time, it was a local driver that won. Admittedly, Bert Shankland broke the Kenyan run with his win in 1966, but he was from nearby Tanzania. It grew to be one of the greatest challenges in rallying; who would be the first European to win the Safari? Carlsson, Hopkirk, Riley, Harper, Harrison, Nicolas (*père*), Consten, Marang, Aaltonen, Makinen, Trana, Pat Moss, Anderson, Verrier, Soderstrom, Lampinen, Zasada, Kallstrom, Munari, Böhringer, Glemser – over a period of 13 years they came, they saw and they lost. It was left to Hannu Mikkola to put his name in the record books with a win for Ford in 1972.

Twice the rally has had only seven finishers, in 1963 and 1968, both times due to heavy rains and on both occasions it was won by Nick Nowicki in a Peugeot 404.

In 1974 the rally was run entirely in Kenya and

Mikkola in an almost improbably clean Ford Escort in East Africa in 1972. Nevertheless, this is the car in which he won that year's Safari.

Japanese cars have an excellent record on the modern Safari rally. This is the Colt Lancer of three times Safari winner, Joginder Singh, seen after his win in 1974 with David Doig.

has stayed that way ever since. To correspond, the title was shortened to Safari Rally in 1975. The most successful driver is Shekhar Mehta with a win for Datsun in 1973 (when he tied on penalties with Harry Kallstrom in another Datsun and the tie was resolved on the first to incur penalty) and his four straight wins, also in Datsuns, from 1979 to 1982. The win by the Toyota Celica Twin Cam Turbo in 1984 was unique in that it was the team's first attempt at the Safari, though team boss Ove Andersson had won it for Peugeot in 1975 and Henry Liddon, his number two, had been competing there since 1965. Both Bjorn Waldegaard (1977, 1984 and 1986) and Joginder Singh (1965, 1974 and 1976) have won the rally three times.

In the World Championship for Makes, the Safari survives as the only example of a rally decided on open roads without special stages or timing to the second. It was also the only rally in the Championship not to be won by a four-wheel-drive car in 1986.

Winners of the Safari Rally

Year	Crew	Car	Class
1953	No overall winner		
	A. Dix/J. Larsen	VW 1200	A
	J. Airth/R. Collinge	Standard Vanguard	B
	D. Marwaha/V. Preston	Tatra T600	C
	J. Manussis/K. Boyes	Chevrolet	D
1954	D. P. Marwaha/ V. Preston	VW 1200	
1955	D. P. Marwaha/ V. Preston	Ford Zephyr	
1956	E. Cecil/A. Vickers	DKW	
1957	A. Hofmann/A. Burton	VW 1200	
1958	No overall winner		
	T. Brooke/P. Hughes	Ford Anglia	Impala
	E. Temple-Boreham/ M. Armstrong	Auto Union 1000	Leopard

	A. Kopperud/ K. Kopperud	Ford Zephyr Mk2	Lion
1959	W. Fritschy/J. Ellis	Mercedes-Benz	
1960	W. Fritschy/J. Ellis	Mercedes-Benz	
1961	J. Manussis/ W. Coleridge/ D. Beckett	Mercedes-Benz 220	
1962	T. Fjastad/V. Schmider	VW 1200	
1963	Z. Nowicki/P. Cliff	Peugeot 404	
1964	P. Hughes/B. Young	Ford Cortina GT	
1965	J. Singh/J. Singh	Volvo PV544	
1966	B. Shankland/ C. Rothwell	Peugeot 404	
1967	B. Shankland/ C. Rothwell	Peugeot 404	
1968	Z. Nowicki/P. Cliff	Peugeot 404	
1969	R. Hillyar/J. Aird	Ford Taunus 20 MRS	
1970	E. Hermann/H. Schuller	Datsun 1600 SSS	
1971	E. Hermann/H. Schuller	Datsun 240Z	
1972	H. Mikkola/G. Palm	Ford Escort RS	
1973	S. Mehta/L. Drews	Datsun 240Z	
1974	J. Singh/D. Doig	Colt Lancer	
1975	O. Andersson/A. Hertz	Peugeot 504	
1976	J. Singh/D. Doig	Colt Lancer	
1977	B. Waldegaard/ H. Thorselius	Ford Escort RS	
1978	J-P. Nicolas/ J-C. Lefèbvre	Peugeot 504 V6 Coupé	
1979	S. Mehta/M. Doughty	Datsun 160 J	
1980	S. Mehta/M. Doughty	Datsun 160 J	
1981	S. Mehta/M. Doughty	Datsun Violet GT	
1982	S. Mehta/M. Doughty	Nissan Violet GT	
1983	A. Vatanen/ T. Harryman	Opel Ascona 400	
1984	B. Waldegaard/ H. Thorselius	Toyota Celica TC Turbo	
1985	J. Kankkunen/ F. Gallagher	Toyota Celica TC Turbo	
1986	Waldegaard/Gallagher	Toyota Celica TC Turbo	

THE ACROPOLIS RALLY. With rallies springing up all over postwar Europe, it was no surprise to find the Acropolis Rally amongst them. With the most gorgeous settings in Europe and some of the toughest rally roads, the Acropolis has always been a challenge and a pleasure.

Among its early winners was Johnny Pezmazoglou, the Opel importer, who had won the original ELPA national rally held in 1952 as a precursor of the international event. Pezmazoglou had an unbroken record of competing in the Acropolis from 1953 until 1985. It became a very popular rally

Walter Rohrl can have had little time for the Greek scenery as he forced his supercharged Lancia on towards victory in the 1983 Acropolis Rally.

with foreign teams and private competitors who were offered help by the Greek Tourist agency.

By the early 1960s it had established its name and was part of the championship year. In 1966, Paddy Hopkirk lost, due to a penalty for alleged illegal servicing, but returned in 1967 finally to give the Mini Cooper the victory for which it had striven for five years. In 1975 Walter Röhrl gave Opel its first World Championship win and went on to be the most successful driver on the Acropolis, having won it three times – the other two were 1978 (Fiat) and 1983 (Lancia).

Winners of the Acropolis Rally

Year	Crew	Car
1953	Papamichael/Dimitracos	Jaguar XK120
1954	Papadoupoulos/Dimitracos	Opel Rekord
1955	Pezmazoglou/Papandreou	Opel Kapitan
1956	Schock/Möll	Mercedes-Benz 300SL
1957	Estager/Mme Estager	Ferrari 250 GT
1958	Villoresi/Basadonna	Lancia Aurelia GT
1959	Levy/Wenscher	Auto Union 1000
1960	Schock/Möll	Mercedes-Benz 220SE
1961	Carlsson/Karlsson	Saab 96
1962	Böhringer/Lang	Mercedes-Benz 220SE
1963	Böhringer/Knoll	Mercedes-Benz 220SE
1964	Trana/Thermaenius	Volvo PV544
1965	Skogh/Berggren	Volvo 122S
1966	Soderstrom/Palm	Lotus Cortina
1967	Hopkirk/Crellin	Mini Cooper S
1968	Clark/Porter	Ford Escort Twin Cam
1969	Toivonen/Kolari	Porsche 911S
1970	Therier/Callewaert	Alpine Renault A110
1971	Andersson/Hertz	Alpine Renault A110
1972	Lindberg/Eisendle	Fiat 124 Spyder
1973	Therier/Delferrier	Alpine Renault A110
1974	Rally cancelled due to petrol crisis	
1975	Röhrl/Berger	Opel Ascona 1.9
1976	Kallstrom/Andersson	Datsun 160J
1977	Waldegaard/Thorselius	Ford Escort RS
1978	Röhrl/Geistdorfer	Fiat Abarth 131
1979	Waldegaard/Thorselius	Ford Escort RS
1980	Vatanen/Richards	Ford Escort RS
1981	Vatanen/Richards	Ford Escort RS
1982	Mlles Mouton/Pons	Audi Quattro A1
1983	Röhrl/Geistdorfer	Lancia Rallye 037
1984	Blomqvist/Cederberg	Audi Quattro A2
1985	Salonen/Harjanne	Peugeot 205 T16
1986	Kankkunen/Piironen	Peugeot 205 T16

Bjorn Waldegard scattering stones in a Toyota Celica on the Acropolis Rally in 1981.

The Greek roads were little different 20 years earlier, when Gunnar Andersson slid his dumpy Volvo PV544 through a dirt road hairpin on the Acropolis.

THE EUROPEAN RALLY CHAMPIONSHIP FOR DRIVERS. The European Rally Championship for Drivers was created in 1953 and survives to this day. To start with, it was the only major rally championship recognized by the governing body, the CSI, but it has now been surpassed in importance by the World Rally Championship Drivers' title. To start with, the European Championship had the pick of the European events but for obscure reasons often ignored major events like the Liège. When the major European rallies became aspirants for inclusion in the World series, the European Championship then spread itself over some 40-odd lesser events and categorized them so that the points scored on each event are proportional to their perceived status.

In the period immediately prior to the creation of the World series in 1973, the European Championship reached its zenith in importance, with drivers like Harry Kallstrom, Pauli Toivonen and Jean-Claude Andruet winning major events and the Championship. Since then, it has been the domain of works-assisted teams with only a few drivers seriously following the entire Championship.

Winners of the European Rally Championship

Year	Driver	Car	Group
1953	H. Polensky	Porsche	
1954	W. Schluter	DKW	
1955	W. Engel	Mercedes-Benz	
1956	W. Schock	Mercedes-Benz	
1957	R. Hopfen	Saab and Borgward	
1958	G. Andersson	Volvo	
1959	P. Coltelloni	Citroën and Alfa Romeo	
1960	W. Schock	Mercedes-Benz	
1961	H-J. Walter	Porsche 356	
1962	E. Böhringer	Mercedes-Benz	
1963	G. Andersson	Volvo	
1964	T. Trana	Volvo	
1965	R. Aaltonen	BMC Mini Cooper S	
1966	L. Nasenius	Opel Rekord	1
	S. Zasada	Porsche 911 T	2
	G. Klass	Porsche 911 S	3
1967	S. Zasada	Porsche 912	1
	B. Soderstrom	Ford Lotus Cortina	2
	V. Elford	Porsche 911 S	3
1968	P. Toivonen	Porsche 911 S	
1969	H. Kallstrom	Lancia Fulvia HF	
1970	J-C. Andruet	Alpine Renault A110	
1971	S. Zasada	BMW 2002	
1972	R. Pinto	Fiat 124 Abarth Spyder	
1973	S. Munari	Lancia Stratos	
1974	W. Röhrl	Opel Kadett	
1975	M. Verini	Fiat Abarth	
1976	B. Darniche	Lancia Stratos	
1977	B. Darniche	Fiat Abarth 131	
1978	T. Carello	Lancia Stratos	
1979	J. Kleint	Opel Kadett GTE	
1980	A. Zanini	Porsche 911	
1981	A. Vudafieri	Fiat Abarth 131	
1982	T. Fassina	Opel Ascona 400	
1983	M. Biasion	Lancia Rallye 037	
1984	C. Capone	Lancia Rallye 037	
1985	D. Cerrato	Lancia Rallye 037	
1986	F. Tabaton	Lancia Delta S4	

Winners of the European Championship Ladies Award

Year	Driver	Car
1972	M-C. Beaumont	Opel
1973	D. Tominz	Fiat Abarth
1974	D. Tominz	Fiat Abarth
1975	M. Mouton	Alpine Renault A110
1976	C. Dacremont	Lancia and Alpine Renault
1977	M. Mouton	Porsche 911 SC
1978	M. Mouton	Fiat Abarth 131
1979	M. Mouton	Fiat Abarth 131
1980	M. Mouton	Fiat Abarth 131
1981	A. Mandelli	Fiat Abarth 131
1982	A. Mandelli	Fiat Abarth 131
1983	A. Mandelli	Fiat Abarth 131
1984	A. Mandelli	Lancia Rallye 037
1985	Not awarded	
1986	Not awarded	

1956

THE TOUR DE CORSE. The first International *Tour de Corse* was won by a ladies crew, Mmes Thirion and Ferrier in a Renault Dauphine. Its original title was the Rally of the Ten Thousand Corners which may have been accurate in the beginning but was soon to be exceeded as the severity and length of the event increased. Traditionally held in November, at the end of the tourist season, it often encountered snow and, in 1961, René Trautmann won the event by being in the lead when it was stopped on the *Col de Vergio* with snowdrifts.

To emphasize its toughness, an award was donated each year to the crew that should complete the rally without road penalty. This accumulated each year that it was not claimed. The men who came closest to collecting the by-then enormous sum were Sandro Munari and Luciano Lombardini whose Lancia Fulvia lost but a single minute on the road in 1967.

Since becoming a World Championship event at the inception in 1973, the *Tour de Corse* has become the host to epic battles between French and Italian teams. So far the score is nine to the Italians and four to the French with a lone Porsche victory for Frenchman Jean-Luc Therier, in 1980. In 1986 the sad accident which claimed the lives of Henri Toivonen and Sergio Cresto in the Lancia Delta S4 triggered off the Group B controversy which still rages.

Winners of the Tour de Corse

Year	Crew	Car
1956	Mmes Thirion/Ferrier	Renault Dauphine
1957	Nicol/de Lageneste	Alfa Romeo Guilietta
1958	Monraisse/Feret	Renault Dauphine
1959	Orsini/Canonici	Renault Dauphine
1960	Strahle/Linge	Porsche SC90
1961	Trautmann/Ogier	Citroën DS 19
1962	Orsini/Canonici	Renault Dauphine
1963	Trautmann/Chabert	Citroën DS 19
1964	Vinatier/Masson	Renault 8 Gordini
1965	Orsini/Canonici	Renault 8 Gordini
1966	Piot/Jacob	Renault 8 Gordini
1967	Munari/Lombardini	Lancia Fulvia HF
1968	Andruet/Gelin	Alpine Renault A110
1969	Larrousse/Gelin	Porsche 911R
1970	Darniche/Demange	Alpine Renault A110
1971	Rally cancelled for financial reasons	
1972	Andruet/'Biche'	Alpine Renault A110
1973	Nicolas/Vial	Alpine Renault A110
1974	Andruet/'Biche'	Lancia Stratos
1975	Darniche/Mahe	Lancia Stratos
1976	Munari/Maiga	Lancia Stratos
1977	Darniche/Mahe	Fiat Abarth 131
1978	Darniche/Mahe	Fiat Abarth 131
1979	Darniche/Mahe	Lancia Stratos
1980	Therier/Vial	Porsche 911S
1981	Darniche/Mahe	Lancia Stratos
1982	Ragnotti/Andrie	Renault 5 Turbo
1983	Alen/Kivimaki	Lancia Rallye 037
1984	Alen/Kivimaki	Lancia Rallye 037
1985	Ragnotti/Thimonier	Renault Maxi 5 Turbo
1986	Saby/Fauchille	Peugeot 205 Turbo 16

1959

Pat Moss won the first of eight outstanding *Coupe des Dames* on the Monte Carlo Rally, spanning a period from 1959 until 1972. Her co-drivers and cars were as follows: Ann Wisdom, Austin A40 (1959–60); Ann Wisdom, Morris Cooper (1962); Ursula Wirth, Saab 96 (1964); Liz Nystrom, Saab 96 (1965); Liz Nystrom, Lancia Fulvia (1968–9); Liz Crellin, Alpine A110 (1972).

1960

The most memorable result ever from a ladies crew was when the world's toughest rally, Liège–Rome–Liège, was won by Pat Moss and Ann Wisdom in a factory-entered Austin-Healey 3000. It was also the first time that a European Championship rally had been won by a ladies team, and it was the first time that this most difficult of rallies had been won by a British crew or car.

1961

SAN REMO RALLY. Possibly to rival that other Mediterranean casino town, San Remo inaugurated in 1961 its International *Rallye dei Fiori* (Rally of the Flowers). It marked an upsurge of interest in rallying within Italy which has survived 25 years and was provoked by the loss of events like the *Mille Miglia*.

International interest grew, and teams like Saab, Ford and Renault came to join the local Lancias. By 1968, when it was a counter for the European Championship, it started to be called the San Remo Rally. There was a period when it combined with the Sestriere Rally to become the Rally of Italy – 1970–2 – but then it was re-established as the San Remo and as a World Championship rally.

Its doses of controversy have been fairly well spaced: Vic Elford's Ford was disqualified from victory in 1966 (its homologation form was wrong and it did not comply with it!); then all the works Lancias ran into the same fuel feed problem within kilometres of the start in 1970 and sabotage was suspected: finally, in 1986, the Peugeot works team was excluded during the rally, a decision ruled to have been wrong and the San Remo results were struck from the World Championship results.

On the more positive side, the 1969 event saw Lancia perform the first planned tyre change in the middle of a special stage, 1974 saw the Lancia Stratos win its first World event after homologation, and, in 1981, the San Remo was the first World Championship rally to be won by a lady,

Michele Mouton in an Audi. Markku Alen is the most successful driver having won it three times (1978, 1983 and 1986).

Winners of the San Remo Rally

Year	Crew	Car
1961	De Villa/De Villa	Alfa Romeo Giulietta TI
1962	Frescobaldi/Malinconi	Lancia Flavia
1963	Patria/Orengo	Lancia Fulvia Coupé
1964	Carlsson/Palm	Saab 96 Sport
1965	Cella/Gamenara	Lancia Fulvia
1966	Cella/Lombardini	Lancia Fulvia HF
1967	Piot/Roure	Renault R8 Gordini
1968	Toivonen/Tiukkanen	Porsche 911 T
1969	Kallstrom/Haggbom	Lancia Fulvia HF
1970	Therier/Callewaert	Alpine Renault A110
1971	Andersson/Nash	Alpine Renault A110
1972	Ballestrière/Bernacchini	Lancia Fulvia 1600 HF
1973	Therier/Jaubert	Alpine Renault A110
1974	Munari/Manucci	Lancia Stratos
1975	Waldegaard/Thorselius	Lancia Stratos
1976	Waldegaard/Thorselius	Lancia Stratos
1977	Andruet/Delferrier	Fiat Abarth 131
1978	Alen/Kivimaki	Lancia Stratos
1979	'Tony'/Mannini	Lancia Stratos
1980	Röhrl/Geistdorfer	Fiat Abarth 131
1981	Mlles Mouton/Pons	Audi Quattro
1982	Blomqvist/Cederberg	Audi Quattro
1983	Alen/Kivimaki	Lancia Rallye 037
1984	Vatanen/Harryman	Peugeot 205 Turbo 16
1985	Röhrl/Geistdorfer	Audi Sport Quattro E2
1986	Alen/Kivimaki	Lancia Delta S4

1962

It is not often that *the same make and model of car wins major races and rallies* in the same year, but in 1962 Sunbeam Rapier MkIIIs won the Scottish Rally (Andrew Cowan) and the Circuit of Ireland Rally (Paddy Hopkirk) and the Touring Car race supporting the Belgian GP at Spa (Lucien Bianchi).

1963

In the absence of a true world championship from FIA, the *RAC decided to award a 'World Cup' for manufacturers*. It comprised five events, the Liège–Sofia–Liège, Midnight Sun, RAC, Canadian Shell 4000 and the East African Safari. It was won by Ford using the Cortina GT and the Anglia on Safari.

The *Tour de France Automobile was won for the fifth consecutive time by a Jaguar*. It was won in 1959 by Ramos in a 3.4 MkI and then an incredible four times in a row by Bernard Consten in Jaguar 3.8 MkIIs.

The first international rally to be won by a plastic-bodied car was also the first major win for the products of Jean Redelé's firm of Automobiles Alpine. The rally was the *Rallye des Lions* in

Jaguar Mk 2 on the Mont Ventoux hill climb in the Tour de France, where Jaguars won the touring category 1959–63.

France and the 1000 cc Alpine 108 was driven by Jose Rosinski and navigated by a lady, Michele Dubosc.

1964

The smallest car to ever win a European Championship rally was the 650 cc Steyr Puch of Sobieslaw Zasada and his wife, Eva, on the Polish Rally of 1964.

1965

In one of the most amazing exclusions from a rally for technical reasons, Peter Harper's works Sunbeam Tiger was thrown out from the *Coupe des Alpes* for having exhaust valves that were too small in diameter compared with its homologation form.

The result of the RAC Rally – and of the European Rally Championship – was *decided on a small hill in Cropton forest*. It was covered in snow and many cars were stuck including the Healey 3000 of Timo Makinen. The Mini Cooper of Rauno Aaltonen passed him on the hill and maintained that advantage to the end of the rally.

1966

Jim Clark set the rally world talking when he took a works Lotus-Cortina MkI on the RAC Rally and kept it amongst the leaders. They were all relieved when first he had one small accident in Scotland (where else) and then went off permanently on an English stage.

1967

THE PORTUGAL RALLY. Portugal's enthusiasm for motor sport and its need for tourism were linked when TAP, the Portuguese airline, sponsored a rally in 1967. With several starting points and a common run into Lisbon featuring navigational sections and special stages, it was firmly following in the Monte Carlo tradition. Its large prize fund and generous support for foreign entries soon brought prestige entries and, in only its second year, it was won by Tony Fall with Paddy Hopkirk second. By the time the World Rally Championship was instigated in 1972, it was worthy of a place in that and has stayed there ever since.

It has had its problems, with Tony Fall being excluded after the finish in 1969 for allegedly carrying a passenger – his wife – on part of the route – the last yards to the last time control. Regrettably, in 1986 it came back to controversy when a car crashed on the first stage, killing four spectators, and the factory drivers went on strike because they said that the spectators were not properly controlled.

It did away with the navigation in 1972 and with the concentration runs for 1974 and has been a straightforward special-stage rally ever since. Through the 1970s it concentrated these on rough and rugged dirt roads but it has been seen of late to be including more tarmac with the intention

Well, in this situation that right front wheel would probably not have been working. The Fiat 131 Abarth was a versatile car which gained the world championship for Fiat in 1977, 1978 and 1980, and in that year Walter Rohrl (here being energetic in a Rally of Portugal) drove them to win the individual title.

of coming nearer to the 50–50 of San Remo. Its sponsors since 1975 have been the port wine companies.

The most successful driver here is Markku Alen with four wins (1975, 1977, 1978 and 1981), all at the wheel of Fiats, and one with Lancia (1987).

Winners of the Portugal Rally

Year	Crew	Car
1967	Albino/Pereira	Renault 8 Gordini
1968	Fall/Crellin	Lancia Fulvia HF
1969	Romaozinho/'Jocames'	Citroën DS 21
1970	Lampinen/Davenport	Lancia Fulvia HF
1971	Nicolas/Todt	Alpine Renault A110
1972	Warmbold/Davenport	BMW 2002 TI
1973	Therier/Jaubert	Alpine Renault A110
1974	Pinto/Bernacchini	Fiat Abarth 124
1975	Alen/Kivimaki	Fiat Abarth 124
1976	Munari/Maiga	Lancia Stratos
1977	Alen/Kivimaki	Fiat Abarth 131
1978	Alen/Kivimaki	Fiat Abarth 131
1979	Mikkola/Hertz	Ford Escort RS
1980	Röhrl/Geistdorfer	Fiat Abarth 131
1981	Alen/Kivimaki	Fiat Abarth 131
1982	Mlles Mouton/Pons	Audi Quattro A1
1983	Mikkola/Hertz	Audi Quattro A2
1984	Mikkola/Hertz	Audi Quattro A2
1985	Salonen/Harjanne	Peugeot 205 T16
1986	Moutinho/Fortes	Renault 5 Turbo
1987	Alen/Kivimaki	Lancia Delta HF

The RAC Rally was cancelled 12 hours before it was due to start thanks to an outbreak of foot-and-mouth disease in Britain.

1968

The first plastic-bodied car to win a European Championship rally was the Alpine Renault A110 with a 1300 cc engine and driven by Jean Vinatier on the Czechoslovakian *Rallye Vltava*.

The FIA introduced *an International Rally Championship for Makes* comprising nine major rallies. The majority were in Europe but by the time it was ready to become the World Rally Championship in 1973, three of those nine were from outside (Safari, Morocco and Press-on-Regardless). Winners: **1968** Ford of Great Britain; **1969** Ford of Europe; **1970** Porsche; **1971** Alpine Renault; **1972** Lancia. It was largely ignored by the press since it was neither a world nor drivers' championship.

Gerard Larrousse was *set to win the first major rally for Alpine Renault* with his A110 1300 cc on the Monte Carlo Rally when spectators threw snow on the Turini stage and he went off, giving the victory to Vic Elford's Porsche. The French team had to wait until Jean Vinatier won the *Coupe des Alpes* that same year to claim their first major win.

1970

Bob Neyret won one rally whilst competing on another. He took a break between the European and South American sections of the World Cup (London to Mexico) rally to enter the Moroccan rally in a works Citroën and won it outright.

1971

One of few appearances by the Porsche 914/6 was on the Monte Carlo Rally in the hands of Bjorn Waldegaard, who had won the two previous Montes with a Porsche 911. He did not like the neutral handling and finished third equal with Jean-Claude Andruet's Alpine Renault A110.

The Renault Alpine 310 first appeared in production in this year, but it was not until 1974 that this 1600 cc successor to the World Championship winning A110 won its first rally. This was the Vercors–Vivarais where it was driven by Bernard Darniche/Alain Mahe. The 310 was later produced with a Renault V6 engine, of which the first were made in 1976. This model won its first international rally with Guy Frequelin at the wheel on the *Criterium Neige et Glace* in 1977.

The Ford GT 70 made its debut appearance on the *Ronde Cevenole* in France, driven by Roger Clark. It was a prototype with a 2.9-litre V6 engine and retired with a broken push-rod. The GT 70 later got a 2-litre BDA engine with more power and less weight and in that form did the *Tour de France* the following year with Francois Mazet, but crashed on the fourth test. His co-driver was Jean Todt, later to be head of Peugeot's competition department.

1972

The Acropolis Rally only inserted one brief halt in its 53-hour northern loop and consequently most crews were falling asleep before getting back to Athens. One co-driver even fell asleep while drinking a bottle of lemonade in the car! This and other incidents led to the formation of the Sleeping Co-drivers Association whose first act was to lobby for proper rest halts.

The ultimate in severity – the Bandama Rally, shortly to become the Ivory Coast Rally – *had no finishers*. Actually one car, the Peugeot 504 of Tony Fall, did finish within the time limits but then the Renault team protested and the results of the event were scrapped. Shekhar Mehta in a Datsun 240Z did complete the route but was definitely out of time. There had been 52 starters, most of whom described the rally schedule as 'ludicrous'.

The World Championship for Rallies

Some 61 years after the first Monte Carlo Rally had been held, the International Sporting Commission (CSI) of the *Fédération Internationale de l'Automobile* (FIA) decided that rallying was worth its own world championship. They changed the old International Rally Championship for Makes into a properly titled World Championship for Rallies. The one thing they did forget was to create a drivers' section of this World Championship which, until 1977, was exclusively for manufacturers.

Rallies and winners of the World Rally Championship

1973

Rally	Crew	Car
Monte Carlo	Andruet/'Biche'	Alpine Renault A110
Sweden	Blomqvist/Hertz	Saab 96 V4
Portugal	Therier/Jaubert	Alpine Renault A110
Safari	Mehta/Drews	Datsun 240Z
Morocco	Darniche/Mahe	Alpine Renault A110
Acropolis	Therier/Delferrier	Alpine Renault A110
Poland	Warmbold/Todt	Fiat Abarth 124 Spyder
1000 Lakes	Makinen/Liddon	Ford Escort RS
Austria	Warmbold/Todt	BMW 2002 Tli
San Remo	Therier/Jaubert	Alpine Renault A110
USA	Boyce/Woods	Toyota Corolla 1600
RAC Rally	Makinen/Liddon	Ford Escort RS
Corsica	Nicolas/Vial	Alpine Renault A110

World Champion Manufacturer, Alpine Renault

1974

Rally	Crew	Car
Monte Carlo	Cancelled due to petrol crisis	
Sweden	Cancelled due to petrol crisis	
Portugal	Pinto/Bernacchini	Fiat Abarth 124 Spyder
Safari	Singh/Doig	Colt Lancer
Acropolis	Cancelled due to petrol crisis	
1000 Lakes	Mikkola/Davenport	Ford Escort RS
San Remo	Munari/Mannucci	Lancia Stratos HF
Canada	Munari/Mannucci	Lancia Stratos HF
USA	Therier/Delferrier	Renault 17 Gordini
RAC Rally	Makinen/Liddon	Ford Escort RS
Corsica	Andruet/'Biche'	Lancia Stratos HF

World Champion Manufacturer, Lancia

1975

Rally	Crew	Car
Monte Carlo	Munari/Sodano	Lancia Stratos HF
Sweden	Waldegaard/Thorselius	Lancia Stratos HF
Safari	Andersson/Hertz	Peugeot 504
Acropolis	Röhrl/Berger	Opel Ascona
Morocco	Mikkola/Todt	Peugeot 504
Portugal	Alen/Kivimaki	Fiat Abarth 124 Spyder
1000 Lakes	Mikkola/Aho	Toyota Corolla 1600
San Remo	Waldegaard/Thorselius	Lancia Stratos HF
Corsica	Darniche/Mahe	Lancia Stratos HF
RAC Rally	Makinen/Liddon	Ford Escort RS

World Champion Manufacturer, Lancia

1976

Rally	Crew	Car
Monte Carlo	Munari/Maiga	Lancia Stratos HF
Sweden	Eklund/Cederberg	Saab 96 V4
Portugal	Munari/Maiga	Lancia Stratos HF
Safari	Singh/Doig	Colt Lancer
Acropolis	Kallstrom/Andersson	Datsun Violet
Morocco	Nicolas/Gamet	Peugeot 504
1000 Lakes	Alen/Kivimaki	Fiat Abarth 131
San Remo	Waldegaard/Thorselius	Lancia Stratos HF
Corsica	Munari/Maiga	Lancia Stratos HF
RAC Rally	Clark/Pegg	Ford Escort RS

World Champion Manufacturer, Lancia

1977

Rally	Crew	Car
Monte Carlo	Munari/Maiga	Lancia Stratos HF
Sweden	Blomqvist/Sylvan	Saab 99 EMS
Portugal	Alen/Kivimaki	Fiat Abarth 131
Safari	Waldegaard/Thorselius	Ford Escort RS
New Zealand	Bachelli/Rossetti	Fiat Abarth 131
Acropolis	Waldegaard/Thorselius	Ford Escort RS
1000 Lakes	Hamalainen/Tiukkanen	Ford Escort RS
Canada	Salonen/Markkula	Fiat Abarth 131
San Remo	Andruet/Delferrier	Fiat Abarth 131
Corsica	Darniche/Mahe	Fiat Abarth 131
RAC Rally	Waldegaard/Thorselius	Ford Escort RS

World Champion Manufacturer, Fiat
FIA Cup for Drivers, Sandro Munari

1978

Rally	Crew	Car
Monte Carlo	Nicolas/Laverne	Porsche Carrera
Sweden	Waldegaard/Thorselius	Ford Escort RS
Safari	Nicolas/Lefèbvre	Peugeot 504 V6 Coupé
Portugal	Alen/Kivimaki	Fiat Abarth 131
Acropolis	Röhrl/Geistdorfer	Fiat Abarth 131
1000 Lakes	Alen/Kivimaki	Fiat Abarth 131
Canada	Röhrl/Geistdorfer	Fiat Abarth 131
San Remo	Alen/Kivimaki	Lancia Stratos HF
Bandama	Nicolas/Gamet	Peugeot 504 V6 Coupé
Corsica	Darniche/Mahe	Fiat Abarth 131
RAC Rally	Mikkola/Hertz	Ford Escort RS

World Champion Manufacturer, Fiat
FIA Cup for Drivers, Markku Alen

1979

Rally	Crew	Car
Monte Carlo	Darniche/Mahe	Lancia Stratos HF
Sweden	Blomqvist/Cederberg	Saab 99 Turbo
Portugal	Mikkola/Hertz	Ford Escort RS
Safari	Mehta/Doughty	Datsun 160J
Acropolis	Waldegaard/Thorselius	Ford Escort RS
New Zealand	Mikkola/Hertz	Ford Escort RS
1000 Lakes	Alen/Kivimaki	Fiat Abarth 131
Canada	Waldegaard/Thorselius	Ford Escort RS
San Remo	'Tony'/Mannini	Lancia Stratos HF
Corsica	Darniche/Mahe	Lancia Stratos HF
RAC Rally	Mikkola/Hertz	Ford Escort RS
Bandama	Mikkola/Hertz	Mercedes-Benz 450 SLC

World Champion Manufacturer, Ford
World Champion Driver, Bjorn Waldegaard

1980

Rally	Crew	Car
Monte Carlo	Röhrl/Geistdorfer	Fiat Abarth 131
Sweden	Kullang/Berglund	Opel Ascona 400
Portugal	Röhrl/Geistdorfer	Fiat Abarth 131
Safari	Mehta/Doughty	Datsun 160J
Acropolis	Vatanen/Richards	Ford Escort RS
Argentina	Röhrl/Geistdorfer	Fiat Abarth 131
1000 Lakes	Alen/Kivimaki	Fiat Abarth 131
New Zealand	Salonen/Harjanne	Datsun 160J
San Remo	Röhrl/Geistdorfer	Fiat Abarth 131
Corsica	Therier/Vial	Porsche 911 SC

Rally	Crew	Car
RAC Rally	Henri Toivonen/White	Talbot Sunbeam Lotus
Bandama	Waldegaard/Thorselius	Mercedes-Benz 500 SLC

World Champion Manufacturer, Fiat
World Champion Driver, Walter Röhrl

1981

Rally	Crew	Car
Monte Carlo	Ragnotti/Andrie	Renault 5 Turbo
Sweden	Mikkola/Hertz	Audi Quattro
Safari	Mehta/Doughty	Datsun Violet GT
Corsica	Darniche/Mahe	Lancia Stratos HF
Acropolis	Vatanen/Richards	Ford Escort RS
Argentina	Frequelin/Todt	Talbot Sunbeam Lotus
Brazil	Vatanen/Richards	Ford Escort RS
1000 Lakes	Vatanen/Richards	Ford Escort RS
San Remo	Mlles Mouton/Pons	Audi Quattro
Bandama	Salonen/Harjanne	Datsun Violet GT
RAC Rally	Mikkola/Hertz	Audi Quattro

World Champion Manufacturer, Talbot
World Champion Driver, Ari Vatanen

1982

Rally	Crew	Car
Monte Carlo	Röhrl/Geistdorfer	Opel Ascona 400
Sweden	Blomqvist/Cederberg	Audi Quattro
Portugal	Mlles Mouton/Pons	Audi Quattro
Safari	Mehta/Doughty	Datsun Violet GT
Corsica	Ragnotti/Andrie	Renault 5 Turbo
Acropolis	Mlles Mouton/Pons	Audi Quattro
New Zealand	Waldegaard/Thorselius	Toyota Celica GT
Brazil	Mlles Mouton/Pons	Audi Quattro
1000 Lakes	Mikkola/Hertz	Audi Quattro
San Remo	Blomqvist/Cederberg	Audi Quattro
Bandama	Röhrl/Geistdorfer	Opel Ascona 400
RAC	Mikkola/Hertz	Audi Quattro

World Champion Manufacturer, Audi
World Champion Driver, Walter Röhrl

1983

Rally	Crew	Car
Monte Carlo	Röhrl/Geistdorfer	Lancia Rallye 037
Sweden	Mikkola/Hertz	Audi Quattro
Portugal	Mikkola/Hertz	Audi Quattro
Safari	Vatanen/Harryman	Opel Ascona 400
Corsica	Alen/Kivimaki	Lancia Rallye 037
Acropolis	Röhrl/Geistdorfer	Lancia Rallye 037
New Zealand	Röhrl/Geistdorfer	Lancia Rallye 037
Argentina	Mikkola/Hertz	Audi Quattro
1000 Lakes	Mikkola/Hertz	Audi Quattro
San Remo	Alen/Kivimaki	Lancia Rallye 037
Bandama	Waldegaard/Thorselius	Toyota Celica Turbo
RAC	Blomqvist/Cederberg	Audi Quattro

World Champion Manufacturer, Lancia
World Champion Driver, Hannu Mikkola

1984

Rally	Crew	Car
Monte Carlo	Röhrl/Geistdorfer	Audi Quattro A2
Swedish	Blomqvist/Cederberg	Audi Quattro A2
Portugal	Mikkola/Hertz	Audi Quattro A2
Safari	Waldegaard/Thorselius	Toyota Celica Turbo
Corsica	Alen/Kivimaki	Lancia Rallye 037
Acropolis	Blomqvist/Cederberg	Audi Quattro A2
New Zealand	Blomqvist/Cederberg	Audi Quattro A2
Argentina	Blomqvist/Cederberg	Audi Quattro A2
1000 Lakes	Vatanen/Harryman	Peugeot 205 Turbo 16
San Remo	Vatanen/Harryman	Peugeot 205 Turbo 16
Bandama	Blomqvist/Cederberg	Audi Quattro Sport
RAC	Vatanen/Harryman	Peugeot 205 Turbo 16

World Champion Manufacturer, Audi
World Champion Driver, Stig Blomqvist

1985

Rally	Crew	Car
Monte Carlo	Vatanen/Harryman	Peugeot 205 Turbo 16
Swedish	Vatanen/Harryman	Peugeot 205 Turbo 16
Portugal	Salonen/Harjanne	Peugeot 205 Turbo 16
Safari	Kankkunen/Gallagher	Toyota Celica Turbo
Corsica	Ragnotti/Thimonier	Renault 5 Maxi Turbo
Acropolis	Salonen/Harjanne	Peugeot 205 Turbo 16
New Zealand	Salonen/Harjanne	Peugeot 205 Turbo 16
Argentina	Salonen/Harjanne	Peugeot 205 Turbo 16
1000 Lakes	Salonen/Harjanne	Peugeot 205 Turbo 16
San Remo	Röhrl/Geistdorfer	Audi Sport Quattro E2
Bandama	Kankkunen/Gallagher	Toyota Celica Turbo
RAC	Henri Toivonen/Wilson	Lancia Delta S4

World Champion Manufacturer, Peugeot
World Champion Driver, Timo Salonen

1986

Rally	Crew	Car
Monte Carlo	Henri Toivonen/Cresto	Lancia Delta S4
Sweden	Kankkunen/Piironen	Peugeot 205 Turbo 16
Portugal	Moutinho/Fortes	Renault 5 Maxi Turbo
Safari	Waldegaard/Gallagher	Toyota Celica Turbo
Corsica	Saby/Fauchille	Peugeot 205 Turbo 16
Acropolis	Kankkunen/Piironen	Peugeot 205 Turbo 16
New Zealand	Kankkunen/Piironen	Peugeot 205 Turbo 16
Argentina	Biasion/Siviero	Lancia Delta S4
1000 Lakes	Salonen/Harjanne	Peugeot 205 Turbo 16
Bandama	Waldegaard/Gallagher	Toyota Celica Turbo
San Remo	Alen/Kivimaki	Lancia Delta S4
RAC Rally	Salonen/Harjanne	Peugeot 205 Turbo 16
USA	Alen/Kivimaki	Lancia Delta S4

World Champion Manufacturer, Peugeot
World Champion Driver, Juha Kankkunen

1973

Best recovery on an event? Markku Alen went off on the first day of the RAC Rally with his Ford Escort RS and fell to 175th overall. By the end of the event he was back up to third overall.

1974

Many rallies fell victim of the so-called petrol crisis and Monte Carlo, Sweden and Acropolis were all cancelled before reason prevailed.

1975

The two *works Ford Escorts of Timo Makinen and Roger Clark failed to progress* more than a few stages through the San Remo rally because *the truck carrying their Dunlop tyres had broken down* in France. The team ran as far as they could on the tyres they had, but when they wore out they had to stop.

1976

When FISA *modified the Group 2 rules for 1976* it was suddenly realized that rallies would lose a lot of competitors, so they allowed the 'old' Group 2 cars to run in rallies as Group 4 cars. Originally Group 4 had been derivatives of two-seater Group 3 cars, but now more manufacturers saw that they could homologate their saloon cars into a category for which the production number was only 400 per annum. The first company to realize this had been Hillman who had put their Imp into Group 4 many years previously.

1978

On the *Criterium du Quebec, John Buffum and Doug Shepherd were disqualified at the finish* for coming to the end of a special stage with crash helmets off and seat belts unfastened. They had suffered a puncture in the stage with their Triumph TR8 and when the wheel was changed had leapt in and continued without bothering with the safety equipment.

The two works Vauxhall Chevette HS 2300s driven by Pentti Airikkala and Chris Sclater *were not allowed to start the Portuguese Rally* as the Lotus cylinder head they were using (and had used earlier on the Swedish Rally) was significantly different from the production version, of which 400 had been built to qualify for Group 4. The Lotus heads had equal valve inclination of 19° instead of the unequal production inclinations of 20° inlet and 11° exhaust. Arguments did not prevail and Vauxhall had to do all subsequent rallies with the Vauxhall head.

1979

It was just as well that he wound up World Champion and that Ford won the Championship for Bjorn Waldegaard was denied victory on the last night of the Monte Carlo Rally when *spectators put rocks in the road* and damaged his Escort. The delay allowed Bernard Darniche to go on to win with a French-entered Lancia Stratos.

1980

When he won the RAC Rally, Henri Toivonen (24) was *the youngest driver to have won a World Championship rally*. This result was also the first World win for the Sunbeam Lotus which went on to win the World Championship for Talbot in 1981. It effectively died when the new masters of the company, Peugeot, started the design and development of the 205 Turbo 16 in 1982.

1981

The Audi Quattro became the *first four-wheel-drive car* to *win a World Championship rally* when Hannu Mikkola won the Swedish Rally. The Jeep Waggoneer of Gene Henderson won the Press-on-Regardless rally in 1972, the year before that rally joined the World Championship.

Hannu Mikkola gained his fourth RAC Rally victory in 1982, to clinch Audi's first world championship with the four-wheel drive Quattro.

Michele Mouton and Fabrizia Pons became the *first ladies crew to win a World Championship rally* when they won the San Remo Rally in their Group 4 Audi Quattro Coupé.

The disqualification of the works Audi Quattros on the Acropolis rally created quite a sensation. It was alleged that the bodywork round the headlamps and two of the four lamps themselves had been removed during the rally to improve cooling. What was alarming was that Audi were not allowed to continue pending the hearing of their appeal against the organizer's decision.

1982

The *Tour de Corse* marked the *debut of Lancia's new 037* but one driven by Attilio Bettega crashed and he was out of action for the rest of the season. On the same rally in 1983 he was fourth and then in 1984, with his new co-driver, Sergio Cresto, he was seventh. But in Corsica in 1985 he left the road, again with an 037, and was killed by a tree branch coming in through the window. Cresto survived that accident unhurt but was to be killed with Henri Toivonen in a Lancia Delta S4 in 1986 in Corsica.

1983

At a mini-rally in Sarlat, Dordogne, to commemorate the death of Jean-Francois Piot, the *Peugeot 205 T16 had its public competition debut* driven by Jean-Pierre Nicolas who had done most of the test

Leading American rally driver of the 1970s and 1980s, John Buffum, in action on home territory in an Audi Quattro.

'Yumping' is one of rallying's attractions and spots like this one featuring Henri Toivonen's Opel Manta 400 on the 1983 Manx can attract many spectators.

driving. The World debut for the car was in Corsica in 1984 where Ari Vatanen crashed and Nicolas came in fourth. They both retired on Acropolis but then Vatanen had three wins in a row – 1000 Lakes, San Remo and RAC (Peugeot did not contest New Zealand, Argentina or Ivory Coast). The second evolution tested in March 1985 and made its debut in Corsica where Bruno Saby finished second with it.

1984

The rally with the most one-upmanship was the 1984 Portuguese event. Firstly, Lancia entered young Henri Toivonen to incite Markku Alen to greater things but Toivonen crashed on stage 6. But Alen's Lancia led and he started first on the very dusty stages. Hannu Mikkola had to battle through dust until he and Audi team-mate, Walter Röhrl, discovered that they could give Mikkola a clear run if Röhrl stopped in the stage and let the leading Audi through. This worked to good effect and it was Mikkola who now led but Alen was still first on the road. Lancia gave him all the help they could by noting both his and Mikkola's intermediate times in a stage from their team helicopter and then relaying it to ground crews who gave Alen 'pit signals'. In the end, the rally went to Mikkola by just 27 seconds from Alen after 425 miles/684 km of stages.

Stig Blomqvist's win in Argentina with the Audi Quattro gave him the unique distinction of being *the first man to win three consecutive World Championship rallies* (Acropolis, New Zealand and Argentina). This was soon equalled by Ari Vatanen (RAC 1984, Monte and Swedish 1985)

and excelled by Timo Salonen in 1985 (Acropolis, New Zealand, Argentina and 1000 Lakes). Both Vatanen and Salonen were driving Peugeot 205 Turbo 16s.

1985

The fifth Rally of Argentina was to *bring to an end the World title chase of Ari Vatanen* who had already won Monte Carlo and Swedish for Peugeot. A high speed encounter with an uncharted bump on just the second stage led to a terrifying crash from which he emerged very close to death. He was to be out of rallying for almost 18 months, making his 'comeback' by driving a Peugeot as course car on the 1986 San Remo Rally.

The same rally saw the *World debut for the Audi Quattro Sport's second evolution* called, confusingly, the S1. Stig Blomqvist retired the car with a broken engine. The next evolution was called an E2 and Hannu Mikkola gave that a debut victory in the non-championship Olympus Rally. That model was used three times by the factory in 1986 before the spectator deaths in Portugal caused them to pull out.

In June, FISA announced that the *current crop of four-wheel drive, evolution Group B cars were too fast*. For 1987 they would be banning the evolutions to the production model that gave so much power and would introduce a Group S with power controlled to 300 bhp which would gradually replace Group B in the World Rally Championship. Less than one year later, when Group B was itself axed in total, Group S was also abandoned – the best-received and shortest-lived international formula that never turned a wheel. Opel built a car to

147

Group S regulations; Peugeot designed one and sued FISA for the money they had wasted.

Did Audi swap cars for Michele Mouton on the Ivory Coast Rally? It was not proved to the international stewards' satisfaction but then the media seemed to have all the evidence and published it afterwards. Also Roland Gumpert, Audi's popular team manager, departed at the end of the season. Mouton had a very unhappy rally anyway; her co-driver, Fabrizia Pons, fell ill during the recce, was replaced by Arne Hertz, only for them to hit a train and write the recce car off on the first day.

The Lancia Delta S4 was homologated into Group B on 1 November and by the end of the month had won its first World Championship Rally, the RAC, with Henri Toivonen. Another S4 driven by Markku Alen was second and another debutante, the Austin-Rover MG Metro 6R4 driven by Tony Pond, was third.

1986

On Saturday 3 May in Ajaccio, Corsica, FISA's President, Jean-Marie Balestre announced at a hastily convened press conference that, subject to ratification by FISA's full Executive Committee, *all Group B cars would be banned from rallies* effective from January 1987, Group S was being abandoned forthwith and that even Group A cars would have to submit to a limit on maximum power for rallying. Initially, this was poorly received by all manufacturers who reckoned that the cars were being blamed for lack of spectator control and poor rally organization, but they later split into two camps thus allowing FISA to go ahead with the proposal.

The FISA decision had been triggered by the deaths on 2 May of Henri Toivonen and Sergio Cresto whose Lancia Delta S4 had gone off the road and completely burnt out with them still inside. But there was never any direct connection made between the accident and the fact that the Lancia was a Group B car. Certainly the actual accident could have occurred to any car and the fire was more likely to be due to the preparation of the individual car rather than the fault of the Group into which it was homologated. In short, the decision was more emotional than rational. World Champions, Peugeot, felt so strongly that FISA was breaking its own rules and breaking them for the wrong reasons, that they initiated a court action against FISA for their own losses as a result of the decision.

Markku Alen experienced the nightmare of every rally driver in New Zealand – *he met a non-competing car on a special stage.* Fortunately he was able to stop his Lancia in time, but the effect on his subsequent performance in the rally was marked and his second place – to Kankkunen – contributed to his losing the World Championship.

The 1000 Lakes Rally became the first international rally where four-wheel drive cars filled the first ten places overall.

At the start of the San Remo Rally, the Manufacturers' World Championship was already Peugeot's for the second year running, but the Drivers' Championship could still go to either Markku Alen (Lancia) or Juha Kankkunen (Peugeot). During a rally which exhibited organizational faults that were not really acceptable at World Championship level, pressure was put on

Ford RS200 made its debut on the 1986 Swedish Rally, where Ford also achieved their best result with it before it was outlawed at the end of that season. After that these sophisticated competition cars were seen in rallycross events.

Austin-Rover's Metro 6R4 was a very promising car, until changed regulations cut its international career short. Malcolm Wilson is about to land on the 1986 1000 Lakes Rally in Finland.

the harassed organizers to take action against the Peugeots for what were alleged to be aerodynamic devices fitted under the cars. The San Remo men went too far, threw out all three works Peugeots before the last night and would not allow them to continue under appeal.

Lancia were then in first three places and Massimo Biasion and Dario Cerrato who were leading Alen slowed up to let him through and win on team orders. Naturally, Peugeot appealed but before all that could be settled there were the RAC and Olympus rallies on both of which Alen beat Kankkunen. So the result of the San Remo appeal would decide the Championship for Drivers. Just before Christmas, after appeals heard in Italy and Paris that said the Peugeots should not have been excluded but failed to rule on the legality or otherwise of the Peugeots, it was left to the FISA Executive, supported by an overwhelming majority of the manufacturers, to take the results of the San Remo out of the count for the World Championship and thus decide that Kankkunen was Champion for 1986.

With Peugeot's World Championship activity coming to a halt with the end of Group B, Kankkunen left them to sign a Lancia contract for 1987 where his team-mate is fellow countryman, Alen.

With the conclusion of this season, there had been 160 World Championship rallies. *The most successful car* has been the Audi Quattro with 21 wins (Audi had two more with the Sport Quattro) while the most successful manufacturer has been Lancia with 28 victories. Hannu Mikkola is way ahead in the drivers' league with 17 wins despite not having won since Portugal 1984 and it is not surprising that his current co-driver, Arne Hertz, heads the co-driver's list with 16 wins though two of his were with drivers other than Mikkola.

1987

Peugeot's Group B 205 Turbo 16 was modified by them by lengthening the wheelbase and increasing the tank capacity to enter the Paris–Dakar endurance rally as a prototype. Having never done this kind of event before, Peugeot survived early problems for Ari Vatanen and Bernard Giroux to emerge as winners by 1 hour 16 mins 36 secs from the Range Rover of past winner, Patrick Zanirolli after 13,000 kilometres of which no less than 8600 km were special stages. This was also the first event in which Vatanen had driven as a competitor since his 1985 accident in Argentina.

First winners of a new-look Group A World Championship rally were Lancia with their newly homologated Delta HF. It was Massimo Biasion who was credited with first place on the Monte Carlo Rally but that was only because Juha Kankkunen who took second place in another Lancia had been instructed to let Biasion pass him by slowing down on the last special stage.

Lancia classics from two eras – the 1972 Monte Carlo-winning Fulvia HF and the 1987 Monte Carlo-winning Delta HF.

ROUND AND ABOUT ON THE ROAD

1771

The *first accident involving a motor vehicle* was when Cugnot's steam tractor, used for pulling guns, hit a low wall in the grounds of the Paris arsenal.

1840

Francis Hill's steam coach covered the 128 miles/206 km from London to Hastings and back without mechanical trouble and was *the first mechanically-propelled vehicle to exceed 100 miles/160 km without a breakdown*. This feat was not to be surpassed for another 40 years.

1865

The Locomotives and Highways Act was *the first piece of British motoring legislation*, though it was originally intended to regulate the use of heavy steam-driven traction engines pulling loads. The Act required three persons in attendance – one to steer, one to stoke and one to walk 60 yards/55 metres ahead with a red flag to warn oncoming traffic. Maximum speeds allowed were 4 mph/6.4 kph in open country and 2 mph/3.2 kph in towns.

1878

The Highways and Locomotives Amendment Act *ordered that such vehicles must be preceded* by 'some person at least 20 yards [18.2 metres] ahead who shall, in case of need, assist horses in passing the same'. In fact the red flag requirement was relaxed, but it was under this and the earlier act that the motor-car first ventured forth upon the roads of Britain.

1893

The world's *first car number plates* were issued in France by the police.

1895

John Henry Knight was convicted and fined for using a motor-tricycle on the highway. He was probably the *first motorist to appear in court*.

1895

The first exhibition of motor vehicles in Britain was organized by Sir David Salomons and held in the grounds of the Tunbridge Wells Agricultural Show on 15 October. Peugeot, Panhard et Levassor and de Dion vehicles were demonstrated.

The Autocar, the *first British motoring journal*, was founded by Iliffe & Sons and dedicated to 'the interests of the mechanically-propelled road carriage'. The editor was Henry Sturmey, who gave his name to the Sturmey-Archer bicycle gear, and it cost 3d (1.25p). The first of the weekly issues appeared on 2 November and *Autocar* continues in weekly publication to this day, making it the *oldest surviving motoring publication in the world*.

The American Motor League became the world's

Sir David Salomons at the tiller of his Peugeot at the first exhibition of motor vehicles in Great Britain at Tunbridge Wells in 1895.

first automobile club. Membership cost $2 and the first meeting was held in November.

Dr Thomas Roberts became the first doctor in Britain to own a car when he imported an 1894 3½ hp Benz. In November he took part in an unofficial drive from London to Brighton, preceded by a boy on a bicycle with a red flag. The journey took 9 hours. In 1982 his great nephew, Dr Michael Roberts, maintained this early link when he took delivery of his first Mercedes-Benz, a 280CE coupé.

1896

The Prince of Wales (later King Edward VII) *took his first ride on a motor-car*, driven by the Hon. Evelyn Ellis, in the Imperial Institute grounds on 16 February.

The 'Emancipation Act' recognized *a new vehicle class* – light locomotive – *into which the new motor cars fell*. The need for three persons in attendance, including one walking ahead, was abolished and the maximum speed raised to 12 mph/19.3 kph. A gong, bell or other warning device had to be carried and lights were required after dark, as they are to this day.

The *Automobile Club de France*, now *the world's oldest car club*, was founded, followed later in the year by Britain's The Motor Car Club (MCC), the brainchild of entrepreneur H. J. Lawson.

The MCC promoted *London's first motor show*, held at the Imperial Institute, South Kensington, between May and August.

Pratt's motor spirit was marketed by the Anglo-American Oil Co., the British subsidiary of Standard Oil of America. Pratt's became Esso petrol in 1935.

The first London to Brighton motoring run was organized by H. J. Lawson and the MCC to celebrate the emancipation of the horseless carriage. On 14 November 35 vehicles set out from Northumberland Avenue for Brighton, stopping for lunch at Reigate, after Lord Winchelsea had symbolically torn up a red flag. That evening 22 participating cars reached Brighton in time for a celebration dinner at the Metropole Hotel.

Charles M. R. Turrell was the first person to drive a car in the Lord Mayor of London's procession. He was accompanied on the imported Daimler by Harry J. Lawson.

'Petrol' was registered as a trade name to describe the petroleum spirit marketed by Carless, Capel &

Leonard. The suggestion for the name came from F. R. Simms, at a time when people were beginning to worry about storing inflammable motor spirit. Simms's logic was that since petrol really meant nothing at all it would allay these fears. Gradually the trade name 'Petrol' came into the common usage in which it survives today. In America the word was not used, the universal term being gasoline right from the start.

1897

The Automobile Club of Great Britain and Ireland was founded by F. R. Simms on 27 January. Under Edward VII's patronage it became the Royal Automobile Club in 1907. The RAC is now *Britain's oldest motoring organization* and is responsible for the modern annual Veteran Car Run from London to Brighton on the first Sunday in November (see 1927).

Shell Transport and Trading was formed to sell motor spirit. It was amalgamated with Royal Dutch in 1906.

The first 'motor wedding' with cars used to transport the bride and groom took place in August. The guests were conveyed in a farm wagon hauled by a traction engine.

The world's first motor-cabs were operated by the London Electric Cab Co. and had solid tyres. As the name implied, they were battery powered. Similar electric cabs were used in New York at about the same time.

The first Land's End to John O' Groats car journey was completed by Henry Sturmey, editor of *The Autocar*, on a 4½ hp Coventry-Daimler on 19 October. He had started from Land's End on 2 October and covered the 929 miles/1495 km in 93½ hours, an average speed of almost 10 mph/16 kph.

1898

The Prince of Wales had his first road journey by car while staying at Warwick Castle. J. S. Critchley drove him from the castle to Compton Verney, about 10 miles/16 km away, on a Daimler on 25 June.

Pratt & Co. introduced special petrol cans at about this time. They were of 2 imp. gallons/9 litres capacity and were the principal means of selling petrol until petrol pumps became common in the 1920s.

The first motor wedding in 1897. The bride is in the car on the left and the groom in the car on the right. Guests were accommodated in the farm waggon, hauled by a traction engine, behind.

The Hon. John Scott Montagu, father of the present Lord Montagu, took the Prince of Wales for a drive in the New Forest on his new 12 hp Daimler in August 1899. The car still exists and can be seen in the National Motor Museum.

1899

The first motor-car accident in Britain resulting in the death of the driver occurred in Grove Hill, Harrow-on-the-Hill, London, on 25 February.

The Hon. John Scott Montagu MP (father of the present Lord Montagu) drove his 12 hp 4-cylinder Daimler to the House of Commons on 3 July, thus becoming the *first person to drive into the precincts of the Palace of Westminster.*

1900

The 1000 Miles Trial, organized by Claude Johnson in his capacity of secretary of the Automobile Club of Great Britain and Ireland, put motoring on the map and gave many people their first sight of a car. The route started in London and then went to Bristol before turning up the west coast to Edinburgh. The return route was via the east coast and the Midlands.

The Prince of Wales (later King Edward VII) *purchased his first car*, a 6 hp Daimler, thus beginning the Royal Family's long association with the marque. Later the same year the Duchess of York (later Queen Mary) was given her first car ride by the Hon. C. S. Rolls on his Panhard.

1901

The first road surveyor to use a car for his work was P. J. Sheldon. Essex County Council provided a 4½ hp de Dion for his use.

American cars were first registered on a statewide basis in New York and California. The *first American plates* were issued in New York and carried the owner's initials, something that is still possible in the USA and Britain today.

The first motor insurance policy was produced by a

Keeping warm in the open cars of 1900 necessitated special motoring clothing, particularly for the ladies. The hats and veils were to ward off the dust clouds that accompanied the early cars on the unmade roads of the day.

Around town at low speeds, the ladies plumped for fashion rather than practicality.

Lloyds underwriter, who treated the car as a ship navigating on land.

1902

Tar was first used on a Macadam surface to prevent dust in Monte Carlo. It was the idea of Dr Guglielminetti, a Swiss. At first the tar was brushed on cold, but soon it was applied hot.

1903

The first coast-to-coast crossing of the USA was made by a Winton car. It took 65 days for the journey but was immobile for repairs for 20 days of that time, mainly due to bad road conditions.

The Motor Car Act in August required *all cars to be registered and carry a number plate*, and *all motor-*

Breakdowns were one of the hazards of motoring in 1904, but those wealthy enough to own a car usually had a chauffeur whose job it was to get his hands dirty on such occasions. Then the passengers could recline in comfort, as in this instance, while their man attended to the motor.

ists to have a driving licence. Registration cost £1 and the driving licence 5s (25p), but there was no driving test to pass and the licence was obtained by filling up a form and paying the fee at a Post Office. Earl Russell was allotted A1, the first London number, and Lord Kingsburgh S1, the first number in Scotland. The Act, which came into force on 1 January 1904, also made dangerous driving an indictable offence.

1904

There were 28,842 vehicles registered in Britain. A year later the figure had risen to 66,703. Figures for cars licensed and in use were respectively 8465 and 15,895.

1905

The Automobile Association was formed in October to warn motorists of police speed traps. AA scouts were provided for this purpose but this became illegal in 1906, so members were then instructed to stop a scout who failed to salute and ask the reason why. The scout would then advise the member to go slowly because of the road conditions if there was a speed trap ahead. The AA's first office was at 18 Fleet Street, where it remained until the move to London's Leicester Square in 1907.

1906

The first petrol pumps were installed in the USA.

The Automobile Club engine rating formula was adopted. A car's horsepower was calculated by the formula $\frac{D^2 n}{2.5}$ where D was the cylinder diameter in inches and n the number of cylinders. This led to decades of long-stroke, small-bore engines.

1909

The Finance Act *imposed a tax of 3d (1.25p) per gallon on petrol*, bringing the cost including tax to 1s 9d (8.75p). The tax was increased to 6d (2.5p) in 1915. A vehicle tax based on horsepower, calculated by the RAC formula (see 1906), was also imposed. The rate was from £2 2s (£2.10) for cars up to 6½ hp, up to a massive £42 for the few cars of over 60 hp. A Road Board was set up to spend the sum raised by taxation of motorists on the improvement of the roads. This new tax soon became known as the Road Fund Tax and applies to this day, though little of the money is now spent on roads.

1910

Driving licences were introduced in Germany.

1911

The first person to drive a car to the top of Ben Nevis in Scotland was Henry Alexander. He did it twice in May that year in a Ford Model T.

1912

The world's first motor museum was founded by Edmund Dangerfield, proprietor of *The Motor* magazine, in Oxford Street, London. It was transferred to Crystal Palace in 1914 and the collection was broken up at the outbreak of World War I.

A typical high street garage in 1912. Note the absence of petrol pumps (not common until the 1920s) and the 10 mph/16 kph speed limit sign behind the front car.

Some of the cars survive in other British museums.

1913

American registrations of motor vehicles exceeded a million for the first time. Of the 1,258,060 vehicles registered, 1,190,393 were cars. By 1921 registrations exceeded 10 million and by 1975 they had topped 100 million.

Henry Ford's Model T was one of the prime movers in taking American car registrations above a million in 1913.

The total of cars registered in Britain exceeded 100,000 for the first time, the actual figure being 105,734.

The first British roadside petrol pump was installed at Shrewsbury, Shropshire. It was not until the 1920s that petrol pumps were a normal part of the motoring scene.

1918

All cars made up to the end of the year are now classified as Veteran by the *Fédération Internationale des Voitures Ançiennes*. Only cars made before the end of 1904, however, are eligible to enter the annual London–Brighton Veteran Car Run (see 1927). Later cars, made up to 1930, are classed as *Vintage*.

1919

The Ministry of Transport was established in September. First Minister of Transport was the Rt. Hon. Sir Eric Geddes.

The world's first traffic lights were installed in Detroit, USA.

1920

The Finance Act *abolished the 6d (2.5p) petrol tax*

Even in the 1920s it was usual to have to swing a starting handle on most cars, but this 1921 Horstmann had an ingenious mechanical kick-starter operated from the driving seat. It beat getting out in the rain when the engine stalled.

Though the world's first traffic lights were in Detroit in 1919, New York had them in the form of this unusual traffic light tower in 1920.

(it was reimposed at 4d (1.6p) per gallon in 1929) and substituted an annual tax of £1 per horsepower, based on the RAC formula (see 1906). This horsepower tax persisted until the late 1940s.

1921

Trade plates of the current pattern were first issued in Britain. 'Limited' plates featured red lettering on a white background, while 'general' plates had white letters on a red background. Unlike normal number plates, they can be, and usually are, transferred from vehicle to vehicle.

Registration documents (log books) were introduced for British cars.

1922

Ford in the USA became *the first car manufacturer to produce over a million cars in a year.* The ubiquitous Model T was delivered to 1,216,792 buyers.

In Britain traffic jams were not unknown in the 1920s. This queue of limousines conducted by liveried chauffeurs is in Ascot, where the horse racing still causes traffic congestion in the 1980s.

1923

British motor vehicle registrations first exceeded a million, but that figure for cars alone was not reached until 1930 (with 1,075,084). There were 2,074,404 cars in 1939 but the figure of 5,080,510 was not reached until 20 years later.

1924

The *Brooklands Gazette* (later *Motor Sport*) appeared in August and was the *first British publication devoted to motor sport*.

The first motorway was opened in Italy between Milan and Verese. Work on this 21-kilometre/13-mile section had started in June 1923 and the new road was opened in September 1924. A length of *autostrada* between Milan and Como followed in 1926.

A London–Liverpool motorway was proposed by John, Lord Montagu of Beaulieu. It was the subject of a Private Member's Bill in Parliament but got no further. London and Liverpool were not to be linked by motorway until the 1970s.

1925

Closed cars outsold open-bodied ones in the USA for the first time.

1926

The Road Fund was raided by the Chancellor of the Exchequer, Winston S. Churchill. For the first time the money was used other than for road construction, allowing the road fund tax to become just an additional Government means of raising revenue – as it is to this day.

1927

White lines were first used as road dividers, in the form of a single white line.

Speedometers became mandatory on cars in Britain.

The vogue for closed cars that became popular in America in the 1920s resulted in cars like this 1924 Chrysler.

The first London–Brighton Commemoration Run, restricted to cars made before 31 December 1904, was sponsored by the *Daily Sketch*. Since 1930 the run has been organized by the RAC, making it the only event for Veteran cars run by a national automobile club.

1928

The first traffic lights in Britain were installed in Wolverhampton. They did not come to London until 1932.

1930

Cars made up until the end of this year, and after 1 January 1919, are classed as Vintage by the *Fédération Internationale des Voitures Ançiennes*. Cars made up until the end of 1918 are designated Veteran.

Third party insurance cover became mandatory under the Road Traffic Act. It made notification of certain accidents compulsory and established driving offences. The 20 mph/32 kph speed limit that had been in force since 1903 was also ended by this Act, though not until the end of the year.

The Highway Code was first issued in draft form.

The 20 mph/32 kph overall speed limit ensured that accidents were not too serious and multiple accidents, like this one at Finchley in North London in 1924, were rare.

An unknown man was murdered by Alfred Rouse and burnt in a Morris Minor on the night of 5–6 November at Hardingstone, Northamptonshire. It was the *first murder that centred round a car.*

The Veteran Car Club, the world's first club for old cars, was formed at the conclusion of that year's London–Brighton run. The founders were S. C. H. Davis (sports editor of *The Autocar*), J. A. Masters and J. A. Wylie. It survives to this day.

1931

Underground car parking came to Britain with the opening of the first such facility at Hastings in December.

The Motor Vehicles (Construction and Use) Regulations made *driving mirrors and safety glass for windscreens compulsory* in Britain.

The first cross-Channel car ferry started operation from Dover to Calais. Cars were slung aboard Southern Railway's *Autocarrier* loaded on pallets.

1933

A tax of a penny a gallon on lubricating oil was imposed in the UK.

1934

The Road Traffic Act imposed a *30 mph/48 kph speed limit in built-up areas, provided for driving tests* for those who did not already hold licences and *instituted pedestrian crossings.*

The horsepower tax on cars was reduced to 15s (75p) per hp (see 1920).

The world's first drive-in cinema was opened at Camden, New Jersey, USA.

1935

America's oldest antique car club was founded in November. The Antique Automobile Club of America is also the world's largest devoted to old cars. The Horseless Carriage Club of America followed in November 1937 and the Veteran Motor Car Club of America in January 1939.

Esso petrol first appeared in Britain (see 1896).

Germany's first autobahn *was opened* between Frankfurt and Darmstadt in May. The Hanover–Berlin motorway followed in 1936.

The new 30 mph/48 kph speed limit came into operation in built-up areas in March and a *new Highway Code was published.*

The world's first parking meter was installed in Oklahoma City, USA, in July. It was invented by Professor H. G. Thuesen and Gerald A. Hale of Oklahoma State University. In August the Reverend C. H. North of the Third Pentecostal Church of Oklahoma City became the *first person to be arrested for a parking meter offence.*

1936

Cat's eyes were installed in the surface of Britain's roads. This British invention made driving at night very much safer and easier.

The Trunk Roads Act made *the British Minister*

One of the first pedestrian crossings in Britain at Cheltenham in 1935. The striped Belisha beacon on the right was named after Minister of Transport L. Hore-Belisha, and the crossing was also marked by dotted lines on the road. The zebra crossing, with black and white stripes, was a post-war addition.

A British speed limit of 30 mph/48 kph in towns came into force in March 1935 and remains to this day.

The world's first parking meters were installed in Oklahoma City, USA, in 1935.

Michelin introduced the world's first low-profile tyre in 1937, bringing improved standards of roadholding for ordinary motorists like the driver of this Citroën Traction Avant.

of Transport responsible for these and not local county councils.

1937

The first drive-in bank was opened in Los Angeles, California, USA.

The first London Motor Show in the new Earl's Court building. Previous London shows had been held at Olympia (since 1905).

1939

Petrol rationing was introduced in Britain, for the first time, on the outbreak of war, and *headlamp masks*, which cut out most of the light, *became compulsory.*

1940

America's first dual-carriageway road, the Pennsylvania Turnpike, was opened in October. It was built along a disused railway line.

British purchase tax was first imposed on cars in October at 33.3% of the ex-works wholesale price. Postwar, the punitive rate of 66.6% was applied to 'luxury' cars costing over £1280 between June 1947 and April 1951. Then, until April 1953, the higher rate was applied to all cars.

1942

Motoring for pleasure in Britain, but not the USA, *ceased* in June to save fuel for the war effort.

1945

The basic *petrol ration for private motoring was reintroduced* and allowed about 200 miles/320 km a month from June.

The October Budget *abolished the annual horsepower tax* based on the RAC formula (see 1906 and 1920) and replaced it with an annual tax based on the cubic capacity of the car's engine. This came into operation for new cars on 1 January 1947, and a year later there was a flat annual fee of £10 for new cars.

1946

Car driving simulators were developed in America by the Aetna Insurance Co. By 1967 over 1000 motoring schools were using them.

The Covenant Scheme to prevent the sale of new cars at black market prices was introduced in the UK in July. Initially an owner had to keep a new car for six months, but in March 1948 this became a year and in September 1950 two years. Covenants did not finally end until January 1953.

France introduced a horsepower tax that discriminated against cars with engines larger than about 2.8 litres. It is still in force, which is why there are no French cars with big engines.

1949

The first regular car ferry service by air was started

by Silver City Airways from Lympne to Le Touquet in France. Later a similar service was operated by British United Air Ferries from Lydd in Kent using Carvairs. The BUAF air ferry to the continent ceased to operate in November 1976.

1950

'Wartime' petrol rationing in Britain came to an end on 26 May, but branded petrols did not appear again until 1953.

1952

The Montagu Motor Museum was founded at Beaulieu, Hampshire, based on the personal collection of vehicles owned by Lord Montagu. Within 10 years the vehicles numbered over 100 and there was a library of motoring books, drawings and photographs. It became the Beaulieu Museum Trust in 1970 and formed the basis for Britain's National Motor Museum in 1972 (q.v.).

In February *hire purchase restrictions were first introduced* in the UK for the sale of motor vehicles. A minimum deposit of 33.3% of the purchase price was required and the maximum repayment period was limited to 18 months. Though deposit percentages and repayment periods have varied, there have been few years since without restrictions.

The last electric trams ran in London in July. Later some of the special tram tunnels were turned into road underpasses. One such takes traffic from the north side of Waterloo Bridge under the Aldwych to emerge in Kingsway. It is one way, in a northbound direction.

1953

The Covenant System, preventing the immediate resale of new cars on the open market, *finally ended,* though expensive cars had been freed earlier.

1956

The Autocar's continental correspondent W. F. Bradley (1876–1971) *retired after 53 years as a motoring journalist* in France. He had contributed to *The Autocar* since 1919, and before that was Paris correspondent of the rival publication *The Motor.*

The Suez Crisis, caused by Col. Nasser of Egypt nationalizing the Suez Canal through which most of Europe's oil supplies passed, brought *petrol rationing to Britain for the second time* on 17 December. Just 200 miles/320 km a month were allowed initially, rising to 300/480 before rationing ended in May 1957.

1957

The size of car number plates in the USA, Canada and Mexico was standardized at 12 inches by 6 inches/30 cm by 15 cm.

Charles Faroux, technical editor of the French *L'Auto,* died. It ended 53 years' service with that publication, the *longest any motoring journalist has worked for the same paper.*

1958

The first parking meters in Britain were installed outside the American Embassy (very appropriately, as they had invented them) in London's Grosvenor Square on 10 July. The Minister of Transport responsible was Harold Watkinson and not, as is widely supposed, his successor Ernest Marples.

Britain's first motorway, the Preston by-pass, *was opened* in December. It is now part of the M6. The first section of the M1 was not opened until 1959.

1959

In the USA life was made easier for motorists on long journeys by *the introduction of a cruise control* so that the driver did not need to keep his foot on the accelerator. The Perfect Circle Co.'s device was the first to appear and used a reversible electric motor.

The first double white lines appeared down the centre of roads in Britain. It was prohibited to overtake in the places so marked.

1960

The Ministry of Transport test for vehicle roadworthiness came into effect on 12 September for all vehicles over 10 years old. They had to be tested annually, and a fee was charged for this and the issue of the required MoT certificate by licensed garages. Brakes, lights and steering were among the original items tested, but other items were added later. From April 1967 the test applied, as it still does, to cars over 3 years old.

The longest skid marks on a public road were left by a Jaguar involved in an accident on the M1 motorway near Luton, Bedfordshire, on 30 June. They were 950 feet/290 metres long, indicative of a speed of over 100 mph/160 kph before the brakes were applied. There was then no motorway speed limit in Britain.

The world's first Veteran and Vintage car auction

was held by Southern Counties Car Auctions in July. The venue was the Montagu Motor Museum (now the National Motor Museum) at Beaulieu.

Self-service petrol was first offered in Britain at a petrol station close to Southwark Bridge, London, in November.

1962

Glasgow's last tram ran in November, but they are still in use in Blackpool. About 40 working trams are preserved at the National Tramway Museum at Crich in Derbyshire.

1963

Three London streets were pedestrianized on an experimental basis. The idea was soon extended to other towns.

The first British number plates to carry a letter suffix were issued in Middlesex in February. The letter A at the end of the number denoted the year, which ran from January to December. In 1967 the year letter changed on 1 January to E and on 1 August to F. Thereafter the year letter ran from August to July. In August 1983 the year letter was changed to a prefix, starting with A again.

Kent and Essex were linked by road with the opening of the Dartford–Purfleet toll tunnel under the River Thames in November. A second tunnel was added later. It is now the only non-motorway part of the M25 ring around London (see 1986).

Automatic disqualification from driving for anyone with three driving licence endorsements within 3 years was introduced with the new Road Traffic Act. It specified 26 offences meriting endorsement.

1964

In Paris *policewomen were used for traffic control duties for the first time*.

Box junctions, marked with yellow crosshatching, were introduced in London. The aim was to prevent traffic blocking junctions when it could not proceed, and this was successful.

A new world record for motorway surfacing was established on a 127-mile/204-km Kentucky motorway in the USA. In 14 hours construction engineers poured 10,614 ft (over 2 miles/3237 metres) of concrete.

1965

The current British road signs using symbols in the continental style came into use on 1 January, fol-

lowing a report by the Warboys Committee. Mandatory instructions are conveyed by circular signs with a red border, information by rectangular ones and warnings of hazards by triangular signs. The traditional British 'Halt' sign was replaced by the more easily understood 'Stop'.

In Britain a 50 mph/80 kph permanent speed limit was imposed on 500 miles/800 km of rural trunk roads, like parts of A5 in the Midlands, in an attempt to reduce accidents.

The continental disc parking system came into operation in the UK at Cheltenham on 10 May. The motorist displayed the time the car was parked on a disc in the windscreen and wardens checked that the time limit was not overstayed.

Almost 100 mpg/2.8 litres/100 km on the road was achieved by W. (Joe) Dembowski, who recorded 96.59 mpg/2.9 litres/100 km driving between the centre of Cheltenham and the centre of Evesham on the morning of 1 July. He averaged 25.75 mph/41.44 kph for the journey in his 2-cylinder Fiat 500D. His technique was to accelerate to 40 mph/65 kph, coast to 20 mph/32 kph and then accelerate again.

The world's longest road tunnel, under Mont Blanc, opened to traffic in July. It links Chamonix in France and Courmayeur in Italy and is 7¼ miles/11.63 km long.

London's car radio-telephone service started on 5 July. The first transatlantic car-to-car call was made by Richard Dimbleby to Max Kaufman, a Montreal cab driver. Both cars had Pye radio-telephone equipment.

The first mobile petrol pump in the UK was operated by European Petroleum near Brands Hatch in Kent. The pump was mounted at the rear of a petrol tanker.

Two German Amphicars crossed the Channel from Dover to Calais in September, despite choppy seas. The Amphicar was powered by a rear-mounted Triumph Herald 1147 cc engine which drove the wheels on land and a propeller in the water.

The Toyota Corolla became *Japan's first car to reach a million*. Production had started in 1957. The same year the 10 millionth Volkswagen Beetle was built.

A 70 mph/113 kph speed limit (including motorways) was imposed in Britain on 22 December as a panic measure by Minister of Transport Tom Fraser after a spate of motorway accidents in fog.

Though introduced as a four-month experiment, it soon became permanent and is with us to this day.

1966

General Motors became the world's first manufacturer to produce 100 million vehicles. The actual vehicle was an Oldsmobile Toronado produced in the Lansing, Michigan, plant on 16 March. The corporation's 100 millionth vehicle produced in the USA followed on 21 April 1967.

Britain's first four-level road junction was opened to traffic at Almondsbury (near Bristol) where M4 and M5 motorways intersect.

Self-service petrol using currency notes was first available in Europe from BP's Lidingo service station outside Stockholm, Sweden. Later in the year a £1 or 10s (50p) note acceptor was installed by BP at Watford in the UK. BP also *introduced blender pumps* to the UK the same year.

The highest circulation for a weekly motoring magazine was recorded by *Autocar* with an Audit Bureau of Circulations average figure of 145,009 copies sold per week for the year. In 1965 *Autocar*'s circulation had been 139,801.

1967

Front seat belts were a mandatory fitting on all new cars registered in Britain after 1 April. Wearing them remained purely voluntary until 1983 (q.v.).

Britain's first Drivotrainer school, using simulators to teach pupils to drive a car, was opened in Nottingham (see 1946).

Sweden changed over to driving on the right of the road in the continental and American manner in September. Iceland followed in May 1968.

The first breath tests for drivers came into force in Britain on 9 October. Anyone suspected of committing a motoring offence could be tested and police officers were equipped with Breathalyzers for the purpose. This was a plastic bag into which the driver blew through a tube of crystals. The crystals changed colour if the motorist was over the limit, but a subsequent blood or urine test at a police station determined whether or not prosecution followed. The new drink-drive legislation made it an offence to drive, attempt to drive or be in charge of a motor vehicle with more than 80 milligrams of alcohol per 100 millilitres of blood. Penalties for a first offence were a fine of £100 or four months imprisonment, or both.

Exhaust emissions regulations in the USA in the 1960s required manufacturers to submit cars for testing at the Federal laboratories at Ypsilanti, Michigan, where this 4.2-litre Jaguar E-type is being prepared for testing.

1968

US Federal Safety Standards came into force on 1 January as the result of lobbying in America by Ralph Nader, among others. An exterior mirror on the driver's side, laminated windscreen, collapsible steering column, two-speed windscreen wipers and front and rear seat belts were among the requirements. It was the thin end of the wedge and ever since additional safety requirements have been added by government. The changes and extra equipment were paid for by the purchaser in higher car prices.

New tyre regulations in Britain came into force on 1 April. They required a minimum of 1 mm of tread depth over three-quarters of a tyre's width. Mixing of radial and cross-ply tyres on the same axle was prohibited.

Europe's first all-plastic petrol station was opened by BP on the A1 at Baldock in Hertfordshire. It used 1¼ tons/1.27 tonnes of plastics and was built by six men in six days.

All new cars on garage forecourts or in showrooms in the UK *were required to display official Government fuel consumption figures* from 1 April. Testing was carried out by manufacturers on rolling roads.

In Tokyo *staggered stop lines at eight junctions were introduced* in a bid to cut accidents. Two-wheeled riders stopped ahead of cars and trucks, so as to be more visible.

Computerized warning signs on British motorways were first tried on the Severn Bridge section of the M4 in June. In the spring of 1969 the signs were extended to the London section of the motorway.

This American presidential car was specially built on a lengthened Lincoln Continental chassis. The steps at the side and rear are for the secret servicemen.

Britain's first ticket-printer petrol pump, which needed no console display, was inaugurated by Graham Hill at Shell's Holloway Service Station in London.

The most expensive American car built to date was the Lincoln Continental Presidential Limousine supplied to the US Secret Service on 14 October. It weighed 5.35 tons/5.44 tonnes (including 2 tons/2 tonnes of armour plate) and was built on a lengthened wheelbase of 160 in/4.06 metres, giving an overall length of 258.3 in/6.56 metres. It cost $500,000 (then £208,000), but is rented by the US Government for $5000 a year.

Long journeys were eased by the introduction of *the world's first combined radio and cassette player*. It was the RN582 from Philips, who had invented the cassette system, and cost 38 guineas (£39.90).

1969

The first drive-in off-licence in Britain was opened by Westminster Wine in Streatham High Road, South London, on 13 March.

Pelican pedestrian crossings came into use in London, Bristol, Lincoln and Reading. Flashing amber lights were seen by drivers, while pedestrians were shown whether it was safe to cross by matchstick-men symbols. A red standing man was shown when traffic had priority and a green walking man when it was safe to cross. A pedestrian push-button activated the signal and there was an audible bleep for blind people.

An additional driving licence group was introduced in the UK for those who had passed their driving tests on cars with automatic transmission. The New Group 1B licence permitted the holder to drive only automatics, whereas those who passed a test on a manual-gearbox car obtained a Group 1A licence and could drive both.

There were 1,056,760 motor vehicle broadcast receiving licences issued in the UK. These were mostly for car radios, but the figure included 79 for televisions in cars. In 1959 the figure for car radios was 415,531 and in 1947 just 24,991.

1970

Mrs Miriam Hargrave (then aged 62) *passed the Ministry of Transport driving test at her 40th attempt*, after 212 lessons, on 3 August. She failed her previous test, the 39th in eight years, after going through a red traffic light.

1971

A separate motor vehicle broadcast receiving licence was no longer required for a radio or television in a car after 1 April in Britain. Like the domestic radio licence itself, the car radio licence was abolished because it was too costly to collect (see 1969).

The first manned vehicle was driven on the moon in August. It was the General Motors Lunar Roving Vehicle with special mesh tyres made from piano wire. It had an aluminium chassis with a 90 in/ 2.29 metres wheelbase and an overall length of 122 in/3.10 metres. Powered by two 36-volt silver-zinc batteries, it had a maximum speed of 10.5 mph/17 kph and each of the four wheels was driven. At the end of the Apollo 15 mission it was left behind on the moon.

The worst motoring accident in Britain took place on the M6 motorway at Thelwall on 13 September.

Eleven people were killed, 60 injured and 200 vehicles were involved.

1972

Britain's National Motor Museum opened to the public at Beaulieu, Hampshire, on 4 July. As well as the cars on display in a brand new purpose-designed building, there were restoration workshops. Research facilities were provided in the BP Library of Motoring and there was also a photographic library (see 1952).

The highest capacity underground car park in Britain was opened in Nottingham in June. There was room for 1650 cars under the Victoria Centre.

1973

Reflective number plates were mandatory on all vehicles registered in the UK after 1 January. They carried black letters and numbers, those at the front on a white background and those at the rear on a yellow one.

A new computerized licence in a plastic wallet replaced the traditional British red-covered book for drivers whose licences were renewed after 1 March. The new licences were issued centrally from the then new Driving and Vehicle Licensing Centre at Swansea, as they have been ever since.

Value added tax, similar to that already used in continental Europe, *replaced British purchase tax on new cars* on 1 April. Unique to Britain was the imposition of a special car tax on the ex-works wholesale price, the total then being subject to VAT. Special car tax has always been at 10 per cent, but VAT was introduced at 10 per cent initially and stands at 15 per cent in 1987.

Multi-tone or musical horns were prohibited on cars registered in Britain after 1 August. It spelt the end for those who liked to drive along playing *Colonel Bogie* on their car horns.

A grooved concrete surface was first used on the 7-mile/11.3-km section of the M40 motorway between Denham and Beaconsfield, opened in August. The transverse grooves were positioned about an inch/2.5 cm apart to aid drainage in wet conditions and reduce vehicle spray.

VASCAR was first used for the successful prosecution of British motorists for excess speed by Essex and Southend Joint Constabulary on 29 October. The initials stand for Visual Average Speed Computer and Recorder and the device was invented by Arthur N. Marshall of Richmond, Virginia, USA. The Indiana State Police first used a mechanical

In the 1970s Malc Buchanan crossed the Irish Sea from the Isle of Man to England in his Volkswagen Beetle, fitted with navigation lights and a propeller.

version in the mid-1960s and later there were some 9000 sets in use in America. VASCAR, made by the Federal Sign and Signal Corporation of Chicago, computes speed against distance to determine average speed and can be used from a stationary or moving police car.

An energy crisis, with long queues for petrol in the western world, resulted from the Arab–Israeli war in the Middle East in October and the interruption of the West's oil supplies. In the USA and Britain there were overall 50 mph/80 kph speed limits (including motorways) to conserve fuel. In most continental countries Sunday motoring was banned, and speed limits were imposed in Germany, Italy and France. In Britain petrol coupons were issued but in the end rationing was not needed as petrol was in short supply anyway. Everywhere small cars and economy motoring received a new impetus. Even in the USA there was a move away from full-size cars and both General Motors and Ford cancelled their Wankel engine programmes.

1974

ARI (Autofahrer Rundfunk Information) radio traffic information broadcasts started in Germany for those with specially-modified Bosch car radios. The scheme was extended to Austria in 1976 and Switzerland in 1980.

Energy-absorbing bumpers to protect the car body from damage in a 5-mph/8-kph collision *became mandatory for 1974 model cars in the USA*. The extra cost put up car prices and the weight increased fuel consumption.

The Trans-Amazonian Highway was completed in

February, connecting the Atlantic coast of South America with the Pacific coast. There were 3340 miles/5375 km of impacted-earth roads.

All new cars in the UK were licensed centrally at the Driver and Vehicle Licensing Centre at Swansea from 1 October. At the same time the old-style vehicle registration log books were replaced by a new document, with the details recorded on a central computer. Later the scheme was extended to include all vehicles previously licensed by local authorities.

1978

EEC Type Approval applied to all cars sold in Britain after 1 April. As in West Germany, a model had to be submitted for government testing before it could be put on sale. The cars most affected were those from the USA and they had to be modified to meet European standards – ironic, as it was America that had started the business of safety legislation for 1968 model-year cars sold there.

A Rolls-Royce Phantom VI limousine with a special high roof was presented to Her Majesty the Queen by the British motor industry to mark her Silver Jubilee in 1977. It is the newest Rolls-Royce in use by the British Royal Family, whose oldest car in current use is a Phantom IV dating from 1950.

The highest authenticated mileage covered by a car was 1,184,880 miles/1,906,879 km in August by a 1957 Mercedes-Benz 180D owned by Robert O'Reilly of Olympia, Washington State, USA.

Mrs Fannie Turner (then aged 77) *passed her written driver's test in America at her 104th attempt* in October.

The first British Motor Show was held at the new National Exhibition Centre in Birmingham where, despite more space, it was more crowded than Earls Court (the venue from 1937–76) had ever been. The British Motor Show replaced the annual London Motor Show and was biennial. Extra halls were used from 1980 to give more space for the exhibits and the 1986 British Motor Show occupied four halls for cars and a further four for commercial vehicles, components and servicing equipment.

1980

Autocar became *the fastest motoring magazine* when British Airways ordered 30 copies a week for in-flight reading on Concorde.

In 1981 Volkswagen Beetle production passed the 20 million mark. The milestone car (left) was built in Mexico but retained the basic shape of the 1938 example pictured (right) with it. No other car has ever been made in such numbers.

1981

The longest taxi fare was for 7533 miles/12,123 km through 10 countries between 19 September and 18 October. The journey was sponsored for charity and the driver was Stephen Tillyer.

1982

The British 'totting-up' system procedure of driving licence endorsements (see 1963) was *replaced by a points system* from November. Offences were graded, the most serious carrying ten penalty points and lesser offences two or three points. Collection of 12 or more points in three years resulted in automatic disqualification.

1983

The wearing of seat belts by front-seat occupants of cars and vans became compulsory from 31 January. It only applies to vehicles registered on or after 1 January 1965, as earlier vehicles were not required to have seat belts fitted.

Motorists who ignored parking regulations in central London faced a new problem from May. *Wheel clamping*, known as the Denver Shoe in the USA where it originated, *was applied*, to immobilize illegally-parked vehicles completely. A motorist had to go to Hyde Park Police Car Pound and pay a fee of £19.50 plus a £10 penalty fine to have the clamp removed. The whole process could take several hours. Originally a special Metropolitan Police vehicle squad were responsible for clamping the vehicles but in 1986 that operation was privatized.

1984

The largest taxi fleet is in Mexico City, is made up of normal taxis, fixed-route *pesaros* and airport taxis, and totals 60,000 vehicles.

The longest distance covered on a standard tankful of fuel was recorded by an Audi 100 Turbo Diesel. Stuart Bladon, navigated by his son Bruce, drove the 1150.3 miles/1851.2 km from Land's End to John O'Groats and back to West Falkirk without refuelling. The journey, under RAC observation, took 22 hours 28 minutes and 53 seconds, an average speed of 51.17 mph/82.35 kph. Fuel consumption was 19.408 imp. gallons/88.23 litres of derv, giving an average of 59.27 mpg/4.76 litres/ 100 km.

The worst recent motorway accident in Britain occurred on the Godstone–Sevenoaks section of the M25 on 11 December in fog. In a multiple pile-up of cars and lorries, some of which caught fire, nine people were killed. Excessive speed in poor visibility was blamed for the accident.

1985

Switzerland began to charge for the use of motorways on 1 January. Motorists had to buy and display a special disc which cost 30 Swiss francs (about £10) and foreign visitors were not exempt. The fine for using a motorway without the disc was fixed at 120 Swiss francs (about £40).

Northern Ireland introduced ten-year driving licences in January. They were different from those in mainland Britain as they also served as identity cards at security checkpoints and so incorporated a picture of the driver sealed into the laminated plastic card. They cost £4.

Computer millionaire *Sir Clive Sinclair introduced his C5 electric three-wheeled 'car'* costing £400. It had a 15-mph/24-kph top speed. The provision of pedals in the cockpit meant it could be driven on the road by anyone over 14. It was not a success and was withdrawn.

London's *Greater London Council brought in a £25 fine for those who parked on pavements and verges* within the capital. This was in addition to any other fine.

On 5 June HRH Prince Charles *formally opened 'Wheels'*, a special facility at the National Motor Museum which transported visitors through the history of the motor-car.

The most expensive driving lesson was given on 20 June by Mike Collins, chief driving examiner of RoSPA Advanced Drivers' Association. He flew

This 1932 Bugatti Type 55 with 2.3-litre supercharged straight-8 engine was auctioned by Sotheby's in London for £440,000 in 1985, setting a new European record.

from Birmingham to Paris to give a 1½-hour driving lesson which cost £266.

The highest auction price for a used Rolls-Royce was the $2,229,000 (then £1,768,000) paid by Jim Pattison on 29 June. He purchased the 1965 Rolls-Royce Phantom V with psychedelic paintwork formerly owned by Beatle John Lennon at Sotheby's New York auction.

The world's largest collection of Rolls-Royce cars was owned by Bhagwan Shri Rajneesh, the Indian mystic, before he was deported from Oregon, USA, in November. The 93 cars in his collection were given to him by his disciples.

The fastest engine change was accomplished by a Royal Marine team from Portsmouth on 21 November on the BBC *Record Breakers* programme. They removed and replaced the engine of a Ford Escort in 42 seconds.

The highest British price for a used car at auction was £440,000 paid for a 1932 Bugatti Type 55 sold at Sotheby's London auction in December. One of only 30 surviving Type 55s, it had once been owned by the second Baron Rothschild.

The country with the most cars in use was the USA with over 130 million, followed by Japan with 27 million, West Germany with 25 million, Italy with 21 million, France with 20 million and Britain with 17 million.

1986

Weldon C. Kocich, a test driver for the Goodyear Tire and Rubber Co., *clocked up 3,141,946 miles/ 5,056,472 km* between 5 February 1953 and 28 February 1986, an average of 95,210 miles/ 153,221 km a year.

The world's largest car auction centre was opened

The world's largest car auction centre, opened by British Car Auctions at Blackbushe, Surrey, in 1986. There were three auction halls, a restaurant and covered parking for 500 cars in the building shown here. Visitors cars were parked in the area shown in the bottom half of the picture.

by British Car Auctions on a 60-acre/24.3-ha site at Blackbushe, Surrey. Facilities include three auction halls, covered viewing for 500 cars, a 350-seat restaurant and parking for 1100 visitors' cars.

The oldest driver in Britain is the Rev. Albert T. Humphrey, who was 100 on 18 May and still drives his Mini. He has averaged about 12,000 miles/ 19,300 km a year for most of his 60 years of driving and has never taken a driving test because they weren't required when he started to drive.

The highest price ever paid for a car at auction was the £4.6 million paid for a 1931 Bugatti Royale with Berline de Voyage body. One of only six Royales built, it was later sold to Texan Thomas Monaghan for £5.7 million.

Fixed penalty fines for minor motoring offences were introduced in Britain in October. Some 250 offences were covered by fines of either £12 for non-endorsable offences or £24 for more serious ones. Motorists who did not accept that they were guilty could opt to go to court in the normal way. If the ticket for the fixed penalty was not paid within 28 days the amount was increased by 50% and courts had power to ensure payment of the fine.

The world's longest urban ring road was completed on 29 October, providing 115.1 miles/185.2 km of motorway around London. The M25 motorway had taken 14 years to build and cost £1000 million. The total length of 119.5 miles/192.3 km around London included 4.4 miles/7.1 km of non-motorway where traffic passed through the Dartford–Purfleet tunnels under the River Thames. The opening was performed by Prime Minister Margaret Thatcher, but the new motorway was unable to cope with peak traffic flows from the outset and rapidly vied for the title of the world's longest mobile traffic jam.

There were *14,500 black taxi cabs and 19,000 drivers in London.*

The world's most expensive car delivered to a customer was the Rolls-Royce Phantom VI State landaulette exported to Malaysia. The rear compartment had a power-operated hood so that it could be converted into an open car and many of the fittings were in solid gold and silver. With UK taxes it would have cost almost £450,000.

The highest-ever new car sales in Britain were recorded with 1,882,474 new cars registered in the year. The previous record was 1,832,027 in 1985.

1987

The National Exhibition Centre, Birmingham, has *the largest parking area in the UK* with space for 15,000 cars and 200 coaches.

The world's largest car park is at West Edmonton Mall, Edmonton, Alberta, Canada. There is space for 20,000 cars and an additional overflow car park for another 10,000.

William Boddy, editor of *Motor Sport* since 1945, holds the *British record for continuous editorship of a motoring magazine.* His association with *Motor Sport* is even longer than that as he ran the magazine during World War II.

The world's two steepest streets are both in San Francisco, USA. Filbert Street on Russian Hill and 22nd Street, Dolores Heights, both have a gradient of 1 in 3.17/31.5%.

The world's longest road is the Pan-American Highway which stretches 17,018 miles/27,387 km from north-west Alaska to southernmost Chile.

Antique automobiles are issued with special number plates in virtually every American State, the District of Columbia and eight Canadian provinces.

The longest annual event for Veteran and Vintage cars is the American Glidden Tour, organized by the Antique Automobile Club and the Veteran Motor Car Club. It usually lasts a week and covers about 500 miles/800 km. In 1908 Mr C. J. Glidden was the first traveller to arrive in Jerusalem by car.

The world's most expensive catalogued model is the Rolls-Royce Phantom VI seven-seater limousine with coachwork by Mulliner Park Ward. It costs £195,595.83 in standard form without extras!

This Oldsmobile Delta 88 Royal Brougham was one of a number of 1987 American cars fitted with a passive restraint seat belt system. The belts are fixed to the door and thus are fastened automatically when the door is closed. Manufacturers in the USA were required by law to fit such devices to a proportion of their 1987 models.

THE MOTOR INDUSTRY

To enable the technical details given in this section to be understood by as wide a circle of people as possible both Imperial inches and millimetres have been used for dimensions. For British and American cars produced up to the 1980s the inch figures are the most accurate and the metric figures conversions. For Continental manufacturers, who have always worked in millimetres, the reverse applies. Engine capacities throughout have been given in litres or cc except for American cars where the capacity in cubic inches is quoted as well. Other abbreviations sometimes found include ohv for overhead valve engines, ohc for overhead camshaft and fwd for front-wheel drive. Where it is stated that a car has 2+2 seating this means that the rear seats are rather cramped and really suitable only for small children.

Alfa Romeo (Italy)

Ugo Stella founded Anonima Lombardo Fabbrica Automobili in 1909, but the first cars bearing the Alfa name did not emerge until 1910, when the last Darracqs had been assembled in the Milan factory. First models, designed by Giuseppe Merosi, had side-valve 4-cylinder engines and were a 24 hp 4.1-litre and a 12 hp 2.4-litre.

Nicola Romeo, an Italian industrialist, took over the factory in 1915 and after World War I the cars were marketed as Alfa Romeos. The RL model introduced in October 1921 had a 2916-cc (75 × 110 mm/2.95 × 4.33 in) 6-cylinder engine with push-rod operated overhead valves, a detachable cylinder head, and engine and gearbox were mounted in the chassis as one unit. The more sporting RLS model had a 76 mm/2.99 in bore, giving 2994 cc, and was marketed as the 22/90. More powerful still was the 1925 RLSS (Super Sport) lightweight version with dry-sump lubrication and 83 bhp. There was also a 1944-cc 4-cylinder 15/20 hp derivative of the RL called the RM, selling for a chassis price of £600 in 1924 compared with £750 for the RL. Less successful was the 6336-cc 6-cylinder 35/50 hp G1 luxury model.

Alfa Romeo Giulietta 2.0 (left) and Alfasud Ti 1.5.

In 1926 Merosi was succeeded by Vittorio Jano (q.v.), who had joined Alfa Romeo from Fiat three years earlier to design their very successful P2 Grand Prix car, and the classic 6C–1500 overhead camshaft 6-cylinder sports model appeared. It was followed in 1929 by a more powerful 1750 model, which was capable of over 90 mph/145 kph in twin cam Sport form and there was even a supercharged version. Eight cylinders in line were the main feature of the 1931 twin-cam 8C-2300, which led to the 2.9-litre supercharged P3 racing car.

In 1930 the company's name was changed to SA Alfa Romeo (previously it had traded under Nicola Romeo's name) and in 1933 it became government controlled, as it remained until 1986. The 1750 and 8C-2300 were replaced by a 2.3-litre 6-cylinder unsupercharged model in 1934, and this continued in modified form as the 2500 into the 1940s.

In 1950 with the arrival of the 4-cylinder 1884 cc 1900 model Alfa Romeos became unitary construction saloons. The 1290 cc Giulietta saloon continued the theme in 1954, and in 1962 a derivative called the Giulia with 1570 cc was added. The larger 130 bhp 2600 saloon arrived the same year, but sporting motorists were not forgotten and in due

course there were open Spyder versions of Giulietta, Giulia and 2600. The 1750 range replaced the 1600s in 1968 and included the sporting GTV Coupé. Top model in the range in 1970 was another coupé, the 2593 cc V8 Montreal.

In 1971 a second factory was opened near Naples to produce the Alfasud, a new small saloon with a flat-four engine driving the front wheels, which proved a great success. Automatic transmission was offered for the first time on the 2000 saloon, a 1962 cc bored-out version of the 1750, in 1972 and the more boxy Alfetta was introduced, later augmented by a coupé. Pininfarina-designed and built open Spyder versions of the 1600 and 2000 appeared in 1972 and continued into 1986, mainly for the American market. The Giulietta name was revived in 1977 for 1.3- and 1.6-litre four-door saloons with gearbox and rear axle as one unit, as on the Alfetta. The prestige Alfa 6 saloon with 2492 cc V6 engine, and no fewer than six carburettors to provide 160 bhp, arrived in 1979 and a year later the same engine with fuel injection was fitted to the Alfetta-based GTV Coupé.

The Arna (Alfa Romeo Nissan Autoveicoli) built in co-operation with Japanese manufacturers Nissan replaced the Alfasud in 1983. The Arna, assembled in Italy, was a cocktail of Nissan Cherry body and rear suspension allied to Alfa Romeo's 1186 cc (Alfasud) engine, front suspension, gearbox and steering. More successful was the larger hatchback version of the Alfasud called the Alfa 33 that also arrived in 1983. Later that year the estate car version of the 33 became the first four-wheel-drive Alfa.

In 1985 new Alfa 75 and 90 models replaced the Giulietta and were available with engines from 1567 to 2492 cc, including two turbo diesels. The 75 was so named to mark 75 years of Alfa Romeo car production.

During 1986 Ford became interested in purchasing the ailing Alfa Romeo company but in the end it was Fiat who took them over, towards the end of the year. Fiat intend to integrate Alfa Romeo and Lancia in the future.

Aston Martin (UK)

The marque's origins go back to a prototype designed by Lionel Martin and Robert Bamford in 1914, followed by a second prototype in 1919. The first Aston Martin production cars appeared in 1922 with 1.5-litre engines and were sold by Bamford and Martin Ltd for £850. The Aston part of the car's name related to the Aston Clinton hill-climb where Martin had scored successes in pre-1914

days with a Singer. At Brooklands in 1922 an Aston Martin nicknamed 'Bunny' took the 15-, 16-, 17-, 18- and 19-hour records – the first small car to capture world records.

The company went bankrupt in 1925 but a new company, Aston Martin Motors Ltd, was formed in 1926, with works at Feltham. A. C. Bertelli designed a new 1½-litre car with an ohc engine and David Brown final drive. It was a sporting car ideally suited to fast touring or racing and soon established a good competition record. The company became Aston Martin Ltd in 1929 and passed into the control of R. G. Sutherland in 1933. A year later came the Mark II with 73 bhp and in 1936 the 2-litre arrived. In Speed Model form the latter had almost 100 mph/161 kph performance.

In 1947 the David Brown group took control of both Aston Martin and Lagonda, with the result that in 1950 the Aston DB2 went into production using the 2.6-litre 6-cylinder twin-ohc engine that W. O. Bentley had designed for Lagonda. From this model evolved the 2.9-litre DB3S which scored 15 international competition wins for the marque, winning the Sports Car World Championship in 1959 (the first British make to do so). The same year the Le Mans 24-hour race was won by the Shelby/Salvadori DBR1, and the DB4 model went into production at the former Tickford coachbuilding works at Newport Pagnell. The 1964 DB5 had a 3995 cc engine with 282 bhp and the DB6 a new body with longer 101.75-in/2584-mm wheelbase and 325 bhp Vantage engine.

Company Developments Ltd took over from the David Brown group in 1972, by which time the DB6 had been replaced by the more modern DBS – first in 6-cylinder and then in 5.3-litre V8 guise. This forms the basis of the current production Aston Martin V8, offered in saloon and convertible versions with a 102.8-in/2611-mm wheelbase.

Low production levels (only DB4, 5, 6 and V8 models topped 1000) and financial crises dogged the company through the 1970s and early 1980s, with several changes of ownership. The company is now controlled by Peter Livanos, part-owner of the American company Automotive Investments.

Aston Martin DB4.

The original William Towns design for the Lagonda with pop-up headlamps.

1934 Audi UW front-wheel-drive saloon.

The futuristic high-performance Lagonda four-door saloon was shown in 1976 and went into production in 1978 with an electronic facia with touch switches. In 1984 changes included three 5-in/127-mm cathode ray tubes used in place of instruments. The 10,000th Aston Martin, a V8 saloon, was built in 1984.

None of these models is built in quantity – total Aston Martin Lagonda production for 1985 was 180 cars. What they do offer is a handbuilt standard of quality with supercar performance. Even the big Lagonda is capable of 140 mph/225 kph, as is the standard V8 model, and all use Aston Martin's own 5340 cc engine, with a plate on each engine giving the name of the man who built it. The V8 Vantage offers real 170 mph/274 kph performance from 370 bhp, while even faster still is the 432 bhp 185 mph/298 kph Special Vantage Zagato which was announced at the 1986 Geneva Motor Show. It was one of just 50 two-seater models coachbuilt by Zagato in Italy, recreating a link between the two companies that goes back to the special 150 mph/241 kph DB4 GT Zagato of 1962. That car cost £5470 and offered 0–60 mph/97 kph in just over 6 seconds. The 1987 Vantage Zagato reaches that speed in 4.8 seconds but costs £95,000 – such is the price of progress! Newest model is the 1987 V8 Vantage Volante which is claimed to be the world's fastest four-seater convertible, capable of 160 mph/257 kph. In March 1987 the Lagonda was restyled with softer lines and triple rectangular headlamps replacing the previous pop-up units.

Audi (W. Germany)

The current German company Audi NSU Auto Union AG was formed in 1969 and, as the name implies, is an amalgam of several older marques. Audi Automobilewerke was formed in Zwickau in 1910 by August Horch after he had left the company which bore his name – Audi being a latinized version of Horch. The first Audi was a 10/28 hp model with which Horch himself scored successes in the Austrian Alpine Trials between 1911 and 1914. A larger 6-cylinder model appeared in 1924 and was followed by the 1928 Imperator model with 4.9-litre 8-cylinder engine. That was the last of the original Audis for in the same year control passed into the hands of J. S. Rasmussen of DKW and in 1931 a small Audi with DKW chassis appeared, while at the same time the first front-wheel-drive DKW, the F1, arrived.

In 1932 Audi, DKW, Horch and Wanderer combined to form Auto Union, symbolized by the current Audi badge with four interlinked circles which dates from that time. The first of the new Audis had 6-cylinder Wanderer engines and front-wheel drive, but there were no Audis after 1939 until the name was revived in 1965. Auto Union and the Audi factory were nationalized in 1945 and it was not until four years later that Audi was re-established at Düsseldorf.

Mercedes-Benz acquired control of Auto Union in 1956, by which time the company was based in Ingolstadt making DKWs. Volkswagen became majority shareholders in 1964 and in the following year a 1.7-litre front-wheel-drive Audi saloon was launched, but it was not until the end of 1968 that the first new Volkswagen-influenced Audi, the 2-litre 100, appeared, giving VW an upmarket model. Aggressive marketing established a quality reputation from which Audi have never looked back. In 1969 the company merged with NSU and until 1977 the front-wheel-drive Ro80 saloon with twin-rotor Wankel engine and semi-automatic transmission was included in the range.

In 1972 came a new smaller Audi, the 80 front-wheel-drive saloon with a 97.2-in/2470-mm wheelbase and 1296- or 1470-cc 4-cylinder ohc engine. Negative offset steering geometry and a diagonal hydraulic split for the disc/drum braking system were unusual features. In 1973 the 100,000th Audi 80 was built and that car was also the millionth Audi. There was a new small model in 1974 called the 50, which became the VW Polo in 1975. The Audi 50 used the VW Golf 1093-cc ohc engine, which in this application gave 50 or 60 bhp, to drive the front wheels and there were front disc brakes. The wheelbase of the three-door hatchback body was 91.7 in/2330 mm and the overall length 137.4 in/3490 mm.

The 1976 front-wheel-drive Audi 100 four-door saloon was altogether much bigger, with a wheelbase of 105.3 in/2675 mm and an overall length of 184.3 in/4680 mm. Engines ranged from the 4-cylinder 1.6- and 2-litre ohc units to the unusual 5-cylinder 2144-cc fuel-injected version producing 100 bhp. In 1977 an Avant hatchback version was added and production of the Audi–NSU Ro80 stopped. In 1978 there was a new 80 model (known as the 4000 in the USA) that was larger with a 100-in/2540-mm wheelbase and 172.6-in/4385-mm length and also looked somewhat similar to the 100. Engines were 1297-cc or 1588-cc 4-cylinder units, with the top GLE model having Bosch fuel injection.

A move upmarket came with the 1979 200 model which used the 100 body with higher equipment levels, four rectangular headlamps, and either the 2144-cc 136-bhp 5-cylinder engine or a turbocharged 170 bhp version. Even more performance was offered by the 1980 4-wheel drive Quattro Coupé which was based on the 80 but with a 99.4-in/2525-mm wheelbase and small boot. All independent suspension, four-wheel disc brakes and 200 bhp from the 2.2-litre 5-cylinder engine made this a very rapid car. The Quattro promoted a revival of interest in four-wheel drive, particularly after it had won the 1981 Lombard RAC Rally. For 1981 there was also an Audi Coupé model which was front-wheel-drive with 1.9-litre 5-cylinder, and later 1.8-litre 4-cylinder, engine.

At the end of 1982 came a completely new and very aerodynamic 100 (5000 in USA) model with flush glass and headlamps, fluted wheel trims and 30% of the unitary bodyshell zinc-plated for corrosion resistance. The wheelbase was 105.7 in/2685 mm and the drag coefficient a class-leading 0.32. Engines were 1781-cc 4-cylinder or 1.9- or 2.2-litre 5-cylinder units. Anti-lock braking was optional on some models. Soon afterwards came a turbo diesel version of the 80, the Coupé was offered with the 2.2-litre engine, and there was a four-wheel-drive 80 Quattro – the first four-wheel-drive Audi saloon. In 1983 the new 200 appeared using the 100's aerodynamic body with the 136-bhp 2.2-litre engine, and there was also a turbocharged version with 182 bhp capable of 140 mph/ 225 kph. In the autumn of 1984 the 5-cylinder 80

1980s Audi 200 Quattro with 4-wheel drive.

models became the 90, and there were four-wheel-drive versions of 80, 90, 100 and 200 models, while the biggest 5-cylinder engine became 2226 cc.

A new, smaller 100.2-in/2545-mm wheelbase 80 model arrived for 1987 with an aerodynamic shape (0.29 C_d) and a fully galvanized bodyshell (a feature introduced on the 100/200 in 1985). A boot which opened down to bumper level and the new Procon-Ten passive safety system, which uses steel cables to pull the steering column away from the driver and tension the seat belts in a frontal accident, were other new features. On the 80 Quattro the Torsen (torque sensing) differential was adopted to regulate automatically the tractive effort between front and rear wheels according to their grip, preventing wheelspin. The new 5-cylinder 90 model sharing the same body arrived later in 1987.

Austin (UK)

Herbert Austin was responsible for the design of the first Wolseleys, but left the company in 1905 to design his own cars. The first Austin was built in the Longbridge, Birmingham, factory and took to the road in April 1906. This big 25/30 hp 4-cylinder was typical of the Austins produced up to 1914, although there were some 6-cylinder models. In 1908 there was even a team of Austin Grand Prix cars.

Austin became a public company in 1914 and after the war for a time there was only one model, the very successful 4-cylinder 20 hp. Their 1.6-litre 12 hp was added in 1921 and joined in 1922 by the revolutionary Seven. Powered by a 747-cc sidevalve four, it was very robust and reliable, and cheap to run. It was built under licence in Germany, America, France and Japan and also raced with great success. It continued in production through the 1930s and was joined in 1932 by the successful 10 hp. In 1947 the big Austin Sheerline and Princess 4-litre models with independent front suspension arrived, with bodies coachbuilt by Vanden Plas. Mainstay of the Austin range, though, was the 1.2-litre A40 in Dorset and Devon form.

In 1952 Austin merged with Morris, who also controlled MG, Wolseley and Riley, to form the British Motor Corporation. Soon afterwards came the popular little two-door A30, the first Austin with a monocoque body. The larger 99.3-in/2522-mm wheelbase A50 Cambridge followed in 1955, by which time most Austins were chassisless, including the new 6-cylinder Westminster.

The Austin Seven made a comeback in 1959, only this model had an 848-cc transverse engine and front-wheel drive allied to great space efficiency. We know it today as the Mini, and in tuned Cooper form (from 1962) it proved very successful in competition. The popular 948-cc ohv A40 Farina also arrived in 1959, followed by the family-sized 1622 cc A60 Cambridge three-box saloon in 1961. Hydrolastic fluid suspension giving a very good ride was the main feature of the bigger 1100 in 1964 and there was considerable interior space, despite an overall length of 146.75 in/3727 mm. A transverse 1098 cc 4-cylinder engine driving the front wheels and Issigonis packaging were the means by which it was achieved. The Minis acquired Hydrolastic suspension for 1965, the same suspension system also being used on the much bigger 106-in/2692-mm wheelbase 1800 model with its transverse 1798-cc 4-cylinder engine and front-wheel drive. It soon replaced the A60, while the 2912-cc Westminster in Mark II guise remained the top Austin model.

A 1275 cc version of the 1100 was marketed as the 1300 in 1968, and that year BMC and Leyland merged to form British Leyland. Last of the big Austins was the 3-litre announced in 1967; so unsuccessful was it that it was relaunched in a modified form only twelve months later. It used the 1800 cabin with a larger boot and longer bonnet to accommodate the 2912-cc 125 bhp 6-cylinder engine which drove the rear wheels. Suspension was Hydrolastic with self-levelling at the rear. With a 114.5-in/2908-mm wheelbase and 180.75-in/4591-mm length it was spacious but also heavy and could only just manage 100 mph/161 kph.

Austin were convinced of the merits of front-wheel drive and used it for their new hatchback Maxi 1500 announced in 1969. It had a new ohc 1485-cc engine and a five-speed gearbox and offered estate car versatility. A more powerful 1748-cc version was added in 1971, and from then on front-wheel drive featured only on BL's Austin models. The popular 1100/1300, which included a 1300GT 70-bhp model from 1970, was replaced in

1973 by the less successful Allegro saloon, which came in a variety of engine sizes from 1100 to 1750 and pioneered the Hydragas suspension. The 1800 was augmented by the 2200 the same year with transverse 6-cylinder engine giving 110 bhp. The wedge-shaped 18/22 series replaced both of them in 1975, and used the same engines but Hydragas suspension. Later that year it became the Princess and then in 1978 the Princess 2 when fitted with the new 1695- or 1993-cc O-Series ohc 4-cylinder engines, though the 2.2-litre six was retained. In 1982 the Princess was fitted with a new 5-door hatchback body and became the Ambassador.

The Metro 'supermini' of 1980 had the modern hatchback body the Mini should have had years before and demonstrated once again the advantages of optimum space utilization in a car that was only 134 in/3404 mm long with an 88.6-in/2250-mm wheelbase. The Mini 998- and 1275-cc engines were used. At the end of 1984 a five-door version was added. The Mini meanwhile continued in production and on 19 February 1986 the 5 millionth Mini was produced at Longbridge.

The 1983 five-door Maestro replaced the Allegro, from which it differed considerably. Engines were the 1275-cc A-plus or the new R-Series 1598-cc ohc units positioned transversely to drive the front wheels through a VW Golf four- or five-speed gearbox mounted end on. Europe's first electronic carburettor control of idle speed, cold-start enrichment and over-run fuel cut-off was fitted, and the top Vanden Plas version was the first European mass-production car to have electronic solid state instruments with a vacuum fluorescent coloured display, digital speedometer and voice synthesizer to give various information warnings like 'low fuel'. The suspension was by coil springs all round, with trailing arms at the rear. It had a 98.7-in/2507-mm wheelbase and an overall length of 159.5-in/4050-mm, with moulded thermoplastic bumpers. Prices ranged from £4555 to £6395 in March 1983.

In April 1984 came the most recent new Austin, the Montego, which was in essence a Maestro with

1987 Austin Metro Vanden Plas 5-door.

a boot added, although its wheelbase at 101 in/ 2565 mm and length at 175.9 in/4468 mm were greater. The 1300 engine was the smallest offered but there was a new S-Series 1598-cc ohc engine that also went into the Maestro at the same time. For the Montego only the 1994 cc O-Series (Ambassador) engine was also available with a Honda five-speed gearbox. Both O- and S-Series engines featured electronic knock sensing for the first time on an Austin. An estate car version of the Montego was added for 1985. Mini, Metro, Maestro and Montego made up the 1987 Austin range.

Bentley (UK)

A fast touring car was W. O. Bentley's aim when he set out to design the first model to bear his name, a natural progression from the DFPs he had raced so successfully in 1912–14. The 3-litre Bentley was announced in November 1919 and the first prototype was on the road early in 1920, but it was not to be until 1922 that any production cars were delivered. Reliability of the long-stroke 4-cylinder engine was proved when a 3-litre won the Le Mans 24-hour race in 1924. The bigger 6-cylinder 6½-litre arrived in 1925 and the 4½-litre in 1927, but it was a lone 3-litre that won the 1927 Le Mans after the other team cars had been damaged in the White House crash. Bentleys won in 1928, 1929 and 1930 too. The 4½-litre supercharged Blower Bentley appeared in 1929, much against W. O. Bentley's wishes and only 50 were built. Though very fast and capable of over 120 mph/193 kph, it was unreliable in races of the day.

Grandest of all the Bentleys built in the Cricklewood factory was the 100 mph/161 kph 8-litre of 1930–1, but only 100 were made before Bentley Motors, which had been dogged by financial troubles from the outset, went into receivership in the Depression of 1931. Plans for a rescue by Napier failed when they were outbid for the company by Rolls-Royce Ltd, who purchased it for £125,256. Rolls-Royce formed Bentley Motors (1931) Ltd as a subsidiary and in 1933 the new Rolls–Royce-designed Bentley 3½-litre appeared. W. O. Bentley worked for the company until 1935 but had no say in the car's design, though he did valuable development work.

The new Bentley was built at Derby by Rolls-Royce until 1940, though the 1939 4¼-litre Mark V was very different from the 3½. After the war Bentley car production resumed at Crewe and the new 4¼-litre Mark VI had a factory-built Pressed Steel body. It was the first complete car to be built by Rolls-Royce and the Rolls-Royce models which

Sir Malcolm Campbell's 1936 Bentley 4¼-litre Vanden Plas tourer.

followed were badge-engineered versions of the Bentley, which itself was built in bigger numbers than any Bentley before or since. A later derivative of the R-type 4½-litre was the Continental, built between 1952 and 1955. With lightweight Mulliner body and sloping tail it was capable of 120 mph/193 kph, making it the fastest four-seater car in the world at the time.

A decline in Bentley's fortunes started in 1955 with the S-series, merely a Bentley-radiatored Rolls-Royce, and this continued with the T-series 6.3-litre V8 which shared the Silver Shadow's monocoque body and mechanicals. The bankruptcy of Rolls-Royce Ltd in 1971 also included Bentley Motors (1931) Ltd, but in 1973 the car division was floated as a separate public company called Rolls-Royce Motors Ltd, of which Bentley Motors Ltd was a subsidiary. The introduction of the Bentley Mulsanne Turbo in 1982 marked a revival in Bentley's fortunes with this special model capable of 135 mph/217 kph and available only as a Bentley. In 1985 the Turbo R was produced with much stiffer suspension giving a more sporting ride with better roadholding and less body roll.

Extensive changes to 1987 models included increased power from the adoption of fuel injection, anti-lock brakes and a memory facility for seat adjustment on Mulsanne and Turbo R. The latter also had completely new seats with increased lateral support. Most expensive Bentley in 1987 was the £95,605 Continental convertible with Mulliner Park Ward body and 6750-cc V8 engine.

BMW (W. Germany)

Originally founded in 1916 as Bayerische Flugzeug Werke to make aero engines, the Munich company's name was changed to Bayerische Motoren Werke in 1922 and the first BMW motorcycle emerged a year later. Car production started in 1928 in a factory at Eisenach with a car

BMW 328.

called the Dixi. This was in fact an Austin Seven built under licence.

The first true BMW, the 4-cylinder 800-cc 3/20 with independent swing axle suspension and a backbone chassis, did not appear until 1932, to be followed a year later by the 6-cylinder 303. Further developments were the 1490-cc 6-cylinder 315 and the 1936 1911-cc 319 models which acquired a sporting reputation and culminated in the 2-litre 328 sports car of 1936 with 80 bhp from triple carburettors and a top speed of over 100 mph/161 kph. The 328 won its first race, the Eifelrennen, at the Nürburgring in June 1936. During the 1935–9 period BMWs were imported into Britain and sold under the Frazer Nash-BMW name.

The Eisenach factory in East Germany was nationalized in 1945, but production of prewar BMWs continued there until about 1955. The first car to emerge from the Munich factory was the 501 in 1952 with 1971-cc 6-cylinder engine, while the 507 Coupé built from 1956–9 was a classic sporting model with 3168-cc V8 engine developing 150 bhp. Maximum speed of this 172-in/4370-mm-long two-seater was about 125 mph/201 kph and it cost almost $9000 in the USA. In 1955 the BMW Isetta bubble car appeared, followed in 1957 by the rear-engined 2-cylinder 700.

A return to the building of proper cars came in 1961 with the Michelotti-styled 4-cylinder 1500 and its larger brother the 1800. They marked the start of the present BMW prestige executive image, which was enhanced by the 2000 coupé of 1965. The 1600 and 2000 saloons of 1966, with 4-cylinder 1573- and 1991-cc engines respectively, were important too and the 1600 two-door saloon was fitted with the 1991-cc 4-cylinder engine in 1968 to produce the 100 bhp 2002. This was a small 98.4-in/2500-mm wheelbase saloon with real sports car performance – 0–60 mph/0–97 kph in about 10.7 seconds and a 110 mph/177 kph top speed. Later the same year the new ohc 6-cylinder 2500 and 2800 saloons were announced, together with the 2800CS coupé, which used the 2800 mechanicals in the 2000CS body. These bigger four-door saloons had a 106-in/2692-mm wheel-

base and an overall length of 185 in/4700 mm. The 2494-cc engine gave 150 bhp and the 2788-cc unit 170 bhp. Suspension was independent all round (self-levelling, too, on the 2800) and there were four-wheel disc brakes.

BMW now had a proper model range and had absorbed Glas along the way in 1967, resulting in the 1600GT with BMW mechanicals in the Glas 1300GT body. In 1971 the 2800 saloon and coupé became 2985-cc 3.0S and 3.0CS models with 180 bhp. At the same time the 1600 became the 1602 and the fuel-injected 2002tii succeeded the 2002. In 1972 the 2000 was replaced by the four-door 520 saloon with a new 3.5 in/90 mm longer 103.9-in/2640-mm wheelbase body but using a developed version of the 1991-cc ohc 4-cylinder engine offered with either carburettors or Kugelfischer fuel injection. Power output was 115 or 130 bhp respectively. The first figure of the number denoted the body and the second two the engine size in litres, a system that still applies.

The 170-bhp 2002 Turbo, the first of the modern European turbocharged cars, with a 130 mph/210 kph top speed, arrived in 1973. That year a version of the 520 with 145-bhp 6-cylinder 2494-cc engine was launched as the 525 and there was a 3.3-litre long-wheelbase model added at the top of the range. For 1975 there was a 1766-cc 518 and a 2788-cc 6-cylinder 165-bhp 528. Later that year the 1602/2002 models were replaced by the 3-Series with engine sizes of 1573, 1754 and 1977 cc respectively for 316, 318 and 320 models, which shared the same 101.0-in/2565-mm wheelbase two-door saloon body. The 630 and 633 big coupé models with 130 mph/209 kph top speed were introduced in 1976.

In 1977 BMW reverted to 6-cylinder engines for some models, with the 320 and 520 sharing the 1990-cc 122-bhp unit and a new 2315-cc fuel injected engine for the 323i. The 528 received fuel injection at the same time, boosting power to 184 bhp. The big saloons came right up to date the same year with the new 110-in/2795-mm wheelbase 7-Series which echoed the styling of the 6-Series coupés. Among the features were high pressure power hydraulics for the brakes, height adjustable seats, central locking and air conditioning. The least powerful 6-cylinder 728 had 170 bhp and in 1979 there was a top 745i version with 3210 cc engine giving 252 bhp. Completely different was the exotic 1978 M1, which was the company's first mid-engined car and had an Ital-styled glassfibre bodyshell and multi-tubular chassis. The 6-cylinder 3453-cc twin-ohc 24-valve engine was mounted longitudinally and produced 277 bhp, giving a claimed 160 mph/257 kph.

In 1981 the 5-Series was re-bodied with the 4-cylinder engine retained for only the 518. The 6-cylinder 520i, 525i and 528i models all had fuel injection. A new feature was the world's first variable service-interval indicator, using a system of coloured lights to denote when a service or oil change was needed. In 1982 for the American market there was a 6-cylinder 528e model with high gearing and a 2693-cc version of the 320 engine giving 121 bhp and developing its torque lower down. The aim of the Eta (efficiency) engine was greater economy and the following year the same engine appeared in the European 525e model.

There were lighter and slightly more aerodynamic 3-Series models in 1982 and for 1983 the 7-Series saloons were available with the new ZF four-speed overdrive automatic gearbox, and there was a 524TD with 115 bhp from a 2443-cc 6-cylinder turbo diesel engine. At the other end of the scale was the 286-bhp M635Csi coupé with 3453 cc engine fitted with a 24-valve head. In 1985 the same engine went into the 5-Series to produce the sporting M5.

For 1987 there were lower, wider, longer and more aerodynamic (C_d 0.32) 7-Series saloons with 111.4-in/2830-mm wheelbase and an overall length of 193.3 in/4910 mm. The cheapest 730i had a 2966-cc 6-cylinder engine giving 197 bhp and the 735i a 3430-cc unit producing 220 bhp. Top model was the 750i with BMW's first V12 production engine, producing over 270 bhp from 4988 cc. On these models Bosch ASC (anti-slip control) to prevent wheelspin was optional and anti-lock braking and Dunlop–Michelin TD safety wheels standard, the latter for the first time on a German car. The 1987 7-Series models were also the world's first to use ellipsoid technology for headlights, resulting in 30% more light output with a sharp 'cut off', while the car's malfunction system could give warnings in six European languages.

British Leyland (UK)

This is the former name of Britain's nationalized motor manufacturer which produces Austin, MG and Rover cars. The name was changed to Rover Group plc (q.v.) in 1986.

Buick (USA)

Inventor David Dunbar Buick built his first engine in 1901 and followed it with an overhead-valve version in 1902. The need for a car to put it in led to the Buick Motor Company's formation on 19 May 1903. The first model of 1904 had a flat-twin engine under the floor and chain drive from the two-speed gearbox. The 2606-cc/159-cu. in overhead-valve engine, unusual at the time, was rated at 16 hp. Problems of finance led to William Durant taking control of Buick in November 1904. Apart from the side-valve 4-cylinder models of 1906–9, overhead valves were to remain a Buick feature into the 1980s.

In 1908 David Buick left the company and Durant formed General Motors, who took over the assets of Buick. Up until 1914 a range of 4-cylinder models was marketed, with 30,000 cars sold by 1910 and exports to Britain where they were sold as British Bedfords and Bedford-Buicks with locally made bodies. Electric lighting and starting were added in 1914, the same year that the first 6-cylinder model was made.

The millionth Buick was built in 1923, when production exceeded 200,000 a year for the first time. In 1924 came front-wheel brakes, detachable cylinder heads and a less rounded radiator. Re-styled 1929 models had 3.8- or 5.1-litre/239- or 309-cu. in engines, while in 1931 all models were straight-8s and synchromesh gearboxes were standard on the top models. The 5.7-litre/348-cu. in engine was Buick's first with over 100 bhp, while independent front suspension was added in 1934.

It was a 1936 Buick 37.8-hp limousine with a 5231-cc/319-cu. in straight-8 engine that took King Edward VIII into exile after the abdication. By that time models had a cruciform-braced frame, hydraulic brakes, and no-draught ventilation. Cheapest and best-selling model was the Series 40, and in 1936 Buick sold 179,533 cars. In 1939 Buick were the first to use flashing indicator signals instead of semaphore arms.

The year 1948 marked two important developments: the availability of Dynaflow torque-

1951 Buick Super Eight with distinctive 'portholes' in the bonnet.

converter automatic transmission on the Road-master; and the new Riviera series which pioneered the convertible body with hardtop. Power-assisted steering was offered in 1952 and power brakes in 1953, the year the first Buick V8 engine of 5.3 litres/324 cu. in arrived. The following year it was used in all models. The 1954 Century had 200 bhp, could exceed 100 mph/161 kph and featured a trendsetting wrap-around wind-screen.

Styling took the lead in 1959 with the arrival of tail fins, while in 1960 the Special was the division's first attempt at a compact car using a 3.5-litre/215-cu. in aluminium V8 engine, which was later to be taken up by Rover after being discarded in 1961 in favour of a 3245-cc/198-cu. in cast-iron V6, the first in an American car. The sporting Riviera coupé came in 1963 and was capable of 120 mph/193 kph from a 6.6-litre/400-cu. in V8 developing 325 bhp. The 1964 Special and Skylark were the first Buicks to have a perimeter-frame chassis. In 1965 the Riviera was the only model without this feature, while the new Wildcat had a 3-in/76-mm longer wheelbase, crash padding on the facia with recessed knobs and switches and optional bucket seats. The same year's Electra 225 had horizontal rear lamp clusters that ran right across the back of the car. The 1966 Riviera shared the Toronado's bodyshell and, with a 119-in/3023-mm wheelbase and 211-in/5359-mm overall length, was very impressive. Recessed headlamps behind the grille bars, face-level ventilation and a rotating drum speedometer were other features. Special and Skylark bodies changed, too, and the 3687-cc/225-cu. in V6 had 160 bhp.

Dual circuit brakes, collapsible steering columns and hazard flashers were standard on all 1967 models, but the big news for that year was an all-new V8, with wedge-shaped combustion chambers, to replace the existing engines dating from 1953. There were 6554- and 7049-cc/400- and 430-cu. in versions, producing 340 and 360 bhp respectively. It was also the final year that Buick offered a V6 engine, which was replaced by an in-line six made by Chevrolet. In 1968 the big cars had revised aluminium brake drums with no fewer than 90 fins to assist cooling, while the 6.6-litre/400-cu. in 340-bhp Skylark GS400 coupé sporting model was supplemented by a 350 version with 5.7-litre/350-cu. in engine, putting out 280 bhp, for younger buyers who could not afford the insurance of the real performance version. At $2903 the GS350 was just $101 cheaper. The Riviera by comparison cost $4589. In 1971 there was a new bigger 122-in/3099-mm wheelbase Riviera with perimeter chassis and a distinctive teardrop-shaped tail. A 7457-cc/455-cu. in V8 gave 370 bhp and there was a computer-controlled anti-skid device called Max Trac. A year later the Riviera had impact-resistant bumpers and there was a new Regal notchback coupé.

The 1974 model Le Sabre coupé featured a return to a body with centre pillar, but more significant was the 1975 Skyhawk compact hatchback coupé. It was based on the Chevrolet Vega and, had it not been for the fuel crisis, would have been the Wankel-engined Chevrolet Chaparral. When GM dropped the Wankel it was replaced by a 3791-cc/231-cu. in V6 in the 97-in/2464-mm wheelbase Skyhawk, which was Buick's first small car for decades and cost $4186. At that price it was more expensive than the bigger Skylark which had an in-line 6-cylinder 4097-cc/250-cu. in engine and cost $3476 in its cheapest form. For 1977 downsizing, to improve fuel economy, came with new Le Sabre and Riviera models sharing a 115.9-in/2944-mm wheelbase and 218-in/5537-mm length. Slightly larger was the new 118.9-in/3020-mm wheelbase Electra, then the biggest model in the range with a length of 222-in/5639-mm, but 11 in/279 mm shorter than before. All the big models had shed about 600 lb/272 kg in weight and the largest engine was the 185-bhp 6.6-litre/403-cu. in V8. A year later this same process was applied to the Century and Regal, which shrank to a 108-in/2743-mm wheelbase. The Regal and Le Sabre were available with an optional turbocharged 3.8-litre/231-cu. in V6 giving 115 mph/185 kph performance.

Buick's first front-wheel-drive model was the new 1979 Riviera which had all-independent suspension and the 3.8-litre/231-cu. in turbo engine as standard. The 1980 Skylark also went front-wheel drive with transverse 2838-cc/173-cu. in V6 or 2471-cc/151-cu. in 4-cylinder engines and a 105-in/2667-mm wheelbase. The 1982 Skyhawk was Buick's version of the 101-in/2565-mm wheelbase GM J-car with 1841- or 1796-cc/112- or 110 cu. in 4-cylinder engine mounted transversely and driving the front wheels. There was also a new front-wheel-drive Century model with 2471-cc/151-cu. in 4-cylinder engine or 3-litre/183-cu. in V6 or 4.3-litre/262-cu. in V6 diesel. In 1983 the only big Buick was the 119-in/3022-mm wheelbase Electra whose biggest engine was a 5.7-litre/350-cu. in diesel, petrol V8s stopping at 5033 cc/307 cu. in.

The new 1984 Electra was a smaller front-wheel-drive car with 3.8-litre/231-cu. in V6 fuel

1987 Buick Century Limited coupé.

1934 Cadillac V12 cabriolet.

injected engine. For 1986 the same engine was turbocharged for a 235-bhp performance version of the Regal. There were also new Le Sabre and Riviera models with transverse front engines, leaving the Le Sabre/Electra station wagon versions as the only rear-drive Buicks and the only ones available with a 5-litre/307-cu. in V8. The 1987 Somerset was fitted with passive front seat belts that fastened automatically when the doors were closed and Buick's first thermoplastic front bumpers (fenders) were fitted to the new Le Sabre T-type coupé.

Cadillac (USA)

Henry M. Leland (q.v.) who founded Cadillac in 1902 with William Murphy, had previously made car engines and other parts for Oldsmobile before building his own cars. His 1½-litre/91.5 cu. in 6½-hp Cadillac of 1903 had much in common with the first Ford, including chain drive, a two-speed gearbox and underfloor engine, but differed in having only a single cylinder. This model continued in production until 1908, in which year the marque won the Dewar Trophy for interchangeability of parts as demonstrated to the RAC at Brooklands. A bigger 30-hp 4-cylinder model appeared in 1906 and 75,000 were sold by 1914. Cadillac became part of General Motors in 1909 and in 1912 the 5½-litre/336-cu. in 4-cylinder model was fitted with Delco electric lighting as standard equipment.

The first V8 model appeared in 1914 and V8 engines were to become a marque feature from then on. A cheaper companion make, La Salle, was added in 1927 with styling by Harley Earl and looked very Hispano-Suiza like. Power came from a 5-litre/305-cu. in V8 and it was built to Cadillac quality standards. Cadillac and La Salle models of 1929 were the first cars to boast synchromesh gearboxes, and also had chromium plating and safety glass. A 7.4-litre/452-cu. in ohv V16 became the top Cadillac model in 1930 and was joined by a V12 in 1931. Other important changes were coil spring front suspension in 1934 and a steering column gearchange in 1938. That year saw the introduction of the smaller Sixty Special with

cruciform-braced lowered chassis and no running boards, while the vee-windscreen, thin pillars and proper integral boot (trunk) gave the model a more modern look.

In 1941 Hydramatic automatic transmission was optional and by 1952 Cadillac owners no longer had the option of shifting gears. Sales had climbed too, from 66,000 in 1941 to nearly 104,000 in 1950, and Cadillac was well established as *the* American luxury car. Wrap-around windscreens and power-assisted steering came in 1954, while the 1957 Eldorado Brougham was the first car with air suspension as standard. By 1966 models had the GM perimeter-frame chassis and massive 7-litre/429-cu. in V8 engines, while interiors had air conditioning and electric seat adjustment. The same year saw Cadillac's first front-wheel-drive car, the two-door Eldorado coupé with V8 engine mounted longitudinally and chain drive to the automatic gearbox alongside. By 1968 engine size had risen to 7736 cc/472 cu. in and disc brakes were optional, becoming standard with the fitment of the industry's biggest V8 (8195 cc/500 cu. in) producing 400 bhp in 1980.

A fuel-injected 5.7-litre/350-cu. in V8 powered the completely new European-style Seville compact in 1975. Marketed as the top model it had a 114-in/2896-mm wheelbase and unitary construction, with self-levelling rear suspension. A new body in 1979 brought the Seville front-wheel drive and all-independent suspension. Safety legislation killed the Eldorado convertible in 1976 and in 1977 both engines and bodies were downsized. The Seville, which had been the first Cadillac with a diesel option in 1978, had a 5.7-litre/350-cu. in diesel as standard in 1980.

The Cadillac version of GM's J-car, called the Cimarron, appeared in 1981 with a 1.8-litre/112-cu. in 4-cylinder engine, front-wheel drive and a manual gearbox. For the large models the 6045-cc/369-cu. in V8s were revised to run on eight, six or four cylinders for economy, while most others had 4087-cc/249-cu. in V8s as standard and automatic transmission with overdrive. In 1984 92% of Cadillacs had petrol V8s, while the others were mostly

4-cylinder 2-litre/121-cu. in Cimarrons, and the Eldorado was offered as a convertible again (until 1985). Both Seville and Eldorado had smaller bodies for 1986. The 1987 Brougham was the marque's only rear-wheel-drive model and the only Cadillac with a 5-litre/307-cu. in V8. As the longest (221 in/5614 mm), tallest (56.7 in/1441 mm) and heaviest (4045 lb/1835 kg) American production car, it needed that engine's 140 bhp. Other models used the 4.1-litre/250-cu. in V8, apart from the small Cimarron which had a 2-litre/121-cu. in 4-cylinder as standard. Typical of the formal Cadillacs was the 110.8-in/2815-mm wheelbase Fleetwood d'Elegance with square styling, though even it had a digital vacuum-fluorescent speedometer. The Fleetwood 60 Special and 75 models were stretched versions with 5 in/127 mm and 23.6 in/600 mm longer wheelbases respectively.

Completely different was the 1987 Allante two-seater convertible which was intended as a serious rival to the imported Mercedes SLs. Not only was the Allante styled in Europe by Pininfarina, it was also partly built in Turin as well. This made history as the completed bodies were flown, 56 at a time, packed in Lufthansa or Alitalia Boeing 747s from Turin to Detroit for final assembly and testing. This created the world's longest (3300 air miles/5310 km) car production line. The monocoque body had a 99.4-in/2525-mm wheelbase, all the usual Cadillac luxury features and a tuned 170-bhp version of the 4.1-litre/250-cu. in V8, installed transversely to drive the front wheels. The Allante opened a whole new chapter for the American luxury car.

Chevrolet (USA)

William C. Durant founded the marque in November 1911 after losing control of General Motors in 1910. It was named after racing driver Louis Chevrolet who helped design the first car, the Six Type C Classic. Price was $2150 and it had a 4.9-litre/

The first Chevrolet of 1912 outside the factory.

299-cu. in engine and 120-in/3048-mm wheelbase with electric lighting and compressed-air starting, but few were sold. Durant's 6-cylinder Little sold well at $1285 but was not as robust. In 1914 it was replaced by the Chevrolet Light Six with 4.4-litre/271-cu. in L-head engine and 112-in/2845-mm wheelbase selling for $1475 and built in the Little factory at Flint. More significant was the 2.8-litre/171-cu. in ohv 4-cylinder with 104-in/2642-mm wheelbase sold as the Baby Grand (tourer) at $875 or Royal Mail (roadster) at $750. The Four-Ninety was a basic simplified version, marketed in 1915 to compete with the Ford Model T also selling at $490, built in New York.

By 1916 Chevrolet sales had reached 62,522 and Durant bought control of General Motors with Chevrolet stock. The 1914 ohv V8, a 4.7-litre/288-cu. in with 120-in/3048-mm wheelbase, was too expensive at $1400 and production ceased in 1918, the same year that Chevrolet started producing trucks. It was the Four-Ninety, later improved and called the Superior, that raised sales to 242,373 in 1922 and 483,310 in 1923 – the millionth Chevrolet being produced on 22 February 1923. In September 1925 the 2 millionth car was built and the Superior had a stronger chassis, new engine and dry-plate clutch. The 3 millionth car, now called Capitol instead of Superior, arrived in 1927 and for the first time Chevrolet sold more cars than Ford. In 1929 the 4-cylinder National was fitted with a 3.2-litre/194-cu. in ohv 6-cylinder engine and became the International. The 2 millionth Chevy six, and 7 millionth car, was built in 1930. Synchromesh arrived in 1932, a vee radiator in 1933 and 'knee-action' independent front suspension in 1934. Hydraulic brakes and the 12 millionth car arrived in 1936, and in 1937 there was a new 3.5-litre/216-cu. in 6-cylinder engine, ladder chassis frame and hypoid rear axle. In 1940 J. M. Fangio won his first major race at Buenos Aires in a Master 85 Coupé.

Postwar cars were little changed, the first new car with 115-in/2921-mm wheelbase and lower wider body arriving in 1949, followed in 1950 by the Bel Air, a low-priced hardtop coupé, and optional Powerglide automatic transmission. The 1953 Corvette can claim to be the first American sports car. Its 110 mph/177 kph top speed was made possible by a glassfibre body and 3.8-litre/235-cu. in 6-cylinder modified production engine, despite an automatic gearbox. A 4.3-litre/265-cu. in V8 arrived in 1955 and was used in saloons and the Corvette, which got a manual gearbox option in 1956 and a 240-bhp 4.6-litre/283-cu. in

V8 in 1957. At Sebring that year the 340-bhp experimental SS Corvette, with tubular chassis and all-independent suspension, caused a sensation.

The 1959 Corvair was a revolutionary compact with a flat-6 air-cooled engine at the rear. Its handling problems became notorious when cited in Ralph Nader's book *Unsafe at Any Speed* in 1965, though by then the original swing-arm rear suspension had been abandoned. In 1962 Chevrolet sales exceeded 2 million in one year for the first time and there was a new Corvette, the Sting Ray. The futuristic body had a 98-in/2489-mm wheelbase, all-independent suspension and coupé or roadster versions. The monocoque Chevy II appeared at the same time with 110-in/2794-mm wheelbase and a choice of 2.5-litre/153-cu. in 4-cylinder or 3.1-litre/189-cu. in 6-cylinder engines. By comparison with the full-sized 210-in/5334-mm-long Impala or Bel Air, it was a compact 183 in/4648 mm long. The intermediate Chevelle, with perimeter chassis frame and 3.1-litre/189-cu. in V6 engine, arrived in 1964 and the V6 was also fitted to the Chevy II.

Chevrolet production was expanded in 1962 with Chevy II models built in Argentina, and Brazilian production started in 1964, followed by South Africa in 1968. The 5.7-litre/350-cu. in V8 Camaro sports coupé of 1967 was Chevrolet's answer to the Ford Mustang and had 295 bhp and front disc brakes. It was followed by a restyled Corvette in 1968 with the basic 5356-cc/327-cu. in engine producing 300 bhp, though power-pack options included a 435-bhp 7-litre/427-cu. in engine giving 0–60 mph/0–97 kph acceleration in about 5.5 sec. The 1970 Monte Carlo coupé, based on the Chevelle chassis, had 5.7-litre/350-cu. in or 7.4-litre/454-cu. in V8 engines. Much smaller was the 97-in/2464-mm wheelbase unitary construction Vega which arrived in 1971. A light alloy 4-cylinder engine, with cogged belt drive to the overhead camshaft, powered it from 2294 cc/140 cu. in. Smaller still was the 1976 Chevette (T-car) powered by a 1.6-litre/98-cu. in ohc engine and having much in common with its European namesake.

By 1977 the big V8s had shrunk to 5.7 litres/350 cu. in and the full-sized models with them. Even the new 1978 Corvette had only 195 bhp. Chevrolet's version of GM's European-sized X-car, the Citation, appeared in 1979. There were coupé or hatchback bodies on a 105-in/2667-mm wheelbase and it had a transverse engine and front-wheel drive with either a 2471-cc/151-cu. in 4-cylinder or a 2838-cc/173-cu. in V6 engine. Another European-sized addition was the 1981

front-wheel-drive Cavalier (J-car) with 1.8- or 2-litre/112- or 121-cu. in 4-cylinder engine. For 1982 it was joined by the X-car-derived Celebrity, while the restyled Camaro became a hatchback with 175 bhp from a fuel-injected 5-litre/305-cu. in V8 in Z28 form. Even the big Impala and Caprice had 3.7-litre/228-cu. in V6s as standard, with V8 or diesel options. For 1983 the Corvette took on a new lease of life with a new plastic/glassfibre 96-in/2438-mm wheelbase body, lift-up rear window and better handling.

The best-selling Cavalier accounted for 400,254 of Chevrolet's 1984 1.45 million production. In June of that year the division launched their smallest car ever, the 88.4-in/2245-mm wheelbase Sprint. Powered by a 3-cylinder 993-cc/61-cu. in transverse engine driving the front wheels, it sold in 1985 for $5151. There was also a 92.3-in/2345-mm wheelbase five-door version. In Japan, where it was built by Suzuki, it was known as the Swift. Later that year another small Japanese import was added; the Spectrum (Isuzu Gemini) had a 1471-cc/90-cu. in 4-cylinder engine, a 94.5-in/2400-mm wheelbase and sold for $6295 in 1985 in three-door form.

Also new for the 1986 model year was the Nova, based on the Toyota Corolla but built in Fremont, California. New United Motor Manufacturing Inc., jointly owned by General Motors and Toyota, was responsible for the actual production of Nova using 170 robots, unique on-site sheet-metal stamping and a Japanese-style 'just-in-time' component supply system. Engines, though, were built in Japan and were the Corolla's 1587-cc/96.8-cu. in 4-cylinder units installed transversely to drive the front wheels. The Celebrity, with 2471-cc/151-cu. in 4-cylinder or optional 2838-cc/173-cu. in V6 engine, was America's best-selling car in 1986 with 408,926 delivered to customers.

For 1987 there was additional emphasis on performance, with turbocharged versions of both Sprint and Spectrum and a bigger 5.7-litre/350-cu. in V8 as an option for Camaro and Corvette, the latter continuing in the additional convertible version offered in 1986. The full-size 116-in/2946-mm wheelbase Impala and Caprice models remained rear-wheel drive, as did the Monte Carlo, and all three had a 4.3-litre/262-cu. in V6 engine as standard. Completely new were the compact two-door Beretta and four-door Corsica, GM's answer to the aerodynamic Ford Taurus/Mercury Sable (q.v.), and replacements for the Citation. With a drag coefficient of 0.329, both cars shared a 103.4-in/2626-mm wheelbase and the Cavalier's 2-litre/

121-cu. in 4-cylinder engine, with an optional 2.8-litre/173-cu. in V6. In 1987 Chevrolet celebrated 75 years of production, and over 110 million vehicles, and is America's best-selling car marque; in 1985 Chevrolet alone produced more cars than Ford, Lincoln and Mercury combined.

Chrysler Corporation (USA)

In 1923 Walter P. Chrysler took over Maxwell and their subsidiary Chalmers and from these companies Chrysler Corporation was formed in 1925. In 1928 Dodge was taken over and the new marques De Soto and Plymouth created. Imperial became a marque in 1954, having previously been a Chrysler model. Manufacture in Australia started in 1951, though chassis had been imported and bodied there from the late 1920s, and continued until 1980, when Mitsubishi took over the factory. Chrysler had purchased a 35% share in Mitsubishi in 1971.

The setting up of Chrysler International, with headquarters in Switzerland, was the preliminary to taking a 25% interest in Simca in 1958 and by 1966 they had acquired a 77% holding. Other European acquisitions followed, with a 40% share in Spanish manufacturers Barreiros in 1963, rising to 77% in 1967. In Britain Chrysler took 45% of the voting shares in Rootes (Commer, Karrier, Hillman, Humber, Singer and Sunbeam) in 1964 and increased this to 77.3% in 1967. The Rootes Group was subsequently re-named Chrysler UK Ltd. Chrysler also had plants in Argentina (1965) and Brazil (1967), the latter being sold to Volkswagen in 1979.

In 1978 Chrysler's European operations in France, Britain and Spain were sold to the PSA Group (Peugeot-Citroën), although Chrysler took a 15% share in PSA and continued to operate Chrysler Europe until 1980 at Peugeot's request. In 1986 Chrysler increased their interest in Maserati from 3.47 to 15.6%, with the intention of stepping this up to a controlling 51% by 1996. Maserati, at present controlled by Alessandro de Tomaso, currently have an agreement to supply Chrysler with 1200 cars a year to be sold as Chrysler-Maseratis in the USA. In 1987 Chrysler purchased Renault's 46% holding in American Car Corporation and signed an agreement with Lamborghini for the Italian manufacturer to design and build a car for Chrysler to sell in the USA.

Chrysler (USA)

Walter P. Chrysler, a former General Motors vice-president, took over Maxwell and its associated

company Chalmers in 1923. The first car to bear his name was the 1924 Six with 70 mph/113 kph performance and four-wheel hydraulic brakes with external contracting shoes. And that was not all – aluminium pistons, pressure lubrication, an oil filter and hydraulic dampers were other features of this medium-priced car. That year 32,000 were sold through Maxwell dealers and led to the formation of Chrysler Corporation in 1925. A new 4-cylinder 3-litre/185-cu. in Chrysler model replaced the Maxwell 4-cylinder for 1926 and the luxury 4.7-litre/289-cu. in 6-cylinder Imperial model with 80 mph/130 kph performance joined the range.

Chrysler reliability was demonstrated at Le Mans in 1928 when 6-cylinder 72 models finished third and fourth. Soon afterwards Plymouth was introduced as a new cheaper 4-cylinder marque, a few weeks before the purchase of Dodge. In August 1928 De Soto was introduced as a marque to compete with Oldsmobile and Pontiac and the first model was a 3.2-litre/193-cu. in side-valve six. New for 1931 were two straight-8s with four-speed gearboxes and thermostatically-controlled radiator shutters. Long bonnets (hoods) and low lines made them look impressive. The 4-litre/248-cu. in CD gave about 80 (later 100) bhp while the top of the range CG Imperial not only had a 21 in/533 mm longer wheelbase but a nine-bearing 6.3-litre/384-cu. in engine producing 135 bhp. Le Baron made many of the CG bodies. These followed the 1930 De Soto 3.4-litre/207-cu. in, sold as the world's cheapest 8-cylinder. Flexible engine mountings arrived in 1932 and synchromesh in 1933.

The Chrysler sixes were fitted with independent front suspension for 1934, but were overshadowed by the revolutionary new Airflow models – 8-cylinder Chrysler and 6-cylinder De Soto – which retained semi-elliptic springing all round. The Airflow body, though, was far from conventional, being of integral construction with radical streamlined styling. There was a waterfall radiator,

1934 Chrysler Imperial Airflow Custom CW straight-8.

faired-in headlamps and a sloping tail containing a luggage compartment. Inside all seats were within the wheelbase and were based on a tubular framework. Unfortunately the streamlined Chryslers and De Sotos did not sell but continued until 1937, though the more conventional Airstream had appeared in 1935. By 1939 both Chrysler and De Soto had steering column gearchanges and hypoid rear axles and both 4.1-litre/250-cu. in sixes and 5.3-litre/323-cu. in straight-8s were marketed up to 1942. Early postwar cars were very similar, though the wooden-panelled saloons and station wagons were distinctive. In 1946 Chrysler purchased the old Graham-Paige factory to build De Sotos. In 1951 Chrysler's 5.4-litre/331-cu. in Firepower V8 engine was announced with hemispherical combustion chambers and four camshafts to operate the overhead valves. De Soto used a 4.4-litre/270-cu. in version of this engine. Power-assisted steering and automatic transmission were options.

When Walter Chrysler died in 1940 the marque was America's number two carmaker, but by 1954 production had dropped dramatically and with a 12.9% market share Chrysler were behind Ford. Imperial became a marque in its own right in 1954, though it remained a big luxurious Chrysler in fact. Improved styling came in 1955, along with a 4.9-litre/300-cu. in V8 to replace the six. The 2 millionth De Soto was produced in 1959, but a year later Chrysler went over to unitary construction and De Soto was integrated into Plymouth.

The more modern Newport models arrived in 1961, while in 1963 Chrysler extended their interests in Europe by acquiring control of Simca and, a year later, of Rootes. First new models were the 1967 Hillman Hunter and Minx with boxy lines and Singer and Humber variants. The Chrysler 180 appeared from Simca in 1970, while in Britain the Minx was replaced by the new Avenger, though in Britain the cars were not badged as Chryslers until 1976, following the arrival of the hatchback Alpine, which was built in France as a Simca. The new hatchback Chrysler Sunbeam appeared in 1978, as did the French-built Horizon and there was even a Sunbeam-Lotus variant in 1979, just before Chrysler pulled out of Europe and sold their French and British interests to the Peugeot-Citroën group, who renamed the cars Talbot.

In the USA Chrysler had been in financial difficulties in the late 1960s with big cars and powerful engines. Even the least expensive Newport series had a 6.3-litre/383-cu. in V8, as did the more sporting 300 series, while 7.2-litre/440-cu. in V8s were optional. The prestige New Yorker had the 440 V8 as standard. In 1971 the 35 millionth car, a Newport Regal hardtop, was built, Bendix anti-skid braking was an option on top models and the previous year's $7.4 million loss was turned into an $82 million profit. The intermediate Cordoba, with 'opera' window in the rear quarter-panel, arrived for the 1975 model year with a 5211-cc/318-cu. in V8 with larger 5.9- or 6.5-litre/360- or 400-cu. in options, and the Imperial had four-wheel disc brakes.

Smaller cars were Plymouths or Dodges, not Chryslers, until the arrival of the 100-in/2540-mm wheelbase transverse-engined front-wheel-drive LeBaron for 1982. It was produced in convertible and 'woody' station wagon versions as well and was powered by a 4-cylinder 2.2- or 2.6-litre/135- or 156-cu. in engine. These K-cars were joined by a longer wheelbase luxury version, the New Yorker, for 1983. For the 1984 model year there was the 97-in/2464-mm wheelbase front-wheel-drive Laser, Chrysler's first sports car with 2+2 coupé body. For those who thought the standard Laser's 99 bhp from 2.2 litres/135-cu. in wasn't enough to propel 2550 lb/1156 kg, Chrysler offered a 146 bhp turbocharged version – the first American front-wheel-drive turbo sports car. The turbo engine was also offered in the New Yorker saloon.

In 1986 the 2.6-litre/156-cu. in Mitsubishi engine was replaced by a 2501-cc/153-cu. in Chrysler in-line 4-cylinder. Largest 1987 model was the four-door Fifth Avenue saloon with 112.7-in/2863-mm wheelbase and an overall length of 206.6 in/5248 mm. It was powered by a 5.2-litre/318-cu. in V8 and was the only Chrysler not to have a 4-cylinder engine. Important new arrivals were the J-Car coupé and convertible versions of the LeBaron, itself not changed. Both were front-wheel drive with 2.5-litre/153-cu. in 4-cylinder engines producing 100 bhp and, for more performance, the 2.2-litre/135-cu. in turbo unit with 146 bhp was optional. Smallest Chrysler-badged model was the 95.9-in/2436-mm wheelbase Conquest (an imported Mitsubishi Starion) with 2.6-litre/156-

Chrysler Fifth Avenue. Their largest 1987 model and the only one with a V8 engine.

cu. in turbocharged engine giving 145 bhp. Most exciting car in the line-up was the Chrysler-Maserati two-door coupé or convertible, built for Chrysler in Italy by Maserati. Though it resembled the Maserati Bi-Turbo it was not the same car at all, being smaller with a 92.9-in/2360-mm wheelbase and only two seats. It was, of course, front-wheel drive and used a 2213-cc/135-cu. in engine with single turbocharger giving 174 bhp.

Citroën (France)

André Citroën had been chief engineer of Mors and his 1.3-litre Type A 4-cylinder was put into production in the former Mors factory in 1919. Features included full electrical equipment and a central change for the three-speed gearbox for a price of 7950 francs. Top speed was 40 mph/64 kph and in 1921 10,000 were built. Citroën's adoption of the herring-bone chevron emblem was in commemoration of the gear-making firm that André Citroën had started in 1913. Success brought the need to expand and Citroën took over Clement-Bayard, and their Levallois-Perret factory, in 1922. There the improved 4-cylinder Type B of 1.5-litres and the 855-cc Cloverleaf, so named because of the pattern formed by its three seats, were built in large numbers. The little Cloverleaf had the advantage of a detachable cylinder head and coil ignition and proved very reliable, if a little slow.

In 1926 Citroën concentrated on the bigger 1,538-cc 12 hp with four-wheel brakes, semi-elliptic suspension and a flat radiator, and this was the first model to be built in the British Citroën factory at Slough, although models had been assembled in London from 1920. British Citroëns continued to be built at Slough until the end of 1965, and there were also factories in Germany and Italy. The first 6-cylinder model, designated C6, arrived in 1929 with a 2442-cc side-valve engine, 116-in/2945-mm wheelbase and a pumped cooling system. The 4-cylinder model was similar,

1934 Citroën 7CV Traction Avant with front-wheel drive.

though with a 4 in/102 mm shorter wheelbase and 1628-cc engine, becoming the 13 hp in the process. A synchromesh gearbox arrived with the addition of the 1½-litre 8CV with box chassis frame in 1932. An 8CV, *Petite Rosalie*, covered 187,500 miles at 58 mph/93 kph and took 43 world records in the process.

The revolutionary Traction Avant appeared in 1934 in 12-hp (7CV) guise with a 1303-cc ohv 4-cylinder engine driving the front wheels. But that was not all, for André Citroën, who had pioneered Budd all-steel bodywork in France in 1925, had adopted a monocoque steel bodyshell with the torsion bar front suspension, engine and transmission mounted on a subframe which was bolted to the body. Also unusual were the wheels at the corners of the car and the gearbox mounted ahead of the engine. Though production was at the rate of 1000 a week, the model bankrupted Citroën, who had to be rescued by Michelin. Top speed was just over 60 mph/97 kph but acceleration was slow, so the engine size was soon increased to 1628 cc and then to 1911 cc, the latter model becoming the Light/Big 15 depending on wheelbase. A more powerful 15CV with 2866-cc 6-cylinder engine was added in 1938, using the Big 15's 121.5-in/3085-mm wheelbase. In 1948 the Traction Avant became the first car to use the new Michelin X radial-ply tyre, and by the time production ended in 1957 over 700,000 had been built.

Cheap basic transport was what Europe needed after World War II, and Citroën's response was the utilitarian 2CV of 1948. A 375-cc flat-twin engine drove the 15-in/380-mm front wheels and there was coil spring suspension all round. A larger 425-cc engine was offered in 1955 and over 5 million had been built by 1976, by which time a bigger 29-bhp 602-cc engine was available. This 2-cylinder engine still powers it today.

Citroën's reputation for unconventional engineering was further strengthened by the DS19 model that appeared in 1955. So far advanced was it that 20 years later some manufacturers still had not caught up. Self-levelling hydropneumatic suspension, power-assisted disc brakes and a semi-automatic gearbox were pretty revolutionary, but the monocoque body had detachable steel panels, front and rear crumple zones, and a smooth aerodynamic shape with a drag coefficient of 0.38. Overnight it set new standards of motoring comfort and safety. The 1911-cc 4-cylinder engine was the one part carried over from the Traction Avant, but despite the sophistication the DS was rugged, as its win of the 1959 Monte Carlo Rally testified.

In 1965 Citroën took over Panhard and the DS received a new short-stroke 1985-cc 4-cylinder engine, the 1911-cc unit being retained for the cheaper ID. A more powerful DS21 with 2175 cc was also added. Final development was the 2347-cc fuel-injected DS23 of 1974, the year that a DS won the World Cup Rally. Technical cooperation between Maserati and Citroën resulted in the 1970 SM, a 140 mph/225 kph Grand Touring model powered by Maserati's four-ohc 2670-cc V6 engine delivering 170 bhp to the front wheels. A five-speed gearbox and DS suspension and disc brakes were fitted as well. Just as unconventional was the smaller 100-in/2540-mm wheelbase GS announced later the same year. It was front-wheel drive, of course, and had hydropneumatic suspension and disc brakes, while power came from an air-cooled 1015-cc flat-four engine. Its aerodynamic shape made 90 mph/145 kph cruising possible on only 55 bhp. Performance was much improved by the 1220-cc engine in 1972, a limited production Birotor Wankel version appeared in 1974 and in 1979 the GS became the hatchback GSA.

In 1974 Citroën took over Ligier, and transferred SM production there, announced their new CX and were in turn taken over by Peugeot. The big CX saloon incorporated a good deal of DS/SM technology for brakes, suspension and steering. It even used the D-Series 1985- and 2175-cc engines, though these were mounted transversely for the first time. The body structure was no longer integral, but was mounted on front and rear subframes which were connected by two longerons to make a perimeter chassis frame. With Peugeot controlling Citroën (instead of Michelin), 1975 saw many changes. The expensive-to-produce SM was dropped and the CX replaced the DS, after 20 years and 1½ million cars.

First rationalized model, in 1976, was the LN, which combined the Peugeot 104 coupé body with the 2CV/Ami 602-cc engine. The larger Visa of 1978 was another model cocktail, for although the basic version had Citroën's 602-cc twin, there was also a Peugeot 1124-cc 4-cylinder engine offered. The later GT model had Peugeot's 1360-cc engine. With the arrival of the BX in 1982 Citroën had a structured range for the first time – 2CV, Dyane, LNA, Visa, GSA, BX and CX. A 104-in/2655-mm wheelbase hatchback, the BX featured a plastic bonnet, bumpers, tailgate and fuel tank plus thin window glass for weight saving. Power came from 1360-cc (Peugeot) or 1580-cc (Citroën) 4-cylinder engines. Despite the usual power hydraulics for suspension and brakes, a major feature of the BX

was the low cost of servicing and ease of replacing units – something that could not be said of the GS, SM or CX. In the spring of 1984 the Visa was offered with a 1769-cc diesel engine and in 1984 there was a GTi version with fuel-injected 105-bhp 1580-cc engine. There was a bigger engined 1905-cc BX GT at the end of that year and a BX estate car in 1985. Most powerful current models are the fuel-injected and turbocharged CX25 GTi and long-wheelbase CX25 Prestige with 168 bhp and a claimed maximum speed of 139 mph/224 kph.

Newest Citroën model is the little AX which went into production in 1986 and slots between the 2CV and Visa. An aerodynamic small three-door hatchback with 90-in/2285-mm wheelbase and 137.8-in/3500-mm overall length, the AX was offered with three new TU-series 4-cylinder engines. The AX10 had a 954-cc unit, the AX11 1124 cc with 55 bhp and the AX14 1360 cc and 65 bhp. Only the latter had a five-speed gearbox, but all models had front disc brakes and all-independent suspension, and were light in weight – the AX10 was only 1411 lb/640 kg.

Daimler (UK)

The origins of the British Daimler company go right back to the purchase of the UK rights to the German Daimler patents in 1890 by F. R. Simms. He imported the first Daimler engine in 1891 and formed the Daimler Motor Syndicate Ltd in 1893. The British Motor Syndicate, headed by H. J. Lawson, purchased DMS in 1895 and formed the Daimler Motor Co. Ltd in January 1896, with Lawson, Simms, Gottlieb Daimler and Evelyn Ellis as directors. The Prince of Wales (later Edward VII) was given a ride on a Cannstatt Daimler in February 1896 and in April a site for the British Daimler factory was purchased at Coventry.

The first Coventry-built Daimler (a 4-hp 2-cylinder with tube ignition, chain drive and tiller steering) of 1897 cost £370 and later that year Henry Sturmey drove from John O'Groats to Lands End in one. The following year the first 4-cylinder 8-hp model was built and in 1900 the Prince of Wales took delivery of a 6-hp model, starting the British Royal Family's patronage of the marque that was to last for over 50 years. Shaft drive arrived in 1901 and battery and coil ignition in 1904, together with the distinctive fluted radiator. In 1905 E.M.C. Instone made fastest time up Shelsley Walsh hill-climb driving a 9¼-litre 4-cylinder 35-hp model. Even bigger was the 1906 45-hp 4-cylinder with 10,604 cc, a gate gearchange and pressed-steel chassis. The year 1909 saw the

Knight sleeve-valved 22- and 38-hp models appear and soon all models used these valves.

A merger with the Birmingham Small Arms Co. Ltd – profitable like Daimler – in 1910 resulted in a name change to the Daimler Co. and the first 6-cylinder 9421-cc model. By 1912 four 4-cylinder models and three 6-cylinder models were offered, spanning 15 to 38 hp. The last 4-cylinder model, the 3308-cc TT4-20, was built in 1921, while the 1923 5764-cc 35 hp was the first model to be fitted with four-wheel brakes and steel sleeve-valves instead of cast iron. For 1926 there were 11 models offered, ranging from the 1872-cc 16/55 at £715 to the massive 8458-cc 45 with 162-in/4115-mm wheelbase at £2250. Those prices were for complete saloon-bodied cars for, unlike many manufacturers, Daimler made most of their own bodies. Pressure lubrication was introduced at that time and at the end of 1926 came the first V12, known as the Double-Six. At first there was only the 50 hp with massive sleeve-valved 7136-cc long-stroke engine – in fact it was two smaller 25/85-hp blocks mounted at a 60-degree vee. Later it was joined by the 3744-cc 30-hp model, and there were even some lowered sporting models built in 1930–1 on the 50 chassis.

The year 1930 marked an important change for Daimler when their fluid-flywheel transmission with steering column control was introduced, for it was to remain a standard feature into the 1950s. In 1931 Lanchester were taken over, with the result that Daimler switched to the poppet valves that they used, the 1932 Daimler 15 being the first model so fitted. Thereafter Lanchesters became cheaper Daimlers. The first straight-8 model appeared in 1934 as a replacement for the V12 with 3.7-litre ohv engine. At the coronation of King George VI in 1937 1000 Daimlers were used by dignitaries, which gives some idea of the marque's importance. That year the 2166-cc 6-cylinder

Daimler Straight-Eight with Vanden Plas pillarless body built for the 1937 London Motor Show.

15 hp became the first model with independent front suspension.

Daimler's 2522-cc Scout car with all-independent suspension and five-speed fluid flywheel played an important part in World War II, and in 1946 the same engine powered the £1340 DB18 Consort saloon. Between 1948 and 1953 there was a distinctive Special Sports model based on this chassis and most had Barker bodies. The DE27 limousine chassis had a wheelbase of 138 in/3505 mm and was powered by the 4095-cc 6-cylinder engine that had been used in Daimler armoured cars. A derivative (DC27) was used as an ambulance, bodied by Barker or Hooper, and was to be found in London and other cities in the 1950s. Barker had been taken over by Hooper in 1938 and the BSA group had then bought Hooper, which explains why many postwar Daimlers had Hooper bodies. The big DE36 straight-8 arrived in 1947 with a 5460-cc engine giving 150 bhp and a 147-in/3734-mm wheelbase. In 1951 Sir Bernard Docker, chairman of BSA, had one of these models gold plated for the Motor Show, where it appeared on the Hooper stand, starting the series of show specials that became known as the Docker Daimlers. The smaller 1951 Regency 3 litre was followed in 1953 by the 2½-litre Conquest (basic price £1066 – hence the name). In 1955 the Regency went to 3½ litres, becoming the 104 mph/167 kph One-O-Four a year later. That model was the first Daimler to be offered with an optional Borg-Warner automatic gearbox in place of the preselector box.

The last straight-8 was built in 1953 and in 1954 the 4½-litre 6-cylinder Regina arrived to provide Daimler's big model. The bigger engine was also offered in the Regency, and in 1955 the Regina developed into the DK400 limousine. Completely new for 1958 was the big and impressive 3.8-litre 6-cylinder Majestic with a modern steel body, Borg-Warner automatic gearbox and disc brakes all round. A new departure for Daimler was the 1959 SP250 (Dart) sports car with glassfibre two-seater body selling for £1395. It too had disc brakes all round to match its 120 mph/193 kph performance, the result of installing Edward Turner's new 2548-cc V8 engine producing 140 bhp in a car weighing 2218 lb/1006 kg. In October 1959 the last of the traditional Daimlers with a separate chassis was announced. The 120 mph/193 kph Majestic Major offered sports-car performance with the luxury of a big saloon and was based on the 3.8-litre Majestic whose 114-in/2896-mm wheelbase chassis and body it shared. The performance came from a completely new 4560-cc V8 engine giving 220 bhp. A stretched 138-in/3505-mm wheelbase version appeared in 1961 as the Daimler Limousine.

Jaguar had bought Daimler from the BSA group in 1960, and the V8–250 which appeared in 1962 looked very like a Jaguar because it used the Jaguar Mark II monocoque bodyshell and suspension. Under the bonnet, though, was the Daimler 2½-litre V8 engine coupled to an automatic gearbox. However, the 4.2-litre Sovereign that replaced the Majestic in 1966 was just a Daimler-badged Jaguar 420. Even the new 1968 Limousine was Jaguar 420G-based with a lengthened 141-in/3581-mm wheelbase, but at least had its own distinctive Vanden Plas body. The 1969 Daimler Sovereign was a badge-engineered Jaguar XJ6 offered with 2.8- or 4.2-litre 6-cylinder engine, as was the 5343-cc V12-engined Double Six that appeared in 1972. In 1980 Limousine production was transferred from Vanden Plas, part of Jaguar since 1974, in London to Jaguar's main factory at Browns Lane. There the Limousine became the first modern British car to be built by group assembly. Daimler's Radford factory now manufactures Jaguar/Daimler engines and other components, with the cars being assembled at Browns Lane.

The Series III Daimlers were replaced in the autumn of 1986 by the new Jaguar XJ6-based Daimler saloon, which was available only with the new all-aluminium 3.6-litre 6-cylinder engine. A four-speed ZF automatic gearbox was fitted as standard (a five-speed manual was a no-cost option), with a special J-gate selector lever to enable the driver to override the automatic gearbox easily. A vestigial fluted Daimler grille and rectangular headlamps blended with the more aerodynamic styling of the new 113-in/2870-mm wheelbase body, which at 196 in/4978 mm long was just over an inch longer than the Series III cars. A revised independent rear suspension layout, incorporating self-levelling and power hydraulics with anti-lock for the brakes, were important changes, as was the Lucas electronic engine management system controlling both ignition and fuel injection. Inside the Daimler leather-trimmed seats, walnut veneer on doors, facia and picnic tables and automatic air conditioning were all standard. The previous Series III Double Six model with 5343-cc V12 engine continued for 1987, the intention being eventually to fit this engine into the new saloon body. The Limousine continued with the XK 4.2-litre 6-cylinder engine and was the most expensive model, with the cheapest the 3.6 saloon launched at £28,495 in Britain. The Double Six then cost £500 more than the new 3.6.

Dodge (USA)

John and Horace Dodge originally built engines for Ford, but in 1914 Dodge Brothers was formed to build their own car, a 3440-cc/210-cu. in 4-cylinder with three-speed gearbox and 110-in/2794-mm wheelbase. It was used by the American army and 70,700 were sold in 1916. By 1924 production exceeded 350,000 a year.

In 1926 Walter Chrysler's interest in Dodge was aroused because the company had many manufacturing facilities that the fledgling Chrysler Corporation lacked. In 1928 Chrysler approached Dodge's owners, Dillon, Read and Co., and used the threat of De Soto competition to persuade them to sell. In July 1928 Dodge was purchased for $175 million. The 4-cylinder car was discontinued but the side-valve 3670-cc/224-cu. in 6-cylinder model that had been introduced in 1927 with 116-in/2946-mm wheelbase and hydraulic brakes continued, forming a low-priced base model. The bigger Senior model was similar to Chrysler's 75 and over twice the price. A straight-8 arrived in 1930 and synchromesh in 1933, while the 1935 version of Chrysler's Airstream had a 3.6-litre/218-cu. in 6-cylinder engine.

Until the 1940s changes followed those of Plymouth and De Soto, so by that time Dodge had independent front suspension, column gearchange and a hypoid rear axle. The postwar 1949 models included the regular-sized Meadowbrook and Coronet with 123.5-in/3137-mm wheelbase and 3769-cc/230-cu. in 6-cylinder engine, plus a Coronet eight-passenger sedan with a 137.5-in/3493-mm wheelbase catering for the chauffeur-driven market most other manufacturers had abandoned. Thinly-disguised Plymouths is the best description of the De Luxe and Special De Luxe models sold in Canada with 111- and 118.5-in/2819- and 3010-mm wheelbases, while the export Kingsway model on the shorter wheelbase

1914 Dodge 3½-litre tourer.

also shared their Plymouth origins and 3563-cc 217-cu. in 6-cylinder engine.

Completely different was the smaller Dodge Wayfarer with 115-in/2921-mm wheelbase and a length of 195 in/4953 mm introduced in 1949. Its bodies were built in the Dodge Main plant and were a two-door sedan at $1738, a business coupé at $1611 and a roadster at $1727. The roadster was a low-priced convertible (the Coronet convertible was $2329) with no power-operation for the soft top and no rear seat. Even the side windows were Plexiglass sidescreens at first, though later converted to wind down. Fluid Drive semi-automatic transmission, sealed-beam headlamps, turn-key starting and vacuum windscreen wipers were other features, while the 3769-cc/230-cu. in engine was shared with the bigger Dodge models. In 1950, despite a strike of 104 days, Dodge production totalled 332,782, of which 75,403 were Wayfarers.

The year 1952 saw the introduction of the Red Ram 3.8-litre/230-cu. in ohv V8 and the demise of the Wayfarer, but the 6-cylinder engine lived on until 1959. The much smaller 106.5-in/2705-mm wheelbase Lancer with 2790- or 3682-cc/170- or 225-cu. in ohv 6-cylinder came in 1961 but was not a success. For 1963 the model range started with the $1808 Dart 170 with 111-in/2819-mm wheelbase, went on through the 119-in/3023-mm wheelbase 330/400/Polara up to the $2960 Custom 880 convertible with 122-in/3099-mm wheelbase and 5902-cc/361-cu. in V8 engine. Automatic transmission was optional and could be had with push-button control. For 1965 the Monaco topped the range with a 6276-cc/383-cu. in V8 giving up to 365 bhp. The Charger fastback coupé was added to the range in 1966 and maintained the performance image with 425 bhp from 6.9 litres/426 cu. in in 1967, and was restyled for 1968.

From 1970 new small Dodges were introduced that were really Japanese Mitsubishis in disguise, for Chrysler had bought a 15% share in that company in 1971. The compact 3.7-litre/225-cu. in 6-cylinder Aspen arrived for 1976 and was followed in 1978 by the first American compact front-wheel-drive model, the Omni. Not only that but it used a 1.7-litre/104-cu. in Volkswagen engine in transverse configuration allied to a VW manual gearbox, and was based on Chrysler's European Horizon model. The Omni coupé later became the Charger. The 1979 Mirada was based on the Chrysler Cordoba, while the big Monaco was replaced by the St Regis (Chrysler Newport) with 3678-cc/224-cu. in six, or 5.2- or 5.9-litre/318- or 360-cu. in V8.

The 1981 Aries compact looked conventional but had a transverse 2.2-litre/135-cu. in Chrysler or 2.6-litre/156-cu. in Mitsubishi engine driving the front wheels. Coupé and convertible versions called the 400 followed in 1982, and the long-wheelbase 600 was also a K-car. By 1983 the biggest cars remaining were the Mirada coupé and its Diplomat saloon equivalent with 112.6-in/2860-mm wheelbases and optional 5.2-litre/318-cu. in V8 engines. For 1984 Dodge had a sports car – the Daytona. This was an Aries-based 2+2 coupé, and there was also a 146-bhp turbocharged version. For 1985 Dodge had Chrysler's new H-bodied car as the 2.2-litre/135-cu. in 103-in/2615-mm wheelbase Lancer, while imported Mitsubishis, which included a four-wheel-drive Vista (Space Wagon) model, sold under the Dodge Colt model name.

The 1987 model range started with the $5799 Omni America with 2.2-litre/135-cu. in 4-cylinder engine. The other sub-compacts were the imported (Mitsubishi Mirage) Colt models in saloon or hatchback form with 1468-cc/90-cu. in or 1598-cc/98-cu. in turbo engines, the smallest fitted to any Dodge models. Completely new were the compact Shadow hatchbacks with 97-in/2464-mm wheelbase and the standard Dodge 2.2-litre/135-cu. in 4-cylinder engine driving the front wheels. The restyled Daytona sport model was available in a Shelby Z performance version with 174 bhp. The sole large Dodge was the 5.2-litre/318-cu. in V8-engined Diplomat with rear-wheel drive.

Ferrari (Italy)

The prancing horse on a yellow shield that serves as the Ferrari badge dates from long before there were any cars bearing that name. It was given to young Enzo Ferrari by the parents of former World War I Italian air ace Francesco Baracca, who had displayed it on his fighter. That was in the days when Enzo Ferrari raced Alfa Romeos, leading to the setting up of *Scuderia Ferrari* in 1929. During the 1930s the *Scuderia* raced Alfa Romeos with considerable success, so it was hardly surprising that the first Ferrari, largely Fiat-based but with a 1½-litre straight-8 engine, should be built for racing in the 1940 GP di Brescia.

The two-seater Vettura 815s were not intended for production (only two were built), any more than the 1947 Ferrari 125 was, but the postwar model formed the basis for the later production cars. The 1½-litre V12 engine had an alloy block with detachable heads and single overhead camshafts, while the 125's chassis was of tubular construction. Boring out this engine and lengthening the stroke produced the 1902-cc 159, that figure being the volume in cc of one cylinder and explaining the sometimes curious Ferrari model numbering. Further lengthening of the stroke for 1948 produced the 1995-cc Ferrari 166, which in coupé form won the *Mille Miglia* that year, which was sold as a road car. Developed from it were the 2340-cc Type 195 and the 2544-cc Type 212.

In 1951 the larger 342 America was developed for export, with a 4.1-litre engine giving 200 bhp. It was enlarged in 1953 to the 4½-litre 375, and again in 1955 becoming the 410 Super America, with a 4962-cc V12 developing 340 bhp and a 110-in/2800-mm wheelbase. The 1954 250 Europa, with 2953-cc engine, was the first of the GT Ferraris and led to the 1956 3-litre 250GT using the same engine but with 220 bhp. The classic 250GT retained the Europa's 102.4-in/2600-mm wheelbase but the 1959 250GT Berlinetta with Testarossa 280 bhp engine had an 8 in/200 mm shorter wheelbase and stayed in production until 1962. Like the models before it, the 250GT established a fine competition record. Disc brakes were fitted from 1959 and by 1961 the Super America had become a 400 with a new 3967-cc engine developing 360 bhp. In 1965 this engine powered the new 330GT, with attractive Pininfarina coupé body, giving 300 bhp at 6600 rpm, while the more powerful Superfast had a 4963-cc V12 producing 400 bhp. Successor to the 250GT was the 275GT with 3286-cc engine and 94.5-in/2400-mm wheelbase Pininfarina body. Even more potent was the rear-engined 250LM with 300 bhp from 2953 cc, though it was hardly a road car. Both these models had independent rear suspension. The 1966 375GTB4 had 300 bhp from the four-ohc engine, while the 275LM replaced the 250.

A new departure was the 206 Dino which went into production in 1968. It had a 1987-cc V6 engine mounted transversely amidships giving 180 bhp in a 90-in/2280-mm wheelbase Pininfarina coupé body and was named after Enzo Ferrari's son. The same engine had been built by Fiat for some time for use in the Fiat Dino. In 1969 the engine size was increased to 2.4 litres and the model became the Dino 246. Also new in 1968 was the 365 GTB4 Daytona, perhaps the first of the modern Ferrari supercars, with Pininfarina-designed and Scaglietti-built 94.5-in/2400-mm wheelbase body. The 4390-cc four-ohc V12 was conventionally positioned at the front and provided 352 bhp, while the aerodynamics meant a top speed of over 170 mph/ 275 kph, compared with the 150 mph/241 kph of cars like the 365GTC.

The year 1969 saw Fiat taking a 50% interest in Ferrari, ensuring that such cars could continue to be built. The 1972 Turin Show saw two new cars; the Berlinetta Boxer 512 and the 365 GT4 2+2. The latter was a restyled version of the previous model, with 106-in/2700-mm wheelbase, seating for four and a 150 mph/241 kph top speed. The Boxer was a totally new design with 99-in/2500-mm wheelbase and 4390-cc engine positioned behind the front seats. Luggage space was under the front bonnet. The horizontally opposed 12-cylinder engine sat on top of the gearbox and the single overhead camshafts were driven by toothed belts for the first time. The 308 Dino with 2+2 seating appeared in 1973 with a new Bertone-styled body on a 100-in/2550-mm wheelbase. Power (255 bhp) was provided by the first Ferrari V8 installed transversely to give a mid-engined configuration. Though the 2926-cc size was new it was actually a 4.4-litre V12 minus four cylinders. A two-seater Pininfarina version joined it in 1975 with glass-fibre body built by Scaglietti, who were now part of Ferrari. For 1977 the Boxer's engine size was increased to 4942 cc with 360 bhp. The 365 became the 400 with longer-stroke 4832-cc V12 and automatic transmission as standard for the first time, while the 308GTS with removable roof section was added. For 1980 the 400 was fitted with fuel injection, added to the 308 later that year. A 1991-cc small-bore carburettor version of the 308 became the 208 with 155 bhp.

In March 1980 the new Pininfarina-bodied Mondial 2+2 replaced the Dino 2+2, but retained the 3-litre mid-engine V8. At the end of 1982 the 308 and Mondial received *Quattro Valvole* (four-valves-per-cylinder) engines and a 208 Turbo with 220 bhp and fuel injection was added for Italy. In 1984 the Boxer was replaced by the new 180 mph/ 293 kph 5-litre 390-bhp Testarossa, and the new 2855-cc twin-turbocharged GTO with 400 bhp and a glassfibre two-seater Berlinetta body by Pininfarina arrived. Both the 308, becoming 328, and Mondial were fitted with a 3185-cc V8 engine in 1985, and the latter was also available as a *cab-*

1987 Ferrari 328GTS with removable targa roof panel.

riolet. The 4.8-litre V12 412 replaced the big 400i and was the first Italian car with an anti-lock braking system as standard equipment.

Fiat (Italy)

Giovanni Agnelli, whose family still run the company today, founded FIAT (Fabbrica Italiana Automobili Torino) on 11 July 1899. Since then the company has grown to an industrial giant that builds not only cars and commercial vehicles, but ships, aircraft, marine engines, roads and bridges as well. On that first Fiat car of 1899 driver and passengers sat facing one another and steering was by tiller, while the transverse rear-mounted 697-cc 2-cylinder engine was rated at 3½ hp. The three-speed gearbox drove through chains. A similar 6-hp model was added in 1900, replaced in 1901 by the 8 hp with vertical 2-cylinder 1082-cc engine mounted at the front under a bonnet.

Exports to France and England started in 1903 with the 12-hp 4-cylinder. This had a front radiator with pumped water circulation and the patented gearbox had the gears, final drive and differential in one unit. Ansaldi were absorbed in 1905, creating Socièta Brevetti Fiat, and the resulting 4-cylinder 15/20-hp Brevetti had *landaulette* bodywork on a 113-in/2870-mm wheelbase with a pressed-steel chassis and shaft drive. The first 6-cylinder model, an 11 litre, appeared in 1907 and Fiat, who had been racing since 1903, won the French Grand Prix and *Targa Florio*. First model to be built in quantity (about 200) was the 1912 Tipo Zero, which had a standard four-seater tourer body and 1846-cc 4-cylinder engine. Other models went up to 9 litres and the 4-cylinder range was marketed in the USA from 1910. There was also a 6-cylinder 3.9-litre model in 1911–12.

With the 1½-litre 4-cylinder 501 of 1919 Fiat became mass producers. Electric welding was used instead of rivets and there were standardized parts and full electrics. By 1926 some 45,000 501s had been made and front-wheel brakes were optional. Similar bigger models were the 2297-cc 505 and

1936 Fiat 500 Topolino.

the 3446-cc 6-cylinder 510. Top of the range in 1921–2 was the Superfiat 40/60 hp with 152-in/3860-mm wheelbase and 6809-cc V12 engine with detachable heads. In England the £1850 chassis price was the same as a Rolls-Royce, though normally the Fiat was complete with a luxurious torpedo body. The smaller 519, a 4766-cc six, shared its four-wheel hydromechanical brakes. More significant was the 1924 509 with 990-cc 4-cylinder ohc engine, flat radiator and thermo-syphon cooling. Fiat's revolutionary hire purchase scheme helped to make it a best seller.

The year 1930 saw assembly of the 2½-litre 6-cylinder 521 in Germany (in a factory purchased from NSU) and the adoption of hydraulic brakes on the bigger 3.7-litre 525. The 1932 508 Balilla marked a new departure, with a 995-cc 4-cylinder engine, hydraulic brakes and an all-metal body. From it developed the more powerful 508S sports two-seater, while the 508 saloon was built under licence in Poland and France (Simca). The streamlined 1500 6-cylinder appeared in 1935 with 110-in/2800-mm wheelbase backbone chassis, independent front suspension, sloping radiator and bonnet with faired-in headlamps; 70 mph/113 kph was possible from 45 bhp.

In Italy the 1936 500 Topolino, with coupé or convertible body, revolutionized personal transport. The tiny 570-cc 13-bhp side-valve 4-cylinder engine was mounted ahead of the radiator, allowing the seats to be positioned in the middle of the 78-in/2000-mm wheelbase, and there was independent front suspension. The bigger four-seater 508C Balilla 1100 with 1089-cc ohv engine followed in 1937, developed into the 1100 in 1939, the unitary construction Nuova 1100 in 1953 and the 1100R with front disc brakes in 1966. The first new postwar design was the 1950 1400 with unitary construction, coil-spring independent front suspension and a 4-cylinder 1395-cc ohv engine. The first V8 model, a 1996-cc 120 mph/193 kph GT coupé with all-independent suspension, known as the 8V, appeared in 1952 and two years later became the first Italian car to be fitted with a glass-fibre body.

The best-selling 600 of 1955 had a 4-cylinder water-cooled rear engine, all-independent suspension and an integral construction body with an overall length of 126 in/3200 mm and the Topolino's wheelbase. In 1960 the engine size went up to 797 cc and it was called the 600D, while by 1966 over 2 million had been sold. The 116-in/2970-mm long Nuova 500 replaced the Topolino in 1957 and had a 16-bhp 479-cc air-cooled 2-cylinder engine at the rear (later versions had 18 bhp from 499 cc). Top speed was nearly 60 mph/97 kph, over 50 mpg/5.65 litres/100 km was easily possible and there were four seats, though minimal luggage space. The model was rebodied as the 126 in 1972, now with a 652-cc engine. The big 1800/2100 6-cylinder saloons appeared in 1959, the latter becoming the 2300 in 1961 and having a 120 mph/193 kph Ghia coupé version. The 1961 1300/1500 4-cylinder family saloons were Fiat's first volume models with front disc brakes. The 1966 Dino, with Ferrari-designed 1987-cc V6 engine producing 160 bhp, was a potent front-engined open sports car, with a coupé version added in 1967. Also in 1966 the significant lightweight monocoque 124 went into production with an 1124-cc 4-cylinder engine, five-bearing crankshaft, 6000-mile/10,000-km service interval and disc brakes all round.

The same year Fiat concluded a technical deal with the USSR to build a factory at Togliatti where the Russian version of the 124, known in export markets as Lada, is currently built by Vaz. Sporting spider and coupé versions used a 90-bhp 1438-cc ohc engine (later cars had 1.6- or 1.8-litre engines) and were sold in Europe and the USA. The Spyder, with 2-litre engine, is currently sold in the USA as the Pininfarina Azzura. The larger 98-in/2505-mm wheelbase 125 arrived in 1967 with 1608-cc ohc engine and is still manufactured in Poland and sold as the FSO.

In 1969 Fiat took over Lancia, acquired a 50% share in Ferrari and had integrated Autobianchi into the group. From the latter's Primula was developed the advanced front-wheel-drive 128, with transverse 1116-cc ohc 4-cylinder engine featuring cogged-belt camshaft drive and all-independent suspension. Also announced in 1969 was the prestige 130 saloon with 2866-cc 140-bhp V6 engine and automatic transmission. Wheelbase was 107 in/2720 mm and there was a distinctive Pininfarina coupé, while later versions had a 3235-cc engine.

First of the new breed of superminis was the front-wheel-drive 127 with 902-cc transverse engine and two-door 87.6-in/2225-mm wheelbase fastback body (later a hatchback). The 850 which it replaced had been in production since 1964 and sold over 3 million; the 127 was to sell nearly 6 million. In 1972 the new X1/9 mid-engined sports car using the 128 engine appeared, and the conventional 132 with 1.6- or 1.8-litre twin-ohc engine replaced the 125 and continued into the 1980s as the 2-litre Argenta. The similar but smaller 131

Mirafiori replaced the 124 saloon in 1974, and was offered in a twin-cam 2-litre Supermirafiori version in 1978. New the same year was the Ritmo (Strada) which used the 1116-cc 128 engine (with optional 1301-cc or 1498-cc variants), suspension and brakes in a new 96-in/2450-mm wheelbase Bertone hatchback body that was welded and painted by robots. Completely different was the boxy 85-in/2160-mm wheelbase Panda hatchback of 1980 with a choice of engines from 652 to 903 cc.

The year 1983 saw the addition of the tall but aerodynamic Uno hatchback with lightweight body and a range of engine options, including a 1299-cc turbo for 1985. Over 2 million Unos had been sold by 1987. A three-box saloon derivative of the Ritmo called the Regata was added to the range in 1984 and the little Panda became available with four-wheel drive. Fiat's new 999-cc FIRE (Fully Integrated Robotized Engine) 4-cylinder engine was fitted to the base Uno in 1985 and the top Panda in 1986. There was a revised body for the Ritmo/Strada in 1985 and for the Regata derivative in 1986.

The new Croma that year marked Fiat's return to the large saloon car market and was the third of the European Type 4 models (following the Saab 9000 and Lancia Thema) to appear. The aerodynamic four-door body had a drag coefficient of 0.32, yet Giugiaro's clever styling meant that it looked very like a booted saloon. A 104.7-in/2660-mm wheelbase was shared with Lancia's Thema (a four-door saloon) but engines ranged from a 1585-cc 4-cylinder through 1995-cc twin-cam units with carburettors or injection to a 2.5-litre diesel and a 2.4-litre turbo diesel. Most powerful version was the 2-litre turbo with 155 bhp.

At the end of 1986 Fiat took over the loss-making state-owned Alfa Romeo which will be integrated with Lancia. This move made the Fiat Group the largest carmakers in Europe.

Ford (USA)

Henry Ford built his first car engine in 1893 while working for the electrical pioneer Thomas Edison in Detroit and the car that this 2-cylinder engine was to propel followed in 1896. A second improved car followed in 1898 and in July 1899 he was chief engineer of the Detroit Automobile Company. That folded in 1900 and was re-formed as the Henry Ford Company in 1901. Two huge racing cars were built and in 1904 with the famous 4-cylinder 999 Henry Ford reached 91 mph/146.4 kph on a frozen lake.

By that time the Ford Motor Co. had been founded (June 1903) and the Model A, with flat-twin engine under the floor and chain drive, had gone into production at a price of $850. It was soon followed by the Model B with a 4-cylinder engine under a front bonnet and the Model C with the flat-twin under a front bonnet. Less successful was the 1905 6-litre 6-cylinder Model K. The Model N of 1906 was the first 4-cylinder model to be mass produced (R and S were de luxe versions of this 15 hp chassis) and led to the 1908 Model T. Originally sold for $850 this lightweight 4-cylinder model was rugged and simple, with transverse leaf-spring suspension. The 2892-cc/176-cu. in side valve engine had a detachable cylinder head and drove through a pedal-operated epicyclic gearbox which made for easy gear-changing. By 1915 assembly-line production topped 300,000 a year, the only colour was black and the price had been considerably reduced to $490. Production reached a million a year in 1922 and when it finished in May 1927 nearly 16 million had been built. In the meantime Ford had taken over Lincoln (q.v.) in 1922.

The 1928 Model A was a conventional 3276-cc/200-cu. in 4-cylinder side valve with three-speed gearbox, sold for $450; a year later it became the first model to have a mass-produced estate car version. The model A chassis with transverse leaf-springing and four-wheel brakes was used for the 1932 V8 whose 65 bhp 3622-cc/221-cu. in engine gave 70-mph/110-kph performance with acceleration to match. Over a million were built in 1935 and two years later a smaller 2.2-litre/136-cu. in version was added, both models getting hydraulic brakes in 1939.

The prewar models continued until 1949, when there was a new body and coil-spring independent front suspension, followed by automatic transmission in 1950, an ohv 6-cylinder in 1952 and an ohv V8 in 1954. For 1955 there were new finned bodies and the Thunderbird two-seater convertible. For 1957 Ford had two wheelbase lengths, 116 in/2946 mm for the cheaper Custom and 118 in/

1957 Ford Fairlane 500 Skyliner's hardtop being retracted into the boot (trunk).

2997 mm for the Fairlane. There was also a retractable hardtop version of the Fairlane called the Skyliner in which the hardtop folded away into the boot (trunk) like a convertible. Standard Fairlane engine was the 4.8-litre/292-cu. in V8 but many had the optional 5.1 litre/312 cu. in. President Eisenhower took delivery of the first Skyliner, air suspension was fitted for 1958 Fairlanes and there was optional three-speed Cruisomatic.

The year 1959 saw improved Ford quality control applied to new bodies on a single 118-in/2997-mm wheelbase and the final fling of the retractable hardtop on the new Galaxie model. All models now had paired headlamps, and the 50 millionth Ford rolled off the line at Dearborn. New for 1960 was the smaller 109.5-in/2781-mm wheelbase Falcon powered by a 2365-cc/144-cu. in six, while the Thunderbird had a 5769-cc/352-cu. in V8.

The sporting compact Mustang of 1964 was a great success, offering over 100 mph/161 kph performance from a 4728-cc/289-cu. in V8. Then in 1965 came real 120 mph/193 kph performance from the Shelby Mustang GT350 giving 306 bhp from the same V8 but costing $4547, whereas the normal Mustang fastback with 3.3-litre/200-cu. in six cost only $2632.

The 1969 Maverick was America's first postwar small car with 105-in/2667-mm wheelbase, an overall length of 179 in/4547 mm and a 2786-cc/170-cu. in engine. Even smaller was the 1970 Pinto, made only as a two-door saloon with 94-in/2388-mm wheelbase and powered by either 1599- or 1993-cc/98- or 122-cu. in European Ford 4-cylinder engines. At just 163 in/4140 mm long, it really was a sub-compact and cost $1930. For 1971 the Mustang had a slightly longer wheelbase for the new Sportsroof fastback body with Kamm tail, and was offered with the new 7-litre/429-cu. in V8 that was standard in the bigger Thunderbird. The intermediate 5752-cc/351-cu. in V8 had its stroke increased to give 6555 cc/400-cu. in to cope with emissions requirements.

For 1974 there was a new Mustang II with shorter 96-in/2440-mm wheelbase and overall length of 175 in/4445 mm, but there was no convertible. Instead there was a two-door notchback, while the fastback had become a hatchback. No longer was there performance, or even the option of a V8 at first, with the standard engine a 2295-cc/140-cu. in 4-cylinder that was also an option on the Pinto. For the Mustang there was also a 2795-cc/171-cu. in German-made V6, while the 2.3 litre/140 cu. in was the first metric engine built in the USA. Ford's subsidiary Ghia had styled the new car, which had its whole front made of plastic and glassfibre.

The Granada, which had no similarities with the European model, was a new intermediate for 1975 with 110-in/2790-mm wheelbase and a 4097-cc/250-cu. in six or optional V8. The Mustang had an optional 4945-cc/302-cu. in V8 and there was a new Elite personal coupé based on the Torino. At the other end of the scale, the massive 120-in/3060-mm wheelbase Thunderbird could be had with a 7544-cc/460-cu. in V8. There was a new, bigger 100-in/2550-mm wheelbase Mustang for 1979 and the top Cobra version had the 2.3-litre/140-cu. in engine with turbocharging. The Maverick was replaced by the Fairmont with 105-in/2680-mm wheelbase and there was a new LTD that was 15 in/381 mm shorter than the previous model and powered by a 5-litre/302-cu. in V8. Next to be downsized was the Thunderbird. The 1980 model was only 200 in/5080 mm long with a 108-in/2755-mm wheelbase and offered with 4.2- or 4.9-litre/255- or 295-cu. in V8 engines.

The front-wheel-drive Escort hatchback was completely new for 1981 and replaced the Pinto. Looking very similar to the European Escort, whose transverse 1599-cc/97-cu. in CVH engine it shared, along with the styling and 94.3-in/2395-mm wheelbase, it was built in the USA. There was also an EXP 2+2 coupé based on the Escort, and a saloon Escort came a year later. For 1982 the sub-compact Futura with 2301-cc/140-cu. in 4-cylinder engine replaced the Fairmont and there was a new 3791-cc/231-cu. in V6 option for Thunderbird and Granada. Biggest engine offered was the optional 5766-cc/351-cu. in V8 for the LTD. This became the LTD Crown Victoria for 1983 with 4942-cc/301-cu. in V8, when a new luxury compact called the LTD replaced the Granada.

In the spring of 1983 the completely new aerodynamic Tempo with 99.8-in/2535-mm wheelbase and 176-in/4470-mm overall length was launched. Looking very like the European Sierra, with which it had very little in common, it featured all-independent suspension and a new cast-iron ohv 2326-cc/142-cu. in 4-cylinder engine driving the front wheels. The old 2.3-litre/140-cu. in ohc engine in turbocharged form giving 145 bhp was optional on Mustang and Thunderbird. The latter was now considerably smaller and more aerodynamic, with 104-in/2640-mm wheelbase and an overall length of 198 in/5020 mm. In 1983 the Mustang could be had with an optional 4942-cc/301-cu. in V8 which restored some performance but for 1984 there was the SVO version with 175 bhp from the

turbo 2.3-litre/140-cu. in engine and a distinctive air scoop on the bonnet for the intercooler intake. By 1985 only the Mustang, LTD, Thunderbird and Crown Victoria had rear-wheel drive and only the latter had a 5-litre/302-cu. in V8 as standard, while Escort and Tempo were offered with the option of 2005-cc/122-cu. in 4-cylinder diesels.

For 1986 there was the completely new Taurus mid-sized saloon and estate car with 106-in/2690-mm wheelbase unitary-construction body with a drag coefficient of 0.32 and all-independent Mac-Pherson strut suspension. Standard engine on all but base versions was a new 2980-cc/182-cu. in V6 producing 140 bhp and driving the front wheels. The base Escort became the Pony and had a larger 1858-cc/113-cu. in 4-cylinder engine, while the 2-litre/122-cu. in diesel was optional only on the Escort and Tempo. A new addition was the fuel-injected Escort GT with high output 1858-cc/113-cu. in engine producing 115 bhp. Standard engine for the Mustang convertible, Thunderbird and LTD was the 3791-cc/312-cu. in V6 with fuel injection, while the 5-litre/302-cu. in V8 was fitted with sequential multiple-port fuel injection and available for Mustang and Thunderbird. Performance versions of these models continued to use the 2.3-litre/140-cu. in ohc turbo engine. The 1987 Thunderbird was more aerodynamic with flush front lamps and full-width tail lamps and there was a Sport version with 4942-cc/302-cu. in V8 engine. The Thunderbird Turbo coupé also had four-wheel disc brakes with an anti-lock system and electronically adjusted rear suspension dampers that automatically firmed up the ride at speed or when cornering hard.

Ford's first American four-wheel-drive car was the 1987 Tempo. The electronically-activated drive to the rear wheels for this additional Tempo model was operated by a dashboard switch. The revised 1987 Mustang was both more aerodynamic and more powerful and the GT version was even more distinctive.

Ford (Europe)

In October 1986 the Ford Motor Company Ltd celebrated 75 years of car manufacture in Britain, which was the first overseas market for Henry Ford's American company. In fact Percival Perry (later Lord Perry) had founded the Central Motor Car Co. in London's Long Acre in 1903 to sell imported Model A Fords, and with the arrival of the legendary Model T in 1909 sales showed great promise – so much so that Perry persuaded Henry Ford to set up a subsidiary company, The Ford

Motor Co. (England) Ltd, in 1911. So successful was this, with 400 cars sold in a year, that Ford soon outgrew the Shaftesbury Avenue premises and the site of a former tram factory at Trafford Park, Manchester, became an assembly plant for Model Ts shipped from America in component form. With an initial workforce of just 60, production began on 23 October 1911. Three thousand Model Ts were built in 1912 and with the coming of the revolutionary moving production line in 1913 sales doubled, and would have reached 10,000 in 1914 had it not been for the outbreak of war. By this time many local components were incorporated and the cars could claim to be manufactured in Britain rather than just assembled. The one thing the new production line techniques could not accommodate was changes in the paint colour, which was why Ford offered only black.

In 1917 Ford opened an assembly plant for the Model T at Cork in Ireland and in the 1920s Trafford Park was expanded. Even so it was obvious that a bigger factory was needed and in 1925, the same year that Model T assembly started in Berlin, 500 acres of land on the banks of the River Thames at Dagenham were purchased and then reclaimed from their marshy state. Henry Ford's son Edsel cut the first turf in 1929 and in October 1931 the Dagenham plant produced its first car, a Model A. Over 300,000 Model Ts had been built in Manchester when production ended in 1927. The more conventional Model A, built also in Germany, had a 3-litre side-valve engine, three-speed gearbox and saloon body. In its British 14.9-hp AF 2-litre economy form it cost £185, which was too much in the 1931 Depression. Henry Ford's answer was the 8-hp Model Y, first displayed at Ford's own motor show at the Albert Hall, London, in February 1932 and the first European Ford. At £120 it was cheaper than both the rival Austin Seven and Morris Eight and offered 60 mph/ 97 kph performance from a 933-cc side-valve engine. A similar model called the Köln was built in the new German factory at Cologne, where production of the Model B had started in 1931. In Britain production economies allowed Ford to reduce the price of the Model Y progressively, a necessary step in order to maintain sales in the Depression, and in 1935 it became the £100 Popular saloon. The same year it was joined by the 1172-cc 10-hp Model C. By 1939 the 8-hp model had become the Anglia and the 10-hp the Prefect, with more rounded bodies that were to continue into the 1950s.

France had a version of the Model Y too in 1934 called the Tracford, which was a front-wheel-drive conversion with engine and gearbox reversed, but better known was the Matford built in the Mathis factory at Strasbourg from 1934 until the war. It was based on the American side-valve Ford V8, which was also built at Dagenham and Cologne from 1935 and in 30-hp 3.6-litre form cost £250 in Britain. Because of the British horsepower taxation system there was a smaller-engined 22-hp version, which paid less tax, built at Dagenham from 1937–9. It also appeared as a Matford.

After World War II the Anglia and Prefect continued in production at Dagenham with the 1172-cc side-valve engine that was also used in the Taunus from Cologne. The 22-hp V8 continued and was built in France as the Vedette with independent front suspension. In Britain the 3.6-litre V8 was called the Pilot. It was in the autumn of 1950 that the first really significant postwar models emerged from Dagenham. The 4-cylinder 1.5-litre Consul and 2.3-litre Zephyr Six had modern styling, unitary construction and MacPherson strut independent front suspension. With their new overhead valve engines they cost £531 for the Consul and £608 for the Zephyr. They sold well and were later joined by the more luxurious Zodiac. In Germany the 12M, 15M and 17M Taunus were completely different, although the 15M and 17M had ohv engines, while in 1954 Ford sold the Poissy factory in France to Simca. The 1953 Popular built at Dagenham was very basic in specification and was the last development of the 1934 10 hp, but sold well because of its low price – just £275 plus £116 British purchase tax. At that figure it was the cheapest car in the world. The 1954 100E Anglia and Prefect had completely new bodies along the lines of the larger Consul/Zephyr but retained the 1172-cc side-valve engine. They were joined in 1955 by the Squire estate car version. The next year the Consul and Zephyr became Mark IIs with a larger body offering seating for six and styling that was distinctly American. The

1965 German Ford Taunus 17M with V4 engine.

Consul's 4-cylinder engine went up to 1703 cc and the Zephyr's to 2.6 litres.

It was the 1960s that were to see massive changes in Ford's models and operations in Europe. It all began in 1959 with the totally new 105E Anglia with distinctive modern styling featuring an inward-sloping rear window. Underneath the new bodywork was a completely new 997-cc overhead-valve engine coupled to Ford's first four-speed gearbox. It was an enormous success and was built at Dagenham at the rate of 1000 a week. Less popular were the bigger, but similarly styled, Classic and Capri of 1961, despite advanced features like four headlamps and front disc brakes. The latter had been offered as an option on the Mark II Consul/Zephyr for 1961 and were standard on the restyled 1962 Mark III Zephyr and Zodiac models. For 1963 the Consul was replaced by the Zephyr 4 with a 1703-cc engine in a new body.

Also new for 1963 was the Consul Cortina with 1198- and 1498-cc 4-cylinder engines in a completely new family-sized body that had been designed for simplicity and light weight by a team of British Ford engineers led by Fred Hart. It was the first British Ford to be completely costed down to the last washer and also the first planned as a complete model range, including estate cars. Before the model was launched in the autumn of 1962 Ford had approached Colin Chapman to produce a sporting version. The result was the quick and distinctive Cortina-Lotus using the Lotus twin-cam version of the 1500 engine. Ford's own more modest performance version, the Cortina GT, also appeared in 1963 and built up a loyal following. The Cortina became Britain's best-selling car over many years, Mark II 1300 and 1600 versions appearing in 1966, and pioneered Aeroflow face-level ventilation with extraction in 1964.

In Germany there was a new model in 1962 also and it looked somewhat similar to the Cortina, although it had been designed in the USA and had front-wheel drive and a V4 engine. Called the 12M it had 1183 or 1498 cc. In 1964 the V4 engine went into the rear-wheel drive 17M, offered as a 1.5 or 1.7 litre, and there was a 2-litre V6 in the 20M. The Corsair of 1963 was a Dagenham-built variation on the Cortina mechanicals with a longer wheelbase and completely different body. In 1965 it was destined to receive the 1.7- and 2-litre German-designed engines, but both V4 and V6 versions were rear-wheel drive. This was the first sign of Ford's design integration in Europe that was to follow and in 1966 the British Zephyr and Zodiac

in new Mark IV guise also had vee engines.

Even more was to come when the Escort was announced in 1968 to replace the Anglia, for the same model was built in Cologne and at Ford's Halewood factory opened in 1963 to supplement Dagenham. This was the first European Ford model from the integrated Ford of Europe, which had been set up in 1967, and was a conventional front-engine rear-wheel-drive saloon or estate car with 1098- or 1297-cc ohv engine. Sporting versions included a GT from the outset, plus the Twin Cam with 1558-cc Lotus engine. Later, in 1970, came the first RS1600 with Ford-Cosworth BDA engine and the Mexico derivative, after the Escort won that year's World Cup Rally. The year 1975 brought a restyled Escort Mark II that was built until 1980, and a 1599-cc engine.

'The car you've always promised yourself' was the slogan in early 1969 that launched the Capri, a sporting two-door coupé with four seats aimed at the family man who really wanted a sports car. It was a new market for Ford, who had not had a similar model before, and was their first European car to be sold with a variety of equipment option packages – and seven engines in Britain. Like the Escort it was also built in Germany, where a different family of engines were used with a 1700 V4 and 2.0-, 2.3- and 2.6-litre V6s. The British versions had a 2-litre V4 and 3-litre V6, in addition to the smaller 1.3 and 1.6 litre. A new body with hatchback third door arrived as the Mark II in 1974 and became the Mark III in 1978. In 1981 the 2.8-litre injected V6 engine was offered and the Capri ended production in 1987.

In 1972 the big Mark IV Consul/Zephyr saloons were replaced by the very much better Granada, though the Consul name and 2-litre V4 engine were retained for the base model until 1974. Again engines were different in Britain and Germany, but from mid-1976 production was in Germany only and the 1977 Mark II Granada used 'commonized' engines – 2-litre ohc Pinto, and 2.3- and 2.8-litre V6s. Similar rationalization had already taken place with the new Mark IV Cortina/Taunus that appeared in 1976 and the German 2.3-litre V6 engine was offered in the Cortina in 1977. Further body changes were made in 1979 and in that guise the Cortina/Taunus continued until 1982, with combined production standing at 6,707,387. Cortinas accounted for 4,279,079 of that total.

Ford had always thought of small cars as 'small profits', but all that changed with the introduction in Germany in 1976 and Britain in 1977 of the

1976 Ford Cortina Mark IV.

company's first small car, the Fiesta, which was also built in a new factory in Spain. It was a three-door hatchback with a transverse front engine driving the front wheels and was designed for economy motoring with simple servicing. Initially there were 957- and 1117-cc engines, but a 1300 was added in 1977 and a 1600 for the sporting XR2 in 1982. Right from the outset there was a luxury Ghia version, Ford having acquired Ghia at the end of 1972.

In 1980 the best-selling Escort underwent a dramatic change. As well as the new hatchback body (there was no saloon version) with all-round independent suspension, there were new engines. The smallest 1117-cc ohv unit came from the Fiesta but the 1300 and 1600 were all-new overhead camshaft CVH (Compound Valve angle Hemispherical head) engines with alloy cylinder heads and hydraulic tappets. These engines were installed transversely and drove the front wheels. In 1982 the sporting XR3 1600 was fitted with fuel injection and a year later came a turbo version and a convertible Escort. A booted saloon version called the Orion arrived in 1983, and the Fiesta received a new nose and the CVH engines the same year. Latest changes to the Escort/Orion came in 1986 with Ford's 1.4-litre CVH lean-burn engine replacing the 1.3 CVH, a new 1297-cc ohv unit and the option of Lucas/Girling SCS (Stop Control System) hydro-mechanical anti-lock braking. This was the first adoption of anti-lock for a small mass-produced model.

At the end of 1982 the best-selling Cortina/Taunus models were replaced by the new aerodynamically-shaped Sierra with a range of engines, but the front-engine rear-wheel-drive layout was retained. Unlike the Cortina, the Sierra was a hatchback and in 1985 was offered with four-wheel drive. The ultimate performance Sierra was the 150 mph/241 kph RS Cosworth fitted with a turbocharged 2-litre 16-valve fuel-injected engine giving 207 bhp and ABS anti-lock brakes. Another completely different sporting Ford that appeared the same year was the mid-engined RS200 coupé with 254 bhp and selectable two- or

four-wheel drive. Designed to win rallies, it was available as a road car for £49,950.

Ford's big-car development had not been neglected and in 1985 the current completely new Scorpio hatchback (called the Granada only in the UK) was announced with a single aerodynamic body. No longer would there be an estate car variant of the big Ford. Power was provided by 1.8-, 2.0- and 2.8-litre engines, while the all-round disc brakes were fitted with ATE electronic control to prevent wheel locking. This was the first mass-produced car in the world to have ABS as standard on all models. High-security Chubb locks were standard, while electrically-adjusted seats, a heated windscreen and (later) four-wheel-drive were options for the top models. This new model was built solely in Cologne. In 1987 new lean-burn 2.4- and 2.9-litre V6 engines replaced the 2-litre 4-cylinder and 2.8-litre V6 in the Scorpio/Granada, and there was a booted version of the Sierra, called the Sierra Sapphire.

General Motors Corporation

The world's largest car producer has headquarters in Detroit, USA, subsidiaries in many countries, and in 1985 the corporation produced 7.1 million cars worldwide, including 4,887,079 in the USA. William C. Durant founded General Motors with Buick in 1908, adding Cadillac, Oakland and Oldsmobile in 1909. Durant lost control of GM in 1910 and went away to found Chevrolet, which in turn became part of General Motors in 1916. General Motors of Canada was added in 1918, being formed out of the merger of the McLaughlin Motor Car Co. and Chevrolet Motor Car Co. in Canada, and in 1925 the corporation spread to Europe with the acquisition of Vauxhall Motors in England. A cheaper Oakland model called the Pontiac became a marque in its own right in 1926, and thereafter Oakland faded out. GM South African Pty Ltd was formed in 1926, and German manufacturers Opel joined the family in 1929. In Australia GM Holden's Pty Ltd was formed in 1931 from the merger of GM (Australia) Pty Ltd and Holden's Motor Body Builder Ltd. With the increasing importance of Japan, General Motors acquired a 34% stake in Isuzu Motors Ltd in 1971. Most recent European addition was Group Lotus plc, comprising Lotus cars and their engineering, research and development consultancy, in January 1986. An attempt to purchase the commercial vehicle part of British Leyland, including Land Rover, came to nothing later in 1986 when the British government withdrew Land Rover from the package.

1987 Chevrolet Nova based on the Toyota Corolla and built in the USA by New United Motor Manufacturing Inc., owned jointly by General Motors and Toyota.

A joint venture with Toyota in the USA resulted in the setting up of NUMMI (New United Motor Manufacturing Inc.) to manufacture an American version of the Toyota Corolla, sold as the Chevrolet Nova, in 1984. The same year the car divisions were regrouped into two business units – CPC (Chevrolet, Pontiac, GM of Canada) and BOC (Buick, Oldsmobile, Cadillac). This reflected the prestige of the various marques, Chevrolet and Pontiac selling the cheapest GM cars in the USA and Cadillac the most expensive. A new GM marque will be added when the Saturn project, started in 1985, comes to fruition. GM's Saturn Corporation was set up to produce small cars in the USA that were cost-competitive with the cheapest Korean and Japanese imports.

Honda (Japan)

When the world's most successful motor-cycle manufacturers turned their attention to cars in 1962 it was natural for some of the motor-cycle design expertise to be applied. Perhaps more surprising was that the first car design was a two-seater sports car that looked remarkably European. Much less conventional were the 356- and 531-cc 4-cylinder twin overhead camshaft engines with water cooling that powered the prototypes, and developed their maximum power of 34 and 40 bhp at 8000 and 9000 rpm respectively. The later Sport 600 had the aluminium alloy engine enlarged to 606 cc with a chain to drive each rear wheel. Suspension was all-independent and the S600 had a wheelbase of 78.7 in/2000 mm. By the 1965 Tokyo Motor Show it had grown up further into the 791-cc S800 made in sports two-seater and coupé versions. Four carburettors ensured 70 bhp at 8000 rpm and there was a four-speed all-synchromesh gearbox and front disc brakes.

It was followed in 1966 by Honda's first saloons. The front-wheel-drive N360 had a transverse air-cooled 2-cylinder engine driving through a constant mesh gearbox. The N500 had a similar engine of 497 cc giving 40 bhp. The advanced air-cooled N600 followed in 1967 and was equipped with safety features like a collapsible steering column and split braking system. In 1968 this model was offered in Hondamatic form, making it the world's smallest car with an automatic gearbox, a three-speed constant mesh device with torque converter. Honda's first full-sized family car, the front wheel drive air-cooled 1300 went on sale in 1969 and featured an 88.6-in/2250-mm wheelbase giving a length of 151.3 in/3843 mm. The 4-cylinder engine produced 100 bhp at 7200 rpm, and the more powerful coupé had a top speed of 100 mph/ 161 kph.

Completely different in design was the new small hatchback Civic of 1972. The transversely mounted 1169-cc 4-cylinder overhead-camshaft engine was water cooled, with the gearbox on the end of the engine. This was Honda's first world car and in 1974 it began to be fitted with the advanced CVCC (Compound Vortex Controlled Combustion) engine which had been announced in 1973 and met both Japanese and American tough 1975 emissions standards. Honda were the first manufacturers in the world to do so. This 1488-cc ohc engine worked on the stratified charge principle and had three valves per cylinder. Power output was 63 bhp, compared with 65 bhp for the same engine with conventional cylinder head. Both 1500 versions were additional to the 1200 Civic. A larger model with a 1599-cc version of the CVCC engine went on sale in Japan and the USA in 1976 and was called the Accord. This was a 94-in/2380-mm wheelbase three-door hatchback with the transversely-mounted 4-cylinder engine driving the front wheels. A coloured light system to indicate the need for servicing and remote operation of the rear hatch were features. A coupé version, the Prelude, and a four-door saloon were added in 1978. The Civic changed too, with the power output of the 1238-cc engine increased to 60 bhp and the body featuring a rear hatch that opened down to the bumper. An additional five-door version had a 4 in/100 mm longer body. In 1979 there was a completely new Civic with larger, and 8 in/ 200 mm longer, body offered on two wheelbases as before, plus an estate car version. The 1335-cc engine and optional five-speed gearbox were new and there was also a 1.5-litre version.

In 1980 the new Quintet, a five-door hatchback, between the Civic and Accord in size and using the latter's 1.6 engine, was announced. The same year's Ballade had the Civic's 91.3-in/2320-mm wheelbase but was a four-door version with a conventional boot. In 1981 it was sold in Britain as the

Triumph Acclaim and was actually built in British Leyland's Cowley factory as a result of a deal with Honda. The gap below the Civic was filled by the small 1200 City hatchback, while the Accord for 1982 had a new body and optional 1.8-litre engine. Though both Accord saloon and hatch shared the new 96.4-in/2450-mm wheelbase, they had different lengths of 174 and 166 in/4410 and 4210 mm respectively. The Prelude coupé version featured pop-up headlamps and was offered in 1983 with an optional anti-lock braking system and a 1.8-litre engine was standard in the new body. The little upright City became Honda's first turbocharged model with 100 bhp from 1232 cc.

For 1984 there was a completely new 1.3- or 1.5-litre Civic, or rather three Civics – the three-door hatchback, five-door tall Shuttle and sporting CRX coupé. The similar-sized Ballade four-door saloon was also built and sold in Britain as the Rover 200 series. Later that year the Shuttle became the first model to be available with four-wheel drive, and a 1590-cc fuel-injected engine producing 125 bhp was offered on the Civic and CRX. More completely new models were added in 1985. The Quint Integra was a new aerodynamic hatchback bridging the gap between the Civic and Accord, offered with the Civic 1.5-litre engine or the double-ohc four-valve-per-cylinder 1.6-litre fuel-injected one. There was a similarly-styled new Accord with longer 102-in/2600-mm wheelbase and 1.8- or 2-litre engines. This came as a four-door saloon, a three-door hatchback or a three-door Aerodeck semi-estate. The 1955-cc double-ohc 16-valve engine with fuel injection was also offered in the Prelude.

For 1986 came the result of Honda's latest collaboration with the Rover Group in the form of the top-of-the-range Legend, the first Honda to be built in Britain for sale as a Honda in Europe. In return Honda would sell Rover's similar 800 model in Japan. With a wheelbase of 108.7 in/2760 mm and a length of 180.4 in/4810 mm, this four-door saloon was bigger than anything Honda had previously built, and marked their entry into the

1987 Honda Quint Integra 5-door hatchback. The mirrors on stalks are peculiar to Japanese-market versions.

executive car bracket. Four-wheel disc brakes and a completely new Honda V6 24-valve ohc engine giving 165 bhp in 2.5-litre form and 145 bhp in 2-litre form mounted transversely and driving the front wheels were featured, and overdrive manual or automatic gearboxes were offered. Honda had come a long way from the 2-cylinder air-cooled minicars of the 1960s, but retained a link in the streamlined hatchback Today introduced for 1986 and powered by a water-cooled 546-cc twin driving the front wheels.

Jaguar (UK)

Though the Jaguar name did not appear on a car until 1935, the marque's origins go back to the Swallow Sidecar Co. formed by William Lyons and William Walmsley in Blackpool in 1922. In 1926 a move into car-body building was made and the first Swallow-bodied Austin Seven was announced in 1927, the year the firm became the Swallow Sidecar and Coachbuilding Co. Lack of space forced a move to Coventry in November 1928 and building on Fiat, Standard and other chassis followed.

It was in 1931 that Bill Lyons' first complete car, the SSI, was announced, based on a specially lowered Standard 16-hp chassis and using that model's 2-litre 6-cylinder engine. The normal Standard 16 stood 68 in/1727 mm tall, but the long-bonneted SSI was only 55 in/1397 mm high and looked like a £1000 car. In fact it cost just £310, exhibiting the value for money that was to become a hallmark of later Jaguars. Cheaper still at £210 was the SSII based on the smaller Standard Nine. The cars sold well and in 1934 S.S. Cars Ltd became a public company and William Heynes joined as chief engineer. With Harry Weslake he redesigned the side-valve Standard engine into an overhead-valve unit which was persuaded to give 100 bhp from 2½ litres. At the end of 1935 this was to power the first SS Jaguar saloon. Earlier in 1935 the first open sports car to carry the company's name, the SS 90, had appeared with the side-valve engine and was succeeded in 1936 by the ohv SS Jaguar 100. In addition to the 1935 2663-cc SS Jaguar saloon and tourer there was also a smaller 1608-cc 1½-litre model. In 1937 the 100 became a 3½-litre and the first steel-bodied 1½-, 2½- and 3½-litre SS Jaguar saloons were produced.

After wartime aircraft work, car production resumed again in 1945, but the wartime connotations of the SS initials resulted in the company's change of name to Jaguar Cars Ltd. It was 1948

Jaguar SS100 sports 2-seater of 1936.

before the new 2½- and 3½-litre saloons and coupés with independent suspension appeared; in the meantime the prewar range was produced, and exported to the USA from early in 1947. The lack of a sports car was put right at the 1948 Earls Court Motor Show where Jaguar showed their brand new XK120 two-seater with 3442-cc 6-cylinder engine. This was the classic XK twin-cam unit (still in production for the Daimler Limousine), that was developed by Bill Heynes, Claude Baily and Walter Hassan. Twin cams, 120 bhp, quiet and easy to make – these were the parameters William Lyons laid down. When told that the power output could be achieved by a simple ohv pushrod unit, Lyons still insisted on the twin overhead camshafts because he wanted the engine to *look* powerful too. Originally it was planned to have a 4-cylinder XK 100-bhp engine also and this 2-litre unit powered Goldie Gardner's streamlined record breaker which reached 176 mph/283 kph at Jabbeke in Belgium in 1948. The following year it was the XK120's turn to prove that it really was fast and on the same road R. M. V. Sutton drove into the record books with 132.596 mph/213.383 kph, making the XK120 the world's fastest production car. This led up to the XK120C (C-type) that scored Jaguar's first Le Mans win as a prototype in 1951.

The 1950 Mark VII ushered in Jaguar's saloon style for the 1950s with a roomy steel body on a conventional chassis. It developed into the Mark VIII in 1956 and the disc-braked 3.8-litre Mark IX in 1958. The D-type which followed the C-type to win at Le Mans in 1954 was usable on the road and cost £3879 in 1956. A more civilized version without the fin was sold as the XK-SS in 1957, but only a few were built before a factory fire halted production. The XK120 developed into the 140 in 1954 and the 150 in 1957. In 1955 there was a new, smaller saloon with 2483-cc short-stroke XK engine. It was Jaguar's first monocoque and was followed by a 3.4-litre version in 1957, and that year Dunlop disc brakes, which had been standard

on the D-type from the outset, were offered on 2.4/3.4 and XK models. The much improved Mark 2 of 1959 had disc brakes as standard and was also offered in 3.8-litre form with a 130 mph/209 kph top speed.

In 1961 that was eclipsed by the streamlined production E-type whose 3.8 litres gave it a top speed of over 150 mph/241 kph, up to that time the fastest achieved by any production car, at a price of £2098 as a two-seater and £2197 as a coupé. For 1962 Jaguar offered their first monocoque big saloon, the Mark X, with a low, wide body and independent rear suspension developed from the E-type, whose 265-bhp engine it shared. By this time Jaguar production was expanding and the new factory at Browns Lane, Allesley, to which all Jaguar production had moved in 1951–2, was unable to cope. Jaguar's acquisition of the ailing Daimler/Lanchester concern in 1960 was therefore more to do with extra space than broadening the range and the Radford factory was to become Jaguar's engine plant. Diversification resulted in the purchase of Guy Motors in 1961, Coventry Climax in 1963 and Henry Meadows in 1964. In 1965 the E-type and Mark X received an enlarged 4235-cc version of the XK engine and a new all-synchromesh gearbox, while the Mark 2 was supplemented by the S-type which was basically a Mark 2 with new rear end and independent rear suspension. Appeal of the E-type was widened with the 2+2 coupé version with longer wheelbase in the spring of 1966 and that autumn the S-type was fitted with a modified Mark X-style front end to become the 420, though S-types continued until 1968. Both 420 and 420G, as the Mark X was renamed, had revised interiors with padded facias.

In July 1966 Jaguar had merged with BMC to form British Motor Holdings, which in turn became British Leyland in 1968, the year that Jaguar's new XJ6 model, in 2.8- and 4.2-litre form, replaced all the saloons except the 420G and Mark 2. Fortunately the XJ6 was classic Jaguar both in performance (120 mph/193 kph) and style, while its ride and quietness set new standards. Jaguar's new 5343-cc V12 engine arrived in 1971 to power the Series III E-type and in 1972 was offered in the saloon, which became the XJ12. A longer-wheelbase saloon body and a coupé were also added from 1973. In 1975 the V12 was fitted with Bosch/Lucas fuel injection and in this form went into the new XJ-S coupé which replaced the E-type. The XJ-S had a maximum speed of over 150 mph/241 kph on 285 bhp and had four seats and air conditioning. Series III XJ saloons appeared in 1979 with higher roofs and deeper windows, fuel injection for the 3.4 litre and 4.2 litre and a five-speed (Rover SD1) manual gearbox for the 6-cylinder cars.

In 1983 the XJ-S was offered with a smaller engine as an alternative to the V12 and there was also a *cabriolet* open two-seater version. The 3590-cc AJ6 (advanced Jaguar) 6-cylinder engine was a completely new aluminium alloy double-ohc unit producing 228 bhp with the aid of four valves per cylinder. In 1986 this engine, with a short-stroke 2919-cc single-ohc 165-bhp derivative, became the power unit for the all-new XJ6 (codenamed XJ40). It was coupled to either a Getrag five-speed manual gearbox or a ZF overdrive automatic with unique J-gate selector that allowed manual control. The body was completely new, but retained the Jaguar line, with electronic instruments and a vehicle-condition monitor displaying a written warning of a problem. Power hydraulics operated the brakes and optional anti-lock and suspension levelling were available. A world first was the use of a clear lacquer over a solid (non-metallic) paint colour. The advanced Lucas electronics, including ignition and fuel injection, prompted Jaguar to develop an equally advanced computer diagnostic system for servicing-dealers. The V12 engine continued to be offered for 1987 in the Series III car, which was otherwise replaced by the outstanding new XJ6, and the XJ-S. The new XJ6 was the first model to be launched by Jaguar Cars plc, the company that was sold off from British Leyland to become independent again in 1984.

Lancia (Italy)

In 1906 Vincenzo Lancia broke away from Fiat, where he had been chief inspector, and formed his own company Fabrica Automobili Lancia e Cia. He continued to race Fiats, on which he had started as a works driver in 1900, until 1908 but did not race his own Lancias. The first model began the trend for using letters of the Greek alphabet as names and was called Alpha. It had a 2543-cc side-valve engine and was notable for its shaft drive. The 6-cylinder 3815-cc DiAlpha followed in 1908 and the 3-litre monobloc 4-cylinder Beta in 1909.

The original works in Turin's *Via Ormea* were augmented by a factory in the *Corso Dante* where the 3½-litre Gamma was built in 1910. That year was the last that Vincenzo himself raced, setting a mile record at 70.2 mph/113.0 kph at Modena in a special Alpha. The 1913 4.9-litre Theta was the first European car with full electrics, and they

An early Lancia Lambda tourer photographed at the factory with 'slave' wheels and wooden tyres.

were designed as part of the car, not a bolted-on afterthought. Postwar, with a detachable cylinder head, it became the Kappa, while 1919 saw a massive 7837-cc narrow-angle V12. The similar 4594-cc ohc V8 followed in the more successful TriKappa in 1922.

Later that year came a revolutionary model called the Lambda, from which all the modern unitary construction cars can be said to have evolved. The integral body/chassis unit was a world first, as was the opening rear boot whose drop-down lid revealed space for a suitcase above the fuel tank. For such a long car (122-in/3100-mm wheelbase) it was surprising that both the 2121-cc narrow-angle V4 engine and the gearbox went under the short bonnet, but Lancia had staggered the bores so that the engine was only 22 in/560-mm long. The Lancia narrow-angle V4 and the sliding pillar and coil-spring independent front suspension were to be features of Lancia models right into the 1950s. With its 70 mph/113 kph top speed and four-wheel brakes, the Lambda was quite sporting, despite its size, and handled well. Some 13,000 were built, the final series having 2570-cc engines producing 69 bhp. The luxury DiLambda of 1929 had a separate chassis and 4-litre narrow-angle V8 engine producing 100 bhp, while centralized chassis lubrication and a massive 137-in/3480-mm wheelbase were other features.

The 1931 2-litre V4 Artena and 2.6-litre V8 Astura were smaller saloons that succeeded the Lambda. An economical small saloon with reasonable performance was what Italian motorists of the 1930s wanted and Lancia provided it in the 1194-cc Astura, the world's first unitary construction saloon (saloon Lambdas had been built on a separate chassis). It was also a pillarless four-door saloon with good roadholding and hydraulic brakes. Considerably more modern in appearance was Vincenzo Lancia's final design, the little 1352-cc monocoque Aprilia which was announced just before his death in 1937. It had independent rear suspension (by torsion bars), 80 mph/129 kph performance with 30-mpg/9.42 litre/100 km economy, and was one of the first aerodynamic European production saloons. It also weighed under 1800 lb/ 816 kg. The 1939 Ardea was really a smaller version of the Aprilia, with a 903-cc engine.

In 1950 the Aurelia four-door saloon replaced the Aprilia, having been designed by Vittorio Jano and Vincenzo's son Gianni. It featured a pushrod 1754-cc V6 engine and led a year later to the Pininfarina coupé version on a shorter wheelbase with 1991-cc (and later 2451-cc) V6 engine. The B20 Aurelia coupé was a classic, and the originator of the modern GT car, with its fastback integral-construction steel body and 100 mph/161 kph performance. That was not a feature of the 1098-cc V4 Appia that replaced the Ardea in 1953 and went on into the 1960s. The much bigger Flaminia of 1956 had a platform-type chassis with the engine and coil-and-wishbone front suspension mounted on a subframe. The first cars had 98-bhp 2.5-litre V6 engines but by 1963 this had been enlarged to 2775 cc with 110 bhp and Dunlop disc brakes all round to cope with the performance.

The 1961 Flavia was the first front-wheel-drive saloon built in Italy and was powered by a 1500-cc flat-four engine, which later became a 2-litre and in that form, as the Lancia 2000, the model continued into the 1970s. The front-drive formula was followed for the 1965 Fulvia, whose original 1216-cc V4 engine was soon enlarged to 1298 cc. By that time there was a very attractive coupé version which was a successful competition car and was destined to be the last of the traditional Lancias. Their fine, but unorthodox, engineering had certainly produced cars of character but these were not sold in sufficient numbers and the result was mounting debts and a poorly-equipped new factory at Chivasso.

In 1969 Fiat bought Lancia for a million lire (about £668) plus Lancia's debts of about £67 million. First new model was the 1972 Beta, a front-wheel-drive saloon using Fiat 1400, 1600 or 1800 twin-cam engines (from the 132) mounted transversely. Four-wheel disc brakes and all-independent suspension by MacPherson struts were features and the 1400 saloon was 5 inches/ 127 mm longer and wider than the Fulvia but only 28 lb/13 kg heavier. A coupé version was added in 1973 on a shorter wheelbase and the unusual HPE (High Performance Estate) version in 1975. The Beta Monte Carlo that appeared that year was a performance two-seater mid-engined coupé styled and built by Pininfarina. The ultimate performance Lancia, though, was the rally-winning Stratos which was built in 1974 and 1975. Based on a steel monocoque was a Bertone-designed wedge-shaped glassfibre coupé body; it used the Fiat Dino 2418-cc V6 engine producing 190 bhp and 140 mph/225 kph in road-going form, though many of the 400 built were rallied with up to 285 bhp.

Lancia's big models did not end for good with the Fiat takeover, for the Gamma saloon and coupé that appeared in 1976 were all new, including the 2484-cc flat-four engine giving 140 bhp. Despite attractive Pininfarina styling the models were not a success, but went on into the 1980s. It was in 1980 that Lancia's reputation suffered a major blow brought about by serious structural rusting of pre-1975 Betas. The fastback saloon was quickly replaced by the conventional booted Trevi, but the coupé, HPE and Monte Carlo models were unaffected, though the Beta designation was dropped. The new five-door hatchback 1300 and 1500 Delta for 1980 was the result of technical collaboration with Saab and benefited from galvanized sections in its construction, as well as an air-blending heater. Later a 1600 with more performance was added, and when turbocharged produced 140 bhp. The ultimate Delta was the S4 which, like the Stratos, was designed to win rallies. It had a 1759-cc twin-cam 4-cylinder light alloy engine with both supercharger and turbocharger giving 250 bhp and 140 mph/225 kph in road form. The engine was installed longitudinally behind the front seats and drove all four wheels, which were braked by discs. At 100 million lire (about £40,000), it was the most expensive Lancia ever. This was not the first Lancia with a supercharger; that distinction goes to the 1982 Volumex version of the Trevi with 135 bhp from 2 litres. The same year the Prisma, in effect a Delta with a boot, was added to the range.

Co-operation with Saab was carried a stage further in 1984 with the new Thema saloon, which was developed with some parts in common with Saab's 9000 and was the equivalent of Fiat's Croma (then unannounced). Engines included 2 litre, 2-litre turbocharged, 2.5-litre turbo diesel and the 2849-cc PRV V6 in a transverse position to drive the front wheels. In 1986 came the range-topping Thema 8.32 with fuel injected Ferrari 2927-cc V8 engine and anti-lock for the four-wheel disc brakes. At the other end of the scale was the small Y10 three-door hatchback with Fiat's 999-cc FIRE (Fully Integrated Robotized Engine) giving 45 bhp or a 1049-cc unit in normal or turbo form with 55 or 85 bhp. The Y10 was also sold under the Autobianchi name, for that company had been owned by Fiat since 1967 and controlled by Lancia since 1975.

Lincoln (USA)

It was Henry Leland, founder of General Motors, who formed the Lincoln Motor Co. in 1920 and marketed a 5.8-litre/354-cu. in V8 which, despite some advanced features like pressure lubrication, was not a commercial success. In 1922 Leland sold the bankrupt company to Henry Ford for $8 million.

Ford continued the Lincoln quality theme and President Coolidge purchased one in 1924. They were also favoured by the police and were capable of 80 mph/129 kph when tuned. The 1931 Model K was the first of the big Lincolns with a 145-in/3683-mm wheelbase and 6.3-litre/385-cu. in V8 giving 120 bhp, a massive third more than the 136-in/3454-mm wheelbase Model L that preceded it, but the slump of 1931 saw Lincoln lose Ford $4.6 million. In spite of this an even grander model, the KB with 7.3-litre/448-cu. in V12 engine with expensive blade and fork connecting rods, was added in 1932. Prices went from about $4300 to $7200, compared with $2900 to $3350 for the V8. In 1933 that was replaced with a smaller 6.3-litre/381.7-cu. in V12 in the 136-in/3454-mm wheelbase chassis and became the KA. The following year KA and KB were amalgamated as the Model K with 136- or 145-in/3454- or 3683-mm wheelbase and 6788-cc/414-cu. in V12 giving 150 bhp.

Completely different was the 1936 unitary-construction Lincoln Zephyr with streamlined fastback shape and faired-in headlamps. A 4.4-litre/267-cu. in V12 provided the power but brakes remained mechanical because Henry Ford distrusted hydraulics. It was this model which formed the basis for the first Continental of 1939, which had started out as a special one-off for Edsel Ford. Postwar both Lincoln and the Continental continued until 1948. The 1949 models were the 125-in/3175-mm wheelbase Cosmopolitan and 121-in/3073-mm wheelbase ordinary Lincoln, the latter sharing a Mercury body. Both were powered by Ford's new 5517-cc/337-cu. in L-head V8 which gave 152 bhp and 100 mph/160 kph performance. A manual gearbox with overdrive was standard and the optional automatic was General Motors' Hydra-Matic! In 1950 the link with the White House was continued when 10 stretched Cosmopolitans were delivered for official use by President Truman (and subsequently Eisenhower, Kennedy and Johnson). For 1952 there were new models

with 123-in/3124-mm wheelbase, Ford's new ohv 5.2-litre/317-cu. in V8 and MacPherson strut front suspension for the first time on any American car. Top model was the Capri, while the Cosmopolitan also used the unique Lincoln bodies.

In 1955 Lincoln and Mercury split into separate divisions. The Lincoln was now 215.6 in/5476 mm long with a 5.6-litre/341-cu. in V8 giving 225 bhp and available with the marque's own Turbo-Drive automatic. It was also the last year of the medium-sized luxury Lincolns (until 1977) and 6-volt electrics. For 1956 the regular Lincoln shared its 126-in/3200-mm wheelbase with the Mark II Continental, which at 233.9 in/5941 mm was 4 in/102 mm longer, and both had a 6030-cc/368-cu. in V8 giving 280 bhp. The Continental Mark II was the first to have the spare wheel shape moulded in the boot lid but even at $10,000 made a loss and was dropped in 1957, the year that fins and 'Quadri-Lite' headlamps arrived for other Lincolns. For 1958 there was a new unit construction Continental with a 7044-cc/430-cu. in V8 developing 375 bhp and 128-in/3251-mm wheelbase. Overall length was a massive 227 in/5766 mm. The 1961 Continental was smaller with a 122-in/3099-mm wheelbase and offered as a four-door saloon or convertible and was now the only Lincoln model. A feature of the convertible was the power-operated hood (soft-top) that stowed itself away in the boot, while both models had unitary body construction with galvanized sections. With the addition of 3 in/76 mm to the wheelbase for 1964 and flat side-windows it remained much the same until 1968. By then Lincolns had front disc brakes and a 345-bhp 7572-cc/462-cu. in V8 – the largest engine in a production car in 1966. A new Mark III Continental in 1968 had a slightly smaller engine and perimeter frame chassis and cost $6585, compared with $5703 for the ordinary Continental.

In 1969 a very special Lincoln was supplied as a presidential limousine. It was armoured, 258 in/6553 mm long and cost $500,000. For 1972 there was a new Mark IV, with Rolls-Royce-like radiator, which cost $8604, while its ordinary Lincoln hardtop counterpart was $7016, and both had concealed headlamps. In 1977 the smaller Versailles, based on the Mercury Monarch, was added, as well as a new Continental and Mark V, though the latter were full size. For Lincoln downsizing came in 1980 with a 5766-cc/351-cu. in V8 the biggest offered, while the Continental had a vertical quarter-window and the Mark VI an oval 'opera' window. Both now had a 117-in/2972-mm wheelbase and overall length of 219-in/5563-mm. For

1987 Lincoln Town Car 4-door saloon.

1982 there was an even smaller Continental that replaced the Versailles, and for the first time a 3.8-litre/231-cu. in V6 engine was standard with a 4.9-litre/302-cu. in V8 optional.

The 1984 Lincoln Mark VII was altogether different with very European streamlined styling, air suspension, a fuel-injected 4942-cc/302-cu. in V8 and electronic instruments including a digital speedometer. Not only was it 13 in/330 mm shorter and 350 lb/159 kg lighter than the Mark VI but it handled like a European car too, and even had a fuel-saving four-speed overdrive automatic gearbox. The Continental and very square Town Car continued in similar form to 1982 but with fuel injection for 1986, and the Mark VII reverted to analog instruments but had four-wheel anti-lock disc brakes. Largest Lincoln in 1986 was the Town Car with 219-in/5563-mm length and 117.3-in/2980-mm wheelbase, the Continental and Mark VII having a 108.5-in/2756-mm wheelbase. All three models were available in special Designer Series, by Cartier, Givenchy and Bill Blass respectively.

Lotus (UK)

The racing pedigree that Lotus enjoys today grew out of the enthusiasm of a London University student named Colin Chapman. With a fellow student he sold second-hand cars in the post-war boom period until a change of climate summarily ended these activities at the end of 1947. An Austin Seven remained unsold and was used by Chapman as the basis of a trials car fitted with a marine plywood body. The chassis was later run with a Ford 10 engine and proved successful in competition. In 1952, with Michael Allen, he formed Lotus Engineering and the first production Lotus, designated Mark 6, emerged from the stables behind the public house run by Chapman's father at Hornsey in North London in 1953. It was offered as a kit with an 87.5 in/2222 mm wheelbase and could be tailored to a variety of engines. Mark 8, 9, 10 and 11 sports racing cars with aerodynamic bodies followed and Lotus Cars Ltd was formed in 1955. In 1957 there were major changes with the announcement of the Lotus Elite coupé. Not only

was it the first closed Lotus, it was also the world's first monocoque glass fibre body with eight box sections reinforced with steel tubing. It had a 1216 cc Coventry-Climax engine producing 75 or 83 bhp and this, combined with an 88 in/2235 mm wheelbase 2-seater that weighed only 1204 lb/546.1 kg, meant that performance was shattering, with 0–60 mph/96 kph in 11 seconds. Stopping was taken care of by disc brakes and there was all-round independent suspension using what are now known as Chapman struts at the rear. The same year the Six was replaced by the Seven, which retained the multi-tubular chassis with alloy panels and cycle wings. The first versions had Ford 100E side-valve engines, but later models were fitted with the ohv 105E or BMC Sprite engines. The Seven remained in production as a kit car until 1973, when the manufacturing rights were sold to Caterham Cars who still build it in modified form with a 1558 cc twin cam Lotus engine as the Caterham Super Seven. A measure of success allowed Lotus to move to a proper factory at Cheshunt in Hertfordshire in 1959. When production of the Elite ended in 1962 it was replaced by the legendary Elan, which set new standards for roadholding and handling and established Lotus as proper car manufacturers. Nevertheless most Elans continued to be supplied in kit form for the owner to assemble, thus avoiding British Purchase Tax. Initially the Elan was a 2-seater sports car powered by a 1499 cc engine but a coupé version and the classic Ford/Lotus twin cam 1558 cc engine soon followed. By 1966 the Series 3 Elan had 115 bhp and could accelerate from 0–60 mph/96 kph in under nine seconds, for it also had a glass fibre body though this was mounted on a backbone chassis. Lotus were now much better known, particularly as a result of their co-operation with Ford in building the Lotus-Cortina from 1963 onwards, and because they were producing more cars so, in 1966, the company moved to bigger premises at Hethel near Norwich. Colin Chapman was a keen flyer and so bought an old airfield site which gave Lotus the advantages of their own airstrip and test track for the first time as well as a modern purpose-built factory. In 1967 the new mid-engined Europa model was introduced for export. It was a 2-seater coupé using the 1470 cc Renault 16 engine and transmission turned round to drive the rear wheels. The 1967 Elan + 2 was the first Lotus to offer 2 + 2 seating, made possible by a 12 in/304 mm increase of wheelbase, to 96 in/2438 mm, on the fixed head coupé body. Lotus Cars became a public company in 1968, at which time production was at the rate of 65 cars a week. In 1970 there was an Elan Sprint model with big valve 126 bhp engine, which was also used in the + 2S 130. The Lotus 907 4-cylinder alloy engine with 16-valve head, developed by Tony Rudd who had joined Lotus from BRM, was first seen in the Jensen-Healey in 1972 and did not appear in a Lotus until 1974. In 1971 Lotus had fitted their own 1558 cc twin cam engine in the Europa and in 1972 produced their own 5-speed gearbox for the 'big valve' Europa Special and + 2S 130/5. Elan and + 2 production at Hethel ended in 1973, after 12,224 and 5200 respectively had been made. Europa production finished the following year after a production run of 9230. The reason was the announcement of the first 4-seater Lotus, available only in fully-built form (no kits). It had a Lotus-designed wedge-shaped body with a rear hatch, interior styled by Giugiaro (q.v.) and was called the Elite. Its debut in May 1974 was a major milestone for Lotus and was a move up market into a totally new sector. Whereas the most expensive model had previously been the + 2S 130/5 at £3486, Elite prices started at £5445. The backbone chassis and GRP moulded body construction continued to be used, but under the bonnet was the Lotus 907 light-alloy 1973 cc 4-cylinder engine producing 160 bhp. In 1975 the Eclat fastback 2 + 2 coupé version with a boot and the Esprit models were added. The very striking 2-seater Esprit was styled by Giugiaro and differed considerably from the Elite/Eclat. The 907 engine was positioned behind the seats to give a mid-engined configuration and drove the rear wheels through a Citroën SM gearbox. To cope with 130 mph/209 kph performance and 0–60 mph/96 kph acceleration in under seven seconds there were disc brakes all round. At the Earls Court Motor Show an automatic transmission version of the Elite, designated 504, was announced demonstrating that Lotus were indeed supplying a wider range of customers than sports car enthusiasts. An Esprit provided James Bond's transport in the 1977 film *The Spy Who Loved Me* and 1978 saw

Lotus Elan SE.

links with the De Lorean Motor Company, to whom Lotus supplied much engineering expertise for the 1981 De Lorean car, and Chrysler UK with whom Lotus co-operated on the Sunbeam-Lotus. A long stroke 2172 cc version of the Lotus engine was first seen as part of the new Turbo Esprit in February 1980 where it gave 210 bhp and 150 mph/241 kph performance. The first 100 cars with the redesigned body were in the colours of Essex Petroleum, sponsors of the Lotus Grand Prix racing team. Later in the year the 2.2 engine in unsupercharged form became standard on all models, which also benefited from a galvanized backbone chassis. In October Lotus Engineering and Technology was formed to offer the company's engineering expertise to other manufacturers and in 1981 Toyota benefited from this in developing their MR-2 model. In 1982 the Elite was dropped and the Eclat replaced by the Excel 2 + 2 with new body and chassis. Colin Chapman died in December 1982 and in 1983 Lotus was restructured with British Car Auctions as the main backers with Toyota, JCB and Schroeder Wagg also holding a sizeable share. The 30,000th Lotus built at Hethel was completed in 1984 and the new V8 engine and Etna concept vehicle were shown publicly. In January 1986 General Motors took control of Group Lotus; a purchase made because of the company's engineering expertise, which continued to be offered to other companies and is demonstrated in developments like the active ride suspension of 1983.

Maserati (Italy)

The first car to bear the Maserati name was the Tipo 26 built for Grand Prix racing in 1926, but the origins of the marque are even earlier. In 1912 Officine Alfieri Maserati was founded by the Maserati brothers – Alfieri, Bindo, Ernesto and Ettore. During World War I they produced Maserati sparking plugs and later built racing cars for Isotta-Fraschini and then Diatto in Bologna. Their own cars followed and earned a good reputation on the world's motor racing circuits. The concern remained under family control until 1937 when they sold out to the Orsi family. Bindo, Ernesto and Ettore continued to work for Maserati in Orsi's Modena factory producing competition cars until 1947, when they left to form Osca (Officine Specializzati Construzione Automobili) in Bologna. The first Maserati road car, the A6, appeared at the Geneva Show the same year and was built in small numbers. It had a 1488 cc 6-cylinder ohc engine producing 65 bhp which with a coachbuilt Pininfarina body meant that about 95 mph/145 kph was possible. It was followed in 1951 by the A6G/2000 which was really just the A6 chassis with a larger 1954 cc engine which gave 100 bhp. From 1954 until 1957 there was a more powerful version with 150 bhp from a twin cam 1985 cc engine produced as well. Unlike the single cam version the rear suspension was by cantilever leaf springs instead of coil. It was not until Maserati abandoned Grand Prix racing in 1957 that the first proper road car to be production-built emerged as the 3500GT. The 3485 cc 6-cylinder 2 ohc engine produced 220 bhp and was fitted in a tubular chassis with 4-wheel disc brakes. Coachbuilt bodies were supplied by Touring of Milan for the closed GT versions and Vignale for the open Spiders. In 1959 there was the 5000GT, which was really the 3500GT re-engineered to accept the ex-racing Maserati 4953 cc V8 engine. Only 32 of these supercars were built and most had bodies by Allemano. The first customer for this 330 bhp car, said to be capable of 170 mph/274 kph, was the Shah of Iran. In 1962 the 3500GT became the first production car to use Lucas fuel injection, and power increased to 235 bhp. The 3500GT coupé developed into the Sebring in 1964 and there was a 4-door saloon called the Quattroporte the same year. This was on a longer wheelbase and had a 4136 cc V8 engine under the bonnet. Final versions of the Sebring had a 3692 cc engine, also used for the Frua-bodied 2-seater Mistrale, and were sometimes called the 3700. In 1966 the Mexico replaced the 5000GT, whose V8 engine it used in a shortened version of the Quattroporte chassis. This produced a 4-seater coupé. A derivative was the 2-seater Ghibli, also new that year and named after a desert wind. It used an enlarged 4719 cc version of the Quattroporte's V8 engine giving 333 bhp. In 1968 co-operation with Citroën resulted in a new Maserati V6 engine being built for Citroën's SM in 1970. The Indy which appeared as a production model in 1969 was offered with either 4.2- or 4.7-litre V8 engines producing 260 or 290 bhp respectively. The 4-seater coupé body was by Vignale and featured paired pop-up headlamps and a typical Italian leather-trimmed interior. Luggage was accommodated in the tail and reached by a rear hatch. Despite its 3638 lb/1650 kg weight it was capable of 160 mph/257 kph. Giving warning of approach in such a fast car was aided by air horns, which were made by Maserati and marketed as accessories for other cars. The 1971 Bora might have looked like a 4-seater but the sloping rear

window and side windows in fact enclosed the 4419 cc V8 engine mounted amidships behind the front seats. A glass partition separated it from the driver and there was a trimmed cover which left space for some luggage on top and the spare wheel behind the engine. The main luggage space though was in the nose. It too was capable of 160 mph/257 kph with superb handling but cost £9970 in Britain in 1972. Less powerful and cheaper was the 1972 Merak derivative which used the same body but with a normal lid over the engine and 'flying buttresses' where the side windows would have been. Under the lid was an enlarged 2965 cc version of the SM V6 producing 190 bhp. This unit was appreciably shorter than the Bora's V8 and allowed room for 2 + 2 seating despite the mid-engined configuration. Giorgio Giugiaro (q.v.) of Ital Design had styled both Bora and Merak but the new front-engined V8 Khamsin (named after an Egyptian wind) was by Bertone and offered 2 + 2 accommodation. It was the first Maserati to feature independent rear suspension, and was added to the range for 1973. Financial troubles followed after Citroën had joined forces with Peugeot and in December 1975 Alessandro de Tomaso took over control of Maserati, though 70 per cent of the company was held by the Italian Government agency GEPI. De Tomaso's 30 per cent share cost him just 210,000 Lire (then about £65), which was accounted for by Citroën taking care of Maserati's 5 billion Lire (about £3.5 million) debts. Indy production ended but a new Kyalami 2 + 2 model based on the de Tomaso Longchamp was added. At the end of 1976 there was a new Quattroporte 4-door saloon with Ital-styled body, standard automatic transmission and a 270 bhp V8 engine. Also new was a 1999 cc V6-engined version of the Merak. The 1982 Biturbo as the name implied had twin turbochargers allied to a different 1996 cc V6 with 3 valves per cylinder installed in what was really a 2-door saloon. Open Spider and 4-door models followed along with 2.5- and 2.8-litre V6 engines. In 1986 Chrysler took a 15.6 per cent share in Maserati and commissioned

1980 Maserati Merak SS.

the new 2.2-litre turbocharged Chrysler-Maserati 2-seater which went on sale in the USA in 1987. That was the first Maserati road car not to carry the Neptune's trident badge that was a symbol of Bologna and had been adopted by the Maserati brothers for their cars.

Mazda (Japan)

The first Mazda vehicle was a motor-cycle-based 3-wheeled truck built in 1931 by the Toyo Kogyo Co. Ltd. which had itself been renamed in 1927 from an earlier company involved with cork making. Although a prototype car followed in 1940, the first production model was not seen until 1960. This was the 2-seater R360 micro-car powered by a 356 cc air-cooled 2-cylinder engine at the rear. The following year Toyo Kogyo, then very small manufacturers, concluded a licence agreement with NSU for the new Wankel engine. This was a move prompted by the need to prove they were different to avoid forced Government amalgamation with another manufacturer. The Carol 360 4-cylinder 358 cc saloon followed in 1962. The first proper car was the Mazda 800/1000 of 1964. This was the first of the Familia models and had a conventional 4-cylinder engine at the front driving the rear wheels. The integral-construction body had a wheelbase of 84.3 in/2140 mm and a length of 143.1 in/3635 mm. The car that really put Mazda on the map was the 1500 Luce that came two years later. Styled by Bertone it was the first European-looking Japanese car and had a 1490 cc ohc engine, optional Borg-Warner automatic transmission and was sold with a warranty for 12,400 miles or a year. Mazda had already shown various prototype Wankel engines at the 1965 Tokyo Motor Show, where they also revealed the Cosmo sports coupé with Wankel engine. This went into production in 1967 as the Cosmo 110S, the number denoting the power output from the twin-rotor (2 × 491 cc) Wankel rotary engine. It had no pistons and a displacement equivalent to a 1964 cc piston engine. Mazda's was the first twin-rotor Wankel engine to reach production, and entailed much original work in Japan to eliminate scuffing of the rotor housing by the apex seals and the development of special materials for the seals. In 1970 the first rotary-engined Mazda saloon was marketed as the RX-2. The same car with 1586 cc 4-cylinder engine was sold as the 616. This pattern was followed with the RX-3/818 in 1971 and the RX-4/929 in 1972. All had twin-rotor versions of the Wankel engine as it had been found that these were smoother running. Mazda had continued to

1987 Mazda RX7 2+2.

make conventional cars as well and there had been a new 1200 4-door Familia saloon with 1169 cc 4-cylinder engine and MacPherson strut front suspension. Biggest model was the 1800 Luce, a conventional 4-door saloon with Bertone styling and 1796 cc 4-cylinder engine producing 104 bhp. The wheelbase was 98.4 in/2500 mm and the length 172 in/4370 mm. In 1972 Mazda produced 379,703 cars and in 1973 the 500,000th rotary-engined car was built in the Hiroshima factory. From 1973 all export cars were fitted with bonded-in windscreens, a move later followed by other Japanese manufacturers. In the USA Mazda proved in 1973 that their version of the Wankel engine could meet the tough emissions standards for 1975, but doing this sacrificed fuel economy – never a Wankel strong point – and the 1973 fuel crisis led to Mazda phasing out their rotary-engined saloons on which most of their production was concentrated. The result was near bankruptcy in 1975. Salvation came in the form of a new conventional small saloon called the 323 in 1977. In America it was known as the GLC – Great Little Car, and in Japan as the Familia. It was a European-loking 3- or 5-door hatchback on a 90.9 in/2310 mm wheelbase powered by a 985 or 1272 cc ohc 4-cylinder engine driving the rear wheels. Also new in 1977 was the larger family-sized 626 Capella, which later sold in Britain as the Mazda Montrose, offered with 1.6- or 2-litre engines. Next up in size was the new Luce saloon with paired vertical headlamps with 1769 or 1970 cc engines. Biggest model in the 1977 range was the Wankel-engined (2 × 654 cc) Roadpacer 4-door saloon which had a 111.4 in/2830 mm wheelbase and sold for 3,780,000 Yen in Tokyo. In 1978 came the RX-7 sports coupé designed expressly for the Wankel engine and not offered with any other power unit. Indeed the compact Wankel made possible a very low bonnet and there was also a lift-up glass hatch for access to luggage behind the 2 + 2 seats. It produced 130 bhp at 7,000 rpm from two 573 cc chambers. Its main market was the USA where it cost $6995 in 1979, the year that Ford increased their stake in Mazda to 25 per cent and an annual production of a million units and a cumulative total of 10 million were reached. The millionth Mazda Wankel engine had been built just a little earlier, on 10 November 1978. In 1980 there was a new front-wheel-drive 323 powered by a range of transversely-mounted ohc engines of 1071, 1296 or 1490 cc. The European-styling of the 323 hatchback was very similar to the European Ford Escort (Mazda had had access to the Ford designs at an early stage) and just to confuse things even further the 323 was sold as the Ford Laser in Australasia and the Far East. The cars had few parts in common and even the body dimensions were different. In 1982 production of a new front-wheel-drive 626 Capella began in Mazda's new robotized Hofu factory and this model was also sold in some markets as the Ford Telstar. The 626 was the first car in the world with electronically variable dampers (shock absorbers), with Normal, Automatic and Sport ride settings. Biggest model was now the 929 Cosmo/Luce range, new for 1982, with Wankel, petrol or diesel engines. The Wankel-engined RX-7 had more power, 4-wheel disc brakes and a rear spoiler. In 1983 the 929 was offered with Mazda's first fuel-injected turbocharged engine, and the first time it had been applied to the Wankel engine. Power went up to 160 bhp, and later the same year the RX-7 was turbocharged. On 1 May 1984 Toyo Kogyo changed their name to the Mazda Motor Corporation. There was a new 323 model in 1985 with 1300, 1500, and 1600 versions. The 1600 turbo version featured fuel injection and a different engine from the ordinary 1600 injection with 4 valves per cylinder and twin overhead camshafts to give 148 bhp. There was also a 4-wheel-drive version of the turbo model. Major changes were made to the RX-7 in 1985 with a new Porsche-like body and unique Dynamic Tracking Suspension System at the rear which could alter the rear wheel alignment for improved stability in cornering. It resulted from Mazda's experiments with 4-wheel steering. Newest model is the 121 3-door small hatchback with 1138 or 1323 cc engine sold in Japan through Ford dealers as the Festiva and made by Kia in Korea for sale in the USA, where Mazda's own new factory at Flat Rock, Michigan, began production in 1987.

Mercedes-Benz (W. Germany)

There have only been Mercedes-Benz cars since 1926, following the merging of the separate Daimler (Mercedes) and Benz companies to form Daimler-Benz AG, though both can claim to have 'fathered' the modern car. The first motor-propelled vehicle was Karl Benz's 3-wheeler for which he was granted a patent on 29 January 1886. It had a 984 cc single-cylinder engine with horizontal flywheel, a mechanically-operated inlet valve and water cooling and was built at Mannheim, where Benz invented the sparking plug the same year. Working quite independently at Bad Cannstatt, Gottlieb Daimler produced a four-wheeled carriage powered by one of his petrol engines (patented in 1883) in August 1886. The vertical single-cylinder 469 cc engine was also water cooled and was positioned in the middle of the carriage with gear drive to the rear wheels. In 1894 Benz's new Velo became the world's first production car and 603 were made in 1903, the year that Benz produced his first 4-cylinder engine which was used in a wide range of Benz cars up to 1914. The first 6-cylinder 25/65 hp model with 6.5-litre engine appeared that year. Mercedes was first used as a car name by Emil Jellinek, the Austro-Hungarian Consul in Nice, to disguise the new 4-cylinder Phoenix Daimler he had entered in the 1899 Nice Speed Week. Mercedes was the name of Jellinek's daughter. In 1900 Jellinek persuaded Gottlieb Daimler to sell him 36 cars with special features along with the sales rights for Austria, Hungary, France and the USA. The resulting 1901 Mercedes 35 hp model was designed by Wilhelm Maybach and also incorporated some ideas from Daimler's son Paul. Behind the new honeycomb radiator was a 5913 cc 4-cylinder engine driving the rear wheels through a 4-speed gate-change gearbox, and there were steel wheels and an angled steering column. It was to be the model for others to copy for decades, and was so successful that in 1902 Daimler registered the name Mercedes as their car trade mark. The famous 3-pointed star had been devised by Gottlieb Daimler to represent the versatility of his engines – on land, in the water and in the air – but was not registered until 1909 and first appeared on Mercedes cars from about 1911. That year there was an important new model, the 37/90 hp for which Paul Daimler had designed a new 4-cylinder engine with overhead valves (3 per cylinder). It was distinguished by the first Mercedes vee radiator bearing the pointed star emblem. Mercedes were also the first make to fit a supercharger to a production car, on the 6/25/40 hp 1½-litre 4-cylinder and 10/40/65 hp 2614 cc models. The first supercharged Mercedes-Benz model after the

Daimler and Benz merger was the 24/100/Type K with 140 bhp from 6246 cc and a top speed of about 90 mph/145 kph. It was the continuation of a former Mercedes model under the new name, but completely new were the 1926 2-litre 38 hp Stuttgart and 3-litre 55 hp Mannheim. The 1928 Nurburg with 4.6-litre engine was the first straight-8 model. The same year's Type S (designated 26 120/180 to denote its German fiscal horsepower, bhp without the blower and bhp with respectively) was a development of the Type K but with a larger 6789 cc 6-cylinder engine and lowered chassis. The performance impression was aided by the long bonnet with triple exhaust pipes coming out of the side on the even more powerful 7-litre SS and SSK versions. More luxurious was the 7.7-litre Grosse model introduced at the 1930 Paris Motor Show, while the 1931 1692 cc 170 model was the first with independent suspension and was followed by rear-engined 130H and 170H backbone chassis versions before being replaced by the more successful 38 bhp 170V in 1936. In 1935 the 260D with 2545 cc 4-cylinder engine was the world's first diesel-engined production car and offered a fuel consumption of about 30 mpg/9.5 litres/100 km. The big and powerful supercharged 540K by comparison returned about 12 mpg/23.5 litres/100 km but was capable of over 100 mph/161 kph. Its 8-cylinder 5401 cc ohv engine produced 115 bhp without the supercharger, which was brought into operation by the driver pressing the accelerator pedal right to the floor. It cost £1890 with cabriolet body in Britain in 1939. Post-war car production started in 1947 with the 170S from the Stuttgart factory and the 6-cylinder 220 and 300 models followed in 1951, the year that Daimler-Benz patented the rigid passenger compartment with front and rear crush zones. The 300 was the first big post-war model with 2996 cc 6-cylinder engine in a 120 in/3050 mm wheelbase body. In 1953 the monocoque 180 model replaced the 170 and like that model was also available as a diesel. The 1952 300SL with multi-tubular spaceframe construction and alloy bodywork with lift-up gullwing doors looked like the sports racing machine it was intended to be and proved it with first and second places in the Le Mans 24-hour race that year. It was powered by a 171 bhp derivative of the 300 saloon's engine and created such a sensation that the factory were forced to put it into production after an order for 1000 cars from the USA. The result was the gullwing steel-bodied 300SL coupé of 1954 which became the first production car in the world to use fuel injection (by Bosch). In this

form the 2996 cc engine produced 240 bhp and gave 130 mph/210 kph performance making it the fastest car in the world at the time. The 300SLR racing car derived from it in 1955 differed a good deal, not least in having a straight-8 engine and inboard drum brakes. Production of the gullwing ceased in 1957 when it was replaced by a roadster version with conventional doors. The smaller 190SL sports model was a normal production car based on the 180/220 engineering with an 1897 cc 4-cylinder engine giving this 2-seater a top speed of just over 100 mph/161 kph. Fuel injection was offered on the 220SE (the E signifying injection) in 1959 boosting the 2195 cc engine's power to 134 bhp and in 1960 there was a new body for the 220 range. In 1963 the 190SL and 300SL were replaced by the much more modern 2-seater 230SL which was offered with optional automatic transmission and a distinctive hardtop. The major talking point of 1963 however was the new luxury 600 model powered by a new 6329 cc V8 engine producing 250 bhp and giving the 126 in/3200 mm wheelbase saloon a top speed of over 125 mph/201 kph. The Pullman limousine version (later offered with six doors) was even larger with a 153.5 in/3900 mm wheelbase and 246 in/6250 mm overall length, making it the world's longest car. The 220 models were replaced by the more modern 230 and 250, the latter with 2496 cc ohc engine, in 1965 and the smaller cars were rebodied in 1968 and the 250SE and 300SE replaced by the new 280 models with 2778 cc engine. In 1969 there was a completely new 3499 cc V8 engine for the new 300SE, identified by paired vertical headlamps, and this engine was also offered in the 280 coupé and convertible. In August 1970 Mercedes built their 3 millionth post-war passenger car engine, a 2778 cc unit with fuel injection for the USA. The SL sports car had become a 250 in 1967 and a 280 in 1968. In 1971 the 350SL replaced the 280SL and used the new 3499 cc V8 engine giving 200 bhp. It was offered as a coupé or roadster with 2 + 2 seating or as the 4-seater SLC coupé with 14.2 in/360 mm longer wheelbase. It was altogether bigger and

1987 Mercedes-Benz 300CE coupé.

more modern and used the engineering of the new S-class saloons which appeared in 280 and 350 guise in 1972. They were joined by 450 models using a long stroke variant of the V8 engine with 4520 cc and 225 bhp in the same 112.8 in/2865 mm wheelbase as the 350, though there was an additional, longer 450SEL. There were 450SL and SLC models too. The 280 models received a new and more powerful 160/185 bhp 2746 cc twin cam engine and the 2778 cc single ohc unit went into the 250. In 1974 the world's first 5-cylinder diesel model appeared as the 240D 3.0/300D with 80 bhp 3005 cc engine. In 1977 it was turbocharged and became the world's first turbo diesel production car. The diesels, of course, were very important in countries like Germany where Mercedes were used as taxis, something the successful marque image in the UK and USA tends to disguise. The smaller models became the W123 series in 1976 with 110 in/2795 mm wheelbase lower and wider bodies and in 1977 were joined by 230T/250T/240TD/300TD estate car derivatives, the T standing for tourism and transport. The biggest engine was then to be found not in the 600, still in production, but in the top S-class model the 450SEL 6.9 introduced in 1975 with a 281 bhp 6834 cc engine, whose dry sump lubrication allowed a 10,000-mile/16,000 km service interval. In 1978 a completely new alloy 4973 cc V8 engine producing 240 bhp was fitted to the 450SL and the following year used in the completely new S-class models along with a 3818 cc derivative. The new lighter bodies were also more aerodynamic and had a 115.6 in/2935 mm wheelbase and long wheelbase versions were offered. The 500SE was capable of 140 mph/225 kph and the 280SE/380SE models could exceed 130 mph/209 kph. They were joined by 380/500SEC coupé versions in 1981, while in 1980 the S-class body was used for the American market 300SD Turbo diesel. A new and smaller 190 series was added in 1982 powered by a 4-cylinder 1997 cc engine producing 90 or 122 bhp. A diesel version with the world's first encapsulated engine compartment to reduce noise was added in 1983 along with a Cosworth-developed 2.3-litre 16-valve version with 185 bhp. The 123 series mid-range models were replaced in 1985 by the new current 124 series with the 190 rear suspension and 110.2 in/2800 mm wheelbase body with the very low drag co-efficient of 0.29. Smallest engine was the 200's 1997 cc 4-cylinder and the largest the 300E's 2962 cc 6-cylinder. The new 260E's 2599 cc 6-cylinder engine was also available in the 190, and there were updated T-range estate cars.

Later in 1985 there were revised engines for the S-class with more power and new 260SE, 420SE and 560SE models. The latter was the Mercedes flagship with 5547 cc 300 bhp V8 and was also available as a coupé. SL models were revised too with a new 6-cylinder 300SL bringing the return of a famous model name and bigger 420/500SL versions. 1985 annual production reached 540,000 cars and Daimler-Benz took a 65.5 per cent share in Dornier. Technological advances were revealed in the 4-Matic 'thinking' 4-wheel-drive system, which was engaged automatically when wheel slip was detected, for the 300E/TE and further risk of skidding under heavy acceleration on the big V8 models was reduced by ASR (acceleration skid control). For the smaller models there was ASD which provided automatic differential locking when one driving wheel started to slip. The 300E was not the first model to have 4-wheel drive as the cross-country Gelandewagen introduced in 1979 had that distinction. 1987 brought new bodies for the 230/300CE coupé models, followed later in the year by a completely new SL range to replace the models that dated back to 1971.

Mercury (USA)

Ford created Mercury as a marque in 1938 with the intention of providing a more up-market Ford to bridge the gap between Lincoln and Ford models. The first Mercury was an enlarged Ford with 3917 cc (239 cu. in) side-valve V8, a 116 in/2946 mm wheelbase and hydraulic brakes. The first really different Mercury came in 1949 with a new semi-fastback curved body style, coil spring independent front suspension and a 118 in/2997 mm wheelbase. The engine remained the V8 but with 4185 cc (255 cu. in) and 110 bhp. In 1951 a 3-speed automatic was offered in place of the manual gearbox with column change, and the following year there was a new chassis and a body with fake air scoop on the bonnet. In 1954 Mercury received Ford's new ohv V8. In 1957 Montclair and Monterey models had a 122 in/3099 mm wheelbase and a 5.1-litre (312 cu. in) engine, with the option of a 6030 cc (368 cu. in) V8 from the Lincoln Premiere. 1958 saw the introduction of the division's Edsel marque intended to slot between Ford and Mercury. The Edsel had a distinctive horse-collar-shaped radiator, no parts in common with anything else, and was the biggest sales flop in Ford's history, losing the Lincoln-Mercury Division a reputed $150 million. Just 110,000 were made in three years of production. To make way for the Edsel, Mercury models went up in size to a

126 in/3200 mm wheelbase and 218 in/5537 mm length. The bigger body was powered by a 6281 cc (383 cu. in) V8 developing 330 bhp. With the demise of the Edsel the Mercury Monterey for 1961 was down to a 120 in/3048 mm wheelbase with 4.8- or 5.8-litre (292 or 352 cu. in) V8 power and there was even an optional 6-cylinder for the first time. The smaller Comet model of 1961 was offered only with 2364 or 2785 cc (144 or 170 cu. in) 6-cylinder engines and had a 114 in/2896 mm wheelbase. For 1963 the line-up started with the Comet, moved up through the larger 116.5 in/2959 mm wheelbase Meteor models, whose cheapest saloon was $2218 and had a 2280 cc (170 cu. in) 6-cylinder engine, to the Monterey. The latter now had a 6384 cc (390 cu. in) V8 and was priced from $2674 for the 2-door saloon to $3343 for the S55 convertible. For 1965 the big Mercurys were even larger with a 123 in/3124 mm wheelbase and engine options included 330 bhp from the 6.4-litre (390 cu. in) V8, while for the top Parklane 4-door hardtop there was even a 7-litre (427 cu. in) performance engine giving 425 bhp. Following on from Ford's success with the Mustang, Mercury had their own similar sporting model, the Cougar, costing $2851 in 1976. Like the Mustang, on which it was based, it had a 4727 cc (289 cu. in) V8 with 200 bhp in basic form but the big Mercury 6.4-litre giving 320 bhp was optional. The following year there was a new Comet Cyclone fastback and for 1971 there was a new Cougar with shallow sloping fastback and Kamm tail fitted with the new 7-litre (429 cu. in) V8. There was also the marque's first compact, the 103 in/2616 mm wheelbase Comet version of Ford's Maverick costing $2193 and powered by a 2786 cc (170 cu. in) 6-cylinder engine. Top model was the 124 in/3150 mm Marquis Brougham costing $4992 with the standard 7030 cc (429) V8 giving 208 bhp in 1972, and sharing the cheaper Monterey's new perimeter-frame chassis and 4-link coil spring rear suspension. In 1973 the Cougar was Ford's last convertible before giving way in 1974 to a bigger version with 114 in/2896 mm

Mercury's semi-fastback saloon of the early 1950s.

wheelbase and 215.5 in/5474 mm length – some 18 in/457 mm longer than before. It also had a perimeter frame chassis and front disc brakes, while engines were 5.7-, 6.6- or 7.5-litre (351, 400 or 460 cu. in) V8s. An addition to the range was the intermediate-sized 109.9 in/2791 mm wheelbase Monarch which like the Cougar featured a distinctive radiator treatment. In January 1975 came the Bobcat, Mercury's first sub-compact small car powered by a 2.3-litre (140 cu. in) ohc 4-cylinder engine. For 1978 the new Zephyr replaced the Comet and for 1979 there was a new downsized Marquis that was 15 in/381 mm shorter and 800 lb/363 kg lighter than the 1978 model. Standard engine was a 4942 cc (302) V8 with the option of the bigger 5766 cc (351) engine that was standard in 1978. Completely new, too, was the sporting Capri hatchback coupé with 100.4 in/2550 mm wheelbase and 179.1 in/4549 mm length. This should not be confused with the German V6 Capri that had been sold by Mercury dealers for several years and was replaced by this new Mustang-based Capri. Standard engines were 2301 cc (140.4) 4 cylinder or 2786 cc (170) V6, though a turbocharged version of the 2.3 with 150 bhp and a turbocharged 4.9 (302) V8 were options. Ford's Escort appeared in Mercury guise as the Lynx to replace the Bobcat in 1980 complete with front-wheel drive and a 1599 cc (87.6) 4-cylinder engine. Like its European namesake whose hatchback body style it shared it had a 94.3 in/2395 mm wheelbase but overall length was greater at 163.8 in/4161 mm. Even longer was the LN7 coupé version at 170.3 in/4326 mm and both versions were hatchbacks. For 1983 there was a new luxury compact Marquis with engines ranging from the 2.3 (140) 4-cylinder to a 3791 cc (231) V6 in a 105.5 in/2680 mm wheelbase body that was 186.5 in/4737 mm long. There was still a big car, the former Marquis renamed as the Grand Marquis with 114.3 in/2903 mm wheelbase and 4.9- or 5.8-litre (301 or 351) V8. The new Cougar coupé was based on Ford's 103.9 in/2639 mm wheelbase Thunderbird with a 3791 cc (231) V6. Completely new was the Topaz which looked like the European Sierra but was not the same car at all with a shorter 99.8 in/2535 mm wheelbase, all-independent suspension and front-wheel drive. Under the bonnet was the 2301 cc (140) 4-cylinder engine that had first appeared in the Capri in 1979. In 1984 the Topaz was offered with an optional 1998 cc (122) 4-cylinder diesel engine and the Merkur XR4Ti was added. The Merkur was in fact a German-built Sierra XR4i fitted with the

2.3-litre (140) turbocharged American engine. For 1986 the Marquis compact was replaced by the completely new aerodynamic Sable with flush window glass and headlamps and an integrated polycarbonate front bumper with air dam. The swept-up tail for this 4-door saloon contributed to a drag coefficient of 0.32. Not only did it have Mac-Pherson strut all-independent suspension and rack and pinion steering but also front-wheel drive. The transversely-mounted engines were either a 2498 cc (152) 4-cylinder or, for most models, a 2980 cc (182) V6 both of which were available with electronic fuel injection, now offered on most Mercury models. Biggest engine available was now the 4942 cc (302) V8 with sequential multi-port fuel injection for Cougar, Capri and Grand Marquis models. For 1987 there was an additional Merkur model, the Scorpio, which was none other than the rear-wheel-drive European model with anti-lock brakes imported from Germany and sold by Mercury dealers. A four-wheel-drive option was offered on the Topaz, and the revised Cougar had flush glass and lamps while the XR7 version had the 4942 cc (302) V8 with electronic fuel injection.

MG (UK)

These famous initials that over the years have become synonymous with sports cars stand for Morris Garages. It was Cecil Kimber, manager of Morris Garages in Oxford, who took a Morris Cowley 4-cylinder model and fitted it with a special body and did other work prior to entering the car in the 1923 Land's End Trial, where he won a gold medal. A 6-cylinder Morris Oxford became an experimental MG in 1924 and in 1925 there was the famous pointed-tail 4-cylinder 2-seater model that is now (incorrectly) known as Old Number One. All these were one-off cars built with the approval of William Morris who owned Morris Garages but led to sales of similar cars to customers, with the 4-cylinder 14/28 as the first MG model. The rounded Morris bullnose radiator was replaced by a flat one in 1927 and MGs followed suit. In 1928 came the first production MG with 2468 cc ohc Morris engine in a new chassis designed by the MG Car Co., personally owned until 1935 by William Morris, and bearing the famous Octagon badge. It cost £485 as a tourer or £555 as a saloon in 1929, compared with £340 and £445 respectively for the 4-cylinder 14/40 which continued to be marketed. Right from the start MG sold open sporting models *and* sports saloons. At the 1928 Motor Show there was a new and very significant MG addition in the form of the first Midget. With a tiny pointed-tail

2-seater body on a 78 in/1981 mm wheelbase it had an overall length of just 123 in/3124 mm and was powered by an 847 cc engine. It was capable of 60–65 mph/97–105 kph, cost £175, and can claim to be the first cheap sports car. The companion Six became the 18/80 in 1929 and such was MG's success that the various assembly buildings in Oxford were bursting at the seams. Sir William Morris (later Lord Nuffield) responded by purchasing some surplus factory buildings from the Pavlova Leather Co. Ltd and creating MG's first proper factory at Abingdon. It was to be the home of the MG car from 1929 until 1980, a facility shared by Riley from 1948 to 1958 and by Austin-Healey from 1958 to 1971. Just 819 MGs were built in Oxford from 1924–9, whereas 12,876 were to be built at Abingdon by 1935. The move to Abingdon brought MG their own chief engineer, H. N. Charles, for the first time and the new Monthlery supercharged model for racing was added in 1931 and led directly to the successful J2 Midget of 1932. It cost £199 10s (£199.50) and was capable of 70 mph/113 kph while the 12 gallon/54.6 litre slab petrol tank gave a range of about 400 miles/644 km. The same year's Magna had a 1271 cc 6-cylinder ohc engine and cost £250, or £289 with a closed coupé body. The bigger Six Mark II version of the 18/80 was also available but was soon to be replaced by the 1086 cc K-type 6-cylinder Magnette for 1933 which led to the 1287 cc 80 mph/128 kph KN Magnette for 1935. The P-type Midget arrived early in 1934 with a new 3-bearing 847 cc engine, proper front wings and a running board all for £220. In July 1935 Sir William Morris sold MG to Morris Motors whose managing director, Len Lord, was not interested in racing successes or costly engineering. The 1936 T-type Midget, though capable of 80 mph/128 kph was fitted with a 1292 cc ohv pushrod engine and simpler hydraulic drum brakes. It cost £222. For the family man there was a completely new and much bigger 2-litre SA saloon for 1936 with box-section chassis of 123 in/3124 mm wheelbase. It cost £375 with a 4-door saloon body. In between this and the Midget came the 1½-litre V-type saloon, introduced at the 1936 motor show, with the Magnette's 108 in/2743 mm wheelbase. With a 1548 cc 4-cylinder engine and 4-door saloon body it cost £325. A still more powerful saloon known as the 2.6-litre appeared in 1938 and cost £442, though an open 4-seater was available for £8 more. The 2561 cc 6-cylinder engine had full-flow oil filtration and an oil cooler while the specially strengthened chassis was in manganese steel and electrically welded. Only 379 customers had a chance to enjoy the TB Midget with its new 1250 cc engine, 2 SU carburettors and 4-speed synchromesh gearbox before the outbreak of war, but it formed the basis of the post-war TC announced in October 1945. That looked little different with the same 94 in/2388 mm wheelbase, knock-off wire wheels and centre-hinged bonnet, but whereas the TB had cost £225 the TC cost £527 in Britain in 1947 (including £115 Purchase Tax). The TC and the TD, with a wider body and independent front suspension that succeeded it in January 1950, were responsible for introducing the concept of the sports car to the USA which was the major market for MG for decades to come. There was only one other MG model offered with the Midget and that was the 1¼-litre YA saloon based on it but with a 5 in/127 mm longer 99 in/2515 mm wheelbase. The TF of 1953 was really a restyled TD with a sloping radiator, faired-in headlamps and steel wheels. The 1954/5 models had a bigger 1466 cc engine giving 63 bhp and raising the top speed to about 85 mph/137 kph. The merger of Austin and Morris in 1952 to form BMC resulted in a new Magnette saloon based on the Wolseley 4/44 but with more performance and stiffer suspension. When the Wolseley developed into the 15/50, the Magnette became the ZB with 68 bhp. The 1955 MGA, launched in September after works cars had run in the Le Mans race in June, featured a completely new and more streamlined Pressed Steel body on the TF chassis and used the 1489 cc 4-cylinder BMC B-series engine also used in the Magnette. It was capable of almost 100 mph/161 kph while the 1588 cc 1600 model introduced in 1959 could reach that magic figure. There was also a fixed-head coupé version from 1956. The first MG with disc brakes was the temperamental Twin Cam produced from 1958 to 1960 with no less than 108 bhp from the 1588 cc engine. With a maximum of over 110 mph/177 kph and disc brakes on all four

Classic MGs: 1977 MGB GT (foreground) and 1953 TF.

wheels it was very rapid indeed on cross country journeys. Final version of the MGA was the 1622 cc Mark II of 1961 and the same engine was used in the Farina-styled Magnette built at Cowley. The new Midget of 1961 was based on the Austin-Healey Sprite with monocoque body and 948 cc engine, though this became 1098 cc when disc brakes were added in 1962. That year saw the end of the MGA after setting a new sports car record with 100,081 built in seven years. The MGB which succeeded it was completely different with a monocoque body and 1798 cc 4-cylinder engine with 95 bhp. For the first time on an MG sports car there were winding windows, and there was a GT version in 1966. The 1967 MGC was the only post-war 6-cylinder model and used the new Austin 2912 cc 145 bhp engine in the MGB body with new wishbone and torsion bar suspension. It was some 350 lb/777 kg heavier than the MGB with all the extra weight at the front, so the handling was poor and only 8964 were built before production ended in 1969. The 1973 MGB GT V8 was prompted by conversions carried out by Ken Costello in 1971/2 when he transplanted a Rover 3.5-litre V8 engine into the GT body, giving 150 bhp for 130 mph/209 kph performance. The Abingdon production cars, with only 137 bhp, were not quite as fast and the model only lasted until 1976, by which time, along with the B itself, there were huge black rubber bumpers to meet American legislation. The Midget was similarly equipped in 1974, together with a 1493 cc Triumph Spitfire engine as a replacement for the 1275 cc unit dating from 1966. During that period of the 1960s the MG radiator was also to be found on the performance version of the BMC 1100/1300 front-wheel-drive models. Midget production ended in 1979 after 223,941 had been built, and with the demise of the MGB in October 1980 the Abingdon factory was closed. This situation had prompted a mass demonstration of MG owners in London when it became known in 1979, for the MGB was Britain's most successful sports car with a total of 511,746 built in a factory that had changed little since the 1930s. There have been no more MG sports cars since but the name was applied to a performance version of the Austin Metro, the first MG made at Longbridge, in 1982. Later that year there was an even quicker turbocharged MG Metro with the 1275 cc A-plus engine producing 93 bhp and giving a 110 mph/177 kph top speed. The 1983 MG Maestro with 1598 cc ohc engine driving the front wheels was a badge-engineered Austin made at Cowley. It had extra performance and was the first European car offered with solid state digital instruments, a trip computer and a voice synthesizer to give warning of faults. The booted Montego with 1994 cc fuel injected engine was added in 1984 and the Maestro was later uprated to this specification. Star of the 1987 range was the 126 mph/203 kph Montego Turbo with 150 bhp from the 2-litre 4-cylinder engine.

Mitsubishi (Japan)

The earliest Mitsubishi model dates not, as might be imagined, from the postwar period but from 1917 when a small number of Model A cars were built. However, car manufacture proper did not start until 1959 when the 500 was produced with a 2-cylinder air-cooled 594 cc engine giving 25 bhp. Even smaller was the 1964 Minica with 359 cc engine in a boxy body, while the 500 had been replaced by the Colt 600 and from then on Colt was to figure prominently and was the name under which Mitsubishis were marketed in some countries including Britain. The 1000 model of 1964 was much more of a real car with 88.6 in/2250 mm wheelbase and a 977 cc 4-cylinder front engine driving the rear wheels. The 1965 Debonair was altogether bigger and was powered by a 1991 cc 6-cylinder engine giving 105 bhp. With dual headlamps, air conditioning, a radio and extras like a door-open warning it was one of the first Japanese luxury cars and cost 1,250,000 Yen – twice the price of the 1000. The 1498 cc Colt 1500, with 70 bhp and similar styling to the 1000 but a longer wheelbase, bridged the gap in 1966. There was also a 3-cylinder 2-stroke Colt 800 fastback saloon. In 1969 Chrysler and Mitsubishi agreed to set up a joint venture company, which became Mitsubishi Motors Corporation in May 1971, with Chrysler holding a 35 per cent share in the new company. Up to that time Mitsubishi had been the car division of Mitsubishi Heavy Industries Ltd. The mainstay of the range was then the Colt Galant family-sized model with conventional engineering and 1.4- or 1.6-litre engines, including a 125 bhp twin cam version for the GTO model. New in 1973 was the 92.1 in/2340 mm wheelbase Lancer with 1187, 1439 or 1597 cc engines. It slotted in between the little Minica (now with more modern styling) and the 95.3/2420 mm wheelbase Galant, also new that year and available as a coupé. In 1976 the Celeste joined the range as a new model but was in fact a coupé version of the Lancer. The same year's Colt 80 2-litre 4-cylinder ohc engine was available in the Celeste, sold in the USA as the Plymouth Arrow, and was exceptionally smooth because of

the use of contra-rotating balancer shafts. It was also used in the bigger Galant. The bigger 99 in/2515 mm wheelbase Galant Sigma arrived in 1976 with a new body and coil spring rear suspension giving improved handling. It was sold in the USA as the Dodge Colt and had the 2-litre balancer engine and a new 1597 cc unit using the same principles. The coupé version was added at the end of the year and was called the Galant Lambda in Japan, the Sapporo in Europe and Dodge Challenger/Plymouth Sapporo in the USA. The first front-wheel-drive model was the 1978 Mirage (Dodge Colt/Plymouth Champ in the USA) with either 1244 or 1410 cc ohc engine mounted transversely and two gearlevers. The additional lever gave in effect an 8-speed gearbox and the stubby range selector was marked 'Power' and 'Economy' for the low and high ranges respectively. The aerodynamic hatchback body had a 90.5 in/2300 mm wheelbase. The Galant Sigma and its Sapporo coupé derivative became even bigger in 1980 with a 99.6 in/2530 mm wheelbase, strut-type independent rear suspension, sloping grilles and rectangular headlamps. Electronics provided a cruise control and various warning systems and engines ranged from 1.6 to 2.6 litres. There was a 2.3-litre diesel and even a turbocharged diesel using a turbocharger made by Mitsubishi Heavy Industries. The 2-litre engine was available with Mitsubishi's own electronic fuel injection. In 1981 the Lancer was available with a 1796 cc fuel injected engine or with 1.8- or 2-litre turbocharged ones. There was a new front-wheel-drive Lancer Fiore, based on the Mirage but with a longer wheelbase and a boot, in 1982 but the old Lancer continued. A new departure was the sporting Starion 2+2 coupé with 4-wheel disc brakes and a 170 bhp 2-litre turbo engine. The Mirage 8-gear concept was also used in the new front-wheel-drive Tredia saloon and Cordia coupé with 96.3 in/2445 mm wheelbases and a liquid crystal display for the instruments. Also new in 1982 was the Shogun/Pajero four-wheel-drive vehicle which replaced the Jeeps Mitsubishi had previously built and was sold in the USA as the Montero. Mitsubishi had taken over Chrysler's Australian operations including the engine factory at Lonsdale, in 1980 and in 1983 Australian-built Colt Sigmas were marketed as Lonsdales in Britain. The Galant went front-wheel drive in 1983 with a more spacious 102.4 in/2600 mm wheelbase body and 1.8- or 2-litre engines with or without turbocharger. The Sapporo coupé version followed in 1984. A new type of vehicle was the Space Wagon/Chariot

1987 Mitsubishi Starion 2000 turbo.

offering van-style passenger carrying with streamlined styling and car levels of comfort. In the USA it was known as the Colt Vista and was offered with the option of four-wheel drive in 1984, as were the Cordia and Tredia. A chic new Minica with 2-cylinder 546 cc engine replaced the old model and was even available in turbocharged form. The totally new 1984 Mirage range had both a 4-door saloon and 3- and 5-door hatchbacks with crisp new styling, and all versions now shared a 93.7 in/2380 mm wheelbase. The 8-speed transmission was replaced by a 5-speed gearbox and there were enlarged 1299 and 1468 cc engines. More powerful was the 1598 cc 120 bhp fuel-injected power unit and there was also a diesel option. In 1986 the old-fashioned Debonair was replaced by a brand new model powered by new ohc V6 engines. The 2-litre unit produced 99 bhp and the 2972 cc Cyclone engine 142 bhp and for the first time the big Mitsubishi had front-wheel drive. Disc brakes all round, electronic fuel injection plus electronic gadgetry were other features.

Nissan (Japan)

Until the 1980s the cars we know as Nissans were marketed in many countries including Britain under the Datsun name. The very first prototype of 1912 was made by Kwaishinsha Motor Works and the first model to be marketed in 1915 was the DAT 31. DAT came from the names of the men involved: K. Den, R. Aoyama and A. Takeuchi. The 2.3-litre Model 41 followed and in 1926 DAT merged with Jitsuyo Jidosha Seizo and a new company called DAT Automobile Manufacturing Co. was formed but concentrated on trucks until 1931. Then a new car was produced and was called Datson – literally son of DAT – but the name was changed to Datsun in 1932 as the sun is Japan's national emblem. The first car produced by the new company Jidosha Seizo in Yokohama in 1933 was based on the Austin 7 and the following year the company name was changed to the present Nissan Motor Co. Ltd. In 1937 there was also a

Nissan 70 model based on the American Graham-Paige, that company supplying help and some tooling. Postwar Nissan concluded an agreement to manufacture the Austin A40 Somerset with BMC in 1952 but a model change meant that the A50 Cambridge was in fact built instead. The first Datsun of any real significance was the 1959 310 Bluebird, though there had been smaller 860 cc 4-cylinder 110, 112 and 113 models with varying wheelbases before that. The Bluebird was offered with new 988 or 1189 cc overhead valve 4-cylinder engines giving 37 or 48 bhp respectively. The wheelbase was 89.8 in/2280 mm and there was independent suspension for the first time. It was joined in 1960 by the bigger Nissan Cedric, initially with 1488 cc but later with 1883 cc, and by the Fairlady 2-door sports car based on a shorter wheelbase version of the Bluebird's chassis. The new 1964 1500 Fairlady used the former Bluebird chassis and there was a new and larger integral construction Cedric 1900. In 1964 Bluebird production at Nissan's new Oppama factory exceeded 10,000 a month, a new record for a Japanese car, made possible by the new Bluebird's monocoque construction. The *Oppama Maru*, Nissan's first ship designed specifically to carry cars for export, was commissioned in 1965. The President luxury model with 2974 cc 6-cylinder engine or a 3988 cc V8 coupled to a Borg-Warner automatic gearbox was launched at the 1965 Tokyo Motor Show. In V8 form it was Japan's most expensive car, costing the equivalent of £3000. The 1966 Cedric had a monocoque body with galvanized steel floorpan. There were 1973 cc ohv Custom Six and 1998 cc ohc Special Six versions, the latter with front disc brakes. The Bluebird SSS had a 1595 cc 90 bhp engine. Prince Motors merged with Nissan in 1966 with the result that the Royal 8-seater limousine they had designed for the Emperor appeared as a Nissan. It was the first Japanese car for Imperial use and looked like a Mercedes-Benz 600. The wheelbase was a massive 153 in/3885 mm and a 6373 cc V8 engine was used. Only two cars were built, both for the Emperor. The 1967 Gloria was a former Prince model using Cedric body panels and engine, although the Gloria Super retained the Prince 2-litre ohc engine. The same engine was used in the new Silvia coupé, based on the Fairlady. The Skyline 1500 was another ex-Prince model, but the Cedric with 4- or 6-cylinder engines was pure Datsun. Most significant newcomer in 1967 was the conventional 988 cc 4-cylinder Sunny 1000 with 89.8 in/2280 mm wheelbase and transverse leaf spring front suspension. The new

1968 Bluebird was larger with a 95.3 in/2420 mm wheelbase and was powered by 1296 or 1595 cc ohc 4-cylinder engines. It was the first Datsun with all-round independent suspension. Nissan exported 132,000 cars to 100 countries, including Britain, in 1968. The 1969 Nissan Laurel was bigger than the Bluebird and had trailing arm independent rear suspension and an ohc 1815 cc engine. It was sold in Britain as the Datsun 1800. The Nissan Fairlady Z coupé replaced the previous model at the 1969 Tokyo Show and was offered with 130 bhp 2-litre ohc or 160 bhp twin cam engines. In 1970 this became the Datsun 240Z with 2393 cc 6-cylinder 150 bhp engine, a combination that was to sell over 700,000 in the next 10 years, particularly in the USA. The 1970 1200 Sunny moved up in size with an overall length of 151 in/3830 mm and a 1171 cc 69 bhp engine to make room for the new Cherry. This was the first front-wheel-drive Datsun and had a 988 cc transverse engine and all-independent suspension. In 1971 Datsun's annual car production exceeded a million for the first time and in 1972 there were new 160B/180B Bluebird models including a 180B SSS coupé with a twin carburettor 115 bhp version of the 1770 cc engine. There was also a 120A coupé version of the Cherry. The Cherry was actually made for Nissan by Subaru (q.v.) as the result of a business agreement in 1968 between Nissan and Subaru's parent company, Fuji Heavy Industries. The Gloria and Cedric were rationalized in 1971 and from then on shared the same body. The Cedric with 2565 cc 6-cylinder engine in the new 105.9 in/2690 mm wheelbase body was seen in Europe in 1972 as the Datsun 260C. The smaller Laurel range was revised with 14 models and 1.8- or 2-litre engines. Completely new was the 140J/160J Violet which was about 4 in/102 mm shorter than the Bluebird whose styling it shared. Engineering was conventional with ½-elliptic rear springs and 1428 or 1595 cc engines. The rebodied 120Y Sunny of 1973 was both wider and longer and there were saloon, coupé and estate car versions. The 2565 cc engine was available in the Laurel for 1974 and

1967 Nissan President Sovereign V8.

the 240Z similarly benefited, becoming the 260Z with 5-speed gearbox. An additional 2+2 version with longer wheelbase gave it more appeal and the 260Z grew into the fuel-injected 2754 cc 280Z in 1975. The 1974 Cherry F-II had a new body, rack and pinion steering, front disc brakes and 1171 or 1397 cc engines. In 1976 Nissan made a record 2,303,703 cars and became the world's fourth largest car producers. Their best selling model continued to be the Bluebird which became Mark II that year and was available with a 2-litre engine for the first time. The 180SSS-ES performance version had fuel injection. Criticism of the Sunny's poor visibility was answered by the 1977 B310 version with slimmer pillars. It also had a new 4-link coil spring rear suspension shared with a new and smaller Violet, whose coupé version was called the Stanza. An additional model was the Silvia/200SX coupé with unique 92.1 in/2340 mm wheelbase body and 1952 cc ohc engine with 5-speed gearbox. Biggest Nissan was the President with 4414 cc V8 fuel-injected engine, ventilated disc brakes, dual air conditioning and a power-operated rear seat. In 1978 there was a more refined, larger, and heavier, version of the Fairlady Z/280ZX and a new Pulsar. This was in effect a new and wider body for the Cherry, which the Pulsar eventually replaced, but just to confuse everyone the Pulsar was known as the Cherry in many export markets. The 200SX/Silvia coupé became a hatchback in 1979 and at the end of the year there was a restyled Bluebird with 99.4 in/2525 mm wheelbase and optional 2-litre 6-cylinder engine. It was sold in the USA as the Datsun 810 Maxima. The gap between the Bluebird and Laurel was bridged by the new Leopard 1.8-litre model in 1980, and there was a turbocharged version of the 280ZX with 200 bhp. At the 1981 Tokyo Show there was a completely new front-wheel-drive Sunny with independent rear suspension and larger 1270 and 1488 cc ohc engines, which also went into the Cherry/Pulsar. Earlier in the year the Stanza and Violet had also gone front-wheel drive. The bigger Skyline was rebodied and offered with engines ranging from 1.8 to 2.8 litres, including two diesels. In 1982 the Cherry became a hatchback with 95.1 in/2415 mm wheelbase and an overall length of 155.9 in/3960 mm and was actually roomier than the Sunny. That model was turbocharged for the first time giving 115 bhp from the 1.5-litre engine, while for economy there was a 1681 cc diesel. The new Micra 3-door hatchback with 90.6 in/2300 mm wheelbase was added at the bottom of the range and its new 988 cc engine was Nissan's first aluminium unit. At the other end of the scale was the Prairie people carrier with 1.5- or 1.8-litre engines driving the front wheels and van-type sliding rear doors. The Cherry body with Alfa Romeo mechanicals was sold in Europe as the Arna (Alfa Romeo Nissan Autovehicoli) in 1983 but was not a success. It was the year for new models with a completely new front-wheel-drive Bluebird/Maxima, Silvia with a new body with pop-up headlamps and a new Cedric/Gloria range. At the end of the year Nissan's first V6 engine, seen earlier in the Cedric, went into the 300ZX and with Nissan's own electronic fuel injection produced 180 bhp in this 2960 cc ohc version. For taxation reasons there was also a 1998 cc version producing 130 bhp, or 170 bhp when turbocharged. The 3-litre V6 went into the Leopard in 1984, giving 230 bhp when turbocharged. The Sunny was rebodied in 1985 with strut-type independent rear suspension and was offered with disengageable four-wheel drive. As the Sentra it was the first Nissan to be produced at a new factory in the USA. The Prairie also had a 4wd option and a 2-litre engine and was sold in America as the Stanza Wagon. V6 engines were offered in the Cedric/Gloria, Bluebird/Maxima and Skyline. The latter was a new car with special HICAS rear subframe allowing four-wheel steering for the first time on a production car. Even the little Micra could be had with a turbocharged engine giving 85 bhp from 988 cc and there was a turbocharged and intercooled 180 bhp 1998 cc engine option for the 300ZX. This was a twin cam 24-valve straight-6 engine and was fitted with the world's first ceramic turbocharger. At the 1985 Frankfurt Show Nissan revealed a prototype of their new mid-engined sports coupé with a 24-valve 4 ohc version of the 2960 cc V6 engine giving 230 bhp. Called the Mid-4, this model was scheduled for production in 1987. Electronics were a major feature of the 1986 Leopard which had an electronic facia, electronic control of the four-speed automatic gearbox, and optional electronically-adjustable dampers (shock absorbers). The 3-litre V6 engine also had variable valve timing and knock sensors to avoid pinking. The new 1986 Stanza 4-door saloon was based on the Bluebird/Maxima and had 1598 or 1809 cc engines, the latter available in fuel injected or turbo form or as a 2 ohc 16-valve version with 145 bhp. Nissan's became the first Japanese manufacturer to build cars in Europe with the opening, by British Prime Minister Margaret Thatcher, of their UK factory at Sunderland on 8 September 1986.

On 30 September the first production Bluebird was presented to the Prince of Wales. That model was a four-door saloon and in 1987 a hatchback version was added.

Oldsmobile (USA)

The world's very first mass produced car was the curved-dash Oldsmobile of 1901. It was the invention of Ransom Eli Olds who had grown up with farm machinery and steam engines and built his first gasoline car in 1895. It followed an earlier steam car and was a buggy with elliptic springs and the engine mounted in the middle. It attracted the attention of E. W. Sparrow who with two friends put up $50,000 to form the Olds Motor Vehicle Company. They made mostly stationary engines until 1899 when one of the friends, S. L. Smith, took over the company. It was after unsuccessful attempts to build a luxury car that Olds went to the other extreme with the $650 curved dash model. It had a single-cylinder 1573 cc engine and chain drive to the rear wheels and succeeded because of its simplicity. Some 600 were sold in 1901 and 2,500 in 1902. Not all the car was made by Olds; the engines were supplied by the Dodge brothers and Leland and Faulconer. In 1904 sales reached 5000 and Ransom Olds left to found Reo. A move back to Lansing from Detroit followed in 1905 and there were new 2-cylinder Double Action 20/24 hp and 4-cylinder 26/28 hp Model S additions selling for $1250 and $2250 respectively. Both had 3-speed gearboxes and shaft drive. Bigger models followed, did not sell and led to the purchase of Oldsmobile by General Motors in 1909. Even bigger models continued and there was an 11,569 cc six with 138 in/3505 mm wheelbase and huge wheels in 1910 called the Limited. After 1912 the biggest model was a 6997 cc six and electric lighting and starting were standardized in 1914. A cheap 4-cylinder and then a 4-litre V8 were added by 1916, the year that Oldsmobile built the millionth General Motors car. It was a 2.9-litre six. In 1924 there was only a 2774 cc 6-cylinder model and the open Sport Touring model was heavily promoted at a time when many manufacturers were concentrating on closed cars. Oldsmobile pioneered chromium-plated brightwork in 1927 and added four-wheel brakes the same year. The 1929 Viking with 4244 cc side-valve V8 was not a success and was followed by a 4-litre straight-8 in 1932. Technical advances included the introduction of synchromesh in 1931 and independent front suspension in 1934. In 1938 (for 1939 models) Oldsmobile were the first to offer automatic transmission, from which the very successful Hydramatic was developed for 1940. It was offered on all models in 1946. 'Futuramic' styling arrived for 1949 with the 125 in/3175 mm wheelbase 98 model and there was a new 4977 cc (303 cu. in) high compression V8 engine with 135 bhp called the Rocket. Installed in place of the 6-cylinder engine in the 119.5 in/3035 mm wheelbase Oldsmobile 76 with GM A-body, it became the Rocket 88, America's first modern high performance car. It dominated NASCAR racing in 1949 and was chosen by the California Highway Patrol as their standard vehicle. In 1950 268,412 Rocket 88s were produced out of a total of 407,877 Oldsmobiles, with the cheapest two-door model selling for $1790. By 1951 all models had the ohv V8 engine, and the 88 had a longer 120 in/3048 mm wheelbase as the Super 88, with one-piece windscreen and wrap-around rear window, plus 160 bhp. Power-assisted steering became an option in 1952 along with GM's Autronic Eye Guide automatic headlamp dipping system. Fins and missile motifs were to follow leading to the 1958 Dynamic Starfire coupé. By then all models were built on 121 or 126 in (3073 or 3200 mm) wheelbases using the GM X-frame chassis and the 98 had a 6076 cc (371) engine giving 260 bhp. The marque's first compact was the 112 in/2845 mm wheelbase F-85 powered by a 3524 cc (215) V8 giving 155 bhp in 1961. It was also the first Olds with unitary construction. The 1962 Cutlass performance version of the F-85 had 185 bhp, while the 1963 Jetfire was turbocharged to give 215 bhp, and the Starfire had 345 bhp from a 6455 cc (394) V8. The 1966 Toronado was the first post-war American front-wheel-drive model and was also the largest and most powerful ever seen. It had a 119 in/3023 mm wheelbase, was 211 in/5359 mm long and was powered by a 385 bhp 6965 cc (425) V8 engine. All that power was transmitted by chain drive to the Hydramatic gearbox. This massive car was a 2-door coupé that could accelerate to 60 mph/97 kph in under 9 seconds and reach 125 mph/201 kph, yet was stopped by all-drum brakes that faded badly if used hard. On 16 March 1966 a Toronado became the 100 millionth vehicle produced by General Motors. A major breakthrough for the whole industry came in 1967 with Oldsmobile's Climatic Combustion Control, which met the requirements of the California Motor Vehicle Pollution Control Board. It used exhaust-heated air to enable carburettors to be adjusted leaner. The same year there were new Delta Custom, Delmont 88 and convertible F-85 Cutlass models, a new 6556 cc (400) V8 giving

340 bhp and optional Delcotronic electric ignition. The 98 had a 7456 cc (455) engine in 1969 and was no less than 224 in/5689 mm long and there was a larger Toronado with the same engine. For 1971 the Toronado was bigger still with a 122 in/3098 mm wheelbase and there was a jumbo-sized 9-seater station wagon with 125 in/3175 mm wheelbase. The Omega compact arrived for 1973, in time for the oil crisis, and was joined in 1975 by the 97 in/2464 mm wheelbase Starfire hatchback costing $4157 (more expensive than the larger Omega) and based on Chevrolet's Vega with 3.8-litre (231) V6 engine. A new Cutlass luxury coupé and a 4.3-litre (260) economy version of the big V8 were added the same year. Both 88 and 98 were new for 1977 with paired rectangular headlamps. The 88 had an aluminium bonnet and was powered by the 3.8 (231) V6. The 119 in/3023 mm wheelbase 98 had a 5.7-litre (350) V8 as standard and there was an optional lighter and more compact 6604 cc (403) V8. Cheapest 1977 model was the $3802 Starfire with 2294 cc (140) 4-cylinder engine, while the best-selling Cutlass cost from $4351. Oldsmobile were the first American manufacturers to offer a diesel engine option, on their 88 and 98 models, for 1978. The 5826 cc (355) diesel V8 produced 120 bhp. Even the Toronado was downsized for 1979, shedding about 1000 lb/453.6 kg and 1 ft/305 mm in length, and getting a 4128 cc (252) V6 engine in the process. There was even an optional 5.7-litre (350) V8 diesel. In the Spring of 1979 there was a new 105 in/2667 mm wheelbase Omega compact with front-wheel drive, ventilated front disc brakes, rack and pinion steering and 2471 cc (151) 4-cylinder or 2838 cc (173) V6 engine. For 1981 there was a rebodied Cutlass Supreme and in 1982 the Cutlass Ciera replaced the Omega. The Ciera could be had with a 2471 cc (151) 4-cylinder, 2966 cc (181) V6 or 4.3-litre (262) V8 diesel. Also new for 1982 was the sub-compact Firenza (based on the J-car) with 101 in/2565 mm wheelbase and a 4-cylinder 1796 or 1991 cc (109 or 121) engine driving the front wheels. The 98 remained the biggest saloon, with rear-wheel drive, on a 119 in/3023 mm wheelbase giving a length of

1966 Oldsmobile Toronado with 6965 cc V8 engine and front-wheel drive.

221 in/5613 mm. The biggest engine available was now the 5.7-litre (350) diesel; the largest petrol unit was the 5033 cc (307) V8. During 1984 the 98 model went front-wheel drive and shrank to a 110.8 in/2814 mm wheelbase with standard 3.8-litre (231) V6. For 1985 there was a new Calais fwd coupé (the saloon came later) on a 103.3 in/2624 mm wheelbase with 2.5-litre (151) 4-cylinder engine costing $8669. 1986 changes included a new fwd Delta 88 on the same wheelbase as the 98, and an even smaller Toronado with 108 in/2473 mm wheelbase coupé body and 3791 cc (231) V6. That engine was optional on the Delta 88 which otherwise had a 3-litre (181) V6. Sole remaining rear-wheel-drive model was the Custom Cruiser station wagon based on the old 116 in/2946 mm wheelbase Delta 88 and powered by a 5-litre (307) V8. In 1987 Oldsmobile offered no fewer than 31 models based on nine different body styles. The Firenza was fitted with a new 2005 cc (122) ohc 4-cylinder engine as standard, and Calais models had passive front seat belts (self-fastening). There was a special luxury Trofeo (Spanish for trophy) version of the Toronado with leather bucket seats and low profile 215/60R-15 tyres on alloy wheels. Leather and real walnut also featured in the interior of the 1987 Ninety-Eight touring sedan, which had a floor-mounted selector for the 4-speed automatic gearbox for the first time.

Opel (W. Germany)

Adam Opel, whose name the company bears to this day, was not involved in car manufacture at all but manufactured sewing machines and later bicycles, of which he became the world's largest producer before his death in 1895. It was his sons who, in 1898, embarked on motor manufacturing when the bicycle industry was in recession. They concluded an agreement with Friedrich Lutzmann to manufacture his machine in the Opel factory at Russelsheim. The first production versions of this 4 hp single cylinder carriage were built in 1899 but only lasted until 1900. An agreement with Darracq followed and until 1902 the Opel brothers imported chassis from France, bodied them and sold them as Opel-Darracqs. The first true Opel was seen at the 1902 Hamburg Show. This 10/12 hp 2-cylinder model had the engine at the front, shaft drive, automatic lubrication and a 3-speed gearbox. A 4-cylinder 20/24 hp model followed in 1903 and a bigger 35/40 hp in 1905, when the arrangement with Darracq terminated. The 1000th Opel to be built was a 2-cylinder 10/12 hp

model in 1906. A variety of models followed including the 4-cylinder 3402 cc 14/20 and 6333 cc 25/40 models which sold in England for £640 and £875 respectively in 1908 when complete with limousine bodies. A factory fire in 1911 ended sewing machine production and allowed modernization, so that the 10,000th Opel was built in 1912. This was the little 6/16 hp model introduced in 1911 and nicknamed the Puppchen (dolly) because of its dainty appearance. At the other end of the scale was the massive 10.2-litre 40/100 model with overhead valves. After World War I a range of 4-cylinder models was sold and in 1923 after a visit to America Wilhelm Opel introduced assembly line production to the Russelsheim factory. The new 1924 4/12 hp 4-cylinder 954 cc model was the first German car to be mass produced but its design led to a dispute with Citroën, whose 5CV it resembled. The result was the longer wheelbase 4-seater 1016 cc version of 1926. Both models were known as the Laubfrosch (tree frog) because of the all-green colour scheme adopted. A Laubfrosch was the 100,000th Opel built in 1924. By 1928 production was at the rate of 250 cars a day and Opel accounted for over 37 per cent of all German car production. Larger models included the 4-cylinder 2613 cc 20/45 and 6-cylinder 3919 cc 30/60. In 1927 Fritz von Opel, grandson of Adam, became interested in rocket-propelled cars and, with help from specialists Max Valier and Friedrich Sander, built Rak 1 using an old Opel racing car as the vehicle. It achieved 60 mph/96.5 kph but the more scientific Rak 2 with 24 rockets in the tail reached 125 mph/201 kph at the Avus track on 23 May 1928. The approaching economic crisis caused the family to form a joint-stock company and in 1929 General Motors acquired control with an 80 per cent holding, extending this to total ownership in 1931. There followed 1-litre, Regent 1.2-litre and 6-cylinder 1.8-litre model ranges under the new regime. The 1934 2-litre was the first Opel with independent front suspension and the 1935 1.3-litre 4-cylinder Olympia was the first mass-produced car with an integral body construction minus chassis. The boxy 1936 1074 cc P4 model was simple, with leaf-spring front suspension, but cheap, and was augmented in 1937 by the Kadett which used the P4 engine in a 92.5 in/2350 mm wheelbase chassis. The Olympia acquired a 1488 cc ohv engine in 1938 and the 2473 cc Kapitan and 6-cylinder 3626 cc Admiral models were added the same year. In 1940 an integral construction Kapitan was the millionth Opel to be made. Postwar production resumed with the

Olympia in 1947 and Kapitan in 1948. In 1953 the Olympia grew into the Rekord, still with the 1488 cc ohv engine. In 1959 the Rekord was available with a larger 1668 cc engine in the bigger 100 in/2540 mm wheelbase body and the Kapitan had a new 2605 cc 90 bhp engine. The Kadett name was revived in 1962 for a new small 993 cc model built in a new factory at Bochum. An American-style larger-bodied Kapitan with Bosch rectangular headlamps and front disc brakes appeared in 1964 and formed the basis for the Admiral model which used the same body and 2605 cc 6-cylinder engine. The top model was the Diplomat, based on the Kapitan but with a Chevrolet 4638 cc V8 engine giving 190 bhp so that 120 mph/193 kph was possible. Automatic transmission was standard on the Diplomat and optional on the Kapitan and Admiral. There was a new 1078 cc 4-cylinder engine with 55 bhp in the new 1965 Kadett which was available in saloon or coupé form. Both Kadett and Rekord had 12 volt electrics for the first time and the latter had a new family of 4-cylinder cam-in-head 1492, 1698 and 1897 cc engines. The larger Admiral was also offered with a 2784 cc ohc 6-cylinder engine. A sporting Rallye Kadett coupé model was introduced in 1966 with front disc brakes, 60 bhp and matt black bonnet panels. There was also a bigger Rekord with revised rear suspension and optional 2239 cc ohc 6-cylinder engine as well as the 1.5-, 1.7- and 1.9-litre units. There were saloon, fastback coupé and estate car versions. The Commodore was an additional model using the Rekord body with a smaller 2490 cc version of the Kapitan engine introduced in 1967, the year that Opels returned to the UK market after being absent since 1939. The 1968 Olympia with 1078 cc engine and front disc brakes bridged the gap between Kadett and Rekord. Opel's own automatic transmission from the new GM Strasbourg factory was an option on the new 1969 Kapi-

1924 Opel 4/12 hp Laubfrosch.

tan and Admiral models which had more powerful engines and new de Dion rear suspension. Bosch fuel injection was optional on the Admiral and Diplomat. Opel's only postwar 2-seater model, the GT, had meanwhile started production, with some bodyshells made by Brissoneau and Lotz in Paris. The striking coupé body with pop-up headlamps was based on the Kadett with 1100 or 1900 engines and was capable of 115 mph/185 kph with the latter. The Rallye Kadett was offered with the 90 bhp 1897 cc engine in 1970 and there was a GS/E version of the Commodore with 150 bhp from Bosch fuel injection. The sporting influence was continued by the new Manta coupé with good handling and performance with 1.6- or 1.9-litre engines. It was so successful that despite a September launch 50,000 were built by the end of the year. The Ascona saloon which followed, with 1584 cc engine, was based on the Manta with 95.7 in/2430 mm wheelbase. The 10 millionth Opel, a Rekord, was produced on 6 September 1971 and the Rallye Kadett was available with a bored-out 1196 cc version of the 1078 engine that was soon to be used in normal Kadett models. The rebodied 1972 Rekord was also better handling and capable of 100 mph/161 kph and 20 mpg/14.1 litres/100 km. At the end of the year it became the first Opel diesel when the new 2068 cc 60 bhp engine was offered in the 2100D. A modern shape with more glass area and better handling were offered in the 1973 Kadett range. The 1975 Manta and Ascona replacements were lower and more modern and also marked the beginning of the integration of Opel and Vauxhall (q.v.) models. They were noted for the excellent safe handling which had developed into a Russelsheim hallmark. This was just as well as there was now a potent Manta GT/E with fuel injection and 105 bhp. The Kadett City hatchback model which followed later in 1975 was the General Motors T-car and closely related to Vauxhall's Chevette. There was a new ohc 1979 cc 4-cylinder engine for the completely new 1977 Rekord making it a comfortable long distance cruiser capable of over 110 mph/177 kph. For the first time there was no Commodore version, but instead new and bigger Senator saloon and Monza coupé models formed the top of the 1978 Opel range, replacing the Admiral and Diplomat. As well as the 2784 6-cylinder engine there was a bored-out 2968 cc version with 180 bhp and both models had independent rear suspension. A 2490 cc Commodore based on the Rekord, which also had a bigger 2260 cc diesel engine option, followed later. The 1979 Ascona was the first Opel to use the new 1297 cc ohc engine which formed the power unit of the first front-wheel-drive model, the hatchback Kadett, launched that autumn. The design allowed a longer wheelbase for more passenger space within a shorter overall length. The 1981 front-wheel-drive Ascona saloon and hatchback (GM's J-cars) were accompanied by a new Manta coupé and hatchback which retained conventional rear-wheel drive. This was particularly beneficial for the Manta 400 2.4-litre competition model, though normal engines were 1.3, 1.6 or 2 litres. A 1796 cc unit was added in 1982 for taxation reasons. There was a revised Rekord for 1983 but the big news was the Corsa, the first General Motors small front-wheel-drive model with 993, 1196 or 1397 cc engines in a saloon or hatchback body. It was the first Opel not built in Germany, for all Corsas were manufactured in the new General Motors factory at Zaragoza in Spain. An advanced aerodynamic shape was the main feature of the new 1984 Kadett hatchback, which was joined by a four-door saloon, four-wheel-drive and open cabriolet versions in 1985. The aerodynamic theme was continued by the 1986 Omega which replaced the Rekord and boasted a drag coefficient of 0.28. This was GM's V-car with longer wheelbase 107.5 in/2730 mm body and 1796 or 1998 cc 4-cylinder engines. There was no longer a Commodore, but the same formula was used for the most powerful Omega which used the 2969 cc 177 bhp fuel-injected 6-cylinder engine from the Senator, and in that form anti-lock braking was standard. Electronically-controlled adjustable damper (shock absorber) settings were a further refinement added in 1987.

Peugeot (France)

The Peugeot family's ironmongery business led to the manufacture of bicycles in 1885 and from there it was but a short step to a steam car in 1889 and a petrol-driven model using a Daimler engine in 1891. This 2-cylinder 4-wheeler had handlebar steering and cycle-type spoked wheels yet was capable of making the journey from Beaulieu-Valentigney to Paris and then to Brest and back – the first long-distance journey by a petrol-engined car, in 1891. In 1895 pioneer motorist Sir David Salomons imported a 4 hp Peugeot to Britain, where C. S. Rolls (later of Rolls-Royce) sold them from his London showrooms. A Peugeot driven by Lemaitre was second in the 1894 Paris–Rouen race, with other Peugeots third and fifth, and André Michelin's pneumatic tyres were first used on a Peugeot in the 1895 Paris–Bordeaux race. In

1899, when electric ignition was first offered, sales reached 300. The following year Peugeots had steering wheels and the first front-engined model ran in the Paris–Berlin race. A new factory at Lille was opened in 1902 and the biggest 4-cylinder models then had pressed-steel chassis and honeycomb radiators. Robert Peugeot broke away to build motor-cycles in 1903 and when he progressed to cars in 1906 they were known as Lion-Peugeots. In 1907 the Peugeot Lion trademark, which had been registered in 1858, was first used on the cars. Most models then had a gated gearbox, as did the first 6-cylinder 60 hp 10.4-litre model of 1908. Then production had risen to 2300 cars a year and there were numerous models from the 10 hp 2-cylinder upwards. The Peugeot family rivalry ended in 1910 with the founding of Société Anonyme des Automobiles et des Cycles Peugeot and a new factory was opened at Sochaux, still the company's main production centre. The 1912 Bébé model was tiny and had been designed by none other than Ettore Bugatti. It had an 856 cc 10 bhp engine driving the rear wheels through twin propellor shafts. The 7.6-litre 4-cylinder Peugeot was designed for racing in the 1912 French Grand Prix, which it won, but more importantly the design's 4 valves per cylinder and twin overhead camshafts formed the basis of future high performance engines to this day. Peugeot had previously raced a V4-engined model and a 12 hp V4 was marketed up until World War I, as was the 2746 cc Type 153B which continued after the war and sold in England for £1075 in 1920. Like the 1437 cc 11 hp Type 163 and other Peugeots it had thermo-syphon cooling (no water pump) and 4 cylinders. The Bébé was succeeded by the little 4 hp 668 cc 4-cylinder Quadrilette which was so narrow that the driver and passenger had to sit one behind the other. It cost £298 in Britain in 1920, and acquired a 719 cc engine in 1926 when the price was reduced to £155. It was then the only model not to have front-wheel brakes, which were eventually added in 1929. Peugeot had acquired the Bellanger and de Dion Bouton factories in 1928 and produced the new 1990 cc 6-cylinder Type 183 the following year. It cost £390 in England in 1929 and was the first of a new series of models. The 1930 1.1-litre small family saloon was designated the Type 201 and thereafter Peugeot models featured this 3-digit numbering with 0 in the middle. The 201's transverse leaf spring front suspension gained it the distinction of being the first mass-produced car with independent front suspension in 1932. That year's 301 model used the same basic specification

but had a 1½-litre engine. The 1934 coupé/
convertible Peugeot with a mechanism to lift the
steel hardtop off and stow it in the boot, thus turning the car into a convertible, was years ahead of
its time. The 1935 Type 601 2-litre 6-cylinder model was to be the marque's last 6-cylinder model
until the mid-1970s, and was joined in 1936 by the
1991 cc ohv 4-cylinder 402, whose main feature
was the streamlined styling. The rear wheels were
covered by spats and the headlamps were hidden
behind the sloping radiator grille. The short
wheelbase model measured 113.4 in/2880 mm between the wheel centres while the extra long version for 6/8-seater coachwork was 129.9 in/
3300 mm. There was also an 'electric coupé' dis-
appearing hardtop version and in 1939 the 402
received a bigger 2140 cc engine with 63 bhp. The
smaller 1133 cc 202 saloon, which cost £198 in
England in 1939, went back into production after
the war in 1946 but was replaced a year later by
the new 203. This had headlamps in the wings and
a sloping tail and was powered by a 1290 cc ohv
engine driving through a 4-speed gearbox with
overdrive top and column change. Hydraulic
brakes and all-independent coil spring suspension
were other advanced features which made the
model a best-seller for a decade. The rugged 403
that joined it in 1955 offered more space and used a
1468 cc engine. It too sold well and earned Peugeot
a well-deserved reputation for sound engineering.
The 203 went out of production in 1960, and the
same year there was a new Pininfarina-styled
boxy 404 which replaced the 403 in 1962. Annual
production meanwhile had risen from 125,000 cars
in 1951 to 237,000 in 1961. The 404 was powered
by a bored-out 1618 cc engine giving 72 bhp and
was noted for the elimination of engine and transmission noise within the body. Indeed it was so
quiet that many rival manufacturers purchased
404s to discover the secret. The 404 was the first
Peugeot offered with fuel injection, by Kugelfischer, in 1962 on the cabriolet version. Styling of
1965's advanced small 204 model had again been
entrusted to Pininfarina and it was initially only
available as a saloon, the estate car following at
the end of the year. An ohc aluminium 1130 cc
4-cylinder engine producing 53 bhp was installed
transversely to drive the front wheels, for the first
time on a Peugeot. The gearbox was in the sump
(Mini-style) and there was a column gearchange.
The 204 had all-independent suspension, front
disc brakes and an overall length of 156.3 in/
3970 mm. The 304 that was added to the range in
1969 shared the 204's 102 in/2590 mm wheelbase

1921 Peugeot Quadrilette.

and technical features for in essence it was a 204
with a bigger boot, though there was a new 1288 cc
engine giving 65 bhp. The distinguishing feature
from the front was that the 304 had the trapezoidal
headlamps introduced on the much bigger 504 a
year earlier. The 504 was conventional with a new
1796 cc engine with 82 bhp, or 97 with injection,
driving the rear wheels. A 107.9 in/2740 mm
wheelbase giving more room for rear passengers,
curved window glass and independent rear suspension were other features. The 404, like the 403
which had sold 1.2 million, continued to sell well
and survived until 1975, by which time 504 sales
had topped a million. Shorter wheelbase 504 coupé
and cabriolet versions were added in 1969 followed
by an estate car version and in 1970 the 504 was
fitted with a 1971 cc engine. There were coupé and
convertible 304s in 1970 and an estate in 1971.
'Europe's smallest 4-door saloon' was the claim
made for the new small front-wheel-drive 104,
which looked like a hatchback but wasn't, launched in 1972. It was the first Peugeot to use an
engine built in the new Douvrin factory shared
with Renault under a co-operation agreement,
while the 104 itself was assembled in a new facility
at the Mulhouse factory completed in 1971. The
954 cc ohc alloy engine produced 46 bhp and was
installed transversely and leaning backwards.
Douvrin's second new engine was the PRV V6,
developed jointly by Peugeot, Renault and Volvo
and used first in the Volvo 264. Peugeot's carburettor version was offered first in the 504 coupé
and convertible in 1974, but the all-aluminium
2664 cc V6 was really intended for the totally new
and bigger flagship 604 model of 1975. That did
not replace the 504 but offered superior accommodation with a 110.2 in/2800 mm wheelbase, and
electric windows and power steering as standard

equipment. At the end of 1974 Peugeot took control of the financially-troubled Citroën and the result was the PSA Peugeot-Citroën group. Later some Peugeot engineering began to appear in small Citroëns. The 305 replaced the 304 in 1977 and continued the same formula with a new body and 1290 and 1472 cc engines giving 60 or 67 bhp respectively, while the new hatchback 104 had an 1124 cc engine and coupé variant added for that year. The 304 estate however continued until the new 305 estate arrived in 1979. By that time the PSA Group had taken over Chrysler's European interests and renamed the marque Talbot. Existing Alpine, Horizon, Sunbeam and Simca models continued under the Talbot name and were joined by the Solara saloon and later Tagora and Samba models. The last Talbots were made in 1986. The 1979 505 Peugeot was in essence a rebodied 504 and as well as the latter's 1971 cc petrol and 2304 cc diesel engines was offered with a new Douvrin-built 1995 cc ohc unit with Bosch fuel injection (also used with a carburettor in the Renault 20). It did not replace the 504, which continued in production as late as 1983, but slotted between it and the bigger 604, which became the first Peugeot to be turbocharged (as a diesel) the same year. Also in 1979 there was a larger and more powerful 1360 cc 72 bhp version of the new 1219 cc Douvrin (Renault 14) engine, which was also offered in the 104. The 205 which arrived in 1983 was essentially a roomier and much more streamlined 104 and shared that model's 95.3 in/2420 mm wheelbase and engines, but the 104 continued in production into 1986. A new departure was a GT version of the 205 with 80 bhp, followed by a GTI version with 1580 cc fuel-injected 105 bhp engine in 1984. The 205 Turbo 16, with 1775 cc turbocharged engine delivering 200 bhp, was a lot quicker as it was a homologation special intended for winning rallies. It was not really the same car at all because the wheelbase was lengthened to allow the engine to be installed transversely behind the front seats and all four wheels were driven. It was possible to buy a road-going example, though, for £25,129. The hatchback 309 introduced in 1985 was the first Peugeot ever to be made in Britain – at the former Chrysler/Talbot plant at Ryton, Coventry. It was powered by 1118, 1294 or 1905 cc engines giving up to 80 bhp in GT form. With a 97.2 in/2470 mm wheelbase it was larger than the 205 and fitted between that and the 305 in the range. Cars made in Britain, like those made in France, were each track-tested at the end of the assembly line, an old Peugeot tradi-

tion. The 505 was restyled in 1985 and the most potent 2155 cc Turbo Injection version then had 180 bhp. For 1987 the 505 became the Peugeot flagship replacing the dropped 604, whose 2849 cc V6 170 bhp engine was used for the top model. That also had anti-lock brakes, the first Peugeot to do so.

Plymouth (USA)

This was Chrysler's low-price marque introduced in July 1928 with a 4-cylinder side valve engine and selling for $725. Right from the start it was Chrysler's volume seller with over 100,000 delivered in the first year. A 6-cylinder model was added in 1933 and independent front suspension in 1934 with many components shared with the more expensive De Soto. In the mid-1930s a 3.3-litre (201 cu. in) engine was standard. The Flight Sweep 4.3-litre ohv V8 appeared in 1955, though the 3.8-litre (230 cu. in) six was still offered. A year later came a major departure from the normal staid models with the introduction of the performance Fury model. More conventional was the Belvedere with 5212 cc (318 cu. in) V8 and 118 in/2997 mm wheelbase. The Valiant compact arrived for 1960 with monocoque body, European styling, 106 in/2692 mm wheelbase and 2.8-litre (170 cu. in) ohv 6-cylinder engine developing 101 bhp. The same year De Soto was integrated into the Plymouth division. The 1964 Sport Fury hardtop was available with V8 engines from 5.2 to 7 litres (318 to 426 cu. in) giving up to 365 bhp, while there was even a Super Stock version of the 426 with 425 bhp. The Valiant-based Barracuda coupé of 1965 had semi-fastback styling with a wrap-around rear window but boasted no more than 235 bhp in its most powerful 4.5-litre (273 cu. in) V8 form, but for 1968 there was an optional lightweight 5.6-litre (340 cu. in) V8 giving 275 bhp. Top Plymouth model was then the $3300 VIP Hardtop with 5212 cc (318 cu. in) V8, a 119 in/3022 mm wheelbase and vertical paired headlamp units. Nearly as big were the 6.3-litre (383 cu. in) Road Runner and 7.2-litre/440 cu. in GTX Hardtop, which offered sports performance from 335 and 375 bhp respectively with optional 425 bhp engines. In 1971 the Cricket sub-compact was added to the range and was actually an Americanized European Hillman Avenger. Mitsubishis were disguised as Plymouths too – the Arrow was actually a Celeste while the 1977 Sapporo coupé was really a Mitsubishi Lambda. At least the Volare which had arrived in 1976 was only a Dodge Aspen clone. Plymouth's remaining full-size mod-

1965 Plymouth Barracuda.

el the Gran Fury was dropped for 1978 to make way for production of the 1.7-litre (102 cu. in) Horizon which bore considerable resemblance to Chrysler's European model of that name and even had front-wheel drive, though the transverse 4-cylinder engine was from Volkswagen. Its Dodge equivalent was the Omni. For 1979 the Horizon was joined by a coupé and the biggest model was the Volare, though in 1980 there was a new full-size Gran Fury with 118 in/2997 mm wheelbase and 3678 cc (224 cu. in) 6, or 5.2- or 5.9-litre (318 or 360 cu. in) V8, but only 130 bhp was available from the most powerful version. For 1981 Chrysler's K-car was introduced as the Reliant with 100 in/2540 mm wheelbase and a choice of 2.2- or 2.6-litre (135 or 156 cu. in) 4-cylinder engines installed transversely and driving the front wheels. New for 1984 was the Caravelle, Plymouth's version of the E-bodied Chrysler New Yorker, with an optional turbocharged engine giving 146 bhp making it the most powerful Plymouth. The smallest Colt models remained imported Mitsubishi Mirages and they had revised styling and 5-speed gearboxes for 1987. Completely new was the compact Sundance 3- or 5-door hatchback with European looks and a 97 in/2464 mm wheelbase. It used the 2.2-litre (135 cu. in) Chrysler engine with fuel injection. The Gran Fury with 5.2-litre (318 cu. in) V8 remained the only rear-wheel-drive Plymouth and the only large model.

Pontiac (USA)

Oakland, which had been part of General Motors since 1909, formed Pontiac as a marque to sell a cheaper model in 1926 but the origins of the marque and the name go back far earlier than that. Pontiac is a town named after an Indian chief who 200 years ago had banded together the Ottawas, Chippewas, Pottawattomis and Miamis. The Indian chief was commemorated as a bonnet mascot into the 1950s. The origins of the car itself go back

to the town of Pontiac in 1893 where Edward M. Murphy founded the Pontiac Buggy Company. Initially he built horsedrawn buggies, but in 1907 he founded Oakland to build motorized buggies using the 2-cylinder engine designed by A. P. Brush. It was particularly apt that the first Pontiac model of 1926 with 3-litre 6-cylinder engine was marketed as 'The Chief of the Sixes'. It cost $825 and was a considerable success with 76,742 sold in the first year, almost double that in 1927 and 210,890 in 1928. There were no more Oaklands after 1931, and Pontiac became the only marque created by General Motors to survive for more than a short time. Success brought a move to a new factory on the outskirts of Pontiac where the glass roof caused it to become known locally as the 'daylight plant', and the factory was linked to the new Fisher Body plant by an enclosed overhead bridge. For 1930 there was a new model very similar to Buick's Marquette, whose 3277 cc 6-cylinder ohv engine it shared. A revamped Oakland V8 was added for 1932 but in 1933 there was a 3654 cc straight-8 that sold, for under $600, to the tune of 89,000. That model had Fisher Body's No Draft Ventilation, which consisted of swivelling quarterlight windows. Dubonnet coil spring independent front suspension, which GM called 'knee-action', and turret-top bodies arrived in 1934. The Silver Streak designation was first carried by 1935 models and the fine chrome strips down the middle of the bonnet were soon to become a Pontiac feature. A column gearchange was optional in 1938 and standard in 1939. By then there was a bigger 117 in/2972 mm wheelbase for the 3654 cc (223) six and a 122 in/3099 mm wheelbase for the 4-litre (249) eight. A new Silver Streak Torpedo with streamlined body cost $1016 in 8-cylinder form and helped to notch up 239,477 Pontiac sales in 1940. In 1941 sales reached a record 283,601 but further successes were cut short by Pearl Harbor. There was no more Pontiacs until 1946 when the mixture was much as before and in 1948 Hydramatic automatic transmission was an option. The new 1949 models retained the Streamliner name for the fastbacks and adopted the Chieftain designation for the normal saloons. Both 6- and 8-cylinder models were built on a 120 in/3048 mm wheelbase and prices started at $1587. Pontiac sold 323,322 cars that year, helped by the image of the car that was built to last 100,000 miles. There were power increases in the following years and a longer wheelbase 124 in/3149 mm Star Chief in 1954 but the big news was Pontiac's first ohv V8 for 1955. The Strato Streak engine produced

180 bhp from 4705 cc (287 cu. in) and had a unique reverse-flow cooling system which fed water from the radiator to the cylinder head, the hottest part of the engine. Power and size were subsequently increased and in 1957, the first year without the Silver Streak bonnet stripes or the chieftain's head, the 5690 cc (347) unit was producing 227–270 bhp according to tune. Chrome and fins were left behind with the 1959 Catalina, followed in 1961 by the compact Tempest with 4-cylinder engine – and gearbox on the rear axle. The Tempest put Pontiac third in the American sales league, and in GTO guise with 6.3-litre (389) V8 giving 365 bhp became a super performance compact capable of 120 mph/193 kph. The 1966 Tempest itself had a new 6-cylinder 3769 cc (230) engine with hydraulic tappets and cogged-belt drive to the overhead camshaft, the first American car to do so. Power output was 165 bhp. Meanwhile Catalina, Star Chief and Bonneville all had lower and wider bodies with curved side windows and used a perimeter-frame chassis. The Canadian-built Parisienne continued to use the 3529 cc (215) six for a while although it was often fitted with a 4638 cc (283) V8. In 1966 Pontiacs were the first mass produced cars to use plastics for external body parts like the front grille, and the Tempest had vacuum-operated central locking of the doors. More charisma was added to the performance image with the 1967 Firebird which had bucket seats and an optional rev counter on the bonnet (hood) that was viewed through the windscreen. Though the 6-cylinder ohc engine was standard there was an optional 6556 cc (400) V8 giving 325 bhp and front disc brakes aided stopping. The Firebird was the first production car to have a Space-Saver tyre (by Goodrich) as standard because the boot (trunk) was so small. Dual circuit brakes and collapsible steering columns were fitted to all models that year and in 1968 the GTO had polyurethane-faced front bumpers painted body colour, a move that eventually led to a whole polyurethane front end on the 1974 Grand Am. The Firebird spawned a Trans Am version in 1969, though the familiar spoilered model did not appear until after the Firebird had received a new body in 1970, but the original shared with the Grand Prix coupé the front bumper divided by the grille. That 1969 Grand Prix on a 118 in/2997 mm wheelbase featured a fastback roofline, an aeroplane-style cockpit and one of the longest bonnets ever on a Pontiac. It was a big car with a 7-litre (428) V8 with 370 bhp available. The new Firebird Trans Am by comparison had a 108 in/2743 mm wheelbase but could call on an even mightier 7456 cc (455) V8 giving 335 bhp, though the standard Firebird engine was the 4097 cc (250) six. Pontiac re-entered the compact market with the 1971 Ventura II which had monocoque construction and a 111 in/2819 mm wheelbase. Even smaller was the 1976 Sunbird sub-compact coupé based on Chevrolet's Monza with a 97 in/2463 mm wheelbase and 2294 cc (140) 4-cylinder engine, both features shared with the Canadian-built Astre introduced a year earlier. The post-oil crisis shrinking came to the Bonneville and Catalina for 1977 along with a new 5033 cc (307) V8 that was 120 lb/55 kg lighter than the previous version. Whereas the 1976 Catalina had a 123.4 in/3134 mm wheelbase and 226 in/5740 mm length, the 1977 model's dimensions were 115.9 in/2944 mm and 213.8 in/5430 mm respectively. Shorter and lighter Le Mans and Grand Prix models followed in 1978 with engines ranging from the 3784 cc (231) six to the 5733 cc (350) V8. Even the Firebird was down to a 6.6-litre (403) V8 producing 185 bhp and by 1980 a 3.8-litre (231) V6 was standard and the turbocharged 4942 cc (302) V8 for the Trans Am was the most powerful available with 210 bhp. The option of the bird bonnet decal, made in plastic by the 3M company and first seen in 1973, continued though. Completely different was the first of a new generation of economy Pontiacs that arrived as the Phoenix fastback in 1979. It had a 105 in/2667 mm wheelbase and was front-wheel drive with a transverse 2835 cc (173) V6 or 2471 cc (151) 4-cylinder engine, the latter going into the Sunbird the same year. In 1981 Pontiac's version of the GM J-car was revealed as the front-wheel-drive J2000 (later called the Sunbird), while the T-car Chevette equivalent was added as the rear-wheel-drive T1000 to replace the old Sunbird. The J-car had a 101.2 in/2570 mm wheelbase and the 3-door T–car a 94.3 in/2395 mm one. They were joined in 1982 by the new 2471 cc (151) 4-cylinder fwd 6000 with 104.9 in/2665 mm wheelbase, while the Bonneville shrank by almost 16 in/406 mm to an over-

1987 Pontiac Bonneville.

all length of 198.4 in/5040 mm on a 108.1 in/2745 mm wheelbase, but remained rear-wheel drive. There was even a new big car, the Parisienne based on the Chevrolet Impala, with 116 in/5395 mm wheelbase for 1984 and it too had rear-wheel drive. There were minor modifications to the Firebird which had lost about 500 lb/226 kg when it was rebodied on a 101 in/2565 mm wheelbase with retractable headlamps in 1982. Completely new for 1984 was the mid-engined Fiero with plastic panels bolted on to a steel space frame. There were four-wheel disc brakes, all independent suspension and a very aerodynamic shape with a drag coefficient of 0.37. There was a shorter 110.8 in/2814 mm wheelbase Bonneville saloon for 1987 with front-wheel drive and a 3.8-litre (231) V6 engine. The only remaining big cars with rear-wheel drive were the Sarari (former Parisienne) station wagon and intermediate Grand Prix.

Porsche (W. Germany)

Ferdinand Porsche had worked for both Austro-Daimler and Mercedes-Benz before he set up his own design business in Stuttgart in December 1930. Designs for a cheap car were completed for both NSU and Zundapp, but came to nothing. The Porsche Type 60 designed in 1934 became the first streamlined Volkswagen (q.v.) Beetle. After the war Porsche returned from internment to find that his son, Ferry, had designed a new Cisitalia racing car and a new sports car. The latter, known now as the Porsche 356, went into production in June 1948 in rented workshops at Zuffenhausen, Stuttgart, where Porsche are based today. The early cars were distinguished by their 1086 cc engines, but later models had 1131 cc versions of the flat-4 air cooled engine which was positioned at the rear. The streamlined two-seater coupé body was a continuation from the Beetle design and featured simple all-independent suspension by torsion bars at the front and swing axles at the rear. The 356 was first exhibited at the 1949 Geneva Motor Show and the following year an example won its class at Le Mans – the start of a long succession of racing achievements. By the time the 356 was first imported to Britain in 1957 the engine size had increased to 1582 cc with 60 or 75 bhp available, while Carrera versions for competition used a 1498 cc 2 ohc engine with 100 bhp or more. The later Super 90 version of the 356 had 90 bhp and was capable of about 110 mph/177 kph, while the final Carrera 2 models had a 1996 cc twin cam 4-cylinder engine producing 130 bhp and 4-wheel disc brakes. Some elements of the Carrera were

used for the classic 911 that went into production at the end of 1964, although it had a new flat-6 1991 cc 2 ohc engine with 6 carburettors and a 5-speed gearbox. The 130 bhp gave a 130 mph/209 kph top speed because of the streamlined shape of the fastback 2+2 coupé body with wedge-shaped nose and faired-in headlamps. In 1965 there was a new 912 which used the 911 body and mechanicals except for a smaller 1582 cc 4-cylinder engine giving 90 bhp. At the 1965 Frankfurt Motor Show the 912 was the first Porsche to have a removable Targa roof panel, for unlike the 956 there were no cabriolet versions of the 911/912 models. The 100,000th Porsche delivered, in 1966, was a 912 Targa. Sportomatic semi-automatic transmission was optional in 1968 and in 1969 the 911's engine size went up to 2195 cc and soon only the cheaper 911T model had carburettors. The 912 was replaced in 1969 by the VW-Porsche 914. This mid-engined 2-seater was designed by Porsche in collaboration with Volkswagen and had front and rear boots (trunks), a removable Targa top and sharp-edged styling by Gugelot Design. The 914 used a VW 411 1679 cc engine but there was also a Porsche 1991 cc version called the 914/6, though only 3360 of these were sold in 4 years. Both models had bodies made by Karmann and were replaced in 1973 by the VW-engined 1971 cc version of the 914, which went out of production in 1975. All 1969 911 models had more interior space because of a 2.4 in/60 mm increase in wheelbase to 89.4 in/2270 mm. The 150 mph/241 kph RS Carrera with 2687 cc 210 bhp engine and distinctive boot spoiler appeared in 1972, by which time the 911 models had 2341 cc engines making them capable of about 140 mph/225 kph. The following year the 2.7-litre engine went into the 911S. The 1975 911 Turbo brought even more performance from a 2993 cc engine producing 260 bhp and could exceed 150 mph/241 kph, though it was not the car to be entrusted to an inexperienced driver in the wet when it was all too easy to lose adhesion at the rear. Porsche had meanwhile been developing another sports car project for Volkswagen/Audi based around the Audi 2-litre engine, with VW Golf front suspension and VW K70 disc/drum brakes. When VW decided not to go ahead with the project Porsche bought back their design and marketed it as the Porsche 924. All previous models had been rear engined and air cooled but the 924's 1984 cc 4-cylinder 125 bhp unit was water cooled and at the front. It drove the rear wheels through a combined rear axle and gearbox. The coupé body had a rear glass hatch and offered 2+2 seating within a 94.5 in/2400 mm wheelbase. A completely different development was the use of a hot galvanized body/chassis unit for the 911 with a six-year anti-corrosion warranty in 1976, following on from the long life Porsche project first seen in 1973. There were also aluminium wheels and bumpers and a stainless steel exhaust system. Engine sizes of the 911 models were increased again in 1977 to 2993 cc for the normal models and to 3299 cc for the turbo which then had 300 bhp. The 1977 range was extended by the addition of the totally new 928 model which followed the design laid down by the 924 but had a longer wheelbase and bigger body, though still only offering 2+2 seating. Under the bonnet was Porsche's all-aluminium 4474 cc V8 engine giving 240 bhp. The steel monocoque body had detachable alloy panels and plastic front/rear ends instead of bumpers. In 1979 it developed into the 928S with 4664 cc V8 engine giving 300 bhp and raising the maximum speed from over 140 mph/225 kph to over 150 mph/241 kph. The ordinary 928 continued to be offered as well. The 924 was similarly given more appeal by the addition of a 924 Turbo version with 170 bhp and four-wheel disc brakes in 1978. This left a gap in the range between the 924 and the 924 Turbo which Porsche filled in 1982 with the 944, which was essentially a revised 924 with a new 2479 cc ohc 4-cylinder 163 bhp engine. There was a new 924S in 1985 with the same body but the 2.5-litre 244's 150 bhp engine, while a turbo version of the 944 was added with 220 bhp. Meanwhile the 911 Carrera had not been neglected and was available as a cabriolet from 1982 and had a bigger 3164 cc engine giving 231 bhp in 1983. The sleek aerodynamic 959, first seen in 1984 in production as opposed to competition form, began production in 1986. It had a twin turbo flat-6 engine at the rear producing 450 bhp from 2850 cc. To cope with all that power there was four-wheel drive and the claimed maximum speed was over 185 mph/300 kph. The galvanized steel chassis had Kevlar body panels and aluminium doors and bonnet. For the fortunate few this homologation special could

The first Porsche 356 model of 1948.

be purchased for around £155,000. The 928 had become Series 2 with the adoption of the bigger 4664 cc 310 bhp V8 engine and Bosch anti-lock braking in 1983, but was further improved for 1987 with a major revision to the V8 engine. Not only were there twin overhead camshafts and 4 valves per cylinder but the power was up to 320 bhp, while more efficient aerodynamics reduced the drag coefficient to 0.32. For 1987 the 944 too received a 16-valve cylinder head and became the 190 bhp 944S in the process. Besides producing 55,000 cars a year, Porsche also have a very successful research centre at Weissach which undertakes engineering and design work for leading European car manufacturers like Alfa Romeo, Fiat, Mercedes-Benz, Volkswagen and Volvo. There design work has even extended to the Contax RTS camera and the cockpit of the European A10 airbus.

Renault (France)

Louis Renault's desire for a 2-seater vehicle caused him to modify his ¾ hp de Dion tricycle in 1898 to produce such a car. He threw away the de Dion's chain drive to eliminate power losses and adopted instead a rear axle with shafts inside the hollow axle tube and a differential. The gearbox to which it was coupled was the first in the world to offer a direct-drive top gear in the manner we now take for granted and was patented on 9 February 1899. Louis Renault's brothers Marcel and Fernand subsidized him to the tune of 500 francs a month from the successful family drapery business, allowing Louis to expand production. This was aided by a win in the *voiturette* class in the 1901 Paris—Berlin race by the single-cylinder 8 hp Renault. The following year Marcel won the Paris—Vienna race with a larger 16 hp model. Its 4-cylinder engine had been designed by M. Viet who had joined the firm of Renault Frères from de Dion. It was the first Renault car to have an engine built by the firm and afterwards went into production as the 1902 Model K 14 hp, but with the engine size reduced from the 3.8 litres of the racing car to a more modest 2554 cc. It was a side valve, of course, with exposed valve springs and archaic gilled-tube side radiators for the thermo-syphon cooling which was to be a Renault feature for many years. More advanced were the 2-shoe internal expanding brakes (patented in 1902) and the tubular chassis. After Marcel was killed in the 1903 Paris—Madrid race Louis gave up racing and concentrated on car production and in 1905 introduced the 2-cylinder 1060 cc AX model with the coal-scuttle-shaped bonnet that was a Renault feature for years afterwards. By 1908, the year in which Fernand died and the company was renamed SA des Usines Renault, there were six models on sale in England. The 8 hp AX cost £306 and was supplemented by bigger 4-cylinder 10/14, 20/30 and 35/45 models, the latter costing £980 and having a 7964 cc engine. Even bigger was the new 50/60 hp model with Renault's first 6-cylinder engine of 9500 cc. This massive model with 156 in/3962 mm wheelbase could reach 75 mph/121 kph and at £1160 cost more than a contemporary Rolls-Royce. Pressure lubrication arrived in 1911 and by the start of World War I, in which Paris Renault taxis were used to transport troops, Renault were making their own detachable wooden wheels and had fitted electric lighting to the bigger models. Postwar all models had electric lighting and starting and the 6-cylinder model became the enormous and impressive 9-litre 40CV in 1921. In 1926 a special lightweight streamlined version was the first car to exceed 100 mph/161 kph for 24 hours. The bigger cars had front-wheel brakes in 1922, and all models by 1925, while in 1923 a new economy 4-cylinder 951 cc KJ model with Michelin disc wheels was added. It cost £320 in Britain. Nearly as big as the 40CV was the JY model added the same year, though it had a 4767 cc 6-cylinder engine. The 1927 Light Six had a 3181 cc engine with detachable cylinder head and coil instead of magneto ignition. The 1929 7125 cc Reinastella was Renault's first straight-8 with front radiator, pumped coolant circulation and servo-assisted brakes. In England the chassis price was £1550. Most models had front radiators and coil ignition by 1931, though there was a reversion to thermo-syphon cooling in 1932. The bigger models had synchromesh gearboxes in 1933 and it was extended to the rest of the range in 1934. A cheaper Nervasport version of the 8-cylinder Reinastella won the 1935 Monte Carlo Rally. By then the 1463 cc 8CV had evolved into the swept-tail Celta-quatre (Airline in England) and the short-chassis Monaquatre which were offered in 1936 with the option of a new 2383 cc side-valve engine and a dashboard gearchange. That was also a feature of the 1938 1003 cc unitary construction Juvaquatre which sold for £140 in Britain. During the war Renault operated under German control and Louis Renault died in prison in 1944, accused of collaboration with the Nazis. Renault was then nationalized with resistance hero Pierre Lefaucheux at the helm. The first cars to appear from the Regie Nationale des Usines Renault were an updated version of the Juvaquatre with hydraulic brakes, and the completely new 4CV. This had a rear-mounted 4-cylinder 760 cc ohv engine and all-independent coil spring suspension. For the British market it was assembled at Acton, as Renault models had been since 1925, and over a million 4CV models had been built in France and Britain by the time production ended in 1961. Thereafter British market Renaults were imported. In 1951 the 4CV's engine size was reduced to 748 cc and a bigger 2-litre Fregate model was announced but was not a big seller. The 1956 Dauphine, which continued the rear-engined theme with an 845 cc unit, became the first French car to sell over two million, despite its poor handling. From 1957 there were tuned Gordini versions with more performance and they led to the Floride sports coupé in 1959. In 1962 the Dauphine was supplemented by the square-shaped R8 with new 956 cc 4-cylinder engine, still in the rear, and 4-wheel disc brakes. The R8 was the first mass-produced car with the latter. The new engine also went into the Floride which was renamed the Caravelle. Cheaper motoring was provided by the new R4 utility model with estate-car-like body, removable seats and a rear door. It was powered by a 747 cc engine driving the front wheels, had all-independent suspension and cost £583 in England in 1961. A year later the engine size was increased to 845 cc and in 1963 Renault had a big car again in the form of an American Rambler built under licence. The 1964 R8 Major had a longer nose and 1108 cc 46 bhp engine. The family-sized 16 model of 1965 pioneered the modern hatchback saloon and was a very versatile people and luggage carrier. The rear seats could be removed, or swung up into the roof, to accommodate large loads. Like the 4 it had all-independent suspension and the use of rear torsion bars for this meant that the wheelbase length differed on the two sides of the car. The 16 was powered by a 1470 cc engine driving the front wheels, and as on the R4 the engine was mounted longitudinally but back-to-front with the gearbox ahead of it. It was available with a 1565 cc engine from 1968, a 3-speed automatic gearbox from 1969, and a more powerful 1647 cc engine from 1973, when a 5-speed gearbox was also available. By the time production ended in 1979 over 1.8 million had been built. The 1968 Renault 6 was a re-bodied hatchback version of the 4, which continued, with 845 cc at first but later 1108 cc. It was followed in 1969 by the 12 which was a conventional 4-door saloon with 1289 cc engine driving the front wheels, a concept to which Renault were now firmly committed. The 1971 15 and 17 were really sporting coupé versions of the 12. Both used the same bodyshell, though the 17 had a slatted rear quarter panel where the 15 had a window, with rear hatch. Both 1289 and 1565 cc engines were fitted and the most powerful 17TS model had fuel injection and 108 bhp. The small hatchback 5 introduced in 1972 was to prove a best seller. Initially available with a 782, 845 or 956 cc engine, it was later offered with 1108, 1289 and 1397 cc units. Suspension was all independent and early cars had a gear-lever that emerged from the facia. Later this was changed to a less precise remote floor change. The moulded plastic bumpers, which absorbed minor knocks, were a first on a production car. The 30TS, introduced in 1975, was Renault's first front-wheel-drive big car and used the PRV (Peugeot-Renault-Volvo) 2664 cc V6 engine in a 105.1 in/2670 mm wheelbase hatchback body with all-independent suspension and 4-wheel disc brakes. The same body was used by the 1647 cc 20 version added in 1976 and later available as a 2 litre. The 14 added to the range in 1976 was like a grown-up 5 but differed considerably under the bonnet where a new 1218 cc alloy overhead camshaft engine was mounted transversely, for the first time on a Renault, and there was MacPherson strut suspension. In 1978 Renault's electronically-controlled automatic transmission (first seen on the 16 in 1969) was offered on the 5; a 5 Alpine won the Monte Carlo Rally and was followed by Alpine/Gordini production versions, and there was a new 4-door family saloon called the 18. This used 1647 and 1397 cc engines and eventually replaced the 12. A deal with American Motors led to the 5 being marketed by them in the USA as *Le Car*, followed later by the 18; in return Renault sold AMC's Jeep models in Europe. By the end of 1980 Renault had a 46 per cent stake in AMC. 1980 saw a mid-engined turbocharged rally version of the 5, a diesel 18 and the new Fuego coupé with curved glass rear hatch that replaced the 15 and 17. In 1981 the 18 was the first Renault family model to be turbocharged with the 1565 cc engine producing 110 bhp, and a year later there were turbo versions of both the 5 Gordini and the Fuego. The big news of 1981 though was the completely new lightweight 9 saloon which was the first European car to be built in the Japanese manner and was offered with 1108 or 1397 cc engines mounted transversely and driving the front wheels. Unusual rocking Monotrace seats had the runners spaced wide apart so rear passengers had more footroom. The 11 model that followed in 1983 was

1959 Renault 4CV 750.

in essence a hatchback version of the 9. The Renault 9 was also built in AMC's Wisconsin plant and sold in the USA as the Alliance, while the 11 was called the Encore. That year the ageless 4 was given a new lease of life with 1108 cc engine in GTL form; by 1986 over 7 million 4s had been built. For 1984 there was a new big model called the 25, a hatchback powered by either 1995 or 2165 cc 4-cylinder engines or the PRV 2.7-litre unit with fuel injection and 142 bhp. There was also a 2068 cc unit in diesel or turbo form. The 25's aerodynamic shape had a drag coefficient of just 0.28 (the best of any production car) and the car bristled with electronics, used not only for instrumentation and voice-synthesized warnings but also engine management. At the end of 1984 the 5 was replaced by a totally new version using the 9/11 engine and transmission installed transversely. Also new was the Espace people carrier built by Matra and using the 25's 2-litre engine. The 2849 cc V6 Alpine-Renault GT was a glass fibre-bodied 2+2 coupé capable of over 140 mph/225 kph and though built by Alpine was marketed through the full Renault dealer network from its launch in 1985. The new aerodynamic 21 with 1721 or 1995 cc engines and diesel options replaced the 18 in 1986 and in 1987 it was sold in the USA by American Motors as the Medallion. AMC Renault's Premier, built in the USA, was a re-skinned 4-door saloon version of the 25, using AMC's 2.5-litre or Renault's new 3-litre V6 PRV engine.

Rolls-Royce (UK)

Henry Royce was a Manchester electrical engineer who built three experimental 10 hp 2-cylinder cars, based on a Decauville he owned, in 1903–4. A meeting in Manchester with the Hon. Charles Rolls, then in partnership with former Automobile Club secretary Claude Johnson and selling foreign cars in London, resulted in Rolls and Co. agreeing to sell the cars produced in the Royce electrical factory in Cooke Street under the name Rolls-Royce. A 10 hp model bearing that name and the now famous radiator shape was exhibited by Rolls at the 1904 Paris Motor Show. For 1905 15 hp 3-cylinder, 20 hp 4-cylinder and 30 hp 6-cylinder models were added and there was also an unsuccessful 3593 cc V8-engined model. A 20 hp model with Rolls driving won the 1906 Tourist Trophy race in the Isle of Man. Royce was a perfectionist who was always improving the product and when he turned his attention to the 6-cylinder model the result was 1906's completely new 40/50 hp model now commonly known as the Silver Ghost. Strictly speaking there is only one car entitled to that name and it was *The Silver Ghost* (now owned by Rolls-Royce Motor Cars Ltd) that played a major part in establishing the company's reputation for engineering excellence. In 1907 it completed 14,371 miles/23,127 km under RAC observation without an involuntary stop and established a new world reliability record. The 40/50 hp model's 7046 cc side-valve engine was built of two 3-cylinder blocks with a 7-bearing crankshaft and had pressure-fed lubrication. The engine was flexibly mounted in the 135.5 in/3442 mm wheelbase chassis and the car cost £985 as a chassis in 1907. Leading coachbuilders supplied the bodies for all Rolls-Royce cars which were sold in this way until 1949. C. S. Rolls & Co. had ceased to trade after the formation of Rolls-Royce Ltd on 16 March 1906, and from 1907 onwards the only Rolls-Royce model was the 40/50. In 1910 the adventurous Rolls was the first man to be killed in a flying accident, but by then he had largely lost interest in the cars anyway. It was left to Royce to improve the 40/50 Silver Ghost successively year by year. Competition successes included the 1913 and 1914 Austrian Alpine Trials and the 1913 Spanish Grand Prix. Many 40/50 chassis were converted to staff and armoured cars during World War I, after which electric lighting and starting were standardized and 4-wheel brakes using a gearbox-driven mechanical servo were added in 1925. The 40/50 had been joined by the smaller 20 hp model with 3127 cc ohv 6-cylinder engine, costing £1100 as a chassis, in 1922. In May 1925 the New Phantom (later called Phantom I) replaced the Silver Ghost and was in essence the latter's chassis with a new

1907 Rolls-Royce *The Silver Ghost*.

overhead valve 7668 cc engine. It was also manufactured in the USA, where Rolls-Royce's Springfield factory had started building Silver Ghosts in 1921. The American venture ended in the Depression of 1931. The 1929 Phantom II, never manufactured in America although sold there, was a completely new, lower chassis with the engine and gearbox in one unit, and the latter was fitted with synchromesh from 1932. Continental versions of the Phantom II with stiffer springing were capable of about 95 mph/153 kph. Meanwhile the 20 hp had grown into the bigger and faster 20/25 with 3669 cc engine in 1929 and this engine was to form the basis for the 3½-litre Bentley after Rolls-Royce's purchase of that marque in 1931. Sir Henry Royce's death in 1933 (he had been created a baronet after the Schneider Trophy air race success in 1931) meant that he never lived to see either the famous Merlin aero engine in service or the V12-engined Phantom III motor car which he had inspired. With a 7340 cc engine developing 189 bhp, the Phantom III offered 100 mph performance that put many contemporary sports cars to shame. It was the first Rolls-Royce to be fitted with independent front suspension, which improved both the ride and handling compared with Phantom II, and despite a shorter wheelbase it offered more room for passengers. It was also fitted with a kneeling version of the Spirit of Ecstasy (Flying Lady) mascot, designed by Charles Sykes for Rolls-Royce in 1911 and fitted to their cars from then onwards. The 20/25 grew into the 4257 cc 25/30 hp in 1936 and this engine size was used in the 1938 Wraith which had independent front suspension. During the war Rolls-Royce concentrated on aero engine manufacture, but the car division engineers also adapted the Merlin engine into the Meteor for the Cromwell tank and then developed its chassis to take the extra power. From 1908 to 1940 every Rolls-Royce car had been made in the Derby factory designed by Royce, but postwar Derby was fully committed to aero engines. The Crewe wartime shadow factory was selected as the postwar home of the Rolls-Royce car which it remains today. The new 1947 Silver Wraith was offered only as a chassis and was powered by an F-head 4257, and later 4566, cc engine. This same unit powered the 1949 Silver Dawn with pressed steel body – the first car made entirely by Rolls-Royce. It was a Rolls-Royce version of the successful Bentley Mark VI and initially was available for export only with a steering column gearchange. The General Motors Hydra-matic automatic gearbox, manufactured by Rolls-Royce, was offered as an option on both models in 1952 (with the bigger engine), and the Silver Dawn had a revised body with bigger boot. The 1955 Silver Cloud, designed by John Blatchley, was completely new but followed the Silver Dawn formula. Until 1959 it used a 4887 cc 6-cylinder engine with automatic transmission but in that year it became the Silver Cloud II with new 6230 cc alloy V8 engine. The same engine went into the new Phantom V limousine, which replaced the Silver Wraith. The Phantom had a 145 in/3683 mm wheelbase and 238 in/6045 mm length, making it the biggest Rolls-Royce model ever, and became the Phantom VI in 1968 when it was the world's first production car with dual air conditioning systems. The 1963 Silver Cloud III with lowered bonnet and twin headlamps was a holding operation until the completely new Silver Shadow was announced in 1965. The first Rolls-Royce monocoque car, it also had power hydraulics providing Citroën-type self levelling and operating the 4-wheel disc brakes. It cost £6557 in 1965 and was to be the most successful model Rolls-Royce had ever produced with various refinements including a more powerful 6750 cc engine in 1969 and rack and pinion steering in 1977 during its 15 years in production. After Rolls-Royce Ltd went bankrupt in February 1971, the Car Division, led by David Plastow, was hived off and almost immediately launched the very successful Corniche 2-door derivative of the Silver Shadow. The 10,000th Silver Shadow (actually a Corniche convertible) followed in December 1971 and in 1973 Rolls-Royce Motors Ltd was launched as a public company. The 1975 Camargue, styled by Pininfarina and built by Rolls-Royce Motors' coachbuilding subsidiary Mulliner Park Ward, was a 2-door personal car based on Silver Shadow mechanicals. It was the world's first car with a bi-level fully automatic air conditioning system, developed at Crewe, and was the world's most expensive car at the time costing £29,250 ($90,000) – about the price of two Silver Shadows. In 1980 Rolls-Royce Motors merged with Vickers and the more modern Silver Spirit replaced the Silver Shadow, on whose running gear it was based. The Silver Spirit was fitted with a revised rear suspension, while American versions were equipped with fuel injection. In 1985 a 4 in/101 mm longer wheelbase Silver Spur version of the Silver Spirit was the 100,000th car made by Rolls-Royce. Rolls-Royce Motors was renamed Rolls-Royce Motor Cars Ltd in October 1986. For 1987 all Rolls-Royce models, except the Phantom, were fitted with fuel injection, and for European markets there was also anti-lock braking, while most models benefited from a package of improvements that included a programmable memory for the seat positions and a plug-in diagnostic circuit. The £195,595.83 Phantom VI, not sold in the USA, was the world's most expensive production car in 1987 and one of the few to retain a separate chassis on which the coachbuilt body was mounted.

Rover Group (UK)

The origins of the group go right back to the merger of Austin and Morris, which also owned MG, Riley and Wolseley, in 1952 to form the British Motor Corporation. In 1967 BMC merged with Jaguar, who also brought Daimler into the group which became British Motor Holdings. The merger of BMH and Leyland in January 1968 created the British Leyland Motor Corporation, then the fifth largest car producers in the world. As well as the makes already mentioned Leyland added Triumph, Rover and Land Rover and Alvis, although the latter no longer made cars. Initially there were two main groups: Austin-Morris, the volume producers, and Jaguar, Rover, Triumph, the specialist car group. The Riley marque was axed in 1969, followed by Wolseley in 1975 and by then the group were in desperate financial trouble which led to nationalization by the British Government that year. The new company was called British Leyland Ltd. Technical co-operation with Honda resulted in 1981 in the Ballade-based Triumph Acclaim, destined to be the last of that marque when production ended in 1984. Jaguar and Daimler became independent again the same year and Morris car production also ended in 1984 with the Ital. In July 1986 British Leyland's name was changed to the Rover Group plc by the new Government-appointed chairman, Graham Day, who came from British Shipbuilders. Only Austin, MG, Rover and Land Rover now remain as Rover Group car marques, with production centred on the Cowley and Longbridge factories that were once Morris and Austin respectively.

Rover (UK)

In 1877 J. K. Starley and W. Sutton formed a partnership to make bicycles in Coventry and the name Rover was first used for a pedal cycle in 1884. The Rover safety bicycle, which was the forerunner of the bicycle we know today, appeared in 1885 and the Rover Cycle Co. was formed in 1896. Starley died in 1901 and the following year the first Rover motor-cycle costing £55 was built. It was followed by the first Rover car, an 8 hp 1327 cc single-cylinder model costing £200, in 1904. That was joined in 1905 by a smaller 6 hp 780 cc model with a wooden chassis, and by the 4-cylinder 1767 cc 10/12 hp and 3119 cc 16/20 hp models. Rovers finished 5th and 12th in the 1905 Tourist Trophy race and at the end of the year the Rover Co. Ltd was formed. In 1907 Rover entered the TT again with a 16/20 hp model with 4-speed gearbox – and it won. There was a 2-cylinder 12 hp model in 1908, joined the following year by the 4-cylinder 2488 cc 15 hp model with distinctive heart-shaped radiator. Both the 8 and 12 were offered with Knight sleeve-valve engines in 1911 and 1912, but from then on the 4-cylinder 12 hp model designed by Owen Clegg was to be the main model. Its actual RAC rating was 13.9 hp and the 2297 cc engine was a monoblock unit and unusually the inlet and exhaust manifolds were cast into the cylinder block. It cost £350, and had electric lighting. Rover had produced a new 3½ hp motor-cycle in 1911 and built over 3000 of them for war use between 1915 and 1919, as well as producing 3-litre Sunbeam staff cars and Maudslay lorries. The 12 hp was on sale again in November 1919, but then cost £750 due to inflation! In 1920 Rover purchased a new factory at Tyseley, where the little 8 hp model designed by Jack Sangster went into production. It had a simple channel-section chassis with ¼-elliptic springs and a 998 cc 2-cylinder air-cooled engine producing 14 bhp. Maximum speed was about 30 mph/48 kph and it cost £300. Rover motor-cycle production ended in 1924 and that year the 8 hp was replaced by the 4-cylinder 1074 cc ohv 9/20 which used the 8 hp chassis. The 1925 14/45 hp was actually the 12 with a new cam-in-head 2132 cc engine designed by Peter Poppe, of White and Poppe. It won Rover the Dewar Trophy from the RAC for making 50 consecutive ascents of the Welsh mountain pass Bwlch-y-Groes. In 1926 the 14/45 became the 2413 cc 16/50 with more performance but Rover's

losses mounted with £123,450 in 1925/6 followed by £77,945 in 1926/27. The result was that Peter Poppe was forced to leave, Jack Starley (son of the founder) was sacked and S. B. Wilks was appointed general manager in 1929. He brought with him from Hillman his brother Maurice and when Spencer Wilks became managing director the Rover quality-first philosophy was established. In the meantime the 10/25 replaced the 9/20 with a larger engine, new chassis and pressed steel body, while the price was reduced from £250 to £189. The 1928 2-litre, designed by Poppe, was the first 6-cylinder Rover and in January 1930 a short chassis Light Six beat the famous Blue Train from St Raphael in the South of France to Calais by 20 minutes, averaging 62.5 mph/100.6 kph for 725 miles/1168 km. The 1930 Meteor was a larger 2565 cc version of the 2-litre and ran until 1933, while the 1932 Pilot was a 6-cylinder version of the 10/25. A new era for Rover started with the 1934 P1 models (10 and 12 hp 4-cylinder and 14 hp 6-cylinder) which established Rover's quality reputation and were supplemented by the big Speed 16 and Speed 20 models. The re-styled P2 of 1937 was offered in a variety of chassis lengths and horsepower ratings from 10 to 20 and was fitted with synchromesh gears in 1939. Postwar the 10 hp 1389 cc model was the first to go back into production, followed by other P2 versions. Independent front suspension came with the 1948 P3 60 and 75 models. They used a new overhead inlet, side exhaust valve arrangement for the 1595 cc 4-cylinder and 2103 cc 6-cylinder engines. The 1.6-litre 60 engine was also used in a new type of utility vehicle called the Land Rover. It came about because Maurice Wilks, Rover's technical chief, wanted a vehicle which would replace the Willys Jeep on his Anglesey estate and be capable of going anywhere and tackling jobs like ploughing and hauling logs. Another factor was that Rover's new Solihull factory needed a stop-gap product to make while the new postwar models were being developed. The first Land Rover had an 80 in/2032 mm wheelbase, permanent 4-wheel drive and could be fitted with all sorts of optional equipment. Longer wheelbase versions, bigger engines, selectable 4-wheel drive and a diesel (in 1957) followed. Far from being a stop-gap it became the mainstay of Rover production and the millionth was built in 1976, by which time wheelbases had been standardized for many years at 88 and 109 in (2235 and 2769 mm). More power came with a 3½-litre V8-engined version in 1979 and the current One Ten was launched in 1983. For the first time it had all-independent coil spring suspension and just the one 110 in/2794 mm wheelbase. In the meantime the completely new P4 75 model with distinctive 'Cyclops' central pass light, a full width body with concealed running boards and the 2103 cc 6-cylinder engine was being prepared for announcement in September 1949. For more than a decade it was to be the main Rover model, fitted with a variety of engines. The first of these was the bigger 2638 cc unit which powered the 1954 90 and at the end of that year there was a bigger boot and wrap-round rear window. The 1957 105R had Roverdrive semi-automatic torque converter 2-speed transmission plus overdrive, while the manual 108 bhp model was called the 105S. The 1958 P5 was a big saloon and the first monocoque Rover on a 110.5 in/2807 mm wheelbase. It was powered by a new 2995 cc 6-cylinder engine. In 1959 front disc brakes were fitted to P4 and P5 and in 1962 the Mark II 3-litre with 121 bhp became a genuine 100 mph/161 kph car for the first time. The last P4 was built at Solihull at the end of May 1964, production of the model totalling 130,342. Despite its 'auntie' image the P4 had also formed the basis for the world's first gas-turbine car, for the 1950 Jet 1 was based on the 75 with the turbine fitted behind the front seats. The P6 2000 which replaced the P4 was altogether different and featured a skeleton body frame with detachable panels, a 4-cylinder 1978 cc ohc engine and de Dion rear suspension with inboard disc brakes. When the Rover sales department learned it had only four seats as well as 4 cylinders they gave up all hope of selling the projected 500 cars a week. In fact demand for the £1,265 2000 was such that Rover were soon struggling to make 800 a week! Rover took over Alvis in 1965 and in 1967 merged with the Leyland Motor Corporation, becoming part of the British Leyland Motor Corporation in January 1968. Prior to this the P5 had been given a new lease of life when Rover managing director Bill Martin-Hurst had acquired the rights

1960 Rover P4 100.

to manufacture a 3528 cc alloy V8 engine that Buick no longer wanted. Fitted with it the 3-litre became the 3.5 P5B in 1967 and the following year the V8 was installed in the 2000 body to create the 3500. This engine also formed the power unit for the 1970 Range Rover, which was a more civilized form of Land Rover with 2-door estate car body, permanent 4-wheel drive, all-independent suspension for off-road use and 100 mph/161 kph performance. A new £25 million production facility at Solihull with a capacity of 30,000 cars a week was commissioned in 1976 to build the SD1 3500 which replaced the P6, and also the P5B which had been discontinued in 1973. The 5-door hatchback body with folding rear seats and wedge-shaped nose was based on a 110.5 in/2807 mm wheelbase (the same as the P5) to give more passenger accommodation yet it weighed only 23 lb/10.4 kg more than the old P6 3500. An increase in engine power to 155 bhp made 120 mph/193 kph possible and there was a 5-speed gearbox as well as automatic transmission. In 1977 2350 and 2597 cc 6-cylinder overhead camshaft engines of Triumph design went into the SD1 to create the 2300 and 2600 models. These models replaced not only the P6 2200 Rover, but also the Triumph 2000/2500 in the British Leyland rationalization. Styling changes followed in 1982 when there was a new 1993 cc 2000 model using the BL O-Series engine and a 2400SD Turbo model with a VM diesel engine. These changes coincided with the move of Rover production from Solihull to the former Morris factory at Cowley, though production of the Land Rover and Range Rover (now with 4 doors) continued at Solihull. The small 1342 and 1598 cc 4-cylinder 213 and 216 models introduced in 1984 were actually based on the Honda Civic under British Leyland's manufacturing and design co-operation agreement with Honda. In 1986 Rover Group (q.v.) became the name for the former British Leyland and there was a new 800 Series Rover to replace the SD1. Though similar to Honda's Legend, the Rover 800 was in fact a joint design with Rover styling, brakes and suspension. The aerodynamic (Cd. 0.32) 4-door saloon body was offered with two engines. The cheaper 820 models had a British designed and built 1994 cc twin cam 16-valve 4-cylinder unit with Lucas fuel injection producing 120 or 140 bhp. The top 825i and Sterling models were fitted with Honda's 2494 cc ohc V6 with Honda PMG-FI injection producing 173 bhp. Both engines were mounted transversely, driving the front wheels through Honda gearboxes and there were 4-wheel disc brakes. Bosch ABS was optional on the 825i and standard on the Sterling which also had air conditioning and an electronic memory facility for the seat positions. All models were comprehensively equipped in the usual Japanese manner and even electric windows and central locking were standard equipment. The one-piece bodysides (windscreen pillar to tail) of the 108.7 in/2760 mm wheelbase 800s were the largest ever on the Cowley assembly line which also built Honda Legends for Europe. Rovers for Japan and the Far East were built by Honda. British prices for the 800 Series ranged from £10,750 for the 820E to £18,975 for the Sterling in October 1986 when the cars were announced. In 1987 the 800 went on sale in the USA under the Sterling name with the 825S costing $19,000 and the 825SL $23,900 – both considerably cheaper than in Britain, and undercutting Honda's Legend in the USA.

Saab (Sweden)

Svenska Aeroplan Aktiebolaget, which we now abbreviate to Saab, was formed in April 1937 to manufacture military aircraft at Trollhattan. Postwar the company decided to diversify into car production and a prototype, styled by Sixten Sason, was shown in 1947. Production of this first model, called the 92, did not start until 1949. It was far from conventional with an aerodynamic (0.35 Cd) body featuring faired-in headlamps and a tiny rear window in the sloping tail. Access to the boot was from within the car. The front wheels were driven by a 764 cc 2-stroke engine with thermo-syphon cooling and there was independent suspension all round by torsion bars. The first 5300 cars were produced in a single colour (green), but for 1953 there were an opening boot and a larger rear window. The following year engine and transmission manufacture moved to a new plant at Gothenburg. The Saab 93 was announced in December 1955 and used the same body with a new 748 cc 3-cylinder engine positioned longitudinally and producing 33 bhp. For the first time there was pumped cooling and a fan, plus 12-volt electrics and a new coil spring rear suspension. A year later this became the first model exported to the USA. The 1956 Sonett (94) was shown as a prototype sports coupé with glass fibre body but only six were built. The nearest Saab were to come to a sporting model at that time was the 1958 Gran Turismo 750, based on the 93 but with extra equipment and 45 bhp. Completely new was the 95 estate car model with 841 cc 2-stroke engine giving 38 bhp and a 4-speed gearbox. It was followed in February 1960 by the 96 saloon version which replaced the

1949 Saab 92.

93. An aerofoil was added to the roof of the 1961 model 95 to keep the rear window clean and ignition was now key-operated. Front disc brakes appeared on the 1962 Sport (Granturismo 850 in USA) which had three carburettors, 52 bhp and a separate oil lubrication system for the 2-stroke engine. No longer did one have to add oil to the fuel tank as well as petrol. An anti-theft provision on 1964 models prevented the ignition key being withdrawn from beside the gearlever unless the latter was in reverse. In January 1965 the 250,000th Saab was built and in May the company became Saab Aktiebolag. In 1967 there was an alternative engine, Saab's first 4-stroke, for the 95 and 96. The 1498 cc V4 engine from Ford of Germany had been used in the Taunus 12M from 1962 and in the Saab installation gave 65 bhp. The glass fibre Sonett II (type 97) went into production in 1967 and after 258 2-strokes had been built the subsequent versions were fitted with the new V4 engine, which was more acceptable in the USA. At the end of the year there was a completely new and much bigger 2-door saloon, again styled by Sixten Sason. Front-wheel drive was retained but a new 1709 cc ohc 4-cylinder engine, built by Triumph for Saab, was used and there were 4-wheel disc brakes with divided hydraulic circuits. The comprehensive heating system had separate controls for the rear and a hot air supply to the rear window. When the 99 went into production at the end of 1968, 2-stroke versions of the 95 and 96 were discontinued, though the V4 95 was to survive until February 1978 and the 96 until January 1980. In 1969 Saab merged with Scania Vabis to form Saab-Scania AB, and car production was started in Finland. The 99 was available with Bosch electronic fuel injection and Borg-Warner automatic transmission in 1970, when a 4-door version was also added. The Sonett III with longer hatchback body went into production the same year and in 1971 received a 1698 cc engine, which also went into American versions of the 95/96. In 1971 the

99's engine was enlarged to 1854 cc by boring it out to 77 mm, increasing the power to 88 bhp, or 95 bhp in the most powerful fuel-injected form. Impact-absorbing bumpers with a cellular structure and an electrically heated driver's seat were other 99 refinements. During the year Saab became the world's first manufacturers to fit a headlamp wash/wipe system (on the 95/96 and 99). The 1972 EMS (electronic manual special) model was the first to use the 1985 cc Swedish version of the Triumph engine which produced 110 bhp. Sonett production ended in the autumn of 1974, after 10,236 had been built, because it could not meet American safety regulations but a Combi Coupé version of the 99 with hatchback rear door was added to the range. The 1977 99 Turbo with 145 bhp was the first European mass-produced turbocharged car. The new 900 3- and 5-door model introduced in 1978 had a 2 in/50 mm longer wheelbase than the 99, whose engines it used. Features included a replaceable filter cartridge for air entering the car that trapped pollen and about 50 per cent of airborne bacteria, and an electronic speedometer. In 1980 an Automatic Performance Control system, which reduced the problem of pinking by using an electronic knock sensor to limit boost pressure on the Turbo, was a world first for Saab but was not seen on production cars until 1982. A 900 4-door saloon was added to the 1981 range and the 2-litre engine was redesigned, becoming known as the H-engine. Production of a 7.9 in/200 mm longer limousine version of the 900 started in Finland in 1981 and it was designated the Finlandia in some markets and the CD in others. A twin cam 16-valve version of the APC Turbo with 175 bhp was announced in 1983 and the following year all models had breakerless electronic ignition. The 1984 9000 hatchback with distinctive wrap-around rear window was the first completely new Saab for 17 years and was an additional, slightly bigger model. It appeared first with the 16-valve turbo engine, but in 1986 a fuel-injected version of the 1985 cc engine without the turbo and with 130 bhp was offered. For 1987 the 9000 was offered with Teves 3-circuit anti-lock brakes and all 900 models were fitted with improved energy-absorbing bumpers. Saab's first convertible model, the 900 cabriolet, went into production in Finland.

Subaru (Japan)

Although one of the smaller Japanese car manufacturers, Subaru are part of Fuji Heavy Industries which was formed in 1953. The six stars in the Subaru badge represent the companies which merged to form FHI, which was based around the former Nakajima Aircraft Co. Ltd that had been Japan's largest aircraft manufacturer until the end of World War II. Today FHI includes aircraft and helicopters, coaches, railway locomotives and cars among its products. The first Subaru car was the monocoque 360 model, looking a little like a Fiat 500, produced in 1958. Its air-cooled 2-stroke 2-cylinder engine developed 16 bhp and there were rack and pinion steering and all-independent suspension. The 1966 1000 FE model was the first full-sized Subaru and was also Japan's first mass-produced front-wheel-drive car. The 977 cc flat-4 engine was water cooled and developed 55 bhp, or 67 bhp for the Sport version which had front disc brakes instead of the standard model's inboard drums. In 1968 Subaru signed a co-operation agreement with Nissan which was to result in Subaru building the Cherry model for Nissan. The FF model with 1088 cc engine succeeded the FE and was the first Japanese car to be fitted with radial-ply tyres. In 1970 there was an additional FF 1300G model with 1267 cc 80 bhp engine and the 360 was replaced by the more modern looking R2. The 1971 Leone coupé was completely new with all-independent suspension (by MacPherson struts at the front and semi-trailing arms at the rear) and front disc brakes. With a 96.6 in/2455 mm wheelbase it was bigger than the FF and also, at 52.9 in/1345 mm tall, lower. The 1361 cc flat-4 engine was offered with 80 or 93 bhp. In 1972 there was an estate car derivative of the Leone fitted with 4-wheel drive, the world's first mass-production road car to be so equipped. In the USA it was known as the Super Star. The Leone saloon was also available with 4-wheel drive in 1975. In 1972 the Rex minicar replaced the R2 and had a more modern body. At the end of 1973 the Rex was fitted with a new 4-stroke 358 cc 2-cylinder ohc engine giving 31 bhp at 8000 rpm. In 1977 Subaru's engines fitted with their SEEC-T exhaust gas recirculation system were the first to meet Japan's tough 1978 emissions requirements. On the Rex this was fitted to the 490 cc engine and there was also a new 1595 cc engine with 80 or 95 bhp for the Leone. For 1978 the Rex had a larger 544 cc engine, still at the rear and giving 31 bhp. In 1979 there was a completely new Leone with saloon and 2- and 3-door coupé bodies. Only the 3-door coupé was offered with the smallest 1299 cc engine, while the 1595 cc 87 bhp unit continued and was augmented by a larger 1781 cc 100 bhp version. A five-speed gearbox was now standard.

For 1980 there were new 4-wheel-drive Leone models in saloon, coupé and estate car form – all with different wheelbases. When the 4-wheel drive was not engaged they were front-wheel drive. That configuration was followed by the new 1981 Rex which also had all-independent suspension and front disc brakes. In 1983 there was an optional 665 cc 37 bhp engine for the Rex as well as the 544, and the following year the latter engine could be had in turbo form with 41 bhp and 4-wheel drive also available. Turbocharging had also been applied to the 1.8 Leone in 1983, giving 136 bhp. A year later the basic 1781 cc engine had an overhead camshaft for each cylinder bank, hydraulic tappets and fuel injection with power boosted to 105 bhp. The 1985 XT coupé offered 2+2 seating in a new body that was lower, longer and considerably more aerodynamic (0.29 Cd) than the Leone saloon. The 1.8-litre fuel-injected turbo engine produced 134 bhp, giving a maximum speed of 125 mph/201 kph and 0–62 mph/100 kph acceleration in 9.5 seconds. There were disc brakes all round and selectable 4-wheel drive, which on cars with automatic transmission was able to engage itself when necessary. Suspension was self-levelling with air springs. On the 4-wheel-drive turbo estate version the electro-pneumatic suspension was even computer controlled, providing automatic levelling at a choice of two ride heights. Damper (shock absorber) settings were also varied automatically to suit the vehicle's speed and load. The Justy 3- or 5-door hatchback, first seen as a prototype at the 1983 Tokyo Show, was added to the range in 1986. The 3-cylinder 998 or 1190 cc engines were mounted transversely and drove through a 5-speed gearbox in addition to which there was selectable 4-wheel drive. The more powerful engine had 3 valves per cylinder and produced 73 bhp. Also new in 1986 was the RX/II 3-door 134 bhp turbo coupé, the first Subaru with permanent 4-wheel drive and a dual-range (high and low ratio) 5-speed transaxle. In 1987 Subaru fitted the Justy with an electronically-clutched

1986 Subaru RX/II, sold as the XT Turbo coupé in the UK.

continuously variable transmission using the steel-belt drive pioneered and supplied by the Dutch company Van Doorne (Daf). This was the world's first production car with a CVT transmission which provided infinitely variable stepless gear ratios, in contrast to an automatic gearbox's three or four ratios which then needed multiplication by a torque converter.

Toyota (Japan)

Sakichi Toyoda invented an automatic weaving loom in 1925 and the Toyoda Automatic Loom Works Ltd were established in 1926 to manufacture it. Success brought diversification and in 1935 his son Kiichiro produced the first prototype car based on the Chrysler Airflow. The first Toyoda AA and AB models that followed had 3389 cc 6-cylinder engines producing 65 bhp. A change of name to the more phonetic Toyota came with the formation of the Toyota Motor Co. in 1937. Both cars and trucks were produced until the war stopped car production in 1942. In 1947 the 100,000th Toyota was produced and there was a new SA model. This aerodynamic two-door saloon had a backbone chassis and independent front suspension. Toyota Motor Sales were formed in 1950 to spearhead Toyota's marketing and a year later the 4-wheel-drive Land Cruiser with 3878 cc 6-cylinder engine appeared. The conventional 1453 cc 4-cylinder Crown saloon was added in 1955 and the smaller 995 cc Corona in 1957, the year that Toyota established a presence in the USA with the sale of some Land Cruisers. The 1961 Publica was the first small model with a 697 cc 2-cylinder air-cooled engine producing 28 bhp and an overall length of 138.6 in/3520 mm. By 1963 there was a much larger Crown with 1897 cc engine, optional Toyopet automatic transmission and a 105.9 in/2690 mm wheelbase body with twin headlamps. There was also an estate car version. The redesigned 1490 cc Corona saloon with 95.3 in/2420 mm wheelbase spearheaded Toyota's exports to the USA and Europe in 1965 and was the first model imported to Britain. The prestige Crown Eight was added to the range at the same time using a new and larger chassis and body than the Crown and was fitted with Toyota's first V8 engine. This light alloy unit was of 2599 cc and produced 115 bhp. At the 1965 Tokyo Show a fastback estate car variant of the Corona and 1988 cc 6-cylinder ohc engine for the Crown were shown. The car that attracted all the attention, though, was the new 2000GT sports coupé with a backbone chassis, all-independent suspension and 4-wheel disc brakes. The 1988 cc twin cam engine had been developed by Yamaha to give 150 bhp and a maximum speed of over 140 mph/225 kph was claimed. Toyota presented a 2000GT to model Twiggy in 1967 and she brought it back to Britain, while a special convertible version was featured in the James Bond film *You Only Live Twice* the same year. More significant was the 1966 Corolla saloon with 1077 cc engine, the first of a line that continues to this day. There was also a new 790 cc Publica and a Servicator for Corona, Crown and Publica models. The Servicator was connected to the speedometer and at specified intervals produced a printed card from a box on the facia giving instructions for the necessary safety checks or servicing. Toyota took over Hino in 1966 and Daihatsu in 1968. For that year there was a 1600 GT version of the Corona with 1587 cc twin cam engine giving 110 bhp and a new 2-litre Crown with perimeter chassis frame. Also new was the big 112.6 in/2860 mm wheelbase Century with pneumatic suspension and a 2981 cc V8 engine. 1968 was also the first year of Corolla exports to the USA and the first year Toyota production exceeded a million. For 1969 there was a larger Mark II Corona with 1587 or 1858 cc engine and front disc brakes, and a fastback coupé version of the Corolla called the Sprinter. For 1970 the Corolla was fitted with a longer stroke 1166 cc engine producing 83 bhp and there was a new Carina, which slotted between the Corolla and Corona, with 1407 or 1588 cc engines. The new Celica coupé shared the Carina's mechanicals but had a completely different body and was Toyota's first mass-produced sporting model. It was sold in the USA with some success from 1971 and the following year Toyota Motor Manufacturing USA Inc was formed to build pick-ups in the USA. The 1972 Crown was available with 1988, 2253 or 2563 cc 6-cylinder engines and there was a 1600GT version of the Celica with a twin cam 1588 cc engine giving 115 bhp. There were even 1000 and 1200 versions of the Publica in addition to the base 800. The 1973 Starlet which appeared in the Publica range was actually built by Daihatsu and was larger than the Publica with more modern styling and a 4 in/100 mm longer wheelbase. A Liftback (hatchback) version of the Celica was introduced during 1973 and it was also available with a 1968 cc ohc engine. For the 2000GT this was a twin cam unit producing 145 bhp. The big Century was also given a more powerful 180 bhp 3376 cc V8 engine. For 1974 there was a new Corona with 1.6-, 1.8- and 2-litre engines, while for the USA a

bigger 2189 cc (133 cu. in.) 4-cylinder was fitted but gave less power than the 1598 unit. The Celica hardtops sold in the USA were also fitted with a bigger 2289 cc (137 cu. in.) engine giving 96 bhp like the Corona's. American emissions requirements were the main reason for the new and bigger 1974 Corolla 30 which had more room under the bonnet and there was also a slightly different and better equipped version sold under the Sprinter model name. Toyota's engineering remained very conventional, though the styling and interior trim were a little garish at times. Between the Corona and Crown in size was the car known in Japan as the Mark II (but sold in Britain as the Corona) with 1.8- or 2-litre engines. The Crown itself was rebodied for 1975 and was fitted with a unique electronic device that locked all the doors as soon as the car exceeded 8 mph/13 kph. On 8 May 1976 Toyota became the first Japanese manufacturer to produce 20 million cars, the figure of 10 million having been reached in 1972. The 20 millionth car was a Corona and was followed in April 1977 by the millionth Celica, a Liftback model. Later that year there was a new body for the Carina/Celica range, following major changes to the Mark II (now called the Cressida in Europe) which had 4-wheel disc brakes and independent rear suspension for the first time. There was also a more luxurious version sold in Japan and the USA under the Chaser name. The Publica name was dropped in 1978 with the arrival of a new hatchback Starlet powered by a 1290 cc 72 bhp engine with 5-speed manual or 2-speed automatic gearbox. The larger Corsa/Tercel was completely new and was Toyota's first front-wheel-drive model, though the completely new light alloy 1452 cc ohc engine was positioned longitudinally. The updated Corona was now available in a 5-door hatchback version and there was a 2-litre twin cam engine with fuel injection – also used in the Carina GT and Celica GT (but not for the USA). A new 4-speed overdrive automatic transmission was available on the Corona, Mark II/Cressida and Crown while for the first time the latter was offered with a 2188 cc 72 bhp diesel option. In 1979 Toyota's production in Japan exceeded 2 million cars for the first time with 2,111,302 built, while in the USA sales exceeded half a million for the first time, reaching 507,816. In 1980 Toyota built 2,303,284 cars and overtook Chevrolet to become the world's biggest car maker and moved into the position of the world's third largest manufacturer behind General Motors and Ford. For 1980 there was a new Crown model and the top Crown Royal version was fitted with a 2759 cc 6-cylinder fuel-injected engine producing 145 bhp. The best-selling Corolla had been rebodied during 1979 and was now fitted with lightweight polyurethane-faced bumpers and there was a 1600 twin cam version. This was the start of major changes to the Toyota range in the early 1980s when the cars became more European both in looks and handling though engineering remained fairly conventional, at least to start with. Both Celica and Carina were new in 1981 following the rebodied Cressida/Chaser/Cresta at the beginning of the year. A new departure was the Celica Supra with 6-cylinder 1988 cc ohc or 2759 cc 2 ohc engines producing 125 and 170 bhp respectively, all-independent suspension and 4-wheel disc brakes in a hatchback coupé body. The same engines were fitted to the equally advanced Soarer 2-door coupé which was also available with a 145 bhp turbocharged version of the 2-litre engine for the first time on a Toyota. There was a new Corona saloon in January 1982, and the similarly styled bigger Camry that followed broke away from the mould in having a new 1832 cc engine driving the front wheels and, unlike the Carina, was also available as a hatchback. At the end of 1982 came Toyota's first 4-wheel-drive car (apart from the Land Cruiser) in the form of the Tercel estate car, while the first turbo diesel engine was seen in the Crown. The 1.8-litre Model F Space Cruiser was completely different, looking like a van but driving like a car and with seating for seven passengers and luggage space. On 1 March 1983 the 10 millionth Corolla built in Japan was produced and the same day Toyota also built their 40 millionth car, a Tercel. The major model change for the year was the Corolla which went front-wheel-drive and was offered with a range of engines producing up to 100 bhp in saloon models. These now had all-independent strut suspension and while the Corolla and Sprinter hatchbacks were almost identical there was a different Sprinter 4-door saloon for the first time. Both models shared most of the underbody structure, including the 95.7 in/2430 mm wheelbase, of the Camry and there was 4-speed automatic transmission for some versions. The coupés were not the same at all as not only did they have a new 1.6-litre 16-valve twin cam engine developing 130 bhp, they also retained rear-wheel drive as the Japanese liked to be able to slide the rear end under power. Thermostatically-controlled front grilles that opened or closed according to engine temperature were a novel feature and the Sprinter had pop-up headlamps. For 1984 the big Crown had a slightly

1987 Toyota MR2.

longer 107.1 in/2720 mm wheelbase while retaining the perimeter chassis frame. Along with this change went independent rear suspension with self-levelling and optional anti-lock brakes. The tilting telescopic steering wheel had a built-in memory so that it could take up the previously selected position when the driver got back into the car. The top Century model continued but with a 190 bhp 3995 cc V8 engine for 1984, while that year's Corona and Carina II models went front-wheel drive. The MR4 coupé that appeared in mid-1984, appropriately, was the first Toyota with a mid-engined configuration, which limited seating to two. In its most potent form it had the Corolla's 1587 cc power unit giving 126 bhp and a 124 mph/200 kph maximum speed. The 1985 Starlet was front-wheel drive with new 999 or 1296 cc engines, while Toyota's first model with twin turbochargers was the high performance 2-litre 24-valve version of the Mark II Cressida/Chaser/Cresta with 185 bhp. Even the Crown was offered with a 160 bhp turbo 2-litre or a 190 bhp 2954 cc 6-cylinder twin cam with fuel injection. There was even a Land Cruiser II with 2.4-litre petrol or diesel engine and coil spring suspension, though the station wagon versions retained leaf springs. For 1986 the Celica (Corona Coupé in Japan) was front-wheel drive with 1.8-litre or twin cam 1587 or 1998 cc engines. The Celica Supra, though, remained rear-wheel drive and became a shorter wheelbase version of the Soarer, which had earlier been offered with a 2954 cc 6-cylinder fuel-injected engine giving 204 bhp, or 230 bhp in turbo form. The new Supra was available with the non-turbo version and like the Soarer had all-independent suspension and all-disc brakes. Toyota's 1985 announcement that they planned to build cars in the USA from about 1988 was a follow-on from the joint manufacturing venture between General Motors and Toyota Motor Corporation started in 1984. The Chevrolet Novas that emerged from the New Motor Manufacturing Inc plant in Fremont, California, were based on the Toyota Corolla and in 1986 were 17th in the US car sales league, ahead of the imported Corolla which was 22nd, up

70 places from 1985. For 1987 there was a new Camry II with much sleeker body and an electronic instrument display, while a new 1998 cc twin cam 16-valve engine with fuel injection provided 132 bhp. The Camry had been Toyota's second best seller in the USA in 1986. For 1987 too there was the ultimate MR2 sports car with 145 bhp, despite a catalyst to control emissions, achieved by fitting an electronically-controlled Roots-type supercharger to the 1.6-litre twin cam 16-valve engine. For those who liked the wind in their hair, there was even a version with a removable targa roof panel. In 1986 Corona production in Japan, since the model's launch in 1957, had reached 5 million, and in January 1987 had risen to 6 million.

Vauxhall (UK)

Marine engines for launches were the main product of the Vauxhall Iron Works, who took their name from the part of London on the south bank of the River Thames where they were situated. The area itself took its name from a corruption of Fulk's Hall, the house of Fulk le Breant. He was a mediaeval mercenary who was granted the manor of Luton by King John for services rendered. Fulk le Breant's heraldic emblem was the griffin, a mythical beast that was half lion and half eagle, and it appears on the Vauxhall badge to this day. The first car produced by the Vauxhall Iron Works in 1903 was a single-cylinder 978 cc model rated at 5 hp. It had a pointed bonnet, tiller steering and two forward speeds with chain drive to the rear axle. It cost £136 in 2-seater form and was capable of about 25 mph/40 kph. An improved 6 hp model costing £150 followed in 1904 and successfully completed a Glasgow to London reliability trial that year. More expensive still was the 12/14 hp 3-cylinder announced in November 1904 at £375. It was the first multi-cylinder Vauxhall and was successful enough to necessitate production expansion and a move to Luton in 1905. It has been the home of Vauxhall ever since. For 1906 there was a smaller 3-cylinder 9 hp and a much larger 4-cylinder 18 hp with shaft drive that sold for

1926 Vauxhall 30/98 OE tourer.

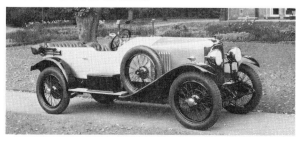

£475. This 18 hp model was the first to feature the fluted bonnet and radiator that were to be a Vauxhall hallmark for over 50 years. Amalgamation of the Vauxhall Iron Works with another engineering company in 1906 resulted in the Vauxhall and West Hydraulic Engineering Co. Ltd being formed, but in 1907 the car side was separated as Vauxhall Motors Ltd. New in 1906 had been the 2526 cc 4-cylinder 12/16 hp (which actually rated 21 RAC horsepower) and this was followed by a 20 hp 3054 cc model designed by Laurence Pomeroy and destined to win its class in the 1908 RAC 2000 Miles Trial. A streamlined version of this type A model was driven at Brooklands by A. J. Hancock at 100.08 mph/161 kph in October 1910, the first car of its horsepower to exceed 100 mph/161 kph. Three modified 20 hp cars with vee radiators were entered for the 1910 Prince Henry Tour in Germany. This reliability trial was named after its originator, Prince Henry of Prussia, and the Vauxhalls acquitted themselves well. Laurence Pomeroy's design was to become the first British sports car when the 3054 cc 4-cylinder C-type Prince Henry went into production for 1912. In the meantime the smaller 16 hp model B, launched in 1909, had been uprated to 26.8 hp by the expedient of adding another two cylinders, making it the first 6-cylinder Vauxhall. From late 1912 Prince Henry models were fitted with a bigger 3969 cc engine and in 1913 the model formed the basis of the classic 30/98 E-type with 4½-litre engine. The 1913 25 hp D-type which used the 4-litre Prince Henry engine in a bigger chassis was to become widely used as an army staff car during World War I, taking King George V to view the battlefield at Vimy Ridge and General Allenby into Jerusalem. Almost 2000 D-types had been made during the war and postwar it and the 30/98 continued in production though now with electric lighting and starting. For 1923 the 30/98 had a new 4253 cc ohv engine with 120 bhp and was designated OE, while the similarly equipped OD became the 23/30. The 30/98 acquired 4-wheel brakes at the same time and went up in price from £1195 to £1220. In this form it was capable of about 100 mph/161 kph with effortless 70 mph/113 kph cruising. Meanwhile the marque's appeal had been widened by the smaller 14/40 hp M-type powered by a 2297 cc engine and costing £595 in 1923. In 1924 Vauxhall pulled out of racing after the 30/98 had scored over 70 wins in hillclimbs and speed trials, though the special GP models entered for the 1914 and 1922 TT races were less successful. Almost as little known today is the 'instruction class' on Vauxhall cars that was run at the Luton factory for owners and chauffeurs in the 1920s. It cost £3 3s (£3.15) for a week's tuition. In 1925 there was a new and bigger 3881 cc 6-cylinder 25/70 hp S-type model which cost £1350 with tourer body. It was the only sleeve-valve-engined model Vauxhall ever made and lasted only until 1927/8. In December 1925 Vauxhall's model emphasis was changed when the company was acquired by General Motors for $2½ million. Vauxhall became GM's first overseas manufacturing plant, with an output of almost 1400 cars in 1925 rising to over 2500 in 1928. That year there was only one model, the new 20/60 R-type with 6-cylinder 2762 cc engine in a 120 in/3048 mm wheelbase chassis, though it was succeeded in 1929 by the similar but bigger 2916 cc T-type, which ended production in 1932 as the 3.3-litre T80. The 1930 Cadet priced at £280 opened up a whole new market for Vauxhall, whose previous models had been much more costly. Even the 17 hp Cadet had a 6-cylinder engine though, and there was a bigger 26 hp model as well. For 1932 the Cadet was the first British car with a synchromesh gearbox and the 1933 Light Six was even cheaper still with a 12 hp version at £195 and the more popular 14 hp at £215. Unprecedented, too, was the availability of 250 Light Six models for dealers to drive away from Luton for the launch. By the end of that year output from Luton was almost 10,000 cars a year. Bigger 2.4-litre 20 hp and 3.2-litre 26 hp Big Six models were added for 1934. The 20 hp sold for £325 and besides General Motors no-draught ventilation also had a novel pedomatic starter. The driver switched on and pressed the accelerator pedal to start the engine. The Light Sixes were succeeded in 1935 by the D-type 12 and 14 hp models with independent front suspension, for the first time on a medium-priced British car. In 1937 the Big Six models were replaced by the G-type 25 hp with independent front suspension, hydraulic brakes (used earlier on some 30/98 models) and a built-in heater. The 1937 10 hp Model H cost £168 and widened Vauxhall's ownership considerably but was also significant as the first British car with integral construction instead of the then conventional chassis plus body. It was powered by a 1203 cc ohv 4-cylinder engine and was capable of 40 mpg/7.0 litres/100 km. A similar 12 hp model added in 1938 had a 6-cylinder engine and there was also a 1781 cc 14 hp version using the same chassis. The successful 10 hp, which had sold 10,000 in five months, continued until 1939 when Vauxhall switched entirely to making Churchill tanks and Bedford

trucks. The latter had been introduced in 1931. In 1946 car production resumed with the pre-war 10, 12 and 14 hp models though the 10 was soon dropped. It was not until 1948 that the first new Vauxhalls arrived in the shape of the 1442 cc Wyvern and 2275 cc 6-cylinder Velox – the first Vauxhalls with steering column gearchange. For 1952 they were rebodied with curved windscreens and 1508 and 2262 cc engines. A de luxe Cresta version of the Velox was added in 1954. Vauxhall celebrated their golden jubilee in 1953 by a record annual output, which exceeded 100,000 for the first time, and the production of their millionth vehicle. The first Victor model of 1957 was criticized for its American styling, which included a wrap-around windscreen and an exhaust pipe that passed through the rear bumper, but it sold well. The 1508 cc Wyvern engine produced 52 bhp in the Victor, which cost £748 or £781 for the Super version. In 1958 the estate car version was the first to be produced by the factory, and there was a new American-styled Velox/Cresta complete with fins. General Motors Hydramatic automatic transmission became an option on this model in 1959, when a PA Cresta was the 2 millionth Vauxhall produced. For 1962 there was a new FB Victor in a more restrained style and a 71 bhp VX 4/90 version was offered for the first time and became the first Vauxhall with front disc brakes. More restrained styling for the Velox and Cresta followed a year later, when the Victor's engine size was increased to 1594 cc. The new small 1057 cc Viva was the big news of 1963 and it took Vauxhall/Bedford sales to a record 342,873 vehicles, with 100,000 Vivas built in the first 10 months after announcement. In 1966 there was a new 1159 cc HB Viva with coke-bottle styling and a luxury Viscount version of the Cresta, which by now had a 3.3-litre engine. The HB Viva was the first model to be built in the new Ellesmere Port factory on Merseyside. The 1967 FD Victor was much more modern, had new 1599 or 1975 cc overhead cam engines and safety features like a collapsible steering column. In 1968 the 2-litre engine was installed in the Viva to produce a GT model and the Cresta's 3294 cc 6-cylinder engine went into the Victor body to create the Ventora. The millionth Viva, the new 1256 cc HC, was built on 20 July 1971 and there was a new coupé version called the Firenza. The updated FE Victor with 1759 or 2279 cc ohc engines arrived in 1972 and these engines were also offered in the Viva and Firenza and were standard for the Magnum luxury version of the Viva in 1973. Considerable changes came in

1975 with the introduction of the Luton-styled Chevette hatchback, with 1300 Viva engine but other engineering from Opel's T-car Kadett, and the Cavalier which was an Opel Ascona, with a sloping nose peculiar to Vauxhall, built in Belgium. It marked the end of Vauxhall's independent engineering, for all that would in future be done by Opel (q.v.) in Germany. The 1976 VX saloons which replaced the Victors were the last to originate from Luton. In 1977 Cavalier production started at Luton and a 1300 version was added to supplement the 1584 and 1897 cc models. In 1978 there was a Sports Hatch Cavalier added and the new, bigger 2-litre Carlton (Opel Rekord with new nose) built at Luton replaced the VX range. Top model in the Vauxhall range was the 2784 cc 6-cylinder Royale, which shared much of the Carlton's engineering but was bigger and offered in saloon or coupé form. It also had independent suspension and disc brakes all round. The Royale was imported from Germany, where it was made by Opel and sold there as the Senator/Monza. For 1980 there was a new Astra (Opel Kadett), with front-wheel drive for the first time on a Vauxhall, to replace the Viva. Initially the Astra was a 1297 cc hatchback, but saloon (Belmont) versions and alternative 1196 and 1598 cc engines were added later. From November 1981 Astras were built at Ellesmere Port. The successful Cavalier which had given Vauxhall an important stake in the fleet market, was replaced by a new front-wheel-drive version of the GM J-car (Opel Ascona) in 1981. The new Cavalier saloons and hatchbacks were made at Luton from the outset and were so successful that the new aerodynamic 1983 Carlton 1800/2000 was imported from Germany to ease production at Luton. For 1984 there was a fuel-injected 1796 cc 115 bhp GTE version of the Astra, but the year's major news was the saloon or hatchback Nova (Opel Corsa), the first GM small front-wheel-drive car. It was built in a new factory in Spain and used 993 ohv, 1196 or 1297 ohc engines. A much more aerodynamic Astra using the previous model's mechanicals followed for 1984. Cavaliers were now offered with 5-speed gearboxes and diesel engines, as was the Astra. For 1987 there was a new Carlton (Opel Omega) with a class-leading aerodynamic body (0.28 Cd) and completely new 1.8- and 2-litre ohc engines with easily varied electronic ignition settings for 95 or 98 octane fuel. All-independent suspension and 4-wheel disc brakes with an anti-lock option were other features. In the Spring of 1987 a top Carlton 3000 GSi model, with 177 bhp fuel-injected 2969 cc

6-cylinder engine and anti-lock brakes as standard equipment, was added.

Volkswagen (W. Germany)

The origins of the Volkswagen (literally the people's car) go back to 1931 when Dr Ferdinand Porsche, then an independent designer, produced some schemes for a low-cost car with 5- and 3-cylinder engines for motor-cycle manufacturers Zundapp. They ran out of money, so Porsche sold the idea to NSU, for whom he built a car with a flat-4 1.5-litre air-cooled engine. That project too was stifled by lack of finance. It was a political dream that changed everything, for Adolf Hitler had recently come to power in Germany and wanted to build a cheap car 'to motorize the people'. Porsche met Hitler on 11 February 1933 and was staggered by the design requirements he had to fulfil. The car had to cruise at 62 mph/100 kph, have a fuel consumption better than 40 mpg/7.0 litres/100 km and seat five people. It was also stipulated that the engine must be air cooled and that the car should sell for less than 1000 Reichmarks. Porsche took up the challenge and the subsequent design was accepted and prototypes produced. In 1937 Daimler-Benz produced a second series of prototypes which looked rather like beetles, hence the Beetle designation that is now so familiar. On 26 May 1938 Hitler himself laid the foundation stone for the completely new factory at Fallersleben (renamed Wolfsburg in 1945) but construction was not finished by the outbreak of war in September 1939. So the thousands of Germans who had been paying 5 Reichmarks a week in a savings scheme to buy one of the new *Kraft durch Freude* (Strength through Joy) cars never took delivery. Instead in 1940 military KdF-wagen with 4-wheel drive began to emerge from the factory, which in April 1944 was 60% destroyed by Allied bombing. After the war both a British Commission, led by Lord Rootes, and Ford of America turned down the gift of the factory and the designs because they thought the car would never succeed. History has shown just how wrong they were. Civilian production of the familiar beetle-shaped car with a divided rear window and 1131 cc flat-4 air-cooled rear engine began in 1945 under the supervision of the British military authorities and 1785 were built that year. Simplicity was an essential part of the Beetle philosophy so the independent front and rear suspension used torsion bars (a system patented by Porsche in 1933) and the drum brakes were cable operated. The body itself was bolted to the platform chassis, which had a 94.5 in/2400 mm wheelbase, and the whole car was just 160 in/4065 mm long. Luggage accommodation was minimal in the front under the sloping bonnet (hood) but was supplemented by a trough behind the rear seats. Clever marketing turned the somewhat noisy air-cooled engine to advantage and the Volkswagen was advertised as the car which never boiled or froze. The first exports, to Holland, began in 1947 and the first Beetle for the USA was shipped from a Dutch port on 8 January 1949. Modifications to the design soon followed with hydraulic brakes in 1950, a synchromesh gearbox in 1952 and a larger 1192 cc engine in 1954. The first VW overseas assembly plant was built in Brazil in 1953 and the millionth Beetle took to the road in 1955. Minor restyling in 1958 included a larger single rear window. In 1961 there was a new 1500 saloon model, added in an attempt to widen the model's appeal but still rear-engined and air-cooled because it was based on the Beetle running gear. The 1493 cc engine gave 45 bhp compared with 34 for the 1200 but it was almost twice the price of the basic Beetle and about the same price as the special Karmann Ghia coupé on the Beetle chassis. There was also a 1500 Variant, which was the first VW estate car. In 1964 Volkswagen purchased a 50% share in Auto Union (Audi), then a subsidiary of Daimler-Benz (Mercedes). More power for the Beetle came with the arrival of the 40 bhp 1300 model in 1965 and at the same time the 1500 estate car was offered with an alternative 1584 cc engine, becoming the basis in that form for the additional new 1600TL fastback saloon. There was no 1600 saloon, though the 1500 saloon with 1493 cc engine was confusingly renamed the 1600A, and both 1500 and 1600 models were fitted with front disc brakes. Later the 1584 cc engine went into the 1600A which then became the 1600L saloon. The 10 millionth VW was built in 1965, the first year that Beetle production topped a million with 1,186,000 made. The following year the Super Beetle with 1493 cc 44 bhp engine, front disc brakes, wider rear track and revised rear suspension was introduced. Maximum speed was now 78 mph/125 kph and the extra performance caused some handling problems because of the model's oversteer. This led to a revised rear suspension layout with semi-trailing arms in 1968, introduced first on 1600 models available for the first time with Volkswagen's automatic gearbox and on 1500 Beetles fitted with the new Fitchel & Sachs semi-automatic transmission. Further diversification came with the bigger 98.4 in/2500 mm wheelbase 411 model later in

1968. It was the first Volkswagen with a monocoque bodyshell and the first with four doors. The 1679 cc 68 bhp engine was still air cooled and at the rear though the front suspension had gone over to the more modern MacPherson strut layout. Top gear was now direct, there were pendant pedals, an alternator and oval headlamps – all for the first time on a Volkswagen. Though the model was only a limited success it did not stop VW production reaching 7600 vehicles a day in 1968, by the end of which the 15 millionth VW had been built and 1,104,000 vehicles exported. In 1969 Volkswagen were the first manufacturers to equip their dealers with electronic and mechanical diagnostic equipment designed specifically for VW models by Bosch. The 1969 VW-Porsche used the 411 engine, was a sporting model which replaced the VW Karmann Ghia and was built by Karmann at Osnabruck. There were also more powerful 2-litre versions marketed by Porsche (q.v.). In August 1970 production of the K70 model started in a new factory at Salzgitter. The K70 was a former NSU model and the first tangible result of the merger of Audi and NSU in 1969. It was the first water-cooled Volkswagen and was also front-wheel drive, being derived from the NSU Ro80 though with a shorter 105.9 in/2690 mm wheelbase. The 1605 cc alloy engine gave 75 or 90 bhp, but like the 411 it was short-lived. The 1600 Super Beetle (1302) with longer nose, through-flow ventilation and MacPherson strut suspension replaced the 1500 in 1970 and grew into the 1303 model with wrap-around windscreen in 1972. On 17 February that year the Beetle passed the Ford Model T's production record of 15,007,033 cars. The completely new Passat (Dasher in USA) model, based on the Audi 80, replaced the 1600 models in 1973 and was offered with 1296 or 1471 cc ohc engines driving the front wheels, and there was a performance TS model with 85 bhp. The 97.2 in/2470 mm wheelbase body, styled by Giugiaro, was available in 2-door coupé, 4-door saloon or 5-door estate versions, the latter the first 5-door Volkswagen. It was followed in 1974 by a hatchback coupé derivative called the Scirocco, which was available with a new economy 1093 cc engine as well as the 1471 cc unit. Both these engines were used in the new Golf hatchback that arrived in June 1974 and was destined to replace the Beetle in Germany in 1978, the same year that production of the Golf started in the USA where it was named the Rabbit. In 1974, however, Beetle production was still running at 3400 a day, twice that of the Passat (Dasher), in Germany. The smaller Polo was

Volkswagen Beetle and new Golf in 1974.

launched in 1975 with 895 or 1093 cc engines and was a VW version of the Audi 50. Even though it was smaller than the Golf with a 91.7 in/2330 mm wheelbase compared with the latter's 94.5 in/2400 mm one, there was some overlap of the two models in Europe and the Polo was not sold in the USA. A completely new performance image emerged for Volkswagen with their 1588 cc fuel-injected 110 bhp GTI Golf and Scirocco models in 1976. A maximum speed of 112 mph/180 kph was not what people expected from Volkswagen and the Golf GTI soon became a cult car with a strong following. Less exciting but more significant was the 1500 diesel version of the Golf announced the same year. It was the first small car with a diesel engine that was acceptably quiet, had easy starting and reasonable performance. The 1977 Derby was a version of the Polo with a boot and the option of a 1272 cc 60 bhp engine and in 1979 the Jetta provided a similar saloon version of the Golf. Early in 1981 the Polo was restyled with a 3-door estate-like body and the booted version became known as the Derby/Polo Classic. Both Scirocco and Passat (Quantum in the USA) had new bodies soon afterwards and the latter was available with the 1921 cc 5-cylinder Audi engine. The additional Santana model was a 4-door booted saloon version of the hatchback Passat/Quantum and was also built by Nissan in Japan. Economy Formel E versions of the Golf/Jetta were marketed in 1981 aimed at those who commuted in heavy traffic. The economy came from stopping the engine, which was restarted by simply depressing the clutch once the traffic queue was on the move again. The best-selling Golf had now taken over the Beetle's mantle, though the latter was still being made in South America in 1987 with over 21 million models built. In 1982 there was increased performance for the Golf GTI with a 1781 cc 112 bhp engine, which was also offered in the Scirocco. In 1983, after 6,005,635 examples had been produced, there was a new Golf which looked very like its predecessor but had a longer 97.4 in/2475 mm wheelbase and a choice of 1272, 1595 or 1781 cc petrol engines plus a 1588 cc 54 bhp diesel

or 70 bhp turbocharged diesel. A new Jetta based on it was announced in January 1984, supplemented later in the year by a GT version with 112 bhp and fuel injection. Volkswagen's Synchro 4-wheel-drive system with viscous coupling was fitted to the Passat at the end of 1984 and offered on the Golf in 1986. In the summer of 1985 a trio of performance VWs arrived. The Passat GT used the Audi 5-cylinder 2226 cc engine with fuel injection and had 136 bhp, while a 16-valve version of the 1781 cc engine giving 139 bhp was available for the Golf GTI and Scirocco GTX. Performance of the latter two models was quoted at 0–60 mph/97 kph in 7.6 seconds and a maximum speed of 130 mph/209 kph. In July 1986 the Volkswagen Group acquired a majority holding in Spanish car manufacturers SEAT, bringing the group's employees up to 385,000 and raising car production to 12,000 a day. Best-selling model by far was the Golf, which reached a peak of 833,614 produced in 1979, with a daily production rate of about 3500. It was the best-selling car in Europe in 1985 and 1986 and, apart from Wolfsburg, was also built in countries as far apart as the USA, Nigeria and Yugoslavia.

Volvo (Sweden)

In 1924 nearly all the cars on Swedish roads were American and this influenced the thinking of Gustaf Larson and Assar Gabrielsson when they set about designing a native product. Three prototypes were completed in June 1926 using bought-out components. The conventional steel chassis was fitted with a 1944 cc side valve 4-cylinder engine and an open tourer body with the usual wooden frame. After the cars had run successfully the two men looked around for finance so that they could start production. In the end it was the SKF bearing company, for which Gabrielsson worked, that provided this plus a name for the new company from one that was on their files but not trading. SKF also provided the new AB Volvo company with a trademark in the form of the circle and arrow which still forms part of the Volvo badge and is the Swedish conventional sign for iron. SKF's finance was sufficient to provide for an initial production of 1000 cars, 500 OV4 tourers and 500 OPV saloons. The first production OV4 (OV standing for *oppenvagn* and PV for *Personvagn* – passenger car) model came off the assembly line on 13 April 1927 and was nicknamed 'Jakob', and was soon followed by the first PV4. The first models had brakes only on the rear wheels and with only 28 bhp were sturdy rather than fast. More performance came with the 3010 cc PV651 (6 cylin-

1938 Volvo PV36 Carioca.

ders, 5 seats) model in 1929 which had 55 bhp and a 116 in/2950 mm wheelbase. The longer wheelbase TR670 was used as a taxi, and later improvements included Lockheed hydraulic brakes, synchromesh and a free-wheel. The 1933 PV653 was fitted with a more powerful 3266 cc 6-cylinder engine and was the first Volvo with a steel body, fabric having been used for the early saloons. A larger PV656 model with vee radiator followed in 1935, when Volvo revealed their more modern PV36 with independent front suspension. Nicknamed the Carioca, the PV36 had been designed by Ivan Ornberg, who had worked for Hupmobile in America, and had aerodynamic lines very similar to the Chrysler Airflow. Only a few examples of this luxury model were sold before the outbreak of World War II, during which car production in neutral Sweden continued with the less expensive PV53 which was adapted to run on gas. The 1944 PV444 saloon was altogether different with independent coil spring front suspension, a distinctive steel body and a 1414 cc 4-cylinder engine producing 40 bhp. It soon enhanced Volvo's reputation for ruggedness and reliability, while in later twin carburettor 70 bhp Sport form it was rallied successfully. The PV444 continued in production until 1958 and then received the new B18 1778 cc 4-cylinder engine to become the PV544, which continued until 1965. By then 440,000 PV444/544 models had been built. In the meantime Volvo launched their much more modern P120 Amazon series, which like the PV544 had an integral construction body with 102.4 in/2600 mm wheelbase. Initially the Amazon was fitted with a 1583 cc engine giving 60 bhp but in 1961 received the new B18 unit that the year before had been fitted to the new P1800 sports car. In a way that was a successor to the P1900 which had been based on the PV444 and was an open 2-seater car with glass fibre body that had been built in California from 1954–7. The P1800 was not open, but was a sports coupé with rakish lines and 2+2 seating. The integral construction bodyshell was from pressed steel and the car was actually built in England by Jensen of West Bromwich from 1960–4, the subsequent P1800S version being built in Sweden until 1968. The model became familiar to many television viewers in Britain as the transport of *The Saint* in the series based on the Leslie Charteris books. Maximum speed even of the early P1800 models was over 100 mph/161 kph. The 121 Amazon saloon's B18 engine produced 68 bhp but the faster 122S had twin carburettors and 80 bhp. From 1962 there was an estate car version also. In 1963 Volvo produced a record 106,000 cars in their Gothenburg factory which was then bursting at the seams, and in April 1964 the King of Sweden opened their new plant at Torslanda 4 miles/6 km away. For 1967 there was a completely new 144 model with 4-wheel disc brakes, a strong passenger compartment with front and rear crumple zones, rubber-faced aluminium bumpers, extensive corrosion protection, a collapsible steering column and split-circuit brake hydraulics. Seat belts, of course, were standard as they had been on all Volvos from 1959. Initially there was only the 144 4-door saloon but it was soon joined by the 142 saloon and 145 estate car. In Volvo terminology at this time 1 signified a passenger car, the second digit the number of engine cylinders and the third the number of doors. In 1968 a 2979 cc 6-cylinder 164 model based on the 144 was added and was identified by a diagonal bar across the radiator and a longer bonnet. In this form the B30 version of the B18 engine gave 145 bhp. The following year the 140 Series and P1800 received a more powerful 1986 cc version of the 4-cylinder engine, now designated B20. In the P1800S the power output was initially 105 bhp but rose to 120 bhp with the fitment of Bosch fuel injection to the 1800E. In the autumn of 1971 the coupé body was given estate car rear treatment with a glass hatch and became the 1800ES. In the meantime the 1½ millionth Volvo, a 164, had been built in May 1969. Both 144 and 164 models were replaced in 1974 by totally new 244 and 264 models with MacPherson strut front suspension, massive bumpers to meet American 5 mph impact requirements and new engines. For the first time both models shared the same body with 109.3 in/2640 mm wheelbase, which meant that the 244 was larger than the 144 and the 264 smaller than the 164. The 2127 cc 4-cylinder B21 engine was a re-engineered overhead camshaft version of the B20, while the 264 was powered by the first of the PRV (Peugeot, Renault, Volvo) engines to be produced in the new

Douvrin engine factory in France. This 2664 cc V6 unit was fitted with Bosch fuel injection for the 264. Estate car 245 and 265 models were also offered and in 1975 there was a long wheelbase version of the 264, called the 264TE, designed and built by Bertone for Volvo. In 1977 the 262 coupé was added to the range. Volvo and Daf had been co-operating since the early 1970s and in 1974 Volvo took over control of Daf, the two companies merging in 1975. The first outcome was the re-engineered Volvo version of the Daf 66 with revised operation of the Variomatic belt-driven transmission. In 1976 there was a new small hatchback Volvo 343 with 1397 cc engine and Variomatic transmission. This continued into 1987, though since 1978 with a 4-speed manual gearbox or automatic transmission and since 1979 with the addition of extra doors as the 5-door 345. In 1978 the 244/245 became the first private car to be fitted with a 6-cylinder diesel engine, a 2383 cc unit giving 82 bhp. A performance GLT version of the 244 was offered in 1979 with 140 bhp from an enlarged 2316 cc fuel-injected engine. In 1980 the 260 Series was fitted with an enlarged 2849 cc V6 engine and in 1982 this unit powered the new big and square 109 in/2770 mm wheelbase 760 saloon, which was also available with the 155 bhp 2127 cc turbocharged diesel first offered in the 245 estate car in 1981. The 340 had been available with a 95 bhp carburettor version of the 1986 cc engine in 1980 and in 1982 fuel injection was added and the new model designated 360. The 1984 740 model was created by installing the 2316 cc engine in the 760 body, and in 1985 there were estate car versions of both 740 and 760 and a coupé version of the 760 called the 780. The new sporting hatchback coupé 480ES announced in 1986 used a 1721 cc 4-cylinder Renault engine, which was also offered in the 300 Series. Volvo's 1987 760 and 240 models were the first in Europe to fit an American-style high-mounted brake light as standard equipment following extensive tests in the USA, where cars are supplied from Volvo's Canadian assembly plant.

1987 Volvo 760GLE.

Car Production Worldwide – Top 20 Countries

	1969	1968	1967	1966	1965	1964	1963	1962	1961	1960
Argentina	153,665	130,351	131,504	133,812	133,734	114,619	75,338	90,648	78,184	*54,000
Australia	371,108	340,950	313,575	280,078	334,953	340,614	307,901	274,092	182,464	*305,096
Belgium	784,207	607,763	455,565	476,245	444,996	325,932	285,161	—	400	194,835
Brazil	280,314	160,683	170,388	144,000	113,520	98,227	85,590	74,746	55,065	37,843
Canada	1,035,551	900,906	720,807	701,537	710,700	560,678	534,103	428,710	327,979	325,752
Czechoslovakia	143,000	—	—	92,640	77,760	42,100	*80,000	*81,200	*77,053	*73,684
France	2,168,462	1,833,047	1,776,502	1,785,906	1,423,078	1,390,312	1,520,827	1,340,328	1,063,595	1,175,301
West Germany	3,312,537	2,862,186	2,295,714	2,830,050	2,733,732	2,650,183	2,414,107	2,109,166	1,903,975	1,816,779
East Germany	115,000	*132,500	*130,000	105,000	102,960	84,200	*80,000	*80,000	*82,000	*77,000
Italy	1,477,366	1,544,932	1,439,211	1,282,418	1,134,444	1,028,931	1,105,291	877,860	693,695	595,907
Japan	2,611,499	2,055,821	1,375,755	877,656	696,176	579,660	407,830	268,784	249,508	165,094
Korea	—	—	—	—	—	—	—	—	—	—
Mexico	*165,164	40,355	30,000	29,160	26,400	20,520	*54,000	*39,000	*24,000	*37,000
Poland	50,000									
Spain	370,955	311,531	274,458	247,006	153,700	117,840	80,500	*112,000	*86,000	*59,500
Sweden	242,887	223,330	193,976	173,499	181,755	160,106	145,672	129,193	109,853	108,382
United Kingdom	1,717,073	1,815,936	1,552,073	1,603,679	1,722,045	1,867,640	1,607,939	1,249,426	1,003,967	1,352,728
USA	8,224,327	8,848,620	7,436,764	8,598,326	9,305,561	7,738,557	7,637,728	6,933,240	5,542,707	6,674,796
USSR	293,600	280,300	251,400	230,400	201,000	184,000	*587,000	*578,000	*555,000	*524,000
Yugoslavia	80,698	59,962	42,338	31,560	35,880	27,840	*29,000	*19,579	*21,688	*16,000

	1970	1971	1972	1973	1974	1975	1976	1977	1978	1979
Argentina	167,000	193,386	200,885	219,439	212,088	185,162	142,072	168,126	133,416	199,646
Australia	391,946	391,242	366,631	376,295	393,741	350,976	385,147	316,394	346,489	403,188
Belgium	781,010	902,493	921,953	969,264	753,916	792,078	1,039,501	1,053,555	1,053,302	1,029,321
Brazil	249,920	342,214	408,712	599,974	708,615	772,122	526,943	463,897	535,442	547,626
Canada	937,219	1,094,631	1,147,280	1,227,432	1,165,635	1,044,822	1,146,264	1,162,427	1,143,425	987,673
Czechoslovakia	130,000	140,000	155,000	160,000	170,100	175,411	178,200	158,987	176,000	174,900
France	2,458,038	2,693,989	2,992,959	2,866,728	2,698,785	2,546,154	2,979,559	3,092,439	3,111,380	3,220,394
West Germany	3,527,864	3,695,779	3,521,540	3,649,880	2,839,596	2,907,815	3,546,900	3,790,544	3,890,176	3,932,556
East Germany	125,000	135,000	125,000	130,000	150,000	—	164,000	167,000	170,967	171,345
Italy	1,719,715	1,701,064	1,732,379	1,823,333	1,630,686	1,348,544	1,471,308	1,440,470	1,508,599	1,480,904
Japan	3,178,708	3,717,858	4,022,289	4,470,550	3,931,842	4,568,120	5,027,792	5,431,045	5,975,968	6,175,771
Korea	—	—	—	—	—	—	25,605	42,284	86,823	113,564
Mexico	*192,147	*210,345	*233,437	*285,568	*350,755	*360,678	*324,979	187,637	242,519	280,049
Poland	54,000	81,500	90,000	100,000	93,688	164,332	216,000	296,211	342,326	357,000
Spain	450,426	452,921	600,559	706,433	704,754	696,124	753,125	988,964	986,116	965,809
Sweden	278,971	287,398	317,962	341,503	326,743	316,386	317,380	235,383	254,256	296,540
United Kingdom	1,640,966	1,741,940	1,921,311	1,747,321	1,534,119	1,267,695	1,333,449	1,327,820	1,222,949	1,070,452
USA	6,550,203	8,583,653	8,828,205	9,667,571	7,324,504	6,717,177	8,497,876	9,213,600	9,175,836	8,433,662
USSR	344,000	529,000	730,000	917,000	1,119,000	1,201,000	1,239,000	1,274,000	1,312,000	1,314,000
Yugoslavia	112,160	114,477	103,733	113,116	171,283	183,182	192,801	231,117	252,075	285,262

	1980	1981	1982	1983	1984	1985
Argentina	227,542	144,083	110,134	134,368	137,206	113,788
Australia	318,048	358,384	378,978	317,239	370,391	383,763
Belgium	882,000	852,013	950,410	972,255	865,297	986,182
Brazil	600,706	406,016	475,112	576,348	538,342	444,628
Canada	846,777	803,117	807,645	968,867	1,021,536	1,077,935
Czechoslovakia	e185,000	e182,000	175,517	177,505	173,483	176,099
France	2,938,581	2,611,864	2,777,125	2,960,823	2,713,289	2,632,366
West Germany	3,520,934	3,577,807	3,761,436	3,877,641	3,790,164	4,166,686
East Germany	176,761	180,233	182,930	e188,000	e202,000	—
Italy	1,445,221	1,257,340	1,297,351	1,395,531	1,439,283	1,389,156
Japan	7,038,108	6,974,131	6,881,586	7,151,888	7,073,173	7,646,816
Korea	57,225	68,760	94,460	121,987	158,503	264,458
Mexico	303,056	355,497	300,579	207,137	231,578	246,960
Poland	364,500	240,338	228,287	270,154	279,135	e283,000
Spain	1,028,813	855,325	927,500	1,141,581	1,176,893	1,230,071
Sweden	235,320	258,261	294,792	344,702	352,585	400,748
United Kingdom	923,744	954,650	887,679	1,044,597	908,906	1,047,973
USA	6,375,506	6,253,138	5,073,496	6,781,184	7,773,332	8,184,821
USSR	1,327,000	1,324,000	1,307,000	1,317,700	1,300,000	1,305,000
Yugoslavia	255,228	239,554	211,372	210,059	235,994	217,755

e = Estimated production figure
* Car and commercial vehicle production
Source: Society of Motor Manufacturers and Traders, FEBIAC (Belgium) and motor manufacturing associations of individual countries.

Top 12 Best Selling Cars in the USA, 1979–1986

1979

1. Chevrolet Caprice/Impala 449,001
2. Oldsmobile Cutlass Supreme 404,068
3. Chevrolet Chevette 375,724
4. Chevrolet Malibu 344,233
5. Ford Fairmont 338,819
6. Chevrolet Citation 308,437
7. Ford Mustang 304,053
8. Chevrolet Monte Carlo 265,877
9. Buick Regal 249,379
10. Ford LTD 245,565
11. Oldsmobile 88/98 223,699
12. Ford Thunderbird 215,698

1980

1. Chevrolet Citation 374,706
2. Chevrolet Chevette 373,988
3. Ford Fairmont 285,272
4. Chevrolet Malibu 267,732
5. Chevrolet Caprice/Impala 261,819
6. Oldsmobile Cutlass Supreme 258,789
7. Ford Mustang 225,290
8. Oldsmobile Cutlass 210,784
9. Buick Regal 199,207
10. Volkswagen Rabbit (Golf) 177,140
11. Buick Skylark 175,741
12. Chevrolet Monte Carlo 165,638

1981

1. Chevrolet Chevette 346,307
2. Chevrolet Citation 300,184
3. Ford Escort 284,907
4. Oldsmobile Cutlass Supreme 266,070
5. Chevrolet Malibu 211,130
6. Chevrolet Caprice/Impala 210,424
7. Buick Regal 208,329
8. Buick Skylark 200,460
9. Plymouth Reliant/Volare 196,997
10. Oldsmobile Cutlass 187,952
11. Ford Fairmont 182,909
12. Volkswagen Rabbit (Golf) 162,445

1982

1. Ford Escort 337,667
2. Oldsmobile Cutlass Supreme 281,120
3. Chevrolet Chevette 231,927
4. Buick Regal 222,169
5. Chevrolet Caprice/Impala 204,193
6. Chevrolet Citation 186,782
7. Oldsmobile 88 180,839
8. Chevrolet Camaro 166,109
9. Cadillac De Ville/Fleetwood 154,229
10. Plymouth Reliant 146,762
11. Buick Skylark 141,766
12. Ford Fairmont 139,056

1983

1. Oldsmobile Cutlass Supreme 331,179
2. Ford Escort 326,333
3. Chevrolet Cavalier 259,397
4. Chevrolet Caprice/Impala 238,930
5. Buick Regal 234,035
6. Oldsmobile Delta 88 228,770
7. Honda Accord 222,137
8. Nissan Sentra (Sunny) 212,719
9. Oldsmobile Cutlass Ciera 191,720
10. Chevrolet Monte Carlo/Malibu 190,945
11. Chevrolet Celebrity 180,627
12. Chevrolet Chevette 178,759

1984

1. Chevrolet Cavalier 377,545
2. Ford Escort 353,578
3. Chevrolet Celebrity 322,189
4. Oldsmobile Cutlass Supreme 302,087
5. Chevrolet Caprice/Impala 258,902
6. Oldsmobile Delta 88 258,293
7. Honda Accord 256,646
8. Ford Tempo 256,532
9. Oldsmobile Cutlass Ciera 242,209
10. Buick Century 217,042
11. Chevrolet Camaro 202,172
12. Ford LTD 196,907

1985

1. Chevrolet Cavalier 431,031
2. Ford Escort 420,690
3. Chevrolet Celebrity 363,619
4. Oldsmobile Cutlass Ciera 333,585
5. Ford Tempo 281,144
6. Honda Accord 268,420
7. Chevrolet Caprice/Impala 245,826
8. Buick Century 234,508
9. Nissan Sentra (Sunny) 225,987
10. Oldsmobile Cutlass Supreme 217,504
11. Honda Civic/CRX 208,031
12. Chevrolet Camaro 199,985

1986

1. Chevrolet Celebrity 408,946
2. Ford Escort 402,181
3. Chevrolet Cavalier 357,120
4. Oldsmobile Cutlass Ciera 329,320
5. Honda Accord 325,004
6. Ford Taurus/LTD 287,037

7. Ford Tempo 265,832
8. Oldsmobile 88 261,260
9. Buick Century 240,747
10. Honda Civic 235,801
11. Chevrolet Caprice/Impala 226,132
12. Nissan Sentra (Sunny) 216,337

Chevrolet Celebrity, America's best-selling car in 1986.

United Kingdom New Car Sales, by make, 1975–1986

1975
Alfa Romeo 8287; Audi-NSU 15,629; BMW 7233; British Leyland 368,687 (Austin/ MG/Morris 291,911, Jaguar/Daimler 12,258, Rover 17,466, Triumph 47,052); Chrysler 95,436; Citroën 22,049; Colt (Mitsubishi) 2983; Daf 6358; Datsun (Nissan) 64,011; Fiat 38,392; Ford 259,124; Honda 10,110; Jensen 429; Lada 5713; Lotus 383; Mazda (Toyo Kogyo) 10,549; Mercedes-Benz 5530; Moskvich 1260; Opel 10,307; Peugeot 14,811; Polski-Fiat 2023; Reliant 1498; Renault 56,665; Rolls-Royce/ Bentley 1354; Saab 7380; Skoda 9353; Toyota 20,270; Vauxhall 87,949; Volkswagen 32,570; Volvo 17,010; Wartburg 1642; others 9135.
Total sales in UK: 1,194,130.

1976
Alfa Romeo 7966; Audi-NSU 12,492; BMW 8621; British Leyland 352,679 (Austin/ MG/Morris 280,407, Jaguar/Daimler 10,401, Rover 12,732, Triumph 49,139); Chrysler 82,905; Citroën 21,001; Colt (Mitsubishi) 6701; Daf 1013; Datsun (Nissan) 68,853; Fiat 48,595; Ford 324,659; Honda 13,328; Jensen 224; Lada 8541; Lotus 544; Mazda (Toyo Kogyo) 10,434; Mercedes-Benz 5825; Moskvich 314; Opel 15,649; Peugeot 18,020; Polski-Fiat 1855; Reliant 2602; Renault 56,855; Rolls-Royce/ Bentley 1438; Saab 6908; Skoda 8952; Toyota 22,094; Vauxhall 114,954; Volkswagen 31,405; Volvo 22,217; Wartburg 338; others 7961.
Total sales in UK: 1,285,583.

1977
Alfa Romeo 8637; Audi-NSU 13,244; BMW 8481; British Leyland 322,067 (Austin/ MG/Morris 248,103, Jaguar/Daimler 9387, Rover 18,669, Triumph 45,908); Chrysler 79,730; Citroën 23,974; Colt (Mitsubishi) 6817; Daf 7; Datsun (Nissan) 82,133; Fiat 66,015; Ford 340,319; Honda 14,430; Jeep (American Motors) 7; Lada 12,286; Lancia 9323; Lotus 432; Mazda (Toyo Kogyo) 12,802; Mercedes-Benz 6981; Opel 16,248; Panther 11; Peugeot 22,632; Polski-Fiat 1501; Reliant 2262; Renault 55,862; Rolls-Royce/Bentley 1215; Saab 4845; Skoda 9447; Subaru (Fuji Heavy Industries) 72; Toyota 24,157; Vauxhall 120,600; Volkswagen 32,714; Volvo 21,772; Wartburg 7; others 2509.
Total sales in UK: 1,323,524.

1978
Alfa Romeo 13,061; Audi-NSU 16,167; BMW 10,506; British Leyland 373,793 (Austin/ MG/Morris 298,219, Jaguar/Daimler 12,812, Rover 33,623, Triumph 29,245); Chrysler 112,562; Citroën 31,957; Colt (Mitsubishi) 10,612; Datsun (Nissan) 101,735; Fiat 72,192; Ford 392,366; Honda 19,480; Jeep (American Motors) 352; Lada 17,974; Lancia 11,764; Lotus 674; Mazda (Toyo Kogyo) 12,810; Mercedes-Benz 6935; Opel 22,199; Panther 218; Peugeot 31,345; Polski-Fiat 3605; Reliant 1453; Renault 69,627; Rolls-Royce/Bentley 1324; Saab 6407; Skoda 9890; Subaru (Fuji Heavy Industries) 1514; Toyota 28,334; Vauxhall 130,993; Volkswagen 47,055; Volvo 29,868; Wartburg 2; others 3165.
Total sales in UK: 1,591,941.

1979
Alfa Romeo 13,638; Audi 16,227; BMW 14,058; British Leyland 336,984 (Austin/MG/ Morris 275,085, Jaguar/Daimler 8035; Rover 32,158, Triumph 21,706); Chrysler/ Talbot 119,433; Citroën 34,015; Colt (Mitsubishi) 10,696; Daihatsu 226; Datsun

(Nissan) 102,395; Fiat 70,626; Ford 485,559;
Honda 17,849; Jeep (American Motors) 429;
Lada 22,270; Lancia 8951; Lotus 697;
Mazda 17,770; Mercedes-Benz 7914;
Opel 27,216; Panther 144; Peugeot 37,980;
Polski-Fiat 6530; Reliant 818; Renault 93,468;
Rolls-Royce/Bentley 1347; Saab 8976;
Skoda 10,243; Subaru (Fuji Heavy
Industries) 3443; Toyota 32,220;
Vauxhall 112,398; Volkswagen 60,061;
Volvo 36,583; others 5111.
Total sales in UK: 1,716,275.

1980

Alfa Romeo 10,219; Audi 13,096; BMW 13,451;
British Leyland 275,798 (Austin/MG/
Morris 225,715, Jaguar/Daimler 5920,
Rover 26,761, Triumph 17,401); Citroën 27,006;
Colt (Mitsubishi) 10,273; Daihatsu 1355;
Datsun (Nissan) 91,893; Fiat 45,267;
Ford 464,706; Honda 22,760; Jeep (American
Motors) 106; Lada 13,043; Lancia 6032;
Lotus 348; Mazda (Toyo Kogyo) 15,370;
Mercedes-Benz 8876; Opel 22,870; Panther 95;
Peugeot 24,333; Polski-Fiat 3989; Reliant 682;
Renault 88,343; Rolls-Royce/Bentley 1315;
Saab 8073; Skoda 7906; Subaru (Fuji Heavy
Industries) 3252; Talbot 90,874; Toyota 34,167;
Vauxhall 109,218; Volkswagen 55,189;
Volvo 38,283; others 4457.
Total sales in UK: 1,513,761.

1981

Alfa Romeo 8030; Audi 15,098; BMW 17,086;
British Leyland 285,071 (Austin/MG/
Morris 240,917, Jaguar/Daimler 5688,
Rover 23,898, Triumph 14,568); Citroën 27,395;
Colt (Mitsubishi) 11,209; Daihatsu 3059;
Datsun (Nissan) 88,209; Fiat 55,505;
Ford 459,365; Honda 15,774; Jeep (American
Motors) 68; Lada 15,508; Lancia 6472;
Lotus 325; Mazda (Toyo Kogyo) 15,594;
Mercedes-Benz 10,667; Opel 18,796;
Panther 42; Peugeot 17,805; Polski-Fiat 2329;
Reliant 308; Renault 72,041; Rolls-Royce/
Bentley 1218; Saab 9461; Skoda 8507; Subaru
(Fuji Heavy Industries) 3312; Suzuki 2533;
Talbot 68,048; Toyota 23,405;
Vauxhall 107,572; Volkswagen 65,123;
Volvo 44,558; Zastava 811; others 4318.
Total sales in UK: 1,484,622.

1982

Alfa Romeo 8928; Audi 18,277; BMW 22,977;

British Leyland 277,260 (Austin/MG/
Morris 199,173, Jaguar/Daimler 6440,
Rover 23,898, Triumph 44,531); Citroën 24,149;
Colt (Mitsubishi) 8640; Daihatsu 4743; Datsun
(Nissan) 93,213; Fiat 43,638; Ford 474,192;
FSO (Polski-Fiat) 3105; Honda 16,333;
Hyundai 2993; Jeep (American Motors) 4;
Lada 16,752; Lancia 5170; Lotus 410;
Mazda 15,139; Mercedes-Benz 12,164;
Opel 7278; Panther 26; Peugeot 19,636;
Reliant 114; Renault 66,147; Rolls-Royce/
Bentley 805; Saab 9474; Skoda 9272; Subaru
(Fuji Heavy Industries) 2700; Suzuki 2763;
Talbot 56,149; Toyota 27,590;
Vauxhall 174,183; Volkswagen 74,157;
Volvo 51,707; Zastava 3101; others 3839.
Total sales in UK: 1,555,027.

1983

Alfa Romeo 7763; Audi 19,235; BMW 25,178;
British Leyland 332,725 (Austin/MG/
Morris 262,609, Jaguar/Daimler 7069,
Rover 24,578, Triumph 38,469); Citroën 25,751;
Colt (Mitsubishi) 8641; Daihatsu 5198; Datsun
(Nissan) 104,684; Fiat 46,254; Ford 518,048;
FSO 4439; Honda 18,796; Hyundai 3412;
Lada 19,225; Lancia 3461; Lonsdale
(Mitsubishi) 504; Lotus 383; Mazda (Toyo
Kogyo) 17,638; Mercedes-Benz 13,506;
Opel 9678; Panther 119; Peugeot 21,342;
Reliant 93; Renault 62,923; Rolls-Royce/
Bentley 633; Saab 9490; Skoda 11,059; Subaru
(Fuji Heavy Industries) 3627; Suzuki 3356;
Talbot 58,153; Toyota 31,683;
Vauxhall 250,409; Volkswagen 81,492;
Volvo 61,250; Zastava 4634; others 4917.
Total sales in UK: 1,791,699.

1984

Alfa Romeo 4266; Audi 19,711; BMW 25,785;
British Leyland 312,054 (Austin/MG/
Morris 264,887, Rover 36,705,
Triumph 10,462); Citroën 24,562; Colt
(Mitsubishi) 9963; Daihatsu 4779; Fiat 47,563;
Ford 486,971; FSO 5419; Honda 18,916;
Hyundai 4989; Jaguar/Daimler 7544;
Lada 15,033; Lancia 2639; Lonsdale
(Mitsubishi) 596; Lotus 547; Mazda (Toyo
Kogyo) 17,505; Mercedes-Benz 14,437;
Nissan 106,360; Opel 12,371; Panther 238;
Peugeot 45,628; Reliant 105; Renault 59,779;
Rolls-Royce/Bentley 630; Saab 8835;
Skoda 11,023; Subaru (Fuji Heavy
Industries) 3673; Suzuki 3391; Talbot 24,891;

Toyota 32,702; Vauxhall 270,437;
Volkswagen 76,892; Volvo 59,072;
Zastava 6190; others 4154.
Total sales in UK: 1,749,650.

1985

Alfa Romeo 3093; Audi 19,989; BMW 33,450;
British Leyland 327,955 (Austin/MG 268,898,
Rover 55,503, Range Rover 3381, other 173);
Citroën 27,479; Daihatsu 4567; Fiat 54,460;
Ford 485,620; FSO 6158; Honda 18,984;
Hyundai 5159; Jaguar/Daimler 8049;
Lada 15,314; Lancia 3077; Lotus 554;
Mazda 17,172; Mercedes-Benz 18,086;
Mitsubishi 11,589; Nissan 105,517; Opel 8102;
Panther 54; Peugeot 44,849; Reliant 625;
Renault 70,622; Rolls-Royce/Bentley 710;
Saab 8375; Skoda 9884; Subaru 3815;
Suzuki 3950; Talbot 28,986; Toyota 34,722;
Vauxhall 295,361; Volkswagen 83,888;
Volvo 59,549; Zastava 7953; others 4691.
Total sales in UK: 1,832,408.

1986

Alfa Romeo 2233; Audi 19,280; BMW 35,898;
Citroën 34,427; Daihatsu 5345; Fiat 61,729;
Ford 515,367; FSO 4558; Honda 20,489;
Hyundai 7495; Jaguar/Daimler 7579;
Lada 20,312; Lancia 3386; Lotus 447;
Mazda 17,982; Mercedes-Benz 19,987;
Mitsubishi 11,811; Nissan 109,914; Opel 4896;
Panther 67; Peugeot/Talbot 80,667;
Reliant 303; Renault 69,261; Rolls-Royce/
Bentley 808; Rover Group 297,466 (Austin/
MG 239,628, Rover 53,521, Range Rover 4226,
other 91); Saab 10,331; Seat 5917;
Skoda 12,775; Subaru 3974; Suzuki 4288;
Toyota 35,802; Vauxhall 279,615;
Volvo 68,972; Volkswagen 99,957;
Zastava 8525; others 4601.
Total sales in UK: 1,882,474.

Top 12 Best Selling Models in the UK

1979

1. Ford Cortina 193,784; 2. Ford Escort 131,667;
3. Mini 82,938; 4. Morris Marina 62,140; 5.
Austin Allegro 59,985; 6. Ford Fiesta 58,681;
7. Ford Granada 52,091; 8. Ford Capri 49,147;
9. Vauxhall Cavalier 46,157; 10. Vauxhall
Chevette 44,197; 11. Datsun Sunny 31,665;
12. Princess 31,253.

1980

1. Ford Cortina 190,281; 2. Ford Escort 122,377;
3. Ford Fiesta 91,661; 4. Mini 61,129; 5. Morris
Marina/Ital 59,906; 6. Vauxhall
Chevette 46,059; 7. Vauxhall Cavalier 41,119;
8. Austin Allegro 39,612; 9. Ford Capri 31,187;
10. Renault 18 30,958; 11. Datsun
Sunny 30,954; 12. Datsun Cherry 30,929.

1981

1. Ford Cortina 159,804; 2. Ford Escort 141,081;
3. Ford Fiesta 110,753; 4. Austin Metro 110,283;
5. Morris Ital 48,490; 6. Vauxhall
Chevette 36,838; 7. Vauxhall Cavalier 33,631;
8. Datsun Cherry 32,874; 9. Vauxhall
Astra 30,854; 10. Mini 28,772; 11. Volkswagen
Golf 26,413; 12. Datsun Sunny 25,737.

1982

1. Ford Escort 166,942; 2. Ford Cortina 135,745;
3. Austin Metro 114,550; 4. Ford Fiesta 110,165;
5. Vauxhall Cavalier 100,081; 6. Vauxhall
Astra 46,412; 7. Triumph Acclaim 42,188;
8. Volvo 300 Series 30,412; 9. Datsun
Sunny 28,767; 10. Ford Granada 28,590;
11. Datsun Cherry 28,117; 12. Volkswagen
Golf 26,311.

1983

1. Ford Escort 174,190; 2. Ford Sierra 159,119;
3. Austin/MG Metro 137,303; 4. Vauxhall
Cavalier 127,509; 5. Ford Fiesta 119,602;
6. Austin/MG Maestro 65,328; 7. Vauxhall
Astra 62,570; 8. Triumph Acclaim 38,406;
9. Datsun Sunny 36,781; 10. Volvo 300
Series 36,753; 11. Volkswagen Polo 32,706;
12. Datsun Cherry 29,229.

1984

1. Ford Escort 157,340; 2. Vauxhall
Cavalier 132,149; 3. Ford Fiesta 125,851;
4. Austin/MG Metro 117,442; 5. Ford
Sierra 113,071; 6. Austin/MG Maestro 83,072;
7. Vauxhall Astra 56,511; 8. Vauxhall
Nova 55,442; 9. Ford Orion 51,026; 10. Volvo
300 Series 35,034; 11. Austin/MG
Montego 34,728; 12. Volkswagen Polo 31,345.

1985

1. Ford Escort 157,269; 2. Vauxhall
Cavalier 134,335; 3. Ford Fiesta 124,143;
4. Austin/MG Metro 118,817; 5. Ford
Sierra 101,642; 6. Vauxhall Astra 76,553;
7. Austin/MG Montego 73,955; 8. Ford

Orion 65,363; 9. Vauxhall Nova 61,358;
10. Austin/MG Maestro 57,527; 11. Rover 200
Series 43,669; 12. Volvo 300 Series 35,558.

1986

1. Ford Escort 156,895; 2. Ford Fiesta 143,712;
3. Ford Sierra 113,861; 4. Vauxhall
Cavalier 113,475; 5. Austin/MG Metro 109,351;
6. Vauxhall Astra 80,067; 7. Austin/MG
Montego 62,658; 8. Ford Orion 55,255;
9. Austin/MG Maestro 51,465; 10. Vauxhall
Nova 48,465; 11. Rover 200 Series 45,197;
12. Volvo 300 Series 39,407.

*Source: Society of Motor Manufacturers and
Traders, London.*

Ford Escort, Britain's best-selling car in 1986.

United Kingdom Car Production by Main Manufacturers, 1975–1985

1975

British Leyland 618,530 (Austin-
Morris 463,163, Jaguar 21,992, Rover/Land-
Rover 60,212, Triumph 73,163);
Chrysler 226,612; Ford 329,648; Jensen 1928;
Lotus 655; Reliant 1395; Rolls-Royce/
Bentley 3120; TVR 132; Vauxhall 98,621.

1976

British Leyland 789,434 (Austin-
Morris 563,975, Jaguar 24,525, Rover/Land-
Rover 68,294, Triumph 132,640);
Chrysler 144,586; Ford 383,220; Jensen 272;
Lotus 931; Reliant 3247; Rolls-Royce/
Bentley 3284; TVR 333; Vauxhall 109,118.

1977

British Leyland 617,260 (Austin-
Morris 454,339, Jaguar 24,851, Rover/Land-
Rover 65,626, Triumph 72,444);
Chrysler 203,549; Ford 406,633; Lotus 1074;
Reliant 2377; Rolls-Royce/Bentley 2843;
TVR 366; Vauxhall 92,237.

1978

British Leyland 590,862 (Austin-
Morris 415,621, Jaguar 26,476, Rover/Land-
Rover 95,642, Triumph 53,123);
Chrysler 230,135; Ford 324,407; Lotus 1200;
Reliant 820; Rolls-Royce/Bentley 3361;
TVR 310; Vauxhall 110,425.

1979

Aston Martin 271; British Leyland 506,904
(Austin-Morris 363,305, Jaguar 13,978, Rover/
Land-Rover 85,688, Triumph 43,933); Chrysler/
Talbot 134,540; Ford 398,694; Lotus 1031;
Reliant 876; Rolls-Royce/Bentley 3358;
TVR 308; Vauxhall 111,850.

1980

Aston Martin 195; British Leyland 419,184
(Austin-Morris 307,032, Jaguar 13,791, Rover/
Land-Rover 67,749, Triumph 30,412);
Ford 342,767; Lotus 384; Reliant 582; Rolls-
Royce/Bentley 3203; Talbot 160,510; TVR 144;
Vauxhall 87,098.

1981

Aston Martin 157; British Leyland 446,277
(Austin-Morris 341,007, Jaguar 14,577, Rover/
Land-Rover 66,169, Triumph 25,524); De
Lorean 7409; Ford 342,171; Lotus 345;
Reliant 89; Rolls-Royce/Bentley 3165;
Talbot 117,439; TVR 164; Vauxhall 69,932.

1982

Aston Martin 134; British Leyland 452,837
(Austin-Morris 299,972, Jaguar 22,046, Rover/
Land-Rover 72,794, Triumph 58,025); De
Lorean 1333; Ford 306,635; Lotus 572;
Reliant 87; Rolls-Royce/Bentley 2436;
Talbot 56,235; TVR 121; Vauxhall 112,669.

1983

Aston Martin 155; British Leyland 517,136
(Austin-Morris 371,872, Jaguar 28,041, Rover/
Land-Rover 67,445, Triumph 49,778);
Ford 318,674; Lotus 642; Reliant 105; Rolls-
Royce/Bentley 1551; Talbot 120,503; TVR 291;
Vauxhall 126,524.

1984

Aston Martin 201; British Leyland 422,425
(Austin-Morris 338,060, Rover/Land-
Rover 79,997, Triumph 5368); Ford 297,235;
Jaguar/Daimler 33,437; Lotus 837;
Reliant 111; Rolls-Royce/Bentley 2238;
Talbot 95,123; TVR 397; Vauxhall 117,397

1985

Aston Martin 184; British Leyland 496,150
(Austin 369,128, Rover 81,764, Range
Rover 14,212, Land-Rover 31,046);
Ford 303,317; Jaguar/Daimler 38,500;
Lotus 638; Peugeot-Talbot 67,257
(Peugeot 5702, Talbot 61,555); Reliant 783;
Rolls-Royce/Bentley 2588; TVR 472;
Vauxhall 152,587.

American Car Production, by make, 1975–1986

1975

American Motors 323,796; Checker 3181;
Chrysler 902,902 (Chrysler division 104,870,
Dodge 354,482, Plymouth 443,550);
Ford 1,808,038 (Ford division 1,301,414,
Lincoln 101,520, Mercury 405,104); General
Motors 3,679,260 (Buick 535,820,
Cadillac 278,404, Chevrolet 1,687,077,
Oldsmobile 654,491, Pontiac 523,468).

1976

American Motors 213,918; Checker 4792;
Chrysler 1,333,402 (Chrysler division 127,466,
Dodge 547,916, Plymouth 658,020);
Ford 2,053,873 (Ford division 1,494,116,
Lincoln 124,880, Mercury 434,877); General
Motors 4,891,891 (Buick 817,670,
Cadillac 312,845, Chevrolet 2,012,338,
Oldsmobile 964,427, Pontiac 784,611).

1977

American Motors 156,984; Checker 4777;
Chrysler 1,236,459 (Chrysler division 130,128,
Dodge 497,232, Plymouth 608,999);
Ford 2,555,867 (Ford division 1,761,374,
Lincoln 190,570, Mercury 603,923); General
Motors 5,259,613 (Buick 801,202,
Cadillac 369,254, Chevrolet 2,133,360,
Oldsmobile 1,079,842, Pontiac 875,955).

1978

American Motors 163,554; Checker 4225;
Chrysler 1,126,168 (Chrysler division 85,596,
Dodge 441,550, Plymouth 599,022);
Ford 2,557,197 (Ford division 1,743,455,
Lincoln/Mercury 813,752); General
Motors 5,284,498 (Buick 810,325,
Cadillac 350,761, Chevrolet 2,346,159,
Oldsmobile 910,252, Pontiac 867,001);
Volkswagen 40,194.

1979

American Motors 184,636; Checker 4766;
Chrysler 936,146 (Chrysler division 77,749,
Dodge 380,315, Plymouth 478,082);
Ford 2,043,014 (Ford division 1,381,604,
Lincoln/Mercury 661,410); General
Motors 5,092,183 (Buick 787,149,
Cadillac 345,831, Chevrolet 2,236,173,
Oldsmobile 1,008,518, Pontiac 714,512);
Volkswagen 173,405.

1980

American Motors 164,725; Checker 3197;
Chrysler 638,974 (Chrysler division 82,463,
Dodge 263,169, Plymouth 293,342);
Ford 1,306,948 (Ford division 929,627, Lincoln/
Mercury 377,321); General Motors 4,064,556
(Buick 783,575, Cadillac 203,991,
Chevrolet 1,737,336, Oldsmobile 783,225,
Pontiac 556,429); Volkswagen 197,106.

1981

American Motors 109,319; Checker 3010;
Chrysler 748,862 (Chrysler division 57,430,
Dodge 325,932, Plymouth 365,502);
Ford 1,320,197 (Ford division 892,043, Lincoln/
Mercury 428,154); General Motors 3,804,083
(Buick 839,960, Cadillac 259,135,
Chevrolet 1,445,353, Oldsmobile 838,333,
Pontiac 521,302); Volkswagen 167,755.

1982

American Motors 109,549; Checker 2000;
Chrysler 600,502 (Chrysler division 114,444,
Dodge 244,833, Plymouth 241,225);
Ford 1,104,044 (Ford division 690,645, Lincoln/
Mercury 413,409); General Motors 3,173,145
(Buick 751,338, Cadillac 246,602,
Chevrolet 994,251, Oldsmobile 759,637,
Pontiac 421,317); Volkswagen 82,246.

1983

American Motors 200,385; Chrysler 904,286

(Chrysler division 234,649, Dodge 358,813, Plymouth 310,824); Ford 1,547,680 (Ford division 1,008,799, Lincoln 106,528, Mercury 432,353); General Motors 3,875,291 (Buick 905,608, Cadillac 309,811, Chevrolet 1,279,106, Oldsmobile 1,050,846, Pontiac 429,920); Honda 55,535; Volkswagen 98,207.

1984

American Motors 192,196; Chrysler 1,247,785 (Chrysler division 403,659, Dodge 465,851, Plymouth 378,275); Ford 1,775,257 (Ford division 1,145,144, Lincoln 168,704, Mercury 461,409); General Motors 4,344,737 (Buick 987,833, Cadillac 328,544, Chevrolet 1,456,733, Oldsmobile 1,065,528, Pontiac 505,766); Honda 138,572; Volkswagen 74,785.

1985

American Motors 109,919; Chrysler 1,266,068 (Chrysler division 414,193, Dodge 482,388, Plymouth 369,487); Ford 1,636,150 (Ford division 1,098,627, Lincoln 163,047, Mercury 374,476); General Motors 4,887,079 (Buick 1,001,461, Cadillac 322,765, Chevrolet 1,169,254, Oldsmobile 1,168,982, Pontiac 702,617); Honda 145,337; Nissan 43,810; Volkswagen 96,458.

1986

American Motors 49,503; Chrysler 1,297,580 (Chrysler division 368,591, Dodge 506,370, Plymouth 422,619); Ford 1,754,235 (Ford division 1,221,871, Lincoln 183,032, Mercury 359,332); General Motors 4,316,143 (Buick 775,966, Cadillac 319,037, Chevrolet 1,499,230, Oldsmobile 927,173, Pontiac 794,737); Honda 238,159; Nissan 65,117; Toyota 13,649; Volkswagen 84,397.

Source: Motor Vehicle Manufacturers' Association of the United States and Society of Motor Manufacturers and Traders.

Canadian Car Production, by manufacturer, 1975–1986

1975

American Motors 48,373; Chrysler 261,265; Ford 324,783; General Motors 406,059; Volvo 13,337.

1976

American Motors 43,191; Chrysler 245,332; Ford 371,305; General Motors 476,949; Volvo 9487.

1977

American Motors 41,717; Chrysler 214,808; Ford 376,785; General Motors 522,291; Volvo 6826.

1978

American Motors 26,286; Chrysler 160,085; Ford 377,172; General Motors 571,683; Volvo 8199.

1979

Chrysler 134,086; Ford 286,416; General Motors 558,405; Volvo 8766.

1980

American Motors 3077; Chrysler 71,530; Ford 249,876; General Motors 512,330; Volvo 9964.

1981

American Motors 37,491; Chrysler 69,149; Ford 209,494; General Motors 478,389; Volvo 8594.

1982

American Motors 30,341; Chrysler 149,434; Ford 283,059; General Motors 334,646; Volvo 10,165.

1983

American Motors 29,448; Chrysler 105,853; Ford 284,549; General Motors 538,639; Volvo 10,378.

1984

American Motors 22,992; Ford 442,049; General Motors 546,009; Volvo 10,486.

1985

American Motors 11,316; Ford 493,560; General Motors 562,981; Volvo 10,078.

1986

American Motors 4,444; Ford 517,478; General Motors 529,055; Volvo 10,388

Source: Motor Vehicle Manufacturers' Association of Canada.

Top 10 Best Selling Cars in Europe, 1984, 1985 and 1986

1984
1. Ford Escort/Orion 546,400
2. Volkswagen Golf 487,846
3. Renault 9/11 470,518
4. Fiat Uno 464,616
5. Opel Kadett/Vauxhall Astra 364,252
6. Ford Fiesta 358,800
7. Opel Ascona/Vauxhall Cavalier 327,578
8. Peugeot 205 317,418
9. Ford Sierra 305,200
10. Renault 5 298,030

1985
1. Volkswagen Golf 599,864
2. Fiat Uno 530,000
3. Ford Escort/Orion 525,200
4. Opel Kadett/Vauxhall Astra 467,855
5. Peugeot 205 462,951
6. Renault 5 405,855
7. Renault 9/11 393,175
8. Ford Fiesta 337,500
9. Opel Ascona/Vauxhall Cavalier 304,145
10. Ford Sierra 293,500

Fiat Uno, second best selling car in Europe, 1986.

1986
1. Volkswagen Golf 696,600
2. Fiat Uno 629,421
3. Opel Kadett/Vauxhall Astra/ Belmont 594,933
4. Ford Escort/Orion 565,928
5. Renault 5 473,345
6. Peugeot 205 462,133
7. Ford Fiesta 356,997
8. Renault 9/11 322,911
9. Ford Sierra 311,223
10. Opel Ascona/Vauxhall Cavalier 283,128

Source: Individual manufacturers' sales figures.

Volkswagen Golf, Europe's best selling car in 1986.

INDEX

Page numbers in *italics* refer to photographs. Where drivers, cars and rallies appear in tables, they are not listed in the index. *C* indicates a picture in the colour section.

Picture Acknowledgements

The pictures in this book have been drawn from the collections of Warren Allport, Anthony Harding, David Hodges and the Publisher. The authors would also like to thank the individual manufacturers who have provided a number of historic and current car photographs from their files. Additional pictures for specific pages have been supplied by the following: Dr Milton Neumann, Okarche, Oklahoma, USA colour 1 (bottom); Associated Press 99; Hugh Bishop 54 (bottom), 64; Neill Bruce colour 2, colour 3 (bottom), colour 5 (bottom); Diana Burnett colour 8 (bottom 2 pictures on left); National Motor Museum 18 (centre); Maurice Rowe colour 5 (top); Nigel Snowdon colour 7 (2nd from top on right), colour 8 (2nd from bottom on left); Quadrant Picture Library/Autocar 2, 7 (top right), 16 (bottom), 25 (top), 43 (bottom), 135, 152 (top), 155 (top left and bottom), 157 (bottom, left and right).